Agrarian Populism and the Mexican State

Agrarian Populism and the Mexican State

The Struggle for Land in Sonora

Steven E. Sanderson

University of California Press · Berkeley · Los Angeles · London

University of California Press
Berkeley and Los Angeles, California
University of California Press, Ltd.
London, England
© 1981 by
The Regents of the University of California

Printed in the United States of America
1 2 3 4 5 6 7 8 9

Library of Congress Cataloging in Publication Data

Sanderson, Steven E
    Agrarian populism and the Mexican state. The struggle for land in Sonora.
    Based on author's thesis, Stanford, 1978.
    Bibliography: p.
    Includes index.
    1. Agriculture   and   state—Mexico—Sonora.   2. Land   reform—Mexico—
Sonora.   3. Agriculture and state—Mexico.   4. Land reform—Mexico.   I. Title.
HD1895.S6S26   338.1'87217   80-14262
ISBN 0-520-04056-2

To Rosalie

Contents

Illustrations and Tables

Preface

As Mexico faces the 1980s, the political and economic crises that plagued the administration of Luis Echeverría Álvarez (1970–1976) have somewhat receded from public consciousness, due at least partly to the sensational oil and natural gas resources divulged in the first years of the López Portillo presidency. While international consumers hungrily eye Mexico's energy wealth, and the Mexican state takes advantage of these more favorable bargaining conditions to improve its loan and trade terms with other countries, the situation in the Mexican countryside remains tense, the last battle over land still unfought. In the wave of new nationalist hopes which swept Mexican political elites during 1977 and 1978, the programs for rural development and land redistribution which for sixty years were the trademark of the Mexican Revolution have been relegated to a diminished position on the national political agenda. Yet the salvation or destruction of the present Mexican regime may well rest with that roughly 40 percent of the Mexican populace who now fill the countryside with their hard work and their poverty. The roots and structure of Mexico's rural economy demand that the agrarian question again be given prominence in public-policy debates.

Nevertheless, in the current flush of Mexican prosperity accompanying newfound power and international attention, the apparent disregard of the rural sector by the new administration is striking. The Ministry of Agrarian Reform has been stripped of much of its power and accused by the president himself of "incompetence" and an "obsession" with land reform. Important commissions and small and medium-sized agricultural projects have been superseded by budgetary requirements for industrialization and the diversion of resources for urban use. The government has reversed traditional political convention, claiming that land reform is no longer the objective of rural development programs but that the landless *campesinos* will instead be "proletarianized" at a fair wage. The federal budget gives short shrift to the agricultural sector, emphasizing a new wave of industrialization through 1990.

But if it is clear that the López Portillo administration is currently paying little attention to rural development and the promises of the Mexican Revolution to the countryside and its people, it is equally clear that the present government's policy reorientation since 1976 stems from the political and economic watershed that marked the last year of Echeverría's presidency. That is, the Mexican government's present policies toward the rural population and the revolutionary ideology of land reform at least partly reflect political exigencies resulting from Echeverría's dubious legacy—a legacy of angry bourgeois opposition to state interference in matters of property; *campesino* mobilization to demand delivery on oft-repeated promises of land reform; and populist demagogy, currency devaluation, and economic contraction. This book tells a part of that conflict's history: the political history of the agrarian reform and its relation to populist politics in decline, beginning with the Revolution and ending with Echeverría's ignominious exit from office and the start of the present administration.

In the early 1970s, Mexican government analysts and scholars alike recognized that the bold and famous land reform which had formed the backbone of Mexican revolutionary ideology was in crisis. Various public officials claimed a lack of land available for redistribution—a claim refuted by the government's own land-tenure statistics, showing a worsening maldistribution of land resources in the countryside. Other partisans said that the issues in modern Mexican society no longer included land reform and "agrarian justice," but hinged instead on increased production and economic growth, after the style of the much-vaunted "economic miracle" of 1940–1970. But the thirty-year period of rapid economic growth which preceded the Echeverría populist revival left many Mexicans marginal to the processes of accumulation and of integration into the modern sectors of the economy, and the well-worn promise of "trickle-down" economics rang hollow to the impoverished *campesino*. Finally the "radicals" of the Echeverría government promised to continue land reform and redistribution until Mexico achieved its stated goals of equity and justice in the countryside—a promise quickly adopted by *campesino* leaders as an old I.O.U. now payable on demand. In an atmosphere of political and economic crisis, the Mexican state seemed, in 1976, dangerously unclear about its goals for agrarian reform and agricultural development.

Nowhere was the political disarray more evident during the 1970s than in Sonora, a state whose revolutionary fame and agricultural wealth were now overshadowed by a surging *agrarista* movement denying the legitimacy of official agrarian politics. Sonora, the homeland of some of the most famous leaders of revolutionary constitutionalism, the heartland of the modern agricultural export economy, the conquered frontier of the nineteenth century—Sonora was challenging the national government and the very ideology of the Mexican Revolution itself.

Though the sometimes bloody events of 1975–1976 captured public attention, they were only a reflection of some deeper underlying processes which had shaped the political attitudes and interests of various parties to the agrarian dispute. If the events of 1975–1976, which we shall analyze in succeeding pages, actually threatened the life of the Mexican government as it has existed in the postrevolutionary period, they also more subtly portrayed the history of the formation of state and civil society in independent Mexico. Sonora's land-tenure patterns developed, not by accident, but as a result of a century-long process of primitive accumulation and capitalist growth. The concentration of capital and dispossession of the peasantry to create a wage-labor force, seedbed for the modern agricultural-export economy in Sonora, also meant the annihilation of the Indians who defended their valuable traditional homelands; disentailment of the clergy, who had held wealth and corporate power outside the reach of the state; and the separation of state and civil society, through the rise of liberalism. Settlement of the frontier required resolving the problems of land and labor markets stunted by the moribund colonial system; improvements in state administration and taxation; and a development plan to spur economic growth and civil order. In short, the growth of independent Mexico depended on the creation of a strong national state.

The shape of modern agrarian politics in the twentieth century was further affected by Mexico's economic weakness in the nineteenth. The processes of concentration and dispossession so necessary to capitalist growth were stunted and distorted by a series of factors outside the control of Mexican society during its formative years: inadequate markets, capital shortages, the influence of foreign investment capital, and imbalances in regional and state development. Standard dependency theories[1] of delayed and unequal development influenced the political

---

1. A large body of literature falls under the increasingly wide umbrella of "dependency theory." As this study progresses, certain tenets of dependency theory will emerge from the historical analysis of Mexico's economic and political development. For a more theoretical presentation than is possible here, the classic work is still Fernando Cardoso and Enzo Faletto, *Dependencia y desarrollo en América Latina*, translated into English by Marjorie M. Uriquidí as *Dependency and Development in Latin America*. Other outstanding contributions to the literature are Guillermo O'Donnell and Delfina Linck, *Dependencia y autonomía*; and Richard R. Fagen, "Studying Latin American Politics: Some Implications of a *Dependencia* Approach." A synthesis of much of the early literature is available in Ronald Chilcote and Joel C. Edelstein (eds.), *Latin America: The Struggle with Dependency and Beyond*; and a good critical review of the literature can be found in Philip J. O'Brien, "A Critique of Latin American Theories of Dependency."

heritage of Mexico, affecting the means and modes of political change, economic progress, and social control. As we shall see, dispossession in nineteenth-century Mexico distorted the distribution of wealth and capital without really contributing concomitant changes in class and market expansion. Wage-labor was concentrated regionally and was thus unable to benefit from prerevolutionary economic growth.

The agrarian difficulties historically faced by Mexican society in fact stem from one main political dynamic, whose nature has occupied political theorists since Hegel: the complex of relations between state and civil society, specifically over the question of property. Underlying the narrative which forms the bulk of this study is the political process of creating legitimate state authority in both the private and public realms: the politics of creating public order and *political consensus* through revolutionary institutions, and *civil consensus* based on the growth of economic, legal, and administrative institutions and depoliticized "rights." The separation of state and civil society in Mexico, under the liberal leadership of the nineteenth century, sought to build on the Bourbon reforms of Spain, to disentail corporate wealth, to protect the institution of private property, and to foster a concept of civic virtue and mass consensus based on the institutions of property, the market, and the yeoman-farmer economy.

The liberal state intended, in Mexico, to remove property from the political realm, to institutionalize in civil law the free exchange of labor and capital, and to emulate the economies of capitalist Europe and the United States. The legitimacy of these aims, however, hinged on a strong and well-extended marketplace and a strong civil society led by a progressive, nationalist producer-class which could universalize citizenship and ensure consensus through economic progress. Liberalism and modernization of the relations between state and civil society, in counterthrust to the colonial institutions of *encomienda, repartimiento,* and *fuero,* ultimately depended on the extension of national benefits to the mass of the citizenry.[2]

Obstacles to this liberal quest, of course, included the very weakness of the national economy, the administrative inadequacy and corruption of the nascent state, and the insecurity of Mexico's territory against the United States. As Chapters 2 and 3 will show, these and other weaknesses distorted the Mexican economy (and thereby the state) and began a new dynamic of dependent development which has continued until today.

In fact, the post-independence struggle to a great extent influenced the formation of the state and the role of civil society in the postrevolutionary

2. The *encomienda,* or "entrustment," was a grant from the Spanish Crown to a conquistador of a right to the tribute of a native community, in exchange for protection and Christian tutelage. The *repartimiento* was a colonial institution by which Indian labor was allotted to various colonists on a temporary basis. The *fuero militar* was a privilege through which the military remained exempt from civil laws.

period (1917–1940). The Mexican state in its postrevolutionary form had to address a complex set of questions about its interventionist nature. Foremost among these questions, of course, lay property. Mexico was an agrarian society whose surplus came from the exploitation of landed property. By making land tenure a political question to be manipulated by the revolutionary state, the leaders of constitutionalist Mexico partially reconstructed the fundamental premise of state restraint under liberalism. The liberal assumption that a free market in property would result in a large middle class sustaining and amplifying the economy was patently inappropriate for Mexico. Land concentration after the Liberal Reform, as we shall see in Chapter 2, painfully exposed its weaknesses.

The agrarian question facing the revolutionary leadership of the 1920s and 1930s (Chapters 4 and 5) was how to manage the distribution of agrarian property as the mainstay of revolutionary legitimacy, while maintaining private property and other civil institutions of capitalist growth. Although the state had intervened before the Revolution to achieve its own version of "balanced growth" in the economy and to protect the leading forces of civil society, the economic rationale of the Mexican economic system and the political rationale of the Mexican state fatally diverged in the last decade of the *Porfiriato*. In the 1970s (Chapters 6 and 7), a similar divergence became one of the issues over which the battle for state survival was fought.

One of the permanent features of Mexican political economy in the last century has been this fundamental difference between the economic rationale employed by the Mexican state, to secure continued legitimation through economic success and bourgeois support, and the political rationale employed to obtain mass support, despite persistent inequities. Not only do these logics sometimes diverge; often they are mutually destructive. Essentially then in the following pages we are dealing in some measure with the struggle of Mexican society, in all its diversity and conflicting interests, to determine the legitimate boundaries of public authority and responsibility under a capitalist system of economic accumulation and growth. While the battle to establish the limits and obligations of the state has taken many forms in the past, the primary importance of the agrarian reform in defining the nature of Mexican state populism has always been recognized. In analyzing the agrarian reform, then, we will touch upon sensitive areas which tie the death of *campesinos* in the crisis of 1975–1976 to the systemic struggle between capital and labor, mediated by an embattled populist state professing obligations to both. We will also discern an implicit link between the results of the events of 1976, seen in historical perspective, and the future of Mexican *agrarismo* in the 1980s.

At another, theoretically less complicated level, this book is a more traditional case study of agrarian-reform politics in Sonora, a state of tremendous symbolic and political value which has remained in relative obscurity in the academic literature. Sonora affords us an interesting view into agrarian politics, not merely because of the events of 1975–1976 which originally stimulated this study, but because of its political and geographic distance from metropolitan Mexico, its rich history of independence, its economic growth and transformation since the Revolution, and the political sophistication of its residents. This study does not depict Sonora as a "modal type" for analysis of the agrarian reform of the Mexican Revolution; it is doubtful that such a representation would make sense for any single state, given the multifaceted nature of agricultural production and agrarian politics in Mexico. But Sonora does serve as a focus for much of the more general public-policy debates regarding the nature of "reform" itself; it is a state of great economic importance; and it has demanded the constant attention of Mexican politicians since the first Spanish incursions into then-hostile deserts which are again today the object of political conflict. To the extent that this study clarifies the complex and rich history of land settlement, policy conflict, and state formation in Sonora, we can include this key state of the northwest in our attempts to analyze rural politics in Mexico.

ACKNOWLEDGMENTS

This study grew out of a doctoral dissertation completed in 1978 at Stanford University. Much of the research was made possible by a generous Fulbright–Hays grant which funded a year of fieldwork in Mexico City and Sonora during 1976–1977. The Fulbright–Hays program enabled me to devote my time exclusively to the topic of my study, and I greatly appreciate that opportunity.

In Mexico City a great many scholars, bureaucrats, and técnicos offered me their time and expertise, contributing greatly to my understanding of agrarian-reform politics in Mexico; many of them cannot be named here because of the delicacy of the subject matter and their relation to it. At the Centro de Estudios Internacionales of El Colegio de México I was able to gain access to some of the more current research on the subject and to use the college's excellent library facilities. Professors Sergio Alcántara, Ricardo Cinta, Mario Ojeda, and Rafael Segovia generously assisted me and offered critical suggestions. Cynthia Hewitt de Alcántara, who has written lively and incisive analysis in related areas, also contributed in this way.

In Sonora I was fortunate to encounter many interesting professionals who aided my field research in a politically sensitive and volatile area. Cynthia Radding de Murrieta of the Instituto Nacional de Antropología e Historia, Alfonso and Maren Mendoza, Leonel Argüelles Mendes, Alejandro Sánchez Meyza, Sergio Miranda, and Jorge Ibarra spent a great deal of time and energy familiarizing me with Sonoran politics and history. I also received help from staff members at the Secretaría de Recursos Hidráulicos, the Departamento de Asuntos Rurales del Estado de Sonora, the Archivo General del Estado de Sonora, and the Universidad Autónoma de Sonora. *Ejidatarios* from Bacame and San Ignacio Río Mayo offered their hospitality and many insights.

At Stanford many others assisted in the preparation and completion of my work. Inés Galindo-Radford of the Latin American Curator's office of the Stanford Library provided many reference and acquisition services over a period of three years. Peter Breiner, David R. Dye, Lawrence Goldyn, and William Smith provided critical remarks on early versions of various chapters and enlightened me in many ways. Editorial and typing assistance were graciously provided by copy editor Marjorie Hughes and the staff of the University of California Press, and by Gaye Passell, Hazel Pridgen, Pat Reichert, and Kathleen Stipek.

The members of my dissertation-reading committee deserve special mention. I was fortunate to enjoy long-standing relationships with each of them and have benefitted from each of their perspectives. Professors Charles Drekmeier and Nannerl Keohane demanded a high standard of scholarship from their students; they pressed me during my years at Stanford to search for theoretical bridges to understanding the events of everyday political life. At the end of this long project, I feel that their diligence and critical capacity have improved my understanding of political theory. Professor Richard Fagen has been both advisor and friend over the past several years. He is unique in the respect he shows his students and colleagues and the role-model he provides them. His intelligence, personal sensitivity, and political integrity have had an important impact on me and my work.

Finally, the mention I swore I would not make in print because of the intimacy it violates: Rosalie Massery Sanderson has carried much of the weight of this study by supporting me, editing drafts, accompanying me to Mexico, and generally being the principal source of my personal strength. I hope this book in some way justifies the sacrifices she has made to make it possible.

S.E.S.

Gainesville, Florida
January, 1980

Abbreviations

ARM	Acción Revolucionaria Mexicana (Mexican Revolutionary Action)
CAAES	Confederación de Asociaciones Agrícolas del Estado de Sonora (Confederation of Agricultural Associations of Sonora)
CAM	Comisión Agraria Mixta (Mixed Agrarian Commission)
‹CAT	Comisión Agraria Tripartita (Tripartite Agrarian Commission)
CCE	Consejo Coordinador Empresarial (Enterprise Coordinating Council)
CCI	Confederación Campesina Independiente (Independent Campesino Confederation)
CCM	Confederación Campesina Mexicana (Mexican Campesino Confederation)
CDIA	Centro de Investigaciones Agrarias (Agrarian Investigation Center)
CDUPS	Centro Director Unificador Popular de Sonora (Popular Unification Center of Sonora)
CLA	Comisión Local Agraria (Local Agrarian Commission)
CNA	Comisión Nacional Agraria (National Agrarian Commission)
CNC	Confederación Nacional Campesina (National Campesino Confederation)
CNOP	Confederación Nacional de Organizaciones Populares (National Confederation of Popular Organizations)
CNPP	Confederación Nacional de Pequeña Propiedad (National Confederation of Small Property)
COM	Casa del Obrero Mundial (House of the World Worker)
CONASUPO	Compañía Nacional de Subsistencias Populares (National Company of Popular Provisions)

CONCAMIN	Confederación de Camaras Industriales (Confederation of Industrial Chambers)
CONCANACO	Confederación de Camaras Nacionales de Comercio (Confederation of National Chambers of Commerce)
COPARMEX	Confederación Patronal de la República Mexicana (Employers Confederation of the Mexican Republic)
CPDS	Comité Pro-Dignificación de Sonora (Dignification Committee of Sonora)
CROM	Confederación Regional de Obreros Mexicanos (Regional Confederation of Mexican Workers)
CTM	Confederación de Trabajadores Mexicanos (Confederation of Mexican Workers)
EPL	Ejército Popular Libertador (Popular Liberation Army)
FCI	Frente Campesino Independiente (Independent Campesino Front)
FEAI	Frente Estudiantil Anti-Imposicionista (Student Anti-Impositionist Front)
FEUS	Federación Estudiantil de la Universidad de Sonora (Student Federation of the University of Sonora)
FONAFE	Fondo Nacional de Fomento Ejidal (National Fund for Ejidal Growth)
FPP	Federación de Pequeña Propiedad (Federation of Small Property-Owners)
FROC	Federación Regional de Obreros y Campesinos (Regional Federation of Workers and Campesinos)
FTS	Federación de Trabajadores de Sonora (Federation of Workers of Sonora)
FTSS	Federación de Trabajadores del Sur de Sonora (Federation of Workers of Southern Sonora)
LCA	Ligas de Comunidades Agrarias (Leagues of Agrarian Communities)
LCAEV	Ligas de Comunidades Agrarias del Estado de Veracruz (Leagues of Agrarian Communities of the State of Veracruz)
LNC	Ligas Nacionales Campesinas (National Campesino Leagues)
MLN	Movimiento de Liberación Nacional (National Liberation Movement)
PCM	Partido Comunista Mexicano (Mexican Communist Party)
PLHINO	Plan Hidráulico del Noroeste (Hydraulic Plan for the Northwest)
PLM	Partido Laborista Mexicano (Mexican Labor Party)
PNA	Partido Nacional Agrarista (National Agrarian Party)
PNR	Partido Nacional Revolucionario (National Revolutionary Party)
PPS	Partido Popular Socialista (Popular Socialist Party)
PRI	Partido Revolucionario Institucional (Institutional Revolutionary Party)
PRM	Partido de la Revolución Mexicana (Party of the Mexican Revolution)
PSF	Partido Socialista Fronterizo (Frontier Socialist Party)

SARH   Secretaría de Agricultura y Recursos Hidráulicos (Secretariat of Agriculture and Water Resources)

SRA   Secretaría de Reforma Agraria (Secretariat of Agrarian Reform)

SRH   Secretaría de Recursos Hidráulicos (Secretariat of Water Resources)

UGOCM   Unión General de Obreros y Campesinos Mexicanos (General Union of Mexican Workers and Campesinos)

UGRS   Unión de Ganaderos Regionales de Sonora (Union of Regional Cattlemen of Sonora)

Chapter 1

An Introduction to

Mexican Populism in the 1970s

After being selected as the ruling party's official presidential candidate for 1970, Luis Echeverría Álvarez began a campaign to resuscitate the neglected populist promise of the Mexican Revolution: the *campesino*-oriented agrarian reform. As he carried his agrarian message to various states, he stopped in Sonora to issue a special pledge of presidential fealty. To the Yaqui Indians gathered in Ciudad Obregón, he declared: "Sonora is the Revolution! I carry Sonoran blood in my being; my forefathers are from these lands, and when you are vigorous, so am I; and if you suffer, I suffer with you."[1] Echeverría issued similar statements throughout his successful campaign.[2] After taking office in December 1970, he continued to cultivate his "special" relationship with Sonora, returning to the Yaqui valley at Christmas in 1973 and 1974 and actively promoting a revival of agrarian populism in the state.

In addition to restating timeworn governmental promises to solve the problems of the Mexican countryside,[3] Echeverría seemed to want to form a genuine policy orientation designed to take up the mantle of Lázaro Cárdenas in attending to the landless rural population. In the years that followed, Echeverría's government expanded CONASUPO,[4] attempted to ra-

1. *El Imparcial*, Jan. 5, 1970, p. 1.
2. *Ibid.*, Sept. 25, 1970, p. 1. On this date Echeverría vowed to create an "*agrarista* and *obrerista* state."
3. *Ibid.*, Dec. 28, 1969, p. 1.
4. *Compañía Nacional de Subsistencias Populares*. CONASUPO controls "price floors" on agricultural goods and provides granaries, warehouse facilities, and retai! outlets with government-controlled prices on basic consumer items.

tionalize policy toward the exploitation of water resources, distributed land and credit, and encouraged technological improvements in farming. The Echeverría *sexenio* (1970–1976) also produced a program for collectivizing the *ejido*,[5] a system of cooperative agricultural and cattle enterprises, and a new Law of Agrarian Reform that departed significantly from the earlier codes of 1934 and 1942.

Despite the appearance of intense agrarian activism, the Echeverría regime almost immediately began to encounter the inherited problems of land invasions, student strikes, and *campesino* rebellions. Finding a means of discouraging independent political activity which fell definitely outside the *echeverrista* concept of reform activism was one of Echeverría's chief political problems. The art of Mexican populist mass mobilization, after all, has been historically as much a problem of controlling mass politics as of exciting the underclasses.

Part of the difficulty in controlling the masses lay in the sluggish bureaucratic structure of the state. After laying the legislative groundwork for renewed agrarian reforms, Echeverría still found the process of land regulation painfully slow.[6] Having participated in the violent repressions of 1968 and 1971, and seeing firsthand the evident weaknesses in exercising political control of the masses through party machinery, the new president sought a means to mobilize the political energies of the Mexican people *within* the existing ideology of the Mexican Revolution. His carefully conceived reformism also allowed him to sound a warning to the privileged classes in Mexican society: a caution to temper privilege with occasional redistribution for the sake of long-term political and economic survival.

In Sonora, a primary forum for the most aggressive *echeverrista* policies, the government employed two basic strategies, designed to deal with some of the major apprehensions of the politically involved populace. The first aspect of the "Sonoran strategy" involved the selection of Carlos Armando Biébrich as governor. In a state where governors have often been the most powerful of landowners themselves, or minions cultivated and selected by large landowning interests, Biébrich departed from the mold in two respects. Echeverría's personal favor seemed to be his principal political stock, and he was only 33 years old. He represented both opportunity and role-model for the politically aware youth of So-

5. The definition of *ejido* varies widely, not only according to the bias of the source but depending on the period. It has been called variously a political unit, an economic–social unit having to do with agriculture and cattle-raising, "the triumph of the Revolution of 1910," and the mode by which the people of the Mexican countryside identify themselves. (See Jerjes Aguirre Avellaneda, *La política ejidal en México* pp. 28–29.) For our purposes, it involves a system of land tenure based in the community, but distinct from communal lands and dedicated—in varying degrees—to agricultural or cattle production. More will be said on this in Chapters 4 and 5.

6. The legislative program consisted basically of the 1971 Law of Agrarian Reform, the 1972 Federal Water Law, and the 1976 Law of Rural Credit.

nora, veterans of the bloody student "revolution of 1967" and intransigent opponents of cynical PRI politics.[7] Biébrich was an ostentatious symbol of youth, an example of party flexibility in the 1970s. Billed by the party as a conciliator, Biébrich counted on the endorsements of ex-governors Faustino Félix Serna and Luis Encinas Johnson. He gave some 200 speeches in the Echeverría campaign and befriended young people and hardened politicos as well. On the other hand, the Sonoran Constitution had to be amended to permit a governor to take office at such a young age. After an electoral campaign distinguished mainly by its lack of opposition, Biébrich ascended to the governorship in late 1973, ready to assume his position of import in the Sonoran populist revival.

The second aspect of the "Sonoran strategy," in keeping with other measures promoting Echeverría's collectivization program, involved an investigation of land tenure in Sonora with an eye toward *ejido*-oriented land reform.[8] In addition to investigating private property-holders, the government claimed by mid-1975 to have purged the ejidal system of some 125,000 Sonoran farmers who had been guilty of abandoning, renting, or not cultivating their lands, contravening the laws regulating agrarian rights (*derechos agrarios*).[9] It appeared, at least on the surface, that perhaps the agrarian reform—and the mass mobilization of the *campesinos*[10] historically associated with it—had gained new life after three decades of decline under more conservative rule. The direction it might take, however, was still unclear.

Suddenly, in the fall of 1975, after a nonviolent invasion of properties belonging to the Dengel family—one of the most notorious *latifundista* families in Sonora—the Judicial Police of the state of Sonora, accompanied by a detachment from the Eighteenth Cavalry of the federal army, opened fire on a group of landless *campesinos*. At dawn on October 23, 1975, more than 20 residents of San Ignacio Río Muerto in the northern Yaqui valley fell wounded at the hands of the Sonoran state authorities; 7 died.[11] In the following days both Governor Biébrich and Colonel Fran-

7. PRI-*Partido Revolucionario Institucional*, the official political party of the Mexican Revolution. The "revolution of 1967" will be discussed at length in Chapter 6.

8. *El Imparcial*, June 16, 1975, p. 1. Earlier, Echeverría had ordered the purchase of 70,000 hectares from private owners for collective *ejidos*. (*Ibid.*, Oct. 23, 1974, p. 1.)

9. *El Imparcial*, July 28, 1975, p. 1. The ejidal system of land tenure prohibits alienation, transmission, cession, rental, mortgage, or encumbrance of ejidal property. (*Ley Federal de Reforma Agraria*, March 22, 1971, Title II, chap. I, art. 52; see also *ibid.*, chap. II, art. 85, for the terms under which individual agrarian rights can be rescinded.)

10. *Campesinos*, literally, are country people. Generally in Mexico they include people outside the classification "peasant," even in its broadest connotations. They are found in widely varying degrees of contact with the land, the market, capital, wage labor, and surplus products. Hence, following Womack's and Wolf's lead, I prefer to refer to *campesinos* merely as country people and thus avoid definitional and class arguments in the abstract. (John Womack, *Zapata and the Mexican Revolution*, p. x; Eric R. Wolf, *Peasant Wars of the Twentieth Century*, p. xi–xv.)

11. *El Imparcial*, Oct. 24, 1975, p. 1. Whether the federal soldiers joined fire with the Judicial Police is still hotly disputed. More on this important sequence of events in Chapter 7.

cisco Arellano Noblecía, head of the state Judicial Police, were forced to resign. Within hours, it seemed, the two main pillars of Echeverría's Sonoran strategy—the glamorous young governor and the budding agrarian reform movement—had both sustained severe damage. Biébrich was deposed, later to become a fugitive. The resurgence of government-orchestrated populism in the countryside rapidly gave way to the outrage of *campesino* groups. After the October massacre, it appeared doubtful that Echeverría could regain his leadership of a successful, peaceful agrarian movement. The next thirteen months of the Sonoran land struggle would bear this out.

The massacre at San Ignacio Río Muerto provided the catalyst for individual heroics, a momentary defiance of the government by the powerless, and a corresponding decline in the power of the already suspect National Campesino Confederation (CNC) and its fellow members of the Pact of Ocampo.[12] New invasions sprang up from the Sonoran countryside as if in response to the treachery of the October killings. While much of the state's political and administrative apparatus reeled from the aftershocks of Biébrich's precipitate fall, the *campesinos* accelerated their demands for land. The new Secretary of Agrarian Reform quickly warned the nation's landowners to beware of newfound *agrarismo*.[13] The *campesinos*, some of whom had waited decades for land, gave that warning substance: "To die of hunger or to die here struggling for our rights, we prefer to die here." Said one invader, "All of my family has died in the country, serving *latifundistas*."[14]

But the momentary burst of unorganized independence died quickly, due partly to the overwhelming government domination of agrarian politics (and systematic elimination of opposition), and partly to the significant land concessions which followed the November 1975 invasions. On November 27 and 28, the national and state governments responded with remarkable speed to the urgent problems of Sonoran land tenure. By a presidential resolution of November 27th, 65,371 hectares were given provisionally into the hands of 604 previously landless *campesinos*. The next day the federal government transferred 4,387 hectares of irrigated land in San Ignacio Río Muerto to 433 *ejidatarios*.[15]

On November 30, the affected landowners, who by then had obtained

12. The *Pacto de Ocampo* is an *echeverrista* pact supposedly assuring more *campesino* participation in agrarian reform. Since 1974 it has mainly disarmed potentially independent organizations as threats to the CNC, which since the 1930s has been the official *campesino* union. (See Moisés González Navarro, *La Confederación Nacional Campesina*.)

13. *El Imparcial*, Oct. 28–29, 1975, p. 1. The new governor of Sonora, Alejandro Carrillo Marcor, and the secretary of agrarian reform, Francisco Barra García, in their warning assured the rights of legally held private property.

14. *Ibid.*, Nov. 23, 1975, pp. 1–2.

15. *Diario Oficial de la Federación*, Nov. 27, 1975; *El Imparcial*, Nov. 28–29, 1975, p. 1. The affected landowners included the Dengel, Bórquez Esquer, and Zazueta families, leading proprietors of the Yaqui valley, who played an important role in 1976 as well.

an injunction (*amparo*) against the agrarian proceedings, declared a general work stoppage, refusing to plant or to irrigate some 128,000 hectares of the richest land in Mexico. The carefully calculated newspaper photograph of stalled agricultural machinery on the streets of Ciudad Obregón[16] overshadowed some of the more transcendent issues at hand in the dispute—issues of equity and social obligation deeply ingrained in the history of postrevolutionary Mexico, and issues of state legitimacy, heightened by continuing failure to meet the terms of the agrarian-reform laws. Invasions resurged, negotiations faltered, and Sonora sank into a political and economic crisis from which it has yet to recover completely.

The battle for land in Sonora continued through 1976, now favoring *campesino* invaders, now encouraging the intransigence of the so-called small proprietor. Echeverría's ambiguous role, encouraging "agrarian justice through the law," made all parties in the dispute feel, at different times, that their point of view was favored. At a January *campesino* rally in Toluca, in the state of Mexico, the president warned *latifundistas* that "Zapata still has his boots on and his horse saddled," evoking the legendary image of the fallen agrarian leader, while redistributing land among the rural poor.[17] In April, however, during a new wave of land seizures, many of them engineered by independent organizations, Echeverría admonished the *campesinos*, assuring them that "the law is the way"[18]—presumably the same law that had led to the invasions.

If there was a single consistency in those highly charged last months of *echeverrismo*, it was the northern bourgeoisie's growing hatred of the president. Never a favorite of the famous "Monterrey Group" or the Hermosillo agro-industrial bourgeoisie, Echeverría soon repelled the generally independent *dons* of the south of Sonora—the Ibarra, Salido, Calles, and Obregón families, among others—who joined with the other factions in their relentless opposition to his waning presidency. The autumn of 1976 provided a medium for their revenge and the forum for the last thrust of *echeverrismo*.

The last quarter of 1976 was more chaotic than anyone could have expected. In September and November, *peso* devaluations rocked the economy while currency speculators made instant fortunes.[19] In October and November, land seizures in Sonora and Sinaloa gained new vigor and threatened the winter wheat planting in the key agricultural-export area of the country. And finally, in the last days of November, the lame-duck president struck a last blow at his enemies, transferring 37,000 hectares of

16. *El Imparcial*, Dec. 1–2, 1971, p. 1. The photo of tractors idle in the city of Ciudad Obregón became a famous symbol of bourgeois resistance to Echeverría.

17. *El Imparcial*, Jan. 6, 1976, p. 1.

18. *Ibid.*, April 20, 1976, p. 1.

19. The two devaluations took place on August 31 and November 22, 1976, and the entire period of September to December was one of monetary disorder and speculation.

irrigated land in Sonora to *ejidatarios*. It would not be until August 1977 that his presidential resolutions of November 18 and 19, 1976, would emerge from behind the closed doors of "in-family" negotiations among the president, official party representatives, official *campesino* organizations, and expropriated landowners. It was by then clear to all that the new administration of José López Portillo definitely did not intend to identify with the unstable agrarian politics of Echeverría.

The first step in analyzing some of the subtle forces at work in this seemingly chaotic sequence of events is to realize that the conflict over land reform, agrarian populism, and economic growth under capitalism is really a historic battle to determine the legitimate boundaries of public responsibility and authority. It represents, in short, the quest to determine the realm of the state versus the dominion of civil society.[20]

An underlying current throughout this study is an attempt to trace historically how the Mexican state—narrowly defined as the institutions of government, but more broadly encompassing aspects of the economy and of private life as well[21]—has transformed itself from the liberal "night watchman" of the early post-independence constitutions of the nineteenth century to an interventionist arbiter of both economic growth and social equity in modern Mexico. To the extent that the postrevolutionary Mexican state has effected a multi-class coalition for development, it has guaranteed its own authority (legitimacy) by limiting the dimensions of class conflict in civil society. But, as we shall see in this study, the willingness of various classes and regional factions to accept state-dictated terms of coexistence has been contingent on their subordination and dependence upon the state—dependence based on the rewards of the agrarian reform, in the case of the *campesinos*, or on the coercive and capital strength of the state, in the case of the development-oriented bourgeoisie. As the *campesinos* are denied the rewards of the official agrarian reform, and as the bourgeoisie finds its own channels of economic and political power, the dominance of the state—and the terms of multi-class populism—are called into question. The obvious consequence of such conjunctures is political crisis.

20. A great deal of literature concerning state and civil society in Latin American has recently appeared, some of which will be cited in the course of this study. Important general works include James Malloy (ed.), *Authoritarianism and Corporatism in Latin America*; Guillermo O'Donnell, *Modernization and Bureaucratic Authoritarianism: Studies in South American Politics*; and Guillermo O'Donnell and Delfina Linck, *Dependencia y autonomía*. A corresponding interest in European theorists of state and civil society—Nicos Poulantzas and Antonio Gramsci, among others—has blossomed in Latin American universities.

21. "The state [is] the set of organizations and relationships pertaining to the 'public' sphere within a delimited territory, which claims from the population of this territory conformity with the expressed content of its commands and supports this claim with superior control of the means of physical violence." (Guillermo O'Donnell, "Corporatism and the Question of the State," in Malloy, p. 50.)

Of course, this schematic presentation is deceptively simple in the abstract. In reality, the dynamic between the state and classes in civil society is often hidden in the minutiae and arcane mechanisms of daily politics. It is a commonplace that politics in Mexico, as in many other countries, exists at different levels among different sets of actors, often for different reasons. An issue such as land reform in Mexico, for instance, can be shaped at the concrete level of legal and administrative casuistry.[22] That is, it is possible to shape the policy position of various presidential regimes within the same constitutional framework and the same basic statutory constraints, and to arrive at very different policy outcomes, depending upon concomitant demands of politics and of the economy. It is also possible to adjust the same set of laws to serve (or appear to serve) sectors of the populace with very different interests. We shall see several examples of this variance in Chapters 5 and 6.[23]

The same issue, land reform, can be addressed through an ideological promise which is used to inveigh against "enemies of the Revolution," or to ensure certain kinds of collective political behavior by relevant sectors of the populace. This is perhaps the key to analyzing the agrarian populist pact in its grand historical context: the capacity of the state to use the land-reform promise to mobilize and demobilize the population for the survival needs of the regime. Thus, the agrarian reform has been used to mobilize and organize the rural working class against pockets of unproductive landowners, and to demobilize the *campesinos* when they verged on independence from the state and the party. This aspect of the state will take clearer shape later in this chapter and become more empirically evident in Chapters 4 through 7.

Finally, land reform is sometimes used as an organizational weapon to pursue often-unrelated personal matters or nonagrarian political struggles. The case of Governor Biébrich partly falls into this area. In Chapter 7 we will see how agrarian reform as ideology was used by Echeverría's subalterns against competing elites in the succession struggle of 1975. It often requires close analysis to see the relationship between their actions and the substantive claims of the agrarian-reform program, or between these small battles and the grand architecture of state and civil society.

But in order to describe the specific issues that comprise the agrarian reform of the 1970s, we must first seek an explanation of more architectonic relationships between state and civil society, landlord and *campesino*, and revolution and ideology. Analysis of Mexican agrarian reform does not involve merely the economic issues of agricultural production

22. Rafael Segovia, in "Tendencias políticas en México," p. 5, contends that political casuistry is a daily fact of life in Mexico.

23. This legal manipulation is a consistent theme of the official agrarian reform, perhaps most obvious in the contrast between public policy under Cárdenas (1934–1940) and his successors in the 1940s who used the same legislative base to different ends.

and the rational distribution of resources. To understand the current problems of the Mexican *campo* and their consequences, we need a theory covering various relations between state and classes, between the national economy and international dependence, between property and productivity, and between ideology and concrete public policy. The theoretical outline presented in Chapter 8 is an abstract analysis of these relations, grounded in the historical experience of twentieth-century Mexico. It will show, in part, how different the Mexican case has been, compared with classical models of Western development.[24] I have attempted in Chapter 8 to introduce an interpretive framework for understanding the events in Sonora in 1975–1976 in the larger context of the genesis of the state in the Mexican Revolution.

In order to establish this historical and theoretical context, to outline the importance of Sonora to the development of Mexican economy and society, and to explain the role of agrarian reform in state development and economic growth, let us start with questions about Sonoran agrarian politics in the 1970s and work toward more general analysis of key relationships among the parties to the dispute: agents of the state, landowners, *campesinos*, and independent political leaders.

At the most elementary level, one question immediately emerges from the Sonoran crisis of 1975–1976: How did the death of seven *campesinos* trigger the fall of the governor and presidential favorite, the state police chief, and the head of the state PRI? There was no similar cry for retribution for the deaths of five Tzotzil Indians in Chiapas in May 1976, or a similar incident in Monterrey in February of the same year.[25] The significance of the Sonoran incident arises from the level of political organization of the *campesinos* and the economic importance of the agricultural-export sector in the state, as well as national political conflicts and historical enmities hidden from the view of most observers of Mexican politics in the 1970s—as we shall see in Chapter 7.

At another level, why was the most productive, most agriculturally capitalized state in Mexico chosen as the stage for an apparent battle between the revived populist state and the captains of state-promoted capitalist growth? Given the severe foreign-exchange and debt problems facing Mexico at the time, it seems unlikely that the government would engage in redistributive activities which would surely reduce the amount of capital produced by the northwestern agricultural-export sector. Was there a genuine confrontation between the state and the politically power-

24. Jan Bazant, in *Alienation of Church Wealth in Mexico: Social and Economic Aspects of the Liberal Revolution, 1856–1875*, makes interesting contrasts between disentailment in Mexico and in parts of Europe; see also Maurice Dobb, *Studies in the Development of Capitalism*, esp. chaps. 4 and 5.

25. *El Imparcial*, Feb. 19, 1976, p. 1; *Análisis Político*, May 26, 1976, p. 5.

ful Sonoran bourgeoisie? If so, who forced this confrontation? Is there evidence supporting the assertion that *echeverrismo* was impelled by the impatient popular classes demanding agrarian action? Was the state trying to recapture the support of the multitude of agrarian workers and *ejidatarios* who had defected from official state-dominated organizations? These questions will also be treated in Chapter 7.

Related to the more general questions about implementation of the agrarian reform, we must also examine the specific public-policy lines of the Revolution historically pursued by various governments, their respective political and economic circumstances, and the effects of those policies on Sonoran land tenure and exploitation. The Echeverría years only become comprehensible in light of the formation of the state and agrarian policy after the Revolution. Rather than presenting land reform as a simple question of land tenure in the 1970s, we must explore the hidden means by which the populist redistribution process formally undertaken by all governments of the postrevolutionary epoch has been subverted over the long run: the tale of illegal monopolization of land through family *latifundios*, land rentals, and *prestanombres*;[26] manipulation of water rights and pumping permits; corrupt management of the land register; credit abuses; and the cynical use of the census as a mode of despoliation, among others.

Behind the story unfolding in Chapters 4 through 7, which includes a measure of each of the issues mentioned above, there lies a more fundamental incongruity which haunts the Mexican search for political stability and economic progress. In the course of examining the formation of the postrevolutionary state, we find one agrarian thorn which never leaves the struggling polity's side: the dilemma which pits the ownership of private property against state authority. The history of Mexican agrarian reform since 1915 is, to a large extent, about this conflict. It has resulted in permanent violence in the countryside, a definite decline in agricultural production since 1965, inconsistent public policies from *sexenio* to *sexenio*, and the continuing misery of the Mexican *campesino*. The conflict between state and civil society over the tenure and exploitation of land has led to an ejidal program with multiple definitions of *ejido*. The government has alternately fostered collectivization (1934–1940 and 1970–1976) and parcelization (1920–1934 and 1940–1970) of community property in the ejidal system. Credit has been alternately withdrawn and offered to the *campesinos*, depending on many occult factors often understood exclusively by the regime. The conflict has become

---

26. *Prestanombres*, literally, is "loaning a name." Often, a *campesino* can earn more by illegally selling his agrarian rights to a landowner, providing a cover (his name) for the latter's exceeding the land limits decreed by law. Illegal renting of ejidal land serves the same purpose.

so great that it threatens to confront the Mexican state with a test of commitment to equity versus aggregate economic growth. It is the test of a basic premise of state legitimacy: the agrarian reform.

> From this derives the historic responsibility of the leaders of the country: If the *ejido* is supported as the predominant form of production in the *campo*, the bases will be established for a more just and democratic society, although to achieve that it would be necessary to overcome certain critical phases; if government action continues to protect and indiscriminately strengthen private property under the controversial proposition that this form of tenure is the only one that assures growing levels of production to meet the internal and external demand for agricultural products, this country will continue to witness the incessant concentration of capital, technology, and income into reduced groups of the rural population; at the opposite pole, the *minifundio* and proletarianization [of the *campesino*] will persist as signs of a misery without horizons.[27]

Why, in this conceptualization of the Mexican "dilemma of development" is it necessary to oppose economic development under a system of private property to equity and distributive justice through a community-owned ejidal structure? From what historical legacy and through what political and economic mechanisms does the "historic responsibility" of the Mexican leadership derive? The answer can be found in an examination of Mexican populism. In Chapters 2 through 5 we will delve into the history of Mexican land tenure since independence, highlighting some facets of the liberal legacy created in the nineteenth century, the reliance upon private property as the sole productive form of proprietorship, the ascendance of the interventionist state, and the gradual entanglement of the Mexican economy with foreign capital and a dependent system of developmental values and expectations. From this analysis and evidence from the formative years of the postrevolutionary state, the answer to part of the "contradiction" of Mexican populism will emerge.

A primary contention underlying this study is that the exigencies of capital formation under a system of private property fundamentally oppose the demands for social justice emanating from the Mexican *campo*. As the Mexican economy develops historically along the lines of dependent capitalist growth, the contradiction becomes more apparent and political responses less adequate. As we unravel the complicated tale of postrevolutionary growth in Mexico, we are in effect discovering several interlocking realities: the history of failed pluralism and populist compromise; the history of the sophistication of the Mexican economy and its leading capitalist factions; the history of a capital-short Third World country dependent upon unreliable external economies for survival; the

---

27. Manuel Aguilera Gómez, "Balance de la Nueva Ley de Reforma Agraria," p. 68.

history of the decline of state power vis-à-vis its class supporters; and, predictably, the history of the proletarianization of the *campesinos* and their failure to advance under the populist scheme.

In the end, to show that this conjuncture of the 1970s is properly a crisis of legitimation, we must—through historically examining the bases of the Mexican postrevolutionary government—establish the limits of reform under a system of private property and populist politics. As we shall see in this investigation, the actual limits of state intervention in civil society vary according to the relative strengths of the classes that make up that society. Porfirio Díaz' intervention in the northwest, in the last decade of the nineteenth century, was quite different in form and substance from that of Cárdenas in 1937 or of Echeverría in 1976. But, though the differences are substantial, there are continuous threads that link the three. Some analytical distinctions employed in Chapter 8 may help to clarify these differences and commonalities. But first we must seek the roots of state intervention and agrarian populism in the nineteenth century, when the terms of Mexican liberalism were founded.

Part I

Prerevolutionary Antecedents: Land and Legitimacy in Mexican History

Analysis of Mexican agrarian reform in the context of national economic growth has been intimately tied to some basic relationships between the Mexican state and civil society. At no time were these ties closer than during the social ferment that swept Mexican society in the years following independence from Spain. In the confusion over centralism versus federalism, amid debates between liberals and conservatives, certain political issues endured throughout the nineteenth century. From the time of the first liberal constitution in 1824, Mexican political society has faced a number of problems: state-building, the future of civil and religious corporations, settlement of the frontier, the formation of national development plans, and the role of the state in the postcolonial economy. Chapters 2 and 3 will examine some of the more important aspects of these issues and their proposed solutions.

As later chapters will show, the nineteenth-century antecedents of the 1910–1917 revolution that are discussed in the following pages had tremendous impact upon every aspect of postrevolutionary society. The political forces that emerged as the voice of Mexican liberalism in the 1850s created a constitution which served as a model for the revolutionary constitution of 1917. The political goal of creating a rural class of yeoman-farmers, another liberal prescription dating from the nineteenth century, imbued the postrevolutionary state's decision to intervene on behalf of the rural dweller, dispossessed of his land by the very limits of the original liberal vision. Liberal colonization schemes, part of the plan to entrench civil order by settling the outreaches of the republic and extending the national network of markets, recurred a century later in the development plans of post–World War II governments. State-led development, a late liberal idea carried to a rather corrupt conclusion under Díaz, continued foremost in the minds of postrevolutionary constitutionalists.

Perhaps more central to our understanding of Mexican society are the limits and contradictions which undermined post-independence order and paved the way for revolutionary insurrection. These limits, discussed in Chapters 2 and 3, included the primitive state of Mexican civil society, which was out of phase with the development designs of the liberal and positivist elites of the time. Such discrepancies between political ideology and civil society allowed liberal political reforms designed to expand the rural smallholding class to be corrupted by the few who could afford to speculate in land. While the process of primitive accumulation advanced, vestiges of precapitalist social relations—e.g., debt peonage and the purchase of land for status—stunted expansion of the wage-labor market, as well as retarding the growth of domestic savings for investment and related necessities of capitalism. Though the small, privileged commercial and financial bourgeoisie ruled during the *Porfiriato*, they often did so through regressive policies inimical to domestic capitalist expansion: foreign concessions, land grants to reactionary *hacendados* and warlords, and closure of the political system to the aggressive middle bourgeoisie.

Such restrictions fomented rebellion by the excluded progressive bourgeoisie of the north, an alliance between *campesinos* and liberals against the old order, and the decline and fall of the *Porfiriato*. Thus there evolved an unlikely combination of revolutionary forces: radicals calling for social justice, traditional *campesinos* fighting for the return of their communal lands, and forward-looking capitalists and development-minded politicians bent on creating an idealized version of mercantile capitalism in the twentieth century.

Land—its disposition, status, and exploitation—has been, for the bulk of post-independence history, the fundamental medium through which the varied forces of state and civil society have played out their roles. In the postcolonial period, it represented to the liberals both a cause of and a solution to Mexico's many miseries. To the Porfirian state, it was the coin of the realm which guaranteed production and growth, as well as the complicity of regional warlords. Land was also the primary reward available to the postrevolutionary political system, through which the state might ensure its legitimacy in the countryside. Beginning with Chapter 2, we will examine various points of the dynamic by which the state and the dominant forces of civil society in Mexico sought to perpetuate the conditions for their existence. This dynamic has come to threaten the legitimacy of the revolutionary state in the 1970s.

Chapter 2

.

The Liberal Legacy

It is not surprising that so much of Mexican history springs from conflict over landed property. As in many traditional agrarian societies, both deities and governments have been called upon to resolve problems around the tenure and cultivation of arable land. While Mexico gradually shed its colonial burden during the nineteenth century, the newly-independent native classes struggled to solve myriad state-building problems: administrative rationality, fiscal stability, territorial integrity, social peace. But these problems were not solved in a vacuum; the struggle to build the "independent" Mexican state of the last half of the nineteenth century represented a difficult labor of transition from a precapitalist to a dependent-capitalist society. The peasant rebellions that fed this transition remained frustrated by regional separation, the intrigues of national leaders, and the scorn of liberal ideologues and conservative *patrones*, plus a host of other national and international factors which impelled the erratic growth of capitalism in agrarian Mexico.

In this chapter we begin to trace the dynamic created by land conflict, liberal policy, and indigenous rebellion during the last century, in which lie the roots of revolutionary social obligation. Here begins a narrative analysis of the land-based ideology legitimizing Mexican liberalism, the forerunner of revolutionary populism. This chapter is not a history of post-independence Mexico; it is instead an attempt to aggregate some of the dominant themes of the time which are important to the formation and development of the postrevolutionary state.

In retrospect, we can see that the individualistic, anti-corporate agrarian ideology proposed by the liberal generations of 1833 and 1856 was doomed from the outset to fail in its goals. "Classic" liberalism, borrowed from France, Bourbon Spain, and the United States, was grossly inappropriate to Mexico's postcolonial situation. But its survival as an ideological framework dramatically affected the Mexican Revolution. The postcolonial liberal quest survived into the twentieth century partly because of the general ascendance of international capital in the 1800s, and partly because the progressive .bourgeoisie, who depended on liberal principles, finally had to resuscitate the reform in order to overthrow the increasingly stilted and corrupt *Porfiriato*. Finally, some credit for its incorporation into revolutionary ideology belongs to the rebellious peasantry, disenfranchised and persecuted by liberal paternalism, but imbued with reform slogans and hungry for the equality promised by liberal leadership. In future chapters we will treat the consequences of these varying relationships in the postrevolutionary era since 1934. For now, let us turn to the nineteenth-century rise of borrowed liberalism.

INDEPENDENCE:
PRELUDE TO DISPOSSESSION OF THE PEASANTRY

Nineteenth-century writers at the scene and contemporary analysts have alike recognized the strong agrarian component of the War of Independence. Liberal José María Luis Mora conceded that in the War of Independence, "the right to property suffered a most formidable attack."[1] Conservative leader Lucas Alamán described the independence struggle as "an uprising of the proletarian class against property and civilization."[2] Eyler Simpson, in his well-known analysis of agrarian Mexico, tells us that the war was a struggle of *proletarios contra propietarios*.[3] Nevertheless, the struggle remained incomplete. For decades after independence, the clergy and the military maintained their corporate privileges which blocked the creation of an independent peasantry. A variety of obstacles—a lack of capital, no domestic market, a tiny proletariat, and government instability, among other factors—retarded the development of a landed middle class, and the industrial bourgeoisie of the era remained insignificant in number and in capital.[4] Instead of fostering capitalist expansion, the colonial legacy encouraged the growth of traditional non-

1. José María Luis Mora, *México y sus revoluciones*, vol. IV, p. 4; cited in Jesús Reyes Heroles, *El liberalismo mexicano*, vol. III, p. 542.
2. Lucas Alamán, *Historia de Méjico*, vol. IV.
3. Eyler N. Simpson, *The Ejido: Mexico's Way Out*, p. 18.
4. Enrique Florescano and María del Rosario Lanzagorta, "Política económica: antecedentes y consecuencias." However, the textile industry did provide an important productive link between capital growth, freedom for the *campesino*, and the disentailment of agricultural resources. (See Charles A. Hale, *Mexican Liberalism in the Age of Mora, 1821–1853*; Howard Cline, "The 'Aurora Yucateca' and the Spirit of Enterprise in Yucatan, 1821–1847"; and Dawn Keremitsis, *La industria téxtil mexicana en el siglo XIX*.)

capitalist *haciendas*. The rigid agrarian structure hobbled bourgeois expansion; not only was the circulation of labor and capital frozen, but state growth was stunted, taxes were ignored, and public debt mounted. Needless to say, *campesino* demands went unattended. Mexico was still prisoner of a stagnated colonial economy.

Conservatism, orphan of colonial Mexico, became more entrenched and obdurate as its political base diminished.[5] The loose coherence of class privilege which had reigned in the colonial epoch now began to atomize into an ever-increasing set of opposing groups. Support for a monarchy evolved into an issue over whether to establish a domestic monarch or invite foreign royalty. More crucial still, the nature of order, the highest value in the conservative armory, was never really resolved. Thus, while the 1824 Constitution was ultimately rejected for its liberal excesses, the authoritarian *Siete Leyes* of Santa Anna were also discarded by indecisive conservative partisans.[6]

The conservatives in one sense helped destroy their own political force by abjuring one of their own constitutive principles. Conservatism, after all, originates with the idea of the shared interests of certain privileged classes, and their ability to act together. By the time of the Mexican-American War of 1846–1848, that set of shared interests and the ability to act politically as a unit no longer existed.[7] Even the question of property divided Mexican conservatives. Lucas Alamán, soul of the post independence conservative movement, defied traditional conservative support for civil and religious corporations by calling for the productive division of land and by attempting to coopt the small, privileged bourgeoisie into the conservative fold. In any event, by 1846 the movement was practically moribund, due to the inability of conservatives to unify, as well as to liberal gains in the public consciousness and the lack of a coherent alternative program. All that remained were the last gasps of the venal Santa Anna.

The liberal cause, allegedly incorporating the needs of the *campesinos* into a project for the nation, had its political problems too. The degree to

5. Lucas Alamán synthesized his view of conservative ideology in seven points: (1) conserve Catholicism; (2) a strong centralist government; (3) oppose federalism and popular elections; (4) support new territorial divisions, for better administration; (5) a strong armed force; (6) no congress; (7) European assistance. (Luis González, "La era de Juárez," pp. 19–20.) Alamán's capsule version of the conservative platform employs a certain amount of license, implying far greater cohesiveness in conservative ranks than actually existed in most of the postcolonial era, especially in 1853 when Alamán wrote the letter containing these precepts. (See also Lilia Díaz, "El liberalismo militante," p. 91.)

6. Santa Anna's *Siete Leyes* (drawn up in 1836) called for reorganization of states into departments, establishment of a *Supremo Poder Conservador* with virtually no restrictions on his authority, and extension of presidential terms to eight years, among other generally centralist, conservative provisions. (Josefina Zoraida Vázquez, "Los primeros tropiezos," p. 29.)

7. Reyes Heroles, *El liberalismo mexicano*, vol. II, p. 344.

which it would struggle for *campesino* demands was bound by its contradictory goals of creating from the same small, badly distributed agrarian population an independent *campesinado* and an army of landless labor. The Mexican liberal vision was further limited by its racism, as we shall see. Moreover, the liberals had to confront the substantial power of the Church; in order to ensure disentailment of the clergy, the liberals would have to strike out at all corporate wealth, including that of the indigenous communities.[8]

In the context of the conflict between conservative and liberal ideologies in the 1821–1856 period, the indigenous communities that survived the colonial period became the target of class war between bourgeois and colonial *patron*, between nascent capitalism and the *ancien regime*. The conservatives argued that Indian uprisings were a product of liberal attacks on the colonial system and the expansion of the economy at the expense of the Indian.[9] The liberals, on the other hand, blamed the *campesino* insurrections on the colonial system itself—the invidious combination of "the cruel yoke of community," "communal vice," and frustration caused by the lack of private ownership.[10] Despite their obvious differences, both conservatives and liberals manipulated the *campesinos*, especially the Indian communities. While conservatives and their allies— *haciendas*, clergy, and parish associations—dreamed of dominating a resurgent corporate society, the liberals pledged to liquidate the "communist" Indians and "repress the colored classes," on behalf of the new order of land tenure.[11]

It would be wrong to infer that the battle over the nature of property took place at a distant and abstract ideological level. It grew out of the daily reality of Mexico's early independence. The ideology—and the public policy—which accompanied liberalism's gradually ascending star partly responded to immediate political problems such as weaning the Indians away from Church influence. Partly the liberals sought to guarantee social tranquility and support of capital, and partly they were convinced of the inherent moral deficiency of communal property.[12] An examination of these three components illuminates much of nineteenth-century public policy and its ideological justification.

The Worldly Power of Religion

> If religious principle is converted into political power, and . . . it pretends to exercise coercive force over the citizenry, to gain profit, [and] impose con-

---

8. Sergio de la Peña, *La formación del capitalismo en México*, p. 118. There was a certain inner conflict in the battle against corporate wealth, since Mexican liberalism, in its early phases, wanted to integrate liberal principles and the virtues of the old society, in the manner of the Bourbon Reforms. (See Reyes Heroles, vol. I, p. 16.)

9. Hale, *Mexican Liberalism*, pp. 244–245.

10. *Ibid.*, pp. 238–239.   11. *Ibid.*, pp. 230–239.

12. Peña, *La formación*, p. 125.

tributions, . . . its degeneration is complete . . . and it becomes an administrative rival to the sovereign.[13]

Mora's statement against the temporal pursuits of the Church in Mexico reveals a clear concern for the survival and sovereignty of the state. Whereas in the early colonial period the Church had played an important "pacifying" role—particularly in the northern missions—the clergy, since the early eighteenth century, had conflicted sporadically with the secular authority of the state. The latest manifestation of that conflict came in the Church's resistance to the conditions of independence. Besides protesting the elimination of its political and cultural power, the Church also continued to resist challenges to its substantial wealth in land and currency. In a capital-starved economy, the Church held a large amount of scarce resources and generally did not employ them in investments for production.[14]

So, in addition to the general anticlerical bias popular in the liberal ideology of the age, the Church was seen as an enemy of liberalism because it represented an impediment to the advance of the Mexican political economy. It was a chief guardian of the old corporate order so closely associated with the colonial epoch. In addition to its obstruction of capital growth, the infamous programs of "reducing" Indians to mission communities under the aegis of Jesuits (and later, Franciscans) prevented the secularization of society and rationalization of the work force in the production of surplus value.[15] As a major organizer of the campesinado, it posed a competitive threat to the administrative consolidation of the state.

In some instances the Church was indirectly responsible for rebellion against the government. A case in point is the 1825 Yaqui Indian revolt in Sonora. The Yaquis greeted independence enthusiastically, expecting more local self-government and less contact with the Yori (white man). But in addition to the usual problems of local corruption and caciquismo, as new citizens they had to pay newly imposed taxes. When they refused to pay the new levy, the army was dispatched to collect the debt. A priest, Pedro Leyva of Cócorit, urged the "new citizens" to resist, and they promptly rose up under the leadership of Juan Banderas. There followed a general rebellion, which surged and receded throughout the century.[16] Needless to say, this rebellion and others of the period did not enhance relations between church and state under the First Republic.

13. Cited in Moisés González Navarro, La Confederación Nacional Campesina, p. 12.

14. Jan Bazant, in his essay "Desamortización y nacionalización de los bienes de la iglesia," shows that the Church wealth that did circulate generally went to hacendados, with no assurance that the investment would be used for production.

15. Edward H. Spicer, Cycles of Conquest: The Impact of Spain, Mexico, and the United States on the Indians of the Southwest, 1533–1960, pp. 288–298.

16. Hubert Howe Bancroft, History of the North Mexican States and Texas, vol. II, 1801–1899, p. 639; see also Spicer, p. 61. The "benefits" of citizenship are stated in more general terms in Michael P. Costeloe, La Primera República Federal de México, 1824–1835, p. 27.

In sum, the conflict between the state and clergy was fundamental; every aspect of the liberal project—from the idea of the virtuous yeoman to the political alliance with northern capital—was opposed by the church, with drastic consequences.

Liberalism in Action: The Concentration of "Civic Virtue"

Because of the popularity of French and North American liberal thought in the post-independence period, concepts of citizenship and civic virtue were closely tied to the creation of a rural middle class to sustain the liberal order. Liberal constitutionalism, incorporated in the 1824 and 1857 constitutions, sprang from the idea that true citizen responsibility rested with the property-holder. A concept of the virtuous citizen obviously meant a great deal in the era of state- and nation-building. It provided a mainstay of legitimacy for the proposed political order. As Mora proclaimed: "Only these [property-holders] possess true civic virtues: beneficence, decorum in person and style, and love of the public good; these are virtues almost exclusive to property-holders."[17] To strengthen the prestige and power of the rural middle class (and of the various sectors of the nascent bourgeoisie), Mora further suggested that only the propertied classes be permitted to exercise the full rights of citizenship.[18]

Consistent with their goal of separating the agrarian bourgeoisie from the conservative *latifundistas*, the liberals forged a political alliance with the incipient mineral, agricultural, and commercial bourgeoisie of the northern and north-central states. The interests of this group included extending the internal market network and guaranteeing the political stability and productive progress of the nation.[19] As corollaries to these general aims, the liberal alliance demanded colonization of the frontier and the dispossession and pacification of the Indians. Naturally, the process of consolidating the liberal forces around a free market of property and the "Europeanization" of the frontier had its counterpart in the degradation of the dispossessed. By the time the process was concluded in the late 1800s, the northern and Yucatecan Indians were decimated by this zealous pursuit of Mora's civic virtue.

Resolving the Indian Problem

In Chihuahua, Sonora, and Durango, the dominant public issue of the immediate post-independence era centered around the elimination, or

---

17. Mora, *Obras sueltas*, p. 183. Mariano Otero also viewed the property-holding class as the embodiment of "enlightenment, morality, the desire for progress, and the sentiments of humanity." (Otero, cited in Reyes Heroles, *El liberalismo*, vol. II, p. 110.) This class was supposed to retrieve the benighted Indian from his misery and reorder the terms of future Mexican development; it was more successful in the latter.

18. Mora, *Obras sueltas*, p. 179.

19. Peña, *La formación*, p. 124.

"pacification," of rebellious Indian tribes. In 1825 the Yaquis of Sonora began an insurrection that would last more or less continuously over a century, and played a significant part in the political economy of the *Porfiriato*. In these three states, the Comanches, Apaches, and Seris, among others, robbed and pillaged with varying intensity.[20] During the 1840s, when these Indian rebellions seemed most severe, the Caste War of Yucatán erupted. Other peasant rebellions surging in Nayarit, Michoacán, Morelos, and Oaxaca further heightened the alarm of white citizens and government functionaries alike.[21]

Indian problems were clearly related to the other public issues of the period. Part of the desire to expand the agrarian property-holding class was based on the liberal conviction that the "Mexican race" was innately superior to the Indian. The various wars of pacification were generally couched in terms of "brothers" versus "barbarians."[22] To Mora, the colonization of the Mexican frontier meant the eventual assimilation of pure Indian races into the "Mexican race." *El Universal*, a conservative organ, went even further: "All activity, we could almost say all intelligence, resides in the Spanish race; luckily the indigenous race . . . is coming to be a kind of auxiliary mass whose importance is invaluable if we know how to direct it well."[23]

In addition to their racial tone, the Indian uprisings, especially in the north, jeopardized the settlement of a stable frontier against the United States, annoyed foreign commercial interests, and generally retarded a strong, rational federal system. As these were key concerns of the liberal governments of the nineteenth century, the Indians and *campesinos* were soon made to regret their transgressions.

The quest to "liberate" the Indians from their communally held land rounded out the liberal formula. Of course the virtues of such action in terms of creating a free rural workforce and more disentailed land are obvious. But the roots of liberal opposition to communal property lay deeper than the surface needs of accumulation. It was partly opposition to the Church and the colonial system, which left the Indians in a state of permanent legal and moral childhood. It derived from Mora's vision of individualism and virtue, and also embodied the more prosaic aspect of creating in "each new proprietor . . . a new defender of institutions and of stability."[24] This civil defense would counter the aggressive tendencies of

20. Bancroft, *History*, pp. 651, 654, 659; Hale, *Mexican Liberalism*, pp. 234–237. Spicer, *Cycles of Conquest*, offers good summary accounts of Seri and Apache activities, though only a brief mention of Comanches.

21. Nelson Reed, *The Caste War of Yucatán*. Reed shows the extreme severity of the Indian problem for national sovereignty. (See Reyes Heroles, vol. III, pp. 644–650, for further hints at the agrarian roots of the caste war; also Luis González, "La era de Juárez," p. 16.)

22. Hale, *Mexican Liberalism*, p. 235.

23. Cited in Florescano and Lanzagorta, "Política económica," p. 105.

24. *El Monitor*, cited in Hale, p. 37.

"communist" Indians who refused to admit that their ancestral lands somehow fit into a larger nation governed by European laws.[25]

ATTACKING THE PROBLEMS:
COLONIZATION AND DISENTAILMENT

The liberal conviction of the necessary supremacy of civil society was a crucial factor in the bias against communal property. We may see in the colonization-pacification programs and in the disentailment of church land the ascendance of civil society at the expense of those sectors of society formerly protected by the colonial state. These programs were defined as leading toward freedom for all, equality before the law, and a just separation of state and civil society, where the latter would reign supreme.[26] One of the greatest contradictions of Mexican political economy in the nineteenth century was the adoption of a market ideology, a market-based conception of freedom, and market-oriented colonization and state-building schemes, when in fact the market was as weak and as regionally limited as state power. Liberal policy meant the exclusion of the vast majority of Mexicans from both citizenship and property. Even though preference was given to "those who before were called Indians,"[27] the capital and political requirements for colonization and proprietorship effectively excluded most of the population from participation in the fruits of the disentailment and sale of national lands. The state would eventually have to replace the market as the main distributor of land and capital, before Mexico's economy could progress. But only under the *Porfiriato* would the state undertake the infrastructure and administrative tasks necessary to construct the roots of a viable national economy.

Colonization

Though colonization never did succeed during the nineteenth century, it was a policy goal from the time of independence from Spain. Since the liberals conceived of the destruction of corporate property as the first step in the redistribution of wealth, free circulation of labor and capital, and the consequent extension of civilization, it seems only natural that colonization became a primary means to achieve their goals. Even though colonization laws began under Iturbide,[28] the influence of liberalism on

25. This struggle between communal land and tribal autonomy versus national supremacy resulted, in the case of the Yaquis and Mayos, in a provision in the 1873 Sonoran Constitution depriving ". . . the Yaqui and Mayo tribes of the rights of citizenship while they maintain the anomalous organization that they have in their towns and *rancherías*, but allowing the enjoyment of those rights to individuals of the same tribes who reside in the organized pueblos of the state." (Cited in Spicer, *Cycles*, p. 67.)

26. Reyes Heroles, vol. II, pp. 275–279.

27. *Ibid.*, vol. III, p. 564.

28. Lucio Mendieta y Nuñez, *El problema agrario en México*, p. 92. Other laws to distribute population which preceded the First Republic include: a Decree of June 4, 1823, to

their content is evident. The occasional overlap of conservative and liberal positions, especially favoring European immigration, does not weaken the contention that colonization *primarily* secured the advance of national capital—in conjunction, of course, with foreign capital.

Two primary aspects of post-independence colonization efforts involved the distribution of land and the distribution of the populace on the land. Two options were exercised to effect the redistribution of land: the settlement of unoccupied national lands (mainly on the northern frontier) and the disentailment of corporate lands. Until the Reform Constitution of 1857, only the former option received sufficient public-policy attention. The distribution of the populace on the land was approached through colonization programs designed to attract military pensioners and foreigners, and through efforts to break up Church-dominated communities by mission-reduction programs. Of course, the anti-Indian campaigns of the last three decades of the nineteenth century would have similar "benefits" for population redistribution.

The first true colonization law, that of January 4, 1823, allowed the government to procure latifundia (with indemnification) in order to effect more equal land division. Though preference was given to nationals, the law also proposed to deal with foreign colonization companies which brought foreigners to Mexico. Despite suspension of the law in April of the same year, it provided a precedent and a structural framework for further forays in this area.[29] Again in 1824 the government decreed a colonization law which essentially embodied the principles of the 1823 law. It also limited the land to be ceded to colonists and forbade the passage of colonized land to *manos muertas* (mortmain).[30]

The colonization efforts of 1823 and 1824 faced the same set of problems that plagued the settlement of the north throughout the century. Conceding land to foreign colonization companies, as would soon become obvious in Texas, threatened to beget a crisis of sovereignty.[31] In the 1830s the new Mexican state found that there was little point in settling

divide land among the permanent army; a Decree of July 19, 1823, conceding unused lands to veterans of the War of Independence; and a Decree of August 6, 1823, conceding unused lands to sergeants and corporals wishing to retire. (Mariano Galván Rivera, *Ordenanzas de tierra y aguas,* pp. 40–41.)

29. Mendieta y Nuñez, *El problema,* p. 92. Foreign colonization was a remarkably consistent facet of Mexican land policy, given the chaos that governed the post-independence period. Though many conservatives opposed such entry of foreigners (as may be seen in the Colonization Law of 1830, which halted immigration to Mexico and put U.S. settlements under military supervision), even Maximilian would later succumb to the idea. For some evidence, see Seymour V. Connor and Odie Faulk, *North America Divided: The Mexican War, 1846–1848,* p. 18; and Gene M. Brack, *Mexico Views Manifest Destiny, 1821–1846,* p. 57. Maximilian's actions on colonization policy are conveniently summarized in José C. Valadés, *Maximiliano y Carlota en México: historia del Segundo Imperio,* pp. 264–265.

30. Galván Rivera, *Ordenanzas,* pp. 45–46, 94.

31. The misgivings were already surfacing in the debates of 1822–1823. Apparently the authorization for Stephen Austin's Texas colonies was given without even knowing the ex-

the frontier if the colonizing state could not control the residents (which was a primary purpose of the Mexican colonization efforts in the first place). Likewise, extending the frontier required a more sophisticated fiscal and administrative network, lacking in the post-independence era.

Disentailment

An equally weighty issue surrounded entailed lands. By the time of the liberal reforms of 1856–1859, it had become apparent that the liberal public-policy position on land tenure must encompass both the distribution of land *and* distribution of the populace on the land. Disentailment was the core of the first part of the project. Colonization would solve the latter. Lerdo de Tejada, author of the famous *Ley Lerdo* and key booster of disentailment, claimed that nine million new landowners had been created by his law. Another observer, however, commented that, due to disentailment, "some rich people added to their fortunes and no poor person found remedy for his poverty."[32] In any event, by the time of the Restoration in 1867, the limits of disentailment were becoming more apparent: disentailed property had become the base ingredient for new latifundia— civil, noncorporate, and virtually impregnable under the Liberal Constitution of 1857. More important, the disentailment effort still had not reached the Indian communities. The battle over their lands would occupy the second phase of disentailment. By the end of the *Porfiriato*, disentailment, which had once been so closely identified with the goals of Mora, yielded the most illiberal concentration of land imaginable.

PURSUING THE RATIONAL STATE

Behind the complicated facade of legislative battle, a fundamental change had taken place in the Mexican state during the struggle to coordinate the future development of the agricultural economy: the statesmen of the post-independence period had gradually come to claim a right of expanded eminent domain. Despite their declared devotion to liberal principles, liberal legislators—and even some conservatives, like Alamán—had argued in the debates of 1822 and 1823 for the rights of the state over corporate property *and over latifundia privately held.*[33] Reyes Heroles sum-

---

act location and dimension of the proposed settlements. The colonization concession proffered to Austin became a central issue in the suspension of the January 4, 1823, law of colonization. See Manuel González Ramírez, *La revolución social de México*, vol. III, *El problema agrario*, p. 112.

32. Cited in Luis González, "La era de Juárez," p. 27.

33. On this point, see the 1822 speech of Gutiérrez de Lara, in the first volume of the *Historia Parlamentaria de los Estados Unidos Mexicanos, de 1821 a 1847* (Mexico: 1877), p. 810; cited in Reyes Heroles, vol. I, p. 139.

marizes their thinking in classical liberal terms: "As property is a product of the social pact, the idea is that the society *or the state, which is its representative*, can and should regulate property with one purpose: to divide it and to foment the circulation of wealth."[34]

This liberal principle permits the market or the state to intervene on behalf of the circulation of capital. At the same time, the conditions of this simple principle change fundamentally if the forces of civil society—mainly, though not exclusively, the market—cannot sustain their function as main agent in this transition of systems of land tenure and exploitation. The *extent* of corporate forms of land tenure also creates difficulties for the liberal state. The principle cited by Reyes Heroles is generally based on the assumption that the state will only act as arbiter of the will of civil society when the latter is incapable of regulating itself. In the case of disentailment, the state conceded much ground to lay *latifundismo* in its zeal to purge its premier enemy, the Church (and later the Indian). The social pact would require not only the productive division of land, but state action to repress the equity demands made by the dispossessed.

The state began, in the middle of the nineteenth century, to undertake an expanded role of marketing agent, governor, source of capital, adjudicator of unoccupied lands, etc. The roles of state and civil society as modeled under the liberal framework had been changed radically, due to the many structural and conjunctural differences which marked the nascent dependent economy. It was in this role distortion that land became a primary question of political legitimacy in post-independence Mexico.

The Reforms of the 1850s

By the time of the reforms of 1856–1859, the liberal forces in Mexico had coordinated a political program based on principles expressed as early as 1810, and partly rooted in the national resentment toward the clergy and the military in the aftermath of the North American invasion of 1846–1848. During the 1840s, the frontier had been ravaged by Santa Anna's futile, humiliating campaigns as well as the various filibusters and invasions by Texans and United States citizens. The invásions and Indian attacks continued into the 1850s, adding to the ignominy of the war and further discrediting conservative rule.[35]

Alamán, embittered by the war and by bourgeois individualism on the rise, blamed colonization for the loss of the frontier to foreigners.[36] But Alamán's vilification of bourgeois society was drowned out by the new

34. Reyes Heroles, p. 130; emphasis added.
35. Brack, *Mexico Views Manifest Destiny*, pp. 54–55, 101–104. See also Gastón García Cantú, *Las invasiones norteamericanas en México*, pp. 170–194; and González Navarro, *La Confederación Nacional Campesina*, p. 20.
36. Alamán, *Historia de Mejico*, vol. V, p. 880.

wave of revived liberalism. Many old liberal slogans against foreigners and the clergy gained new currency after the defeat of 1848.[37] To Alamán's contention that bourgeois egoism could never provide the foundations for any political institution[38] came the liberal retort that the very foundation of all political institutions and of the national spirit was to be found in the organization of property.[39] None of these statements was particularly new, but the political crisis of Mexico in the 1850s gave them new life. After a generation of false starts, Mexican liberalism was becoming the dominant ideological force in national politics.

Still unresolved, however, were the problems of creating a rational state. During this period in Mexican history it appears that the ideological sophistication of the political elite outstripped their capacity to act through existing political institutions. Still eluding the grasp of all parties to the political struggle of the 1850s was a national government with the administrative authority to preside over the federal system.[40] The tax system was ineffectual and in grave disrepair after Santa Anna. By 1853 approximately half of Mexico's territory had been lost through war and the Gadsden Purchase. Commercial agriculture, especially in the central states of the Bajío region and in Morelos, Puebla, and Tlaxcala, had been virtually destroyed by internecine warfare, from independence to the reform. Fear of United States domination of Mexico exacerbated the problems of maintaining an already fragile economy.

The liberals, emboldened partly by the failure of postwar compromise governments, sought to gain power by politically exploiting the economic crisis of the period. Conservatives, in turn, refused the *modus vivendi* offered to them by moderate liberals and sealed their future by beginning a search for a foreign monarch. Mexico was polarized, and any notion of a program of economic and political development would have to await the arrival of a dominant political force.[41] That force would not appear until Porfirio Díaz became president.

Probably the single most important reason that the new force of liberalism failed to express itself in a national government was the opposition— increasingly violent—of the now-dissolving conservative movement. Despite the liberals' substantial gains in the early 1850s, they still commanded a *military* force often inferior to that of the champions of reaction. The fight for final supremacy began with a conservative call for "*religión y fueros*"; it would not end until the Republic was restored in 1867. From the outbreak of the bloody Three Years War—almost imme-

37. Manuel Otero, "Consideraciones sobre la situación política y social de la República Mexicana en el año 1845," in *Obras*, vol. I, pp. 104, 120–125, 127.
38. Alamán, vol. V, pp. 919–920.
39. Otero, "Ensayo sobre el verdadero estado de la cuestión social y política que se agita en la República Mexicana" (June 1, 1842), in *Obras*, vol. I, p. 27.
40. Florescano and Lanzagorta, "Política económica," p. 76.
41. *Ibid.*, p. 89.

diately after Juárez' assumption of power—until the end of the Second Empire in 1867, the liberals had to delay implementation of the reform programs while they struggled for mere survival.

The Second Empire and the Restored Republic

Even while the Three Years War was reaching a conclusion in late 1861, the strange partnership between Mexican conservatives and European monarchs was being established. Thus, shortly after the defeat of conservative forces in 1861, the French invasion began. The period known as the Second Empire (1864–1867) represented essentially a holding action by conservatives, who, having lost on the battlefield, hoped for a restoration of the privileges denied them under the liberal reforms of 1856–1859. In his short three-year term, Emperor Maximilian, of course, had little real opportunity to show his long-range plans for Mexico. But the forces of conservatism that guarded his flanks were gravely disillusioned by his confirmation of all Juárez' basic reforms. Maximilian's moderate land policy, far from the monarchist dreams of a restructured corporate order, disappointed his once-ardent reactionary admirers. Like Juárez, Maximilian saw the necessity for exploiting national lands through auctions, colonization schemes, mortgages, etc.

Partly because of the moderate stance Maximilian took toward property, the Restored Republic (1867–1876) was able to impress its image on Mexican history as the beginning of the end of post-independence chaos. The Restored Republic could also benefit from the already accomplished destruction of Church wealth, which had taken place during the reform. It represented a regime whose juridical base had preceded it. But the reform laws were in one important sense a false foundation for the liberal dream. Much of the wealth generated by the disentailment of corporate lands was lost in the Three Years War and the subsequent French occupation. Without an adequate fiscal system based on administrative reform and national solvency, no credit could be generated to expand the productive base of agriculture. Due to profound inequities in wealth and social position, the sale of national lands more closely described a *rotation* of capital among a small elite than a free *circulation* of capital in a well extended marketplace. The existence of such a traditional landholding elite accelerated the concentration of wealth and retarded the decomposition of traditional *haciendas*. Rural communities, stripped of the colonial protection of municipal land tenure, were ravaged by *hacendados*, speculators, merchants, and public officials.[42]

Even the radical liberals had to accept these lay latifundia, because, in effect, there was no way to attack them. To protect individual private

---

42. Jorge Calderón Salazar. *Algunos aspectos de la dinámica económica y social de México en el período 1920–1935*, pp. 14–15.

property was an integral part of liberal faith; lay latifundia, regardless of their productivity, fell under that protection.[43] Speculation, outrageous violations of Indians' rights, falsified land surveys, and intimidation all worked swiftly to dispossess the *campesinos* of the now-illegal ejidal land they held.[44]

In addition to failures in the legal machinery designed to create the base for the new agrarian bourgeoisie, the Restored Republic faced other obstacles to its development. To colonize and populate Mexico was a task of generations, requiring concessions to foreign capital, economic infrastructure, a large army, credit, etc., that were simply not available at the time. The workforce was estimated to be two million, or one worker for every 100 hectares (250 acres) of land; in the words of Luis González, this population was "scarce, rustic, dispersed, dirty, poor, stagnant, sick, badly fed, boastful, heterogeneous, ignorant, and xenophobic."[45]

The Restored Republic did engage in an administrative reform which served to rationalize some of the daily functions of the government and order the liberal vision. What had been the liberal dream of independence now became a set of semi-programmed priorities—to populate the nation, to produce a net agricultural surplus, to stimulate small property and the free circulation of labor. The liberals of 1867 dreamed of railroads and highways which would uncover Mexico's potential wealth. Through renewed programs of colonization, the Indians could be pacified and integrated into a new, more dynamic mode of production.

But the liberal programs never really assaulted the global problems the Mexican system was suffering. Again, the regime endured rebellions every year from 1867 to 1876, from virtually every region of the country.[46] The Indian populations, hostile still, rejected incorporation as an "auxiliary mass" in the new society. Capital, especially foreign capital, would not respond to credit pleas emanating from a country appearing to be under siege. Without capital, even the most modest designs for infrastructure growth were doomed. In sum, the situation in 1876 cried out for a combination of enforced peace, growth, and political strength. And, as liberalism ended what Leopoldo Zea called its "combative phase," Porfirio Díaz stood ready to design its future as the philosophy of order and capitalist growth.

43. Hale, *Mexican Liberalism*, pp. 225, 301–302.
44. Wilfrid Callcott, *Liberalism in Mexico, 1857–1929*, pp. 38–40.
45. Luis González, "El liberalismo triunfante," p. 180.
46. *Ibid.*, p. 184.

Chapter 3

Porfirian Progress

> To you belonging to the family of pauperism, to you that cannot resign yourselves to work in order to carve out . . . an independent, unencumbered position in life, these words go out to you warning you not to come to Sonora. . . . Sonora offers all of its elements, all of its riches, to men of enterprise, to men who come to exploit it with strong spirit and manly force, making themselves useful to society with great and positive benefits for themselves as well.[1]

With this curious half-warning, half-advertisement, historian Francisco Dávila in 1894 signalled that a remarkable change had taken place in the northwest since the beginning of Porfirio Díaz' dictatorship in 1877. Only a few years had passed since Sonora and Sinaloa had been barely able to sustain commerce, isolated from the nation—surviving, it seemed, on the ferocious energies of their sparse populations. But those few years nurtured a climate for increased investment and an aggressive, development-oriented public-policy stance by the Mexican national government. The northwest was finally "investment property."

In the 1860s the civil war in the United States had injected the Mexican agricultural economies of Nuevo León, Chihuahua, Sinaloa, and Sonora with new vigor.[2] Cotton boomed, and with it the Pacific coast ports of Guaymas, Mazatlán, and Manzanillo grew in importance.[3] Foreign and national merchants prospered in the coastal boomtowns of the Gulf of Cal-

---

1. Francisco T. Dávila, *Sonora histórico y descriptivo*, p. 326; cited in Héctor Aguilar Camín, "La Revolución sonorense, 1910–1914," p. 17.
2. Enrique Florescano and María del Rosario Lanzagorta, "Política económica," p. 85.
3. Inés Herrera Canales, "Comercio exterior," pp. 148–149.

ifornia. Of course, their importance to foreign trade made settling the frontier more important than ever to the growth-oriented Díaz regime.

Another boost to the exploitation and settlement of the northern frontier came as a result of the speculative actions of many government officials.[4] Throughout the Porfiriato, fortunes were made through land legislation, wars of pacification, colonization and survey concessions, and the manipulation of water rights. While aggregate economic growth sometimes resulted from such activities, the type of growth and its limitations later caused serious problems of legitimacy for Porfirio Díaz, as we shall see in this chapter.

Other key factors which contributed to the historical conjuncture known as the Porfiriato include the lively remains of the liberal development plan of the Restored Republic. It was obvious by the time of Juárez that an essential prerequisite for national economic development was an adequate system of railroads.[5] Without such a network, the internal market system could never develop in a country so segmented by rugged mountain ranges and heavy-handed local bandits and warlords. Likewise, the producers who had flourished during the short-term export boom of the United States' Civil War and Reconstruction period could not continue to compete with growing Yankee markets without being included in the North American chain of western railroads. Happily for Porfirian plans, the western frontier of the United States was beginning to consolidate in the 1870s, drying up some former sources of windfall profits and, at the same time, stabilizing as a market. International finance capital, riding the wave of imperial boom, became more inclined to invest in the future of Díaz' Mexico.

A resurgence of northern mining provided a major enticement for new capital. Decimated by the myriad problems of colonial Spain, gold and silver mining in Mexico did not regain their 1805 production levels until 1843, and then only briefly. After 1875 the production of precious metals rose steadily and rapidly until the Revolution of 1910.[6]

These circumstances signified that the frontier had to be settled, capitalized, and controlled with the substantial—albeit costly—assistance of foreign capital. The goal was ambitious: nothing short of transformation

4. Many legislators who would soon find a place in the Porfiriato made their fortunes through the disentailment, and made sure that they flourished in the years that followed. (See Manuel González Ramírez, La revolución social de México, Vol. III. El problema agrario, pp. 143–146.)

5. Fernando Rosenzweig, "El desarrollo económico de México de 1877 a 1911," p. 406.

6. Ibid., p. 408; and Sergio de la Peña, La formación del capitalismo en México, p. 111. In 1881 W. C. Greene bought the mines of Cananea, Sonora, for 350,000 pesos. That same year other Yanqui companies bought interest in various Chihuahuan mines. (See Luis González, "El liberalismo triunfante," p. 207.) New investment was further stimulated by the extremely lenient mining codes of 1884 and 1892. For specifics of the Cananea mines, see C. L. Sonnichsen, Colonel Greene and the Copper Skyrocket.

of the Mexican economy through the internationalization of northwestern development. The beneficiaries, unfortunately, were limited in number to those who funded, defended, or comprised the organizational body of Porfirio Díaz' dictatorship. Among the pariahs surrounding this small coterie were, first, the excluded elite—those who felt continual frustration at being a part of the development network, yet outside the charmed Porfirian circle of privilege. Beyond these forgotten elite were the poor: the peasantry, the *peones*, and the working class, the propertyless masses whose patience would eventually reach its limits in the rigid inequality of the Porfirian regime.

PORFIRIAN DEVELOPMENT PLANS

One of the key functions of the phase of primitive accumulation which precedes industrial capitalism involves the concentration of wealth through dispossession of its former owners.[7] This process of creating a class of the dispossessed concomitantly bolsters the reserve army of labor necessary for the production of surplus value. In analyzing the *Porfiriato*, we must take into account additional factors, which disturbed the relations of primitive accumulation and, in the end, contributed to the morbidity of the Porfirian state. In addition to considering the conscious growth plans of an interventionist state, we must consider the structural conditions which characterized Mexico in the nineteenth century: a maldistributed workforce, which would create problems of stability as well as accumulation; a high proportion of foreign interest in investment planning, and related foreign domination of frontier development; and a poorly organized national market system which, coupled with low wages and an infantile industrial sector, sealed off the opportunities for domestic economic expansion. Even more crucial are two corollaries to the structural problems of the Porfirian regime: class weakness and liberal *agrarismo*. These two characteristics of the final phase of primitive accumulation in Mexico changed the terms of capitalist development for generations.

Because of the class weakness of the bourgeoisie—their regional separation, proprietary and sectoral interests, and unresolved feelings toward foreign capital—the state was required to take command of capitalist development, which had been a shared, though vague goal since the formation of the Republic and the decline of conservatism. In Sergio de la Peña's words, "a prepotent state was being formed that assumed the empresarial labor of the bourgeoisie, in part because of the indecision of the latter."[8] Once the Porfirian state inextricably identified itself with the course of Mexican de-

7. Maurice Dobb, *Studies in the Development of Capitalism*, chap. 5, *passim*, but esp. p. 185.
8. Peña, *La formación*, p. 180.

velopment, it became responsible for the failures of the economy, the stagnation of the bourgeoisie, and the international exploitation of Mexican wealth, as well as the entire litany of social abuses that finally destroyed the regime.

The role exchange that took place between state and civil society in the last quarter of the nineteenth century was an outcome of the Jacobin liberal ideology, which contained a concept of distributive agrarian justice contrary to the development goals of the times. After the advent of foreign finance capital and the development of a state–class alliance for capitalist development, notions of agrarian equity and an economy sustained by a large agrarian middle class no longer had currency with government policy-makers and the captains of Porfirian growth.[9]

The agrarian ideology of the reform had aptly criticized the backward *haciendas* and demanded parcelization of the Indian *ejidos*. It had proposed that the state act as an arbiter of its version of progressive social justice (for the small proprietor, at least), even extending to the realm of land tenure. The Díaz regime, perhaps more cognizant of the wrenching contradictions facing the liberal path of parcelization and market development, chose to defend dispossession and aggregate economic growth without concerning itself with ethical problems of concentrated land tenure. The *Porfiristas* chose to ignore—or, worse, encourage—the abuses of the *hacienda* while dispossessing *ejidatarios* for reasons of development and regime survival. The ideology of reform liberalism was not in tune with the advance of primitive accumulation. Those who adjusted to the new reality embraced positivism; others lay waiting for a resurgence of combative social liberalism.[10] But the myth of the happy yeoman lay dormant until the last years of the *Porfiriato*.

"Veins of Iron": The Growth of the Railroads

Clearly one of the most crucial aspects of modernization of the Mexican economy involved expansion of the national railroad network. An integrated, modern system of railroads would have the virtue of consolidating the fragile linkages among regionally isolated markets. It would also provide a potential boom for the unsettled north by incorporating agricultural production (which had surged during the United States Civil War) into the American southwest.

The railroad network to the Mexican northwest was set up to connect

9. This must of course be qualified in light of several land-reform measures proposed in the last decade of the *Porfiriato*. (See Daniel Cosío Villegas (ed.), *Historia Moderna de México*, vol. III, pp. 192–195.) Nevertheless, these measures failed, and certainly they did not represent the main current of Porfirian thought on land tenure.

10. Leopoldo Zea, *El positivismo en México. Nacimiento, apogéo y decadencia*, pp. 276–278. The positivist developers, proposing a new philosophy of order, called for "less promises and more order; peace and work instead of impossible laws."

Table 1

Railroad Expansion, 1876-1910[a]

PERIOD	KILOMETERS CONSTRUCTED
1876-1880	433.2
1880-1884	4,658.0
1884-1898	6,350.0
1898-1910	7,108.0

[a]Data derived from Francisco R. Calderón, "Los Ferrocarriles."

important agricultural and mining areas with both the United States and the hub of the Mexican Republic.[11] The mission of the railroad was to create the *venas de hierro* through which the future development of Mexico's economy would course. Table 1 shows the vigor which accompanied the mission of railroad expansion.

The virtues of the railroad extended to political advantage as well. A government-dominated railroad system lent itself naturally to control of insurrectionary groups. In 1896, Porfirio Díaz frankly admitted that a compelling reason for opening national lands and subsidizing railroad expansion was to control the Indians.[12]

Related to the exploitation of geographically isolated areas of Mexico was the attraction of foreign capital. Though Mexican legislators feared developing the frontier in conjunction with foreign capital—undoubtedly with the problems of 1846–1848 in mind—the exigencies of Porfirian development eventually swept away their opposition. Foreign capital won the support of the regime. Two more facets of Porfirian frontier progress were then in motion: foreign capitalization of Mexican development, and the demarcation and colonization of "national lands."

The Great Survey Concessions

Always mindful of the difficulty in defeating the Indians as well as the rich prize that awaited the successful *conquistador*, Porfirio Díaz promoted foreign colonization schemes and land speculation with the same watchwords he used to justify the expansion of the railroads: "Peace and prosperity."[13]

11. Ángel Bassols Batalla, *El Noroeste de México: Un estudio geográfico-económico*, p. 351.
12. *Informe del Ciudadano General Porfirio Díaz,* . . . *entre el 1° de diciembre 1884 y 30 de noviembre de 1896*, p. 90.
13. *Ibid.*

The increased role of the state as guarantor of economic development and private property, as is apparent in Díaz' frontier programs, partly reflects this strategy for settling the wild, potentially rich nomadic pastures of the north. Administrative and fiscal reforms, consolidation of the foreign debt, and the national integration of markets and transport, all justified an attempt to cultivate foreign interest in capitalizing and settling the promising outer reaches of the Mexican nation. Since support for lay latifundia was essential to maintaining power and concentrating capital, unfettered exploitation of enemy Indian communities and their lands came to represent both a statement of mutual interests between regime and *hacendado* and a state commitment to regional development.

In an important sense, settlement of the frontier was the beginning of what might be called the great "agricultural contradiction" of the *Porfiriato*. In order to effect the transition of Mexican society from its chaotic precapitalist agrarian economy to a modern agricultural and industrial producer, *the agricultural sector would have to operate on behalf of the formation of capital*. That is, land under the new order would have to act as capital and not as a nonrational source of social status. On the other hand, in order to settle the frontier, pacify or destroy the Indians, curry favor with regional *caciques*, and keep the military loyal, *the Díaz regime had to use land not as capital, but as a bribe often unrelated to production*. The survey concessions in one aspect represent the first phase of this bribe.

On September 15, 1883, under the nominal reign of Manuel González—chief foil for Díaz' plans at the time—the Law of Colonization was revised, allowing the government to name commissions of engineers or private companies to survey national lands, previously left more or less to whomever claimed them. Up to one-third of the territory surveyed was granted as compensation for the work of the concessionaires.[14] This provision, along with previous colonization and land-tenure laws, was the nucleus of the Porfirian dispossession program.[15] This program amounted to an enclosure movement, in which any lands not clearly titled were redistributed to survey companies and regime favorites.[16]

Land redistribution during the next two decades completely reordered the ownership of the Mexican countryside and stripped thousands of their way of life. A comparison by decade of public-land titles issued to claimants, and the surface area involved, is given in Table 2; the titles listed represent slightly more than one-fourth of the total land alienated during the *Porfiriato*. More than 20 million hectares of additional public land was

14. González Ramírez, *La revolución social; El problema agrario*, p. 112.
15. Moisés T. de la Peña, *El pueblo y su tierra*, pp. 281–282; and George M. McBride, *The Land Systems of Mexico*, p. 74.
16. Clark W. Reynolds, *The Mexican Economy: Twentieth-Century Structure and Growth*, p. 136.

Table 2

Baldíos[a] Adjudicated, 1867-1906[b]

PERIOD	NUMBER OF TITLES	AREA (hectares)	AREA/TITLE (hectares)
1867-1876	880	1,423,872	1,618
1877-1886	3,662	5,408,631	1,474
1887-1896	2,370	3,063,698	1,292
1897-1906	1,022	1,016,401	994
			Average
Totals	7,934[c]	10,912,602	1,369

[a]These figures do *not* include lands given in compensation for survey work. This table covers only *denuncias*, or public claims to untitled or "inadequately titled" land. *Baldíos*, according to the 1894 law, were lands which had never been alienated by the nation or legally destined for public use. For the text of the law, see Wistano Luis Orozco, *Legislación y jurisprudencia sobre terrenos baldíos*, Book Two.

[b]Data in the Table are compiled from Manuel González Ramírez, *La Revolución Social de México*, p. 165; and George McCutchen McBride, *The Land Systems of Mexico*, p. 74.

[c]These totals do not agree with those of Cosío Villegas, though both admit to being tentative, given the incompleteness of the data available. This dispute over land data is a permanent condition of research into Mexican land tenure. For various reasons there is little agreement among authors even over the most basic data; controversy often extends to misstatements in the same primary sources of data. I have used the most-often-cited primary-source figures in my research. Wide variations are footnoted.

given to survey companies alone for the discovery and survey of *baldíos*. The bulk of land purchases were also made by companies, adding substantially to their control over a good part of the 49 million hectares they surveyed.[17]

Three-fourths of the titles doled out during the *Porfiriato* (but less than 2 percent by area included) were from ejidal subdivisions; only 2 percent were destined for colonists; and less than 1 percent by number (311 titles) represented the survey companies' shares.[18] In the states with the most public land available—and the smallest indigenous population—the parties involved effected an extremely quick transfer of lands. In Chihuahua, some 7 million hectares went to 7 concessionaires; in Durango, 2 million hectares were given to 2 grantees; and in Oaxaca, 3.2 million hectares went to 4 concessionaires. Similar solutions prevailed in Coahuila, Nuevo

17. Jesús Silva Hérzog, *El agrarismo mexicano y la reforma agraria*, p. 117.
18. Cosío Villegas, *Historia Moderna*, vol. VIII, p. 196.

León, Tamaulipas, Tabasco, and Puebla.[19] In Sonora, concessions from the survey of public lands alone yielded 2,624,974 hectares for 81 owners, including over 1.7 million hectares to a single individual.[20] In all, some 38,774,280 hectares of public land were distributed to *hacendados* and survey companies during the Porfiriato.[21]

Much of the land adjudicated came from unoccupied national lands. Simpson contends that only about 2.2 million acres of communal lands were allotted in severalty during the *Porfiriato*—an enormous amount of land, but only about 2.2 percent of the total land area distributed.[22] A very high proportion of the total land on the market during the *Porfiriato* fell into the category of survey concessions and claims by *denuncia*, as outlined in Table 2. These claims to land through *denuncia*, needless to say, were hardly contested equally. From the provisions of the Law of 1894, no corporation or community (i.e., *ejido*) could legally own or contest real-estate titles.[23] All of the communities that had until then survived the Reform disentailment were suddenly thrown into the war between local *hacendados*, land speculators, concessionaires, generals, and public officials, without the necessary skills to maintain possession of their lands even in parcel form. Large companies and wealthy individuals with political power and contacts within the regime were much more likely to use the *denuncia*. Needless to say, the Porfirian bureaucracy was not disposed to hinder them in their pursuit of land. Indian lands—or what was left of them—became the booty of the new frontier.

Survey concessionaires were also notorious for marking the best land for their own, inventing *baldíos* by personally judging the validity of titles to land already occupied, and intimidating whoever opposed them.[24] Between the survey and land companies and the Mexican *hacendados* seeking to extend their domains, the traditional *campesino* community was destroyed.

As a result of the colonization, survey, and expropriation of "national lands," by 1910 only 4.2 percent of rural heads of families owned any property; 95.8 percent did not.[25] One person in a thousand—834 persons,

19. McBride, *Land Systems*, p. 75.
20. Cosío Villegas, vol. VIII, p. 149.
21. This figure (*ibid.*, p. 196), does not square with the 134.5-million-acre figure given by Eyler N. Simpson in "The Mexican Agrarian Reform," p. 5. Since Cosío Villegas and González Ramírez roughly agree in their figures, their data are used here.
22. Simpson, p. 5.
23. This law only restated the principles set forth in the 1857 Constitution. Though the *Ley Lerdo* of 1856 had protected the *ejido* from the general disentailment of Church property, Article 27 of the Reform Constitution made no such provision. See Wilfrid Hardy Callcott, *Liberalism in Mexico, 1857–1929*, p. 5.
24. Cosío Villegas, vol. VIII, pp. 188–190.
25. Data are conflicting here, too. The government publication from the Secretaría de Economía, Dirección General de Estadística, *Estadísticas sociales del Porfiriato, 1877–1910*, p. 218, cites 95.8 percent as the landless proportion of the rural population; Silva Hérzog (*El Agrarismo*, p. 123) cites 96.9 percent from the Census of 1910.

0.1 percent of the rural population—owned 21.3 million acres; 18 percent of the rural population were classified as farmers, 82 percent as peons.[26] In all but one state, Baja California, over 92 percent of the rural population held no property. At the extreme was Oaxaca, the birthplace of Juárez and Porfirio Díaz, where only 499 people (0.2 percent) out of a population of over 900,000 owned any property.[27] Mexico was a rural country owned by a few men who generally controlled their vast lands with a distant, but watchful eye.

Colonization Fails

Throughout the nineteenth century, Mexico suffered labor shortages in many regions. In some areas this historical scarcity of wage labor was abetted by the labor demands of the railroads, hostile Indians, epidemics, tropical heat, and similar hardships. With the advent of a purposive regime brandishing an ambitious development project, this situation had to change. Dispossession programs that robbed workers of alternative means of survival supplied part of the answer; they were supplemented by debt peonage, forced labor, and deportation programs. But plainly the government still felt that the bulk of the manpower shortages faced by nineteenth-century Mexico could be attacked through foreign colonization.

Repeated failures of these programs were to aggravate opposition to the Díaz dictatorship in the late 1890s among both *campesinos* and local landholders in many labor-scarce areas. Eventually, of the 12,000 colonists who arrived on Mexico's shores, only a scattered few would endure.

The state responded to these labor-distribution problems in its last twenty years with a curious mixture of bribe and brute force, the legendary *pan y palo* (bread and a stick) that guided Porfirian decision-making. But it could hardly be expected that a workforce suffer proletarianization and loss of land *and* be expected to weather relocation as well. Likewise, one could hardly expect the rising middle bourgeoisie to accept the continual frustrations of a regime blending capitalist growth with an antiquated seigneurial system of land tenure and exploitation. For, despite the retrospective aura of the *Pax Porfiriana*, the epoch was one of radical change in the forms and relations of production. Class oppositions were heightening between *hacendado* and *peon*. When all exits for the dispossessed peasantry finally closed, Porfirian progress would show its lack of flexibility.

ECONOMIC DEVELOPMENT DURING THE PORFIRIATO

Most surveys of the *Porfiriato* remark on the tremendous growth that characterized the 1877–1910 period. But growth is a many-sided process

26. *Estadísticas sociales del Porfiriato*, p. 218.
27. McBride, *Land Systems*, pp. 98, 154.

which redounds to the benefit of certain classes and to the detriment of others. Porfirian growth, in particular, benefitted the social forces dominant in the regime. Among these dominant forces we can count the *hacendados*, the commercial bourgeoisie, and foreign capital, along with a coterie of fifty or so *científicos*. Besides assuring their own wealth, these leaders of the *Porfiriato* succeeded in developing a pattern of aggregate economic growth for the country. Let us examine the nature and extent of that growth, as it affects the nature of the land struggle in the northwest.

The most impressive advances made during the *Porfiriato* came from the export sector, mainly agriculture and mining. Between 1877 and 1901, mining and metallurgy grew at a rate of 7.3 percent annually, manufacturing at 2.8 percent, and agricultural, cattle, and forestry products at 6.1 percent. From 1901 to 1910, growth was even more accelerated in most of the categories mentioned. But the export-led development that characterized the *Porfiriato* depended on increased exploitation of natural resources, cheap labor, and high levels of foreign investment and technology.[28] As the supply of one or another of these inputs became scarce, the Díaz regime tended to try to squeeze more value out of the other factors. Most often, the victims of these efforts to compensate for weaknesses in the economy were the workers, especially the rural *jornaleros* (day-workers).

In agricultural development, there were two conflicting tendencies. Producers for the domestic market tried to monopolize land and crops to reduce the amount of land under cultivation, thereby maintaining artificially high prices.[29] On the other hand, the export sector, as noted above, depended on increased production for expanding international markets. Often there was little interaction between the two factions. Overall, between 1877 and 1907 agricultural production sustained only 0.65 percent annual growth rate. While export goods and primary goods for the internal market rose at an annual rate of 4.21 percent during the *Porfiriato*, the share of land and labor reserved for domestic food production began to evaporate; the predictable results are summarized in Table 3. The effect of this change in the structure of production was dramatic in terms of aggregate growth data.

More dramatic, however, were complaints of mass hunger heard by local officials and journalists—horrifying reports that "from Culiacán to Álamos nothing is being eaten but the roots and trunks of *mezcal* plants."[30] The domestic food requirements of Mexico were being neglected for the sake of cash crops, primarily destined for international sale. Corn, beans, chile, and squash, the staples of the Mexican poor, were subject to neglect, drought, frost, and local monopolies. Backward tech-

28. Reynolds, *The Mexican Economy*, pp. 21–23. As Reynolds duly notes, growth in agriculture came almost entirely from the export sector.
29. Luis Cossío Silva, "La agricultura," p. 2.
30. *Ibid.*, p. 20.

Table 3

Shares of Agricultural Production,

1887-1907[a]

(percent)

CATEGORY	1877	YEAR 1894	1907
Maize	52	42	33
Other food and drink for internal market[b]	34	30	29
Primary goods for the internal market[c]	10	13	17.6
Export goods	4	15	20

[a]Data elaborated from Luis Cossío Silva, "La Agricultura."

[b]Activity in this sector would appear even more sluggish if it were not for a lively alcoholic beverage industry which buoyed up production for the internal market.

[c]Consisting primarily of sugar, cotton, tobacco, and cacao.

nology, wildly fluctuating prices, and ruthless speculators further reduced staple production. Corn production declined by 20 percent during the *Porfiriato*, almost 50 percent on a per-capita basis. Beans declined by 25 percent, or 75 percent per capita.[31] The situation became so extreme that the mortality rate appeared to increase as a function of the bad corn harvests. And still the *hacendados* were not inclined to plant more basic foodstuffs.[32]

The marked differences among *hacendados* producing for different markets reveals complex regional and sectoral divisions in the landholding class. Several gradations existed between producers for foreign markets, raw-materials producers for domestic markets, and traditional subsistence producers. The smooth generalization that the *hacienda* as an institution did not aid economic development does not stand up under scrutiny.[33] To understand the *hacienda*, we must analyze the variety of class tensions and factions which plagued Mexican society during the *Porfiriato*. To view the *hacienda* as a uniform entity, drawing no distinction between capitalist *hacendados* and regressive advocates of a sei-

31. Charles C. Cumberland, *Mexico: The Struggle for Modernity*, p. 204.
32. Rosenzweig, "El desarrollo económico," p. 440.
33. Callcott, *Liberalism in Mexico*, p. 166.

gneurial system of rural social relations, is to gloss over a key facet of the *Porfiriato* as a period of social change. Many traditional *hacendados* performed as a rentier class, exploiting the *peones* without regard for technical change or productivity, satisfied with a rent that would be "sure, perpetual, and firm."[34] On the other hand, with the arrival of extensive external commerce, more diversified markets and investment opportunities, and the chance for profit in agricultural export, a number of *hacendados* betrayed the canons of their class and became leaders of the bourgeois resistance to Porfirio Díaz.

The relevance of these distinctions, then, surpasses mere acknowledgment of intraclass tension among landholders. These differences keyed regional attitudes toward the regime. Progressive bourgeois revolutionaries in the countryside—e.g., Francisco I. Madero—fought the irrational waste of land resources which characterized *hacendados* of the traditional sort. Likewise, progressives fought against the *tiendas de raya* and debt peonage which were especially prevalent in areas with a scarce supply, gravely reducing the labor market.[35] To the progressive bourgeoisie, then, the state in league with the traditional *haciendas* and their peons represented an obstacle to the creation of a more balanced and rational land and labor market.[36] To the *campesinos*, the backward *hacendado* conveyed a more immediate image of permanent indebtedness and dependence. Despite their class opposition, these *campesinos* and the bourgeoisie were to ally themselves, at least momentarily, for the seizure of state power.

Objective economic and social conditions continued to press toward that radical change of power. The aggregate economic gains already mentioned were substantial, both in absolute production levels for export-related activities and in more durable infrastructure investment. As an economy which was led by the state, however, the occasionally-impressive sectoral growth did not match the gross imbalances which threatened the regime's survival. Though agricultural production grew 21 percent from 1888 to 1910, the population grew some 61 percent.[37] Less and less of

34. Rosenzweig, p. 427.

35. Friedrich Katz, "Labor Conditions on Haciendas in Porfirian Mexico," p. 8, fn. 20. The *tienda de raya* was a *hacienda*-owned store through which a great number of *peones* became indebted. It provided a large margin of profit for the *hacendado*, who arbitrarily set prices and often sold low-quality merchandise at exorbitant prices; it also allowed the conservative *hacendado* to circumvent the market to a great extent, by avoiding transactions in cash and selling products made on the *hacienda*. The debt peonage thus created also represented a means of dividing peasant labor against itself. *Acasillados*, privileged wards of traditional *haciendas*, often fought against peasant uprisings from free villages. The assimilation of half of the rural populace into the hacienda system by 1910 shows an undeniably anticapitalist tendency of the system. (Sergio de la Peña, *La formación*, p. 192.)

36. *Ibid.*, p. 136.

37. Cossío Silva, "La agricultura," p. 3. The population grew from 9.4 million to 15.16 million between 1877 and 1910, according to census data from Cosío Villegas, vol. VIII, pp. 5–10.

domestic agricultural production was channeled to serve the needs of the Mexican populace. The most backward units of production provided the bulk of domestically consumed comestibles. The working classes, in addition to being ill-fed and ill-paid, were abused on their jobs, prevented from organizing, and continually subjected to the frequent economic contractions the *Porfiriato* suffered.[38] Four of every five Mexicans depended on the land for survival; by 1910 only four in every hundred owned any land to depend on. The rest—mostly agricultural workers—found that their salaries (when paid in cash) dropped between 15 and 30 percent from 1877 to 1911.[39] The situation in the *campo* was plainly desperate.

SONORAN DEVELOPMENT

In 1875, at the close of the era of strongmen Ignacio Pesqueira and Manuel María Gándara, Sonora was crippled by years of internecine squabbles, imperial intervention by the French, North American filibusters, conspiracies by the United States government to annex the state, and the ever-present Apache, Pápago, Yaqui, and Mayo rebellions. The principal cities, Álamos, Guaymas, Hermosillo, Ures, and Arizpe, had been taxed into economic stagnation by the government of Ignacio Pesqueira.[40] The *Porfiriato*, faced with a declining Sonoran population, a wobbly economy, and Indian raids, had to rely on foreign capital, land concessions, the modern labor force, and progressive capitalist *haciendas* to effect the striking transformation witnessed by historian Dávila at the opening of this chapter.

Sonora, dating from the late *Porfiriato*, has always been a prime factor in the transition from precapitalist to capitalist society. In the nineteenth century this northwestern border state contained all of the elements that provoked the changes brought about during Porfirian development: Indians warring against the government; rich commercial elites on the coast; competition for labor among mining companies, *hacendados*, and United States companies; rapid railroad development; steadily building foreign investment; and a booming system of agricultural capitalism. Sonora produced a governor who ascended to the vice-presidency of the nation; it also provided some of the revolutionary forces responsible for his overthrow.

The Sonoran boom of the *Porfiriato* took many forms, according to re-

38. Compounding the damage done by bad crop years which reduced the need for agricultural labor in 1878, 1883, 1884, 1888, 1892, 1900, 1901, 1904, 1909, and 1910, the industrial sector was unable to absorb population migrating to the cities. See Cossío Silva, "La agricultura," pp. 21–22; also Roger D. Hansen, *The Politics of Mexican Development*, p. 21; and Rosenzweig, "El desarrollo económico," p. 438.

39. Rosenzweig, p. 447.

40. Rodolfo F. Acuña, *Sonoran Strongman: Ignacio Pesqueira and His Times.*

gion and economic sector of activity. In the north and in Álamos, mining companies from the United States revamped the decaying remains of the colonial system of mineral extraction. Probably the most illustrious example of *Yanqui* presence in Sonora's mines was Colonel William C. Greene, whose Cananea Consolidated Copper Company gave rise to the Cananea Realty Company, the Cananea Cattle Company, the Greene Consolidated Gold Company, the Yaqui River Gold and Silver Company, and the Bonanza Belt Copper Company, in addition to timber lands, sheep ranches, railroads, and other activities.[41] North American mining entrepreneurs invested some 33 million dollars in Sonoran mining, creating towns overnight around the nearly 5,400 mining properties that existed by the end of the *Porfiriato*.[42]

Commercially, Guaymas had boomed for some time, but it too fell under the economic woes besetting Sonora under Pesqueira. Under the *Porfiriato*, despite the Yaqui and Mayo wars, Guaymas remained a key commercial center and wellspring of finance capital for development schemes in other parts of the state. Guaymas merchants helped finance the Sonora and Sinaloa Irrigation Company of Carlos Conant Maldonado. Likewise, commercial agriculture, within the limits of unstable markets and speculation, boomed in Guaymas and Hermosillo, as well as in the southern valleys. Corn, wheat, garbanzos, oranges, and tomatoes all thrived in a select number of advanced commercial *haciendas*.[43]

As a result of agricultural, commercial, and mining activities throughout the state, the cities of Sonora grew rapidly. From 1890 to 1910, Álamos increased its population by 35 percent, thanks largely to the mining boom of the last decade of the *Porfiriato*. The granaries of the state—Hermosillo, Ures, Arizpe, Magdalena, and Altar—grew apace.[44]

In typical Porfirian fashion, Sonora's railroads marked the key to the early phase of the economic boom. In 1882, the Guaymas–Nogales run of the *Ferrocarril de Sonora* concession was completed. Five years later the line was bought out by Southern Pacific. Another foreigner, the Englishman F. H. Seymour, built trunk lines to the northern mines, as did the Moctezuma Copper Company owners and Colonel Greene. Even the Richardson Construction Company joined in financing railroad construction in Sonora.[45] Though many of the lines were never completed, the infusion of foreign capital and economic activity stimulated Sonora and the nation after the post-Civil War letdown.

Above all, these many aspects of the Sonoran boom represented a triumph of liberalism over the old order. Despite the profoundly antiliberal

41. C. L. Sonnichsen, *Colonel Greene and the Copper Skyrocket*, chap. 14.
42. Aguilar Camín, "La Revolución sonorense," pp. 110ff.
43. *Ibid.*, pp. 70ff.
44. *Ibid.*, p. 90.
45. Claudio Dabdoub, *Historia del Valle del Yaquí*, pp. 304–306.

overtones of the *Porfiriato* in general, and the horrific slaughter of Indians perpetrated in the last two decades of Díaz' reign, the agricultural, mineral, and commercial barons who rode the crest of Sonora's growth represented the political forces which had ended the reign of conservative Manuel María Gándara. When his successor Ignacio Pesqueira was unable to impose the Indian peace necessary to commerce and to maintain taxes at an acceptable level, the liberal bourgeoisie rebelled against him under the leadership of one of their own, the customs chief of Libertad, Francisco Serna.[46] The liberals, who formed regional clubs to organize their political voice and economic power, were not rigidly committed to any single person or idea. Their allegiance to the Díaz regime, and their later opposition to it, revolved basically around the question of pacifying the Indians with federal troops and receiving necessary stimuli to continue the Porfirian boom.

In the rich river valleys of Sonora, the advent of a progressive capitalized commercial bourgeoisie and a higher level of foreign investment brought with it more evidence of glaring differences between social classes in the countryside and the brutality with which that inequality could be enforced. Above all, with the continual need for foreign exchange to generate more economic growth, the internationalized sector of agriculture and mining had to be cultivated. Despite the gross fluctuations in international demand for rubber, henequen, garbanzos, and other key Mexican export items, capitalist enclave production required a steady labor supply, low wages, good land, and social stability. At the same time, the "denationalization" of key sectors of the Porfirian economy incensed many regional leaders and traditional supporters of the *Porfiriato*. Encroachment on the regional labor supply, in the cases of Sonora and Sinaloa, became a major issue dividing the Díaz regime and progressive *hacendados* during the Yaqui deportations at the turn of the century (mainly 1902–1905).[47]

Growth and the Indians

The goals of Porfirian development in Sonora extended, not surprisingly, to advancing mining and export agriculture, pacifying and dispossessing the Indians (especially the Yaqui and Mayo), and securing the frontier for Mexican development against the United States. Ramón Corral, infamous director of the Yaqui deportation program, governor of Sonora (1895–1899), and vice-president of the nation under Porfirio Díaz, remarked in 1888 on the difficulties of achieving these goals in his home state. His annual report of that year (as vice-governor) was a virtual chronicle of grievances against the bellicose Indians. Fiscal crisis was a seem-

46. Acuña, *Sonoran Strongman*, pp. 123ff.

47. Evelyn Hu-Dehart, "Development and Rural Rebellion: Pacification of the Yaquis in the Late *Porfiriato*," pp. 72–73.

ingly unalterable fact of life in Sonora dating from Pesqueira, increasing partly due to the Yaqui and Mayo wars of 1885 and continued Pápago raids in the northern community of Altar.[48] Corral proposed to solve the problem by reducing the Indians until, like the Mayo, they were "convinced of their impotence."[49] The Yaqui, Seri, and Pápago, however, continued to raid, each for their own reasons. Corral entreated the Yaqui to return from their mountain hideouts so that the government could protect them, "distributing the land, establishing them in pueblos organized civilly," instead of their traditional communities. The Yaqui response was war. The Pápago, threatened by ranchers and government, moved north to Arizona; the Seri continued to raid until almost eliminated.

The Yaquis had warred, in the company of other tribes, for virtually the entire post-independence period. They fought at different times for Federalists, Centralists, Liberals, and the French.[50] Their goals were autonomy and separation from the white race; to an extent they enjoyed autonomy by constantly besieging a weak state government and protecting the entrance to the Yaqui Valley at Boca Abierta. Their geographical position caused Sonora to be cut off from the Republic for much of the nineteenth century. But during the *Porfiriato*, the stakes changed, as the Yaqui became a potential laboring force and their rich land the nucleus of northwestern development plans.

After the capture and execution of the rebel Yaqui leader José María Leyva (Cajeme) in 1887, the federal government began its two-pronged attack on the Sonoran development project: the proletarianization of the Indians and the exploitation of the Madgalena, San Miguel, Sonora, Mayo, and Yaqui river valleys.[51] Yaqui lands were summarily declared *baldíos* so that concessionaires could subdivide and resell them. Pima and Ópata communal holdings to the north were declared destroyed, the survivors supposedly living as independent farmers. Companies from as far away as Kansas City bought their lands.[52] The engineer Colonel Ángel García Peña arrived in Sonora with a delegation from the National Geographic Commission (*Comisión Nacional Geográfica Exploradora*) to survey, subdivide, colonize, and irrigate those river valleys and to settle the native populace under military authority. Though the Yaqui retreated again to the Sierra del Bacatete, most of the valley was settled under the firm hand of the military. García Peña, in return for his public service, became proprietor of 13,000 choice hectares in the Mayo river valley.[53]

48. Estado de Sonora, *Informes dados por el Ciudadano Ramón Corral, Vice-Gobernador Constitucional del Estado de Sonora, 1888*, p. 33.
49. *Informes dados por el Ciudadano Ramón Corral, 1889*, p. 11.
50. Hu-Dehart, "Development and Rural Rebellion," p. 74.
51. Francisco R. Almada, *La Revolución en el Estado de Sonora*, p. 20; Hu-Dehart, p. 76.
52. Aguilar Camín, "La Revolución sonorense," p. 44.
53. Other public servants who benefitted from the domination of the Yaqui and Mayo river valleys included governors Rafael Izábal, Luis Torres, and Don Ramón Corral himself.

The Great Concessions

Although the Indian wars were certainly far from over, the occupation of the state of Sonora by federal troops and the geographic commission began an epoch in which Indian communities would be despoliated for the purposes of capitalist economic development. During the 1890s the agricultural lands and vast open ranges of the Sonoran desert would yield to the Sonora and Sinaloa Irrigation Company, the Richardson Construction Company, the Sonora Land and Cattle Company, and the Wheeler Land Company. These concessions brought economic growth and agricultural export to Sonora. They also brought white settlers to displace Indians, land speculators to create urban subdivisions, and irrigation canals to divert the rivers they conquered.[54]

The main focus of the Sonoran boom in the 1890s was on the rich lands of the Yaqui and Mayo valleys. In the decade 1892–1902, nine major canals were constructed on the right of the Mayo river, and nine more on the left.[55] Financiers from the Bank of Sonora and other important entrepreneurial groups provided funds for the first irrigation and colonization concessions in the Yaqui and Mayo valleys. Carlos Conant Maldonado, an original rebel against Pesqueira in 1873, later a miner in Quiriego, received in 1890 a federal concession for the survey of the Mayo, Yaqui, and Fuerte rivers and for the use of the waters of the three most powerful rivers of the region.[56] By the terms of the concession, one-third of the area surveyed would become property of the concessionaires and the government would be required to sell them an additional third at 90 centavos per hectare—a potential total of one million hectares.[57] In December 1891, Conant formed the Sonora and Sinaloa Irrigation Company, of which he held 25 percent; the remainder was held by a combination of Mexican and North American investors. By 1900, however, after many fits and starts, the company broke down under the grandeur of the project itself, and Conant became merely another *latifundista*, along with his major partners.

The concession did not die with the Sonora and Sinaloa Irrigation Company, however. In 1904, a Los Angeles company headed by three brothers named Richardson acquired the Yaqui valley concession.[58] Under the Richardson Construction Company and the Yaqui Land and Water Company, the Richardsons opened the concession to colonists from the

---

Civilian *latifundistas* included the concessionaire Carlos Conant Maldonado, José María Parada, Jesús Salazar, and Albino Almada, among others. (*Ibid.*, pp. 16, 42, 86.)

54. Almada, *La Revolución*, p. 26.

55. Acuña, *Sonoran Strongman*, pp. 132ff.

56. The text of the concessions can be found in the appendix to Dabdoub, *Historia del Valle*, pp. 403ff.

57. *Ibid.*, p. 272.

58. William Richardson had first scouted this land as a railroad engineer, so the Richardsons' arrival paralleled the arrival of the Sonoran boom in the 1880s.

United States with tantalizing posters and advertisements in American newspapers. The sale price to North American colonists was 26 dollars per hectare.

With the sale and development of concession land came increased competition for scarce water resources, since the Richardson Company was responsible for providing water to the Yaqui valley. When, in 1909, the Richardson Concession was granted the rights to 45 percent of the yearly flow of the Yaqui river, the older farmers of the area cried out in anger against the *Yanquis* and the federal government.[59] The Richardsons asked for even more concessions in return for the construction of "La Angostura" dam on the upper Yaqui, but their plans were dragged under by the Madero rebellion in 1910.

With the arrival of the new leaders of Porfirian economic development, the need for agricultural laborers also rose. The northwestern laborer had always been scarcer, generally better paid, and more modern than his traditional counterpart of the *mesa central*.[60] In the agricultural boom of the 1890s, the pacification programs—along with dispossession—partly represented a purely instrumental need for more workers.

Warriors and Peons

After the early pacification of the Mayo (1887) and the resulting labor benefits for local agricultural interests, hopes were high for a similar "accommodation" with the Yaqui. The government had generally been optimistic in the past. In 1881, upon taking command of the Sonoran military zone, General Bernardo Reyes had remarked: "The majority of those people [Yaquis] are susceptible to civilization. . . . The lands they inhabit should simply be occupied, pursuing the few that are necessary, leaving the rest some part of the land conveniently distributed."[61]

But the Yaquis, despite the steady decimation of their ranks by war and starvation, were to prove stubborn defenders of their land. They outstayed the Mayo capitulation in 1887, the death of two great leaders (Cajeme and Tetabiate), and removal from their homeland in 1902–1905. By the time of the Constitutionalist battles of the Revolution (1914–1915), there existed in the military a hatred for the Yaquis that would later set a violent stage for postrevolutionary recovery in Sonora. Exhausted by the Indians' interminable energy, the *Boletín Militar* of the Expeditionary Force to the Northwest in 1914 coldly remarked that "all of the Yaqui prisoners caught bearing arms were immediately shot, proving that the best Yaqui is a dead Yaqui."[62] During the thirty years between these two different assessments

---

59. Dabdoub, pp. 314–315.
60. Katz, "Labor Conditions," p. 34; Adolfo Gilly, *La Revolución interrumpida*, pp. 16–17.
61. Quoted in Aguilar Camín, "La Revolución sonorense," p. 35.
62. Quoted in Almada, *La Revolución,*. p. 218.

of the situation in the Yaqui Valley, the tribe itself had undergone the trials of attempted pacification, starvation, deportation and slavery, and extermination through massacre.[63] Nevertheless, they would not quit fighting until 1929, after leaving an indelible mark on the agrarian history of Sonora.

The warring Indians were linked to Sonoran economic progress, as they were in other parts of Mexico. In addition to obstructing the redistribution of their traditional homelands, the Indians—again primarily the Yaquis—disturbed the trade network of the merchants of such ports as Guaymas and Mazatlán. Due to the American Civil War, westward expansion, and the arrival of the railroad in the late 1880s, Guaymas was booming with foreign trade in primary goods. It sustained two and a half times the commercial volume of the capital, Hermosillo. Between 1891 and 1910, Guaymas' population increased by over 140 percent.[64] But the continual wars between the government and the Yaquis, and the related separation of Guaymas' commercial elite from bourgeois *hacendados* to the south, cost Guaymas dearly in terms of economic advance and political power in Hermosillo. By the time of World War I, Guaymas had seen its best years as an international port.[65]

The uncooperative Indians also caused intense strains on an already overextended labor force. Since Olegario Molina, the Secretary of Development, Colonization, and Industry, also owned a large henequen plantation in Yucatán, the policy of deporting Yaquis became the favored remedy to Yucatecan labor problems as well as Indian unrest in Sonora.[66] But by 1907 only about 2,000 peaceful Yaquis actually lived in the Yaqui River valley, the warring groups being forced to other areas of Sonora, to the Sierra, or to the port of Guaymas for deportation. Because the deportation was inspired by development as well as retribution, more deportees had to be selected. In 1907 the government ordered the deportation of even peaceful *peones* of Yaqui descent, living mainly outside the valley.[67]

The local bourgeoisie, especially in northern and central Sonora, opposed the federal government in its deportation program, not out of horror of a system that could arrest entire families and deport them, but out of a narrow proprietary interest.[68] The government accused local *hacen-*

---

63. Hu-Dehart in "Development and Rural Rebellion," gives an excellent account of the Yaqui deportation programs by which the government solved the Indian problem in Sonora and the labor shortages in Yucatán and Guerrero, where key export crops were grown. This policy followed several pacification attempts, notably the flawed Peace of Ortiz (1897), which was followed in 1900 by the massacre of some 400 Yaquis at Mazocoba. (See also Jesús Luna, *La carrera pública de don Ramón Corral*, esp. pp. 37–55.)

64. Aguilar Camín, pp. 63–64.   65. Almada, p. 24.

66. Hu-Dehart, p. 84.   67. *Ibid.*, pp. 72, 88.

68. Hu-Dehart (p. 81) cites a Sonoran *hacendado* from Moctezuma dealing with the government over the disposition of several Yaquis. "There are in this jail, by disposition of the

dados of harboring fugitive Yaquis as peons and obstructing the federal deportation policy. The hacendados returned with a volley condemning the government for depriving them of laborers.[69] The seemingly incidental conflict between state and bourgeoisie over the nature of the labor force was actually a symptom of a much deeper conflict within Porfirian society.

THE BREAKDOWN OF PORFIRIAN POWER

The rudiments of the Porfirian development plan and its impact, including some of the human conflict and misery that leavened the slow process of bourgeois revolution, have been seen in this chapter. But there are some primary points at which the story of Porfirian land tenure and development transcends its own immediate context to show the underlying dynamic of a dependent enclave economy.

Most important, especially in terms of the future populist "social contract" of postrevolutionary days, was the transformation of the relationship between state and civil society that took place during the *Porfiriato*. In Chapter 2 we noted that the state, under liberal doctrine, could act as the authorized representative of civil society in the determination of property relations and the development of the economy. We also noted, however, that this form of representation carried with it certain dangers for the continued legitimation of the regime. The *Porfiriato*, the first regime to carry out an economic development plan after independence, in one sense became the victim of its own role as intervener in the Mexican economy. As leader of the plan for national development, source of infrastructure investment, and chief liaison with foreign capital, the Porfirian regime was held responsible for the inequalities and fluctuations that characterized the enclave economy. The legacy of state intervention on a grand scale began with the *Porfiriato*. It would reappear in a similar, equally delicate form in the postrevolutionary state.

Another devastating weakness in the Porfirian dynamic stems from the basic inflexibility of the class structure it fostered. Because of a lack of capital, poorly-extended market network, and a large proportion of the citizenry living outside the market economy, the leading class factions of the *Porfiriato*—merchants, foreign concessionaires, and primary-goods exporters—could not expand sufficiently. Because of the nature of goods produced and the lack of a domestic market for most of them, the economic well-being of Porfirian Mexico lay in the hands of foreign financial

government, seven Yaquis, four with families; I think they are *pacíficos*, who for some circumstance did not have their passports. We have an extreme shortage of laborers and I beg that you, if it is not compromising to you, arrange in my name the release of these *indios* so that I can have them as servants."

69. *Ibid.*, p. 82.

giants and commodity speculators. A stable, "neutral" market did not exist.

Another aspect of this same class rigidity reveals itself in the form of unemployment and below-subsistence wages. The maldistributed work-force, widely varying modes of production in different regions, peonage, slavery, sharecropping, and unequal sectoral growth combined to create bottlenecks in the transition from peasant to wage-laborer, or from rural worker to urban migrant. An adequate supply of jobs in advanced cap-italist sectors must accompany the dispossession of the peasantry to form a new wage-earning class. Because of the externally dependent agricul-tural economy and the fledgling manufacturing sector, the *Porfiriato* was unable to accomplish this necessary task. Thus, for example, after a severe economic contraction in Arizona in 1907 and 1908, simultaneous mine closings in northern Mexico, and a bad harvest in 1909, even the relatively privileged workers of northern and northwestern Mexico were left out of the substantial benefits of Porfirian progress.[70] Such instability was an early portent of the fall of Díaz.

We have already discussed briefly the use of property as a bribe rather than as a tool in the construction and expansion of an advanced capitalist economy. It provided what we have termed the great "agricultural contra-diction" of the *Porfiriato*: advancing to a fully productive agricultural economy, which would buttress future industrialization, was accom-panied by the contradictory necessity of supporting traditional *haciendas* and outmoded social formations in order to gain the social peace neces-sary for foreign investment. This fundamental contradiction shows many of the structural limitations of Porfirian development. It could not sustain the social order on a class basis; instead it resorted to caste and semifeudal modes of social relations. The *Porfiriato* could not advance the interests of capital beyond a certain limited level, due both to external dependency and to the very terms of its own internal legitimacy.

Even more basic than the "agricultural contradiction," the imperma-nence of Porfirian rule manifested itself in the regime's incapacity to en-able the working class to survive and improve its own condition. From the policies against the Indian peasants-turned-dayworkers to the lack of at-tention given to the production of domestic foodstuffs, the *Porfiriato* failed to address one of the most revolutionary tenets of capitalist ideol-ogy: that "success" (or at least employment and sustenance) can be found in the marketplace with other values. Once it allied itself with land-hungry peasants, opposition to the regime took a qualitatively different course.

70. See Katz, "Labor Conditions," p. 46. Between 1900 and 1907, production had de-clined by some 40 percent in the northwest. The added pressures on the labor force as a result of the 1907–1908 crisis certainly did nothing to relieve the already disastrous con-dition of the working class. (See Reynolds, *The Mexican Economy*, p. 105.)

Finally, compounding these and other developmental inequities that characterized the *Porfiriato* was the haunting image of the Liberal Reform. Throughout the century, liberals had awaited the chance to implement their programs for land distribution, economic development, and political reform. Chafing in opposition to the structural and political constraints of Díaz' reign, liberal partisans attempted to reorganize the reform movement throughout Díaz' 30-year tenure. Against the liberal opposition that finally began to congeal at the turn of the twentieth century, Porfirio Díaz had but one response: repression. Set in the context of anti-reelectionism, the reconquest of Mexican soil from foreigners, and financial and administrative reform, the liberal-inspired rebellion of 1910 is curiously reminiscent of the principles behind the Constitution of 1857. As we shall see, the consequences this time would be amazingly different.

Part II

The Creation of Order
in Postrevolutionary Society

In the aftermath of the revolutionary insurrection of 1910–1917, the political forces which had become allies to overthrow the *Porfiriato* faced a twofold problem: the reconstruction of state authority with a new base of legitimation, and reorganization of the mode of production under a new system of economic growth. The postrevolutionary state also had to carry within it the symbols of national order, since the civil order had dissolved with the old regime. As we shall see in Chapter 4, the task that faced the national leadership during the 1917–1935 period was complicated by several factors. To enumerate these factors is to chronicle the struggle for political power and a share in the system's rewards which took place during the formation of Mexican populism in the 1920s.

First, the revolutionary alliance itself contained internal conflicts. Its leadership mainly came from the aggressive middle-sized agricultural bourgeoisie of the north, who envisioned the expansion of Mexican society under capitalism, with free elections and a liberal constitution. But the regional *campesino* leadership, under the banners of Zapata and Villa, fought the Revolution for the promise of regaining their traditional lands, lost during the Liberal Reform of 1856–1859. A conflict between bourgeois *caudillos* and *campesino* militants thus developed over the question of private versus ejidal property and related issues of agrarian redistribution. It became, through the medium of state power and the legal-administrative system, a struggle of the Constitutionalist element of the revolutionary alliance to limit the concessions given to the dispossessed.

This simple reduction, however, is further complicated by the realities of postrevolutionary Mexican society. Constitutionalism, though it originally offered no advance beyond the limited liberal rebellion led in 1910 by Francisco Madero, faced the difficult problem of creating a durable "social peace," so necessary for future capitalist growth and investment. Against the backdrop of sporadic agrarian uprisings challenging the newly asserted authority of the state, the Constitutionalists groped for a method of giving substance to the "solemn promise" of agrarian reform. This involved nothing less than a guarantee of social obligation to the masses in the context of a system based on the defense of private property and private accumulation.

In fact, this challenge and the state's responses are the keys to the developmental problems of the postrevolutionary order. Equipped with a legislative and bureaucratic approach to *campesino* rebellion against the inadequate agrarian reform, the Constitutionalists—and their successors in power—encountered several political bottlenecks which seemed insoluble. The *ejido* represented to the bourgeois revolutionaries only a step to efficient, productive private holdings, while to the *agraristas* it meant either restored communal lands or the first step toward modern collectivization of land tenure. The state viewed the agrarian-reform machinery as a means of aggrandizing state power over rebellious *campesinos*; the *campesinos* often viewed it as an extension of the regime's social obligation to them. Both bourgeois and *campesino* were disappointed in the dualism and indecision that characterized the "engine of economic growth," the agrarian reform. Finally, the state viewed its extended powers of eminent domain as a means of protecting claims to legitimate private property by eliminating reactionary *hacendados*. The *campesinos*, in their view of the populist pact, expected fast and strict adherence to the agrarian laws.

Into the quickening fray stepped Lázaro Cárdenas, just as the Revolution appeared to be consolidating around a personally run political party and institutionalized *latifundismo*. It is to Cárdenas' credit that he accomplished in six years what other presidents had not completed in eighteen. As we shall see in Chapter 5, Cárdenas intervened on behalf of the masses in order to integrate them into a system of capitalist production dominated by the state. Viewed by contemporary analysts as a socialist, Cárdenas in fact coopted or destroyed the independent left. Cárdenas, the defender of the village and *ejido*, also consolidated state power against the potential threat of local autonomy (a real threat, at least in the case of Sonora and Román Yocupicio). Through the party, he solidified the political rules of the new order that had been laid out in the constitution. He organized the postrevolutionary system of state-led capitalism, which "took off" during the World War II boom of 1941–1945. And he mediated class struggle in civil society with the authority of the populist state.

The principal instrument of Cárdenas' populist mobilization, as we shall see, was the agrarian reform that he used to defeat Calles in 1935. Agrarian reform during the 1930s represented institutionalization of the *ejido*; construction of a political weapon against the vestiges of the old order; the promise of social obligation through land redistribution; and, most important, the development of agricultural production as midwife to industrial transformation in Mexico.

Final judgment on the Cárdenas years, as controversial as that period now is in Mexican historiography, must acknowledge the contradictions of one-party populism—contradictions resulting in the eventual subordination of the working class and *campesinos*, and the change of legitimation which followed in the "counter-reform" of the 1940–1970 period. Once the common people were subordinated to the state through the party, they became permanently dependent upon the benevolence of the state for continuation of the populist pact—benevolence that was not forthcoming from Cárdenas' successors. The agrarian reform was left to its legal base, a base forever changing and shrinking under successive presidents, their reforms, and their interpretations of the law. And finally, Cárdenas left it to the state to ensure political equality through populist mediation among classes, when civil society was inherently unequal under the rules of private accumulation. While the power of capital increased in civil society (and thereby in the state), the common people had no such private means to aggrandize wealth and power. Thus the Cárdenas epoch we will examine in Chapter 5 represented not only the rescue of the Revolution from the chaos of the 1920s, but its subsequent surrender to capital in the 1940s.

Chapter 4

The Reorganization of Power

In the shadow of Victoriano Huerta, the usurper of Francisco I. Madero's government, the once-modest *maderista* rebellion that had broken out in the fall of 1910 continued to evolve into full-scale revolution. On August 29, 1913, barely six months after Huerta's assassination of Madero, General Lucio Blanco, commander of the Constitutionalist forces in Nuevo León and Tamaulipas, decreed the first revolutionary land expropriations in favor of the *campesinos* and soldiers who had fought against Díaz and Huerta.[1] Three years had passed since Madero had issued the call for rebellion against Díaz to begin November 20, 1910, "from 6 p.m. forward."[2] What had originated as a movement for "effective suffrage and no reelection"[3] had leaped forward to an agrarian-based revolution founded on yet-undefined principles of land distribution and rights for the underclasses.

Still unsettled, however, were the terms by which an essentially liberal *maderista* revolt, with vague hopes of restoring small property-holdings, could transform itself to meet the deep-seated needs and aspirations of the masses of people who were the main source of support for the war against the old regime. Early hints of liberal *agrarismo* had quickly triggered a more general *campesino* revolution outside the network of national *maderista* and Constitutionalist leadership.[4] A fight for the material benefits which would derive from reorganization of the bases for political legitimacy and economic control pervaded the formative years of the postrevo-

1. Jesús Silva Hérzog, *Breve historia de la Revolución mexicana*, vol. II, pp. 56–59.
2. "Plan de San Luis Potosí," reprinted in *ibid.*, vol. I, p. 162.
3. Charles C. Cumberland, *Mexican Revolution: Genesis Under Madero*, p. 63.
4. Moisés González Navarro, "Mexico: The Lopsided Revolution," p. 209.

lutionary regime. From the 1912 declarations of Luis Cabrera to the birth of the National Revolutionary Party (PNR) in 1929, this transformation took place within earshot of the conspicuous *campesino* resistance to concepts of peace and justice that excluded them.

PRELUDE TO INTERNAL CONFLICT

The language of the Plan of San Luis Potosí issued by Madero in October 1910 was circumspect in adhering to the Constitution of 1857. It called for returning land to the dispossessed who had been victimized by Porfirian colonization and survey laws, but mentioned nothing of *ejidos* or communal lands.[5] Madero had declared his intentions directly in 1909:

> I am very much in agreement that the division of property will contribute greatly to the development of agriculture and the national wealth. I believe more. I believe that the division of property will be one of the strongest bases of democracy.[6]

But the revolutionary army consisted, to a great extent, of dispossessed indigenous *ejidatarios* and *rancheros* who had lost their lands and thus become the rural proletariat of the *Porfiriato*.[7] In fact, the Revolution quickly outstripped its *maderista* leadership in its goals for agrarian reform, presenting dissonant notes which would plague the revolutionary regime for a generation.

On one hand, the growing militancy of the *campesino* forces served the military needs of the revolutionary agricultural bourgeoisie. In this aspect, the goals of bourgeois and *peon* were sublimated in a common struggle against the old regime.[8] But the means of achieving their conflicting class goals could not have been more different. The agrarian goals of the *maderista*, and later the Constitutionalist leadership, were limited to reviving legal protection under the Constitution of 1857 and assuring the sanctity of private property.[9] One facet of the postrevolutionary search for

5. "Plan de San Luis Potosí," pp. 157–168.

6. Cited in Stanley R. Ross, *Francisco I. Madero: Apostle of Mexican Democracy*, p. 92fn.

7. Ross, one of Madero's best-known biographers, rightly comments that Madero was not the prime mover of the Revolution, but helped to prepare and organize popular support for the movement, becoming a symbol for the discontented. (*Ibid.*, pp. 116–117.)

8. This symbiosis between *campesino* and revolutionary *agricultor* was clearly present in Sonora, as we shall see in this chapter. For more general comments, see Antonio Gramsci, "State and Civil Society," in *Selections from the Prison Notebooks*, p. 213.

9. As Madero put it, the goals of the 1910 rebellion were that "the law should be complied with and should protect all citizens; . . . the government should be concerned with the improvement of the situation of the workers . . .; and national lands, instead of passing into the hands of a few favorites of the government who do not exploit them properly, . . . or who dispose of them to foreign companies, should be divided among small proprietors. This would augment the well-being of many citizens as well as . . . of the Republic. . . . The only way to make a people strong is to educate them and to elevate their material, intellectual, and moral level." (Cited in Ross, *Madero*, p. 92.)

order derived from the political leadership's attempt to legislate agrarian reform to a *campesino* class whose conceptions of the reform not only had progressed beyond the bulk of the legislation, but who had lost faith altogether in legislation as a method of political change, and could now back up their discontent with their military potential.

Another dissonant note stemmed from the character of the postrevolutionary state itself, and the limited perspective of the *campesino* militants toward a national state. Given the acknowledged liberal bias of most early land-reform proponents within the government, postrevolutionary *agrarismo* seemed destined to take on a traditional legislative-bureaucratic character, after the style of the 1856 reforms. A chief mission of the revolutionary Constitution of 1917 and its statutory supports was to affirm the rules of political and economic order for the new society. In the tradition of Mora's liberal state, providing the organizing principle or set of rules around which society could find order was among its primary functions. The *campesinos* and their *caudillos* Zapata and Villa never really appreciated this fundamental need for organization at the national level. Thus their concern for local justice and immediate resolution of local land conflicts caused them to be viewed in official circles as unappreciative malcontents subverting the duly constituted authority of the state.

Finally, another source of conflict among revolutionary partisans resulted from pressures from the agricultural bourgeoisie and segments of the *hacienda* system which still survived. From the power of the progressive *hacienda* to the strong cultural heritage of positivism, the agrarian reform was infected from the beginning with a frequently anti-revolutionary rationalism and little sensitivity to the momentous project the state was undertaking.[10] But let us pursue these matters in a more concrete setting.

LEGISLATING THE REVOLUTION

Antonio Manero, a contemporary observer of the Mexican Revolution, contended that "the problem of property is the fundamental problem of

10. "Progressive *hacienda*" signifies one economically advanced, not necessarily politically progressive. Pastor Rouaix, himself one of the more progressive *agraristas* of the second decade of the twentieth century and crucial contributor to Articles 27 and 123 of the Constitution of 1917, drily reasoned that "first, an *hacienda* should be acquired which has been seen as appropriate for a hydraulic irrigation system, the system will be constructed, and then the division of land will proceed in lots of eight hectares that will be sold to the *campesinos* under liberal terms of payment. To pretend to do the opposite is to start the program from the finish." As Marco Antonio Durán points out, the Revolution was forced to "start from the finish" to realize some change in land tenure immediately, even in the absence of capital, planning, infrastructure, etc. This did not necessarily imply ignorance, but recognition of the lack of resources to conduct the reform "rationally." (Durán, *El agrarismo mexicano*, p. 17.)

the Revolution."[11] In his view, a popular one at the time, the problems of the Revolution fell into the general categories of property, administration, banking, legislation, and public education. But, reflecting the regional, political, and class divisions which had fomented the Revolution, the forces that had overthrown Díaz and Huerta could not decide how to resolve the problem of property definitively. One camp, headed by Madero, advocated small property as the future of Mexico; the other, following Zapata, Múgica, and other *agraristas*, espoused a system of *ranchero* and ejidal land tenure more deeply founded in the agrarian traditions of the country. The chief spokesman of the former point of view was Luis Cabrera.

> The creation and protection of agrarian small property is a problem of great importance to guarantee the smallholder against the great property-holders. In order to accomplish this, it is urgent to undertake throughout the country a series of reforms leading toward equal footing . . . for great and small rural property.

Cabrera envisioned *ejidos as a step to private property* in the liberal tradition:

> It is necessary to think of the reconstitution of *ejidos*, assuring that they are inalienable, taking the lands that are necessary from the large neighboring properties, some by means of purchase, others by expropriations for the sake of the public interest with indemnification, some by rental or forced sharecropping.[12]

Legislation Before 1917

Cabrera was the principal author of Venustiano Carranza's famous Decree of January 6, 1915, which began the tortuous process of legislating agrarian reform. The decree was based firmly on the principle of safeguarding private property. The concessions given to *ejidos*, as in Cabrera's 1912 statement, were merely temporary, an allowance for the Indians' failure to grasp the concept of private property adequately.[13]

Unfortunately for Cabrera's vision, however, small family holdings were still subject to the same structural malnutrition they had suffered since 1856. Credit and infrastructure were nonexistent. Public law and enforcement were inadequate. Existing political machinery served entrenched landowners, not dispossessed *campesinos*. So, despite liberal

11. Antonio Manero, *The Meaning of the Mexican Revolution*, p. 17. At the time of this comment, Manero was a Professor of Practical Cases in Financial, Banking, and Stock Exchange Operations at the Superior School of Commerce and Administration of Mexico.

12. Luis Cabrera, "La reconstitución de los ejidos de los pueblos como medio de suprimir la esclavitud del jornalero mexicano," speech given in the Chamber of Deputies, December 3, 1912, reprinted in *La cuestión de la tierra*, p. 281.

13. González Navarro, "The Lopsided Revolution," p. 211.

hopes, the two trends that actually were to dominate early agrarian reform efforts were the concentration of large holdings and the fragmentation of small holdings into uneconomical *minifundios*,[14] a situation not unlike the prerevolutionary one, with slightly more emphasis on the small-holder. The legal basis for this perversion of liberal intentions lay in Cabrera's (Carranza's) very proclamation. To ensure that the parties to the Reform of 1915 understood its purpose clearly, he forcefully declared its intent

> . . . not to revive the ancient communes nor to create others similar to them, but only to give the land to the miserable rural population that lacks it today, in order that [the populace] may fully develop its right to life and liberate itself from the economic servitude to which it is now reduced; moreover, it must be noted that proprietorship of the land will not be vested in the commune of the pueblo, but will be parcelled out in full dominion with only such limitations as are necessary to prevent avid speculators, especially foreigners, from monopolizing such property.[15]

The law then went on to nullify illegal land invasions and occupations of communal land, forests, and waters, and to restore title to the villages concerned. Perhaps most significantly, it also created the National Agrarian Commission (CNA) as overseer of the agrarian-reform process.[16]

Though the ostensible purpose of the law was to satisfy the clamor for agrarian reform, an equal purpose was to maintain that reform within the boundaries of private property. Restitution of indigenous lands and creation of communally worked—if not communally owned—*ejidos* made the former *hacendado* Carranza uneasy. After only twenty months of an already-muted reform program, Carranza decreed the Administrative Accord of September 19, 1916, denying state governors the right to distribute lands provisionally, even to *pueblos* designated by local Agrarian Commissions. This in effect halted the *carrancista* agrarian reforms.[17]

It is clear that Carranza had never really savored the possibility of positive agrarian reform; his Decree of January 6, 1915, had been vague, limited to existing agricultural communities, and bureaucratically over-

14. Rodolfo Stavenhagen, "Aspectos sociales de la estructura agraria en México," p. 16. A *minifundio* is generally a plot of less than ten hectares, depending on the quality of the land.

15. *Ley de 6 de Enero de 1915 que declara nulas todas las enajenaciones de tierras, aguas y montes pertenecientes a los pueblos, otorgadas en contravención a lo dispuesto en la ley de 25 de Junio de 1856*; reprinted in Arnaldo Córdova, *La ideología de la Revolución mexicana*, pp. 453–457.

16. The provisions for restoring communities' rightful titles and creating the CNA later created conflict between the agrarian-reform legislation and its own administrative network. Even with all the ambiguities and shortcomings of the Decree of January 6, 1915, the CNA proved too adventuresome for Carranza.

17. Manuel Aguilera Gómez, *La reforma agraria en el desarrollo económico de México*, p. 128. This accord was abrogated on December 10, 1921, by Álvaro Obregón, after Carranza's death and the start of a new chapter in *el agrarismo mexicano*.

weight, even before he cancelled it. After he withdrew even that tentative commitment, the agrarian question was sure to remain unresolved in ideological as well as legislative terms.

In addition to the plainly defective nature of the Decree of January 6, 1915, the Constitutionalist faction faced significant competition in the countryside from local leaders. Zapata's November 28, 1911, Plan of Ayala; the Agrarian Law of the Sovereign Revolutionary Convention (October 26, 1915); and the Agrarian Law of General Francisco Villa (May 24, 1915), all challenged the Carranza reforms. Meanwhile, the petulant Carranza had already shown the limits of his personal attitude toward land reform by vengefully transferring erstwhile *agrarista* General Lucio Blanco to Sonora in retaliation for his early land-reform attempts in the northeast.[18] Other regional opponents also plagued the regime, fragmenting the sources of Constitutionalist support. A key element of the conflict among revolutionaries, then, arose from the differing class bases of the two main approaches to agrarian reform—one generated by a liberal, elite culture, and the other by a mass movement of dispossessed *campesinos*. Naturally, the Yaquis figured among the latter.

Earlier, in accordance with his agrarian-reform plans, Madero had attempted in 1911 to pacify the Yaquis in Sonora by signing an agreement with them for the irrigation, cultivation, and eventual parcelization of traditional lands. The government was to provide wages, schools, mules, and tax-exempt status to the Indians. This accord was supposed to gain for Sonora some measure of internal peace from the Yaquis.[19] But the uprisings continued. By the time of his annual report to the Legislature in 1912, Governor José María Maytorena—a man with considerable reputation for fairness with the Yaquis—felt compelled to conclude that "one cannot arrive at a generous solution with that tribe."[20] Maytorena advocated repressing the Yaquis and parceling their *ejidos*. Madero's compromise with the Indians had not lasted long, precisely because he had not

18. Manuel González Ramírez, *La revolución social de México*, vol. III, *El problema agrario*, p. 212. Ironically, Blanco was chastised for dividing up the *hacienda* Los Borregos of Félix Díaz, nephew of Don Porfirio and archreactionary supporter of coup attempts against the Revolution. Blanco was later murdered, some say by future president Plutarco Elías Calles. (See the blatantly anti-Calles work of Fernando Medina Ruiz, *Calles: un destino melancólico*; p. 63; also Jean Meyer, *La Cristiada*, vol. II. *El conflicto entre la iglesia y el estado, 1926–1929*, p. 187.) Edwin Lieuwen, in *Mexican Militarism: The Political Rise and Fall of the Revolutionary Army, 1910–1940*, p. 31, mistakenly gives Carranza credit for Blanco's reforms.

19. Ross, *Madero*, p. 183. Carlos Randall, the interim governor of Sonora at the time, spoke highly of the prospects for peace and the end of the Yaqui "stain on civilization" and "threats to public tranquility." (*Informe del C. Gobernador Interino del Estado, Sr. Carlos E. Randall, presentado el 1° de Septiembre de 1911 ante el H. Congreso del mismo, al hacer entrega del ejecutivo al Gobernador Constitucional, Sr. José María Maytorena*, p. 6.)

20. *Informe presentado por el C. José María Maytorena, Gobernador Constitucional del Estado de Sonora, ante la XXIII legislatura del mismo, y contestación del presidente de la Cámara, C. Flavio A. Bórquez*, 1912, p. 7.

recognized that there were two simultaneous revolts occurring in Sonora— the revolt of white political elites and *caciques*[21] leading the masses against the limits of *porfirismo*, and the revolt of the Yaquis against the white man.

The white man's struggle was fragmented by regional interests in conflict over political power; they called upon the Díaz bureaucracy—still intact—to perform revolutionary acts, and summoned the old oligarchy to join in exploitation of the budding Sonoran economy.[22] The white revolt in Sonora used the *campesinos* and the Indians to achieve political supremacy, not agrarian reform. The *maderista* forces in Sonora restored the system of *rurales*, the dreaded rural police force which symbolized Porfirian repression; they warred intermittently against the Yaquis, and resisted worker-organization efforts in Cananea and other northern mining centers.[23] Madero's proposed peace-offering to the Yaquis was a sop to encourage native support for struggles among elites from Guaymas, Hermosillo, Huatabampo, and Agua Prieta. That struggle was to continue through the 1920s, led by Adolfo de la Huerta of the port of Guaymas; Plutarco Elías Callés, representing the "frontier brokers" of Agua Prieta and the northeast; and Álvaro Obregón of Huatabampo and the southern valley farms. Their interests, as in Porfirian times, lay in "social peace" and foreign capital investment, not land reform.

As if the participation of old-order bureaucrats and *hacendados* in the *maderista* and Constitutionalist reforms were not weight enough for the fledgling Revolution, international considerations played an important part in the attitudes of Mexico's future leaders. The Cananea Consolidated Copper Company of the American William C. Greene was still a major presence in Sonora, still a much-needed liaison between Yankee and Mexican capital, and still intransigently opposed to worker organization.[24] The Yaquis, in their eternal war against the *Yori*, had provoked many international claims against the Mexican government. The development plans of the Richardson Construction Company, the Wheeler Land

21. *Cacique*, in its popular context, signifies a person who exercises power through control and manipulation of public authorities. It describes a phenomenon of political mediation "characterized by informal and personal exercise of power to protect individual economic interests, or those of a faction." (Luisa Paré, "Caciquismo y estructura de poder en la Sierra Norte de Puebla," p. 36.)

22. Héctor Aguilar Camín, *La frontera nómada: Sonora y la Revolución mexicana*, p. 163. The allure of the bourgeois revolution was such that even Luis Torres—Porfirian general, author of the anti-Yaqui economic development of the Yaqui River Valley, and last pre-revolutionary governor of Sonora—in March 1911 found his son distributing insurrectionist literature among the Indians. (*Ibid.*, p. 151.)

23. *Ibid.*, pp. 167, 240.

24. Ralph Roeder, in *Hacia el México moderno: Porfirio Díaz*, vol. II, pp. 263–314, presents an interesting brief narrative of issues and attitudes in the strike at Cananea in 1906 and the consequences for the *Porfiriato*. The importance of foreign capital extended far beyond the Cananea Consolidated Copper Co. See also C. L. Sonnichsen, *Colonel Greene and the Copper Skyrocket*, chaps. 16 and 17.

Company, and other agro-commercial interests depended upon achieving social peace and eliminating threats to private property. The nadir of national relations with the Yaquis was reached in 1905 when four American stockholders of the Yaqui Smelting and Refining Company and the Mina Grande Mining Company were killed in a Yaqui assault on their car.[25] Many other complaints were lodged against the bellicose tribe, so that even during the *maderista* revolt, *rurales* under the cruel leadership of Luis Medina Barrón pursued the rebels.[26]

As we have seen, much of the development that took place in Sonora during the late *Porfiriato* involved export goods to the United States. With the traditional worries of diplomatic recognition, international markets, and continued foreign capital investment, it is little wonder that the revolutionary leaders approached land reform as another irritant to relations with the United States. That trepidation, however viewed, proved disastrous for the *campesinos*.

The Carranza reform did little to right the inauspicious beginnings of *agrarismo* in Sonora. In the style of his national leadership, Carranza encouraged the most conservative revolutionary ideas. In mid-1913 a Dr. Samuel Navarro wrote approvingly to Carranza that, like the First Chief himself, the Sonoran rebels had "the sanest radical ideas." To them, the first political order of business for the Revolution was to elaborate the "agrarian reform," by which they meant a "solemn promise" to the rural classes that their economic condition would improve in the future. Land division was discarded as too incendiary, a dangerous prospect because of its potential for bringing about new *campesino* uprisings.[27] Throughout the Carranza presidency, the Yaqui wars strained the regime and pressured the political leadership for a more satisfying agrarian reform, something broader and bolder than the "solemn promise" of future rewards.[28] They represented only one facet of general *campesino* discontent with the Revolution, which had yet to dispense any benefits even to its most loyal

25. Eduardo W. Villa, *Compendio de historia del estado de Sonora*, pp. 455–466.

26. Aguilar Camín, *La frontera nómada*, chap. 4, *passim*, esp. p. 190. Rafael Izábal, Porfirian governor of Sonora, had ordered the 11th *Cuerpo Rural de la Federación* to be formed under Medina Barrón, whose continuation under Maytorena points to some of the darker uses of the old guard during the Revolution. See also Villa, *Compendio*, p. 456.

27. Isidro Fábela, *Documentos históricos de la Revolución mexicana*, vol. I, pp. 12–15.

28. See *Informe que rinde al H. Congreso del Estado de Sonora el Gobernador Provisional C. Adolfo de la Huerta, por el período de su gobierno, comprendido entre el 19 de Mayo de 1916 al 18 de Junio de 1917*, pp. 9–11 and 32, for evidence of the scanty *carrancista* agrarian reform. De la Huerta claimed that 67,773 hectares had been restored (*restituciones*)— some to cooperatives, some to small proprietors, and the rest for communal use. Only the lands in the Sonoran desert, however, were left in commons. All land of agricultural value was distributed in parcels of four to eight hectares. No land was distributed in the Yaqui valley, and only two *ejidos* in the Mayo valley were affected. The same tendency is clear in the next reports: *Informes que rinde el C. General Plutarco Elías Calles, Gobernador Constitucional del Estado de Sonora, ante la XXIV legislatura del mismo, 1918–1919*. Given the limited attention paid to land redistribution, it is not surprising that all of the reports make some reference to the warring Yaquis.

supporters. The "solemn promise"—embryo of a more comprehensive social obligation to the masses—had not yet been accepted.[29]

Article 27 of the 1917 Constitution

In the 1917 Constitutional Convention, Venustiano Carranza, First Chief of the Constitutionalist Army (and thereby interim president of Mexico), attempted to regain some semblance of order among his revolutionary cohorts. Corruption was prevalent among regional leaders, and banditry and anti-Constitutionalist resistance divided the country. Postrevolutionary society thus far included radical agrarians, anarchists, socialists, syndicalists, liberals, and positivists, among others. Carranza, having declared war on the *agrarista* supporters of Villa and Zapata on behalf of the Constitution list elite, decided, not surprisingly, to mold the state's chief document after its liberal predecessor. In his proposed draft of the new constitution,

> . . . the liberal spirit and the form of government established [in the Constitution of 1857] would be preserved intact; . . . the reforms would be limited to eliminating the inapplicable parts, . . . cleansing it of all the additions which were inspired only by the intent of using them to enthrone dictatorship.[30]

But the Carranza proposal failed to recognize that years of revolution had changed not only the demands of the countryside for agrarian justice, but also the consciousness of the convention delegates. Instead of adopting a document that failed to even mention agrarian reform (among other pressing social issues), the convention leaders began a limited legalistic attempt, through Article 27 of the Constitution, to fulfill the hopes of the *agraristas* still bearing arms in the Mexican hinterland.

Article 27 is the legal expression of the expanded right of eminent domain (discussed briefly in Chapter 3). At least two important paragraphs of its text merit attention.

> The ownership of lands and waters within the limits of the national territory is vested originally in the nation, which has had the right to transmit title thereof to private persons, thereby constituting private property.
>
> The nation shall have at all times the right to impose on private property

29. For more detail on the Yaqui rebellions in the revolutionary period, see Claudio Dabdoub, *Historia del Valle del Yaqui*, chaps. 9 and 10; Aguilar Camín, *La frontera nómada*, *passim*; and Francisco R. Almada, *La Revolución en el Estado de Sonora*, *passim*.

30. Mexico, *Diario de los debates del Congreso Constituyente, 1916–1917*, vol. I, p. 262. A crucial historical difference between Constitutional liberalism in 1917 and that of 1857 is that the *Porfiriato*—through its development plan—had made the liberal protection of private property a necessity for economic progress. In place of this borrowed liberalism of 1857, Madero's and Carranza's represented the rising agro-mineral-commercial bourgeoisie. But the demands of that class for private property fell between two strong opponents: the Porfirian *hacendados* and conservative elite, and the dispossessed and desperate *campesinos*. The new state, in succeeding years, had to destroy the former and control the latter for the sake of capitalist growth and social peace.

such limitations as the public interest may demand, as well as the right to regulate the development of natural resources, which are susceptible to appropriation, in order to conserve them and equitably to distribute the public wealth. For this purpose, necessary measures shall be taken to divide large landed estates; to develop small landed holdings; to establish new centers of rural population with such lands and waters as may be indispensable to them; to encourage agriculture; to prevent the destruction of natural resources; and to protect property from damage detrimental to society. Settlements, hamlets situated on private property, and communes which lack lands or water or do not possess them in sufficient quantities for their own needs shall have the right to be provided with them from adjoining properties, always having due regard for smaller landed holdings. . . . Private property acquired for the said purposes shall be considered as taken for public use. . . .[31]

It is readily apparent that Article 27 involves the state's right of eminent domain over national territory. But there are at least two ways of considering the role of a state protecting private property in a capitalist society. One formula cedes the private right over property to the state *in the last instance*, as a regulatory measure designed to protect the institution of private property in general.[32] Thus a state—representing civil society at large—can infringe upon individual proprietary rights when they conflict with specific "societal needs" (public highways, railroads, etc.) that the state is obliged to fulfill. In fact, one could argue from this viewpoint that the *primary* function of the capitalist state is to protect private property, and that eminent domain is merely an artifice employed to that end. In the second paragraph of Article 27, however, it becomes apparent that the state's role here is more broadly described, including division of land, development of small proprietors, establishing new centers of population, and so on. Mexico's postrevolutionary populism, based on the promise of the equitable distribution of property as well as protection of the institution of private property in civil society, is first codified in Article 27. The emphasis obviously rests more on accruing state power than on truly including "the masses" in a popular government—a distinction which often escaped politicians who lauded Articles 27 and 123 as evidence of equality.

Formal recognition of the state as an expression of the will of a class society also heralded the weakness of Mexican civil society. Given the chaos which reigned over the Mexican economy during the Revolution, and the Constitutionalists' tenuous grasp of the sources of postrevolutionary power, compromises between government and class—and among

31. This translation of relevant portions of Article 27 of the 1917 Constitution is taken (with slight changes) from Eyler N. Simpson, "The Mexican Agrarian Reform: Problems and Progress," pp. 8–9
32. This was the liberal conception so prevalent in nineteenth-century Mexico (see Chapter 2).

classes—were best carried out through state-administered reforms. The symbols of order resided with the state, not with the economy or any of the revolutionary classes. Amid peasant rebellion, worker organization and radicalization, and economic decline, the revolutionary bourgeoisie and middle class turned to the coercive apparatus of the state. In the absence of overt military control of the country, the Constitutionalist forces, supported by the agricultural and commercial bourgeoisie, nevertheless dominated Mexican society by controlling the elite aspects of revolutionary ideology and official, authoritative land reform. The problems of postrevolutionary organization thus involved not only consolidating groups which had supported the Revolution wholeheartedly, but also those which had opposed the old system conditionally—not as revolutionaries themselves, but as "middle classes" who merely wanted their position in the new society guaranteed.[33] The state could make that guarantee and gain their support only with a populist ideology that created social peace. Steeped in the liberal precedents of the nineteenth century, and relying on an expanded right over property, the political leadership slowly gravitated toward the populist pact.

According to General Francisco Múgica, *agrarista* general and member of the Commission on the Constitution at the 1917 convention, the soldiers there—generally *campesinos* and workers—actually wanted to socialize private property, but were intimidated by the impressive array of powerful and learned revolutionaries who were opposed. To them, Article 27 also represented a compromise.[34] By limiting the size of holdings of private property and by restoring or granting village lands, the article was clearly reformist—thus it gained *agrarista* support. But though Article 27 obligated the National Congress to pass a set of enabling laws regulating its provisions, the nature of such legislation was left unresolved. Many of the local legislative struggles of the 1920s stemmed from such proposals.[35]

Such crippling limits to the reforms of Article 27 lay hidden in the transitory clauses, where it was left to the states to fix maximum limits on individual land tenure. Practically all of the subsequent state laws allowed landlords to retain possession of their properties until expropriated; gave landowners the right to choose the land they would relinquish; and allowed them to sell excess lands or to divide them voluntarily, as they wished.[36] In Chihuahua, *latifundistas* were still legally able to own 44,000 hectares *after* the state reform laws were put into effect. In Coahuila, the limit was 35,000 hectares; in Durango, 20,000; and in Querétaro,

---

33. Wilfrid Hardy Callcott, *Liberalism in Mexico, 1857–1929*, p. 291.
34. Joe C. Ashby, *Organized Labor and the Mexican Revolution Under Lázaro Cárdenas*, p. 143.
35. Simpson, "The Mexican Agrarian Reform," p. 36.
36. *Ibid.*, p. 37.

heart of agricultural production in the nineteenth century, a landowner could still preserve some 12,500 hectares of arable land.[37] In Sonora, ownership of up to 10,400 acres of different classes of land was legally permissible. The states became new postrevolutionary centers of power— power built on a combination of traditional *caciquismo*, increased military potential due to the Revolution, and the license which it had afforded them.

Sonora passed the first *Ley Agraria* in the Republic, almost simultaneously with Zacatecas.[38] The basic legislation guiding Sonoran land reform came during the governorship of Plutarco Elías Calles, on July 3, 1919. The new agrarian law stated in its first article that "the present law has as its objective the creation and growth of small private property (*pequeña propiedad*) in the state."[39] There was no mention in the law of *ejidos*, except to acknowledge zones designated "originally [*primordialmente*] as *ejidos* of pueblos" (Chapter 4, Article 14).[40]

The Calles law dictated limits on land tenure, but provided also that proprietors of cattle pastures or nonirrigated cultivable land could irrigate all of their land, without fear of losing any of it by exceeding the 100-hectare limit on irrigated land (Chapter 4, Articles 17 and 19). As virtually no major irrigation work had been undertaken at this time, this was clearly a provision that favored the wealthy farmer with access to credit, pumps, canals, and other resources for land improvement.[41] This provision sustained the concentration of land tenure in Sonora which had begun during the *Porfiriato*; it was definitely a law favoring the advanced *hacendados* who, not incidentally, were leaders of the Constitutionalist movement in Sonora.[42]

Like other state laws, the Calles law provided that *latifundistas* could subdivide their own excess land (Chapter 5, Article 22) and that they be allowed to choose the land they would keep (Chapter 5, Article 26). In some areas of the waterless desert, of course, this meant little more than a convenience to the landholder. But allowing *latifundistas* to dispose of their own excess land and choose their own remaining lot gave rise to de-

37. Aguilera Gómez, *La reforma agraria*, p. 122.
38. Antonio G. Rivera, *La Revolución en Sonora*, p. 496. Rivera, a deputy in the state constitutional convention and 24th Congress of Sonora, proposed the *Ley Agraria* in 1919.
39. *Ley Agraria de 27 de Junio de 1919.*" All further references to this law are in the text.
40. These zones were more fiction than fact, since the Yaquis—traditional occupants of the most important zone—were still not settled, and would not be until 1929.
41. In fact, until 1933 only three *ejidos* received irrigation rights in Sonora as a result of the agrarian reform, bringing under cultivation an insignificant 1,813 hectares of the total land distributed during the period. (Nathan L. Whetten, *Rural Mexico*, p. 620.)
42. In addition to supporters of Obregón such as the Salido family (owners of the important *haciendas* Rosales, Tres Hermanos, and Santa Barbara) and the Valderráin family (owners of El Naranjo), Maytorena himself owned eight *haciendas* in the valley of San José de Guaymas. De la Huerta, in the tradition of progressive Sonoran agriculture, joined the Revolution to benefit from it commercially. Calles himself found both his future and his political obligations through his paternal relatives, the great cattle-ranchers Elías.

lays, speculation, *prestanombres*, intrafamilial exchanges, transfers of ownership from one municipality to another, and many other modes of subverting real agrarian redistribution.

Before any action was taken to divide the *latifundios*, the burden fell on the petitioner to provide relevant data concerning the specific land he wanted (Chapter 6, Article 30). In addition, the petitioner had to prove possession of draft animals and other equipment to cultivate the land, or the means to acquire them; and either cattle (fifteen to thirty head) or the means to acquire them for any pasture-land petitioned (Chapter 6, Article 31). Finally, preference was given to Mexicans who had fought in the Constitutionalist army, *those who fought in the campaigns against the Yaquis*, and their successors (Chapter 6, Article 32). This clearly excluded most Yaquis—who still resided in their mountain redoubts and could not participate within the limits of the law's provisions, in any event.[43]

If, somehow, a *campesino* were literate, capitalized, and not a *peon* or Yaqui, and he managed to gain provisional possession of a piece of land, more hurdles awaited. He had to cultivate the entire *predio* (plot) within the first year of possession. He had to pay an annual mortgage, plus municipal and state taxes. And, with all this, he was ineligible to apply for private credit that involved any lien on the land. Public credit, of course, was unavailable. Any violation of these conditions or failure to bring in a crop permitted deprivation of his agrarian rights and forfeiture of his land, which was then put up for auction (Chapter 7, Articles 34 and 35).

The Calles law sustained a corrupt tradition of legally manipulating reforms to the advantage of the privileged classes. From at least the Reform days of the mid-nineteenth century, the authors of reform seem also to be either the primary beneficiaries or agents for privileged groups and classes. At this level, the agrarian reform started to take the form of legal and administrative casuistry—i.e., circumvention by the powerful of the objective intent of the law. Since the Revolution, the legal phrasing and interpretation of agrarian reform has allowed flexibility in land-tenure limits, as we have seen in the Calles law. Every legal and financial burden imaginable has been imposed upon the often illiterate, always under-

43. This stated preference for soldiers of the Revolution apparently did not extend to the Mayo residents of Sebampo, Etchojoa, in the Mayo valley. The residents had occupied their land for years when the *Compañía Limitada de Terrenos y Colonización* bought it from the Secretary of Agriculture and Growth in 1896. In 1903 the Company sold the residents 3,511 hectares of their own land, thanks to a loan from the *hacendado* Robinson Bours. Francisco Salido then received 400 hectares of the newly-purchased land in payment for survey work. The residents instituted proceedings to recover the rest of their lands, but meanwhile had to go to fight the Revolution. Afterwards, only five of the original co-proprietors remained, and the remainder of their lands were fraudulently bought from them by the state agrarian delegate. At present, descendants of the original co-proprietors of Sebampo are still petitioning for restitution. After some 80 years, their chances of winning are virtually nil, since the law must protect property-owners of ten years' standing or more, and the new proprietors' documents are in order.

capitalized *campesinos*, despite the advent of ejidal credit banks under Cárdenas. As we shall see in Chapter 7, even taxation policy has been wielded against the *ejidatarios* by state legislatures, often in flagrant disregard of federal law. In this tradition of falsely contrived legislation, the Calles document provides the first insight into the national agrarian-reform plans of the *jefe máximo*. Such plans continued long after his demise.

Sonora's legislation was by no means unique. Without the presence of Porfirio Díaz, the nation suddenly lacked a supreme arbiter of internecine warfare. The country was divided into regional fiefdoms dominated by famous *caciques* whose names comprised a veritable litany of heroes of the Revolution: Felipe Carrillo Puerto in Yucatán, Saturnino Cedillo in San Luis Potosí, Lázaro Cárdenas in Michoacán, Garrido Canabal in Tabasco, Adalberto Tejeda and Úrsulo Galván in Veracruz, and of course, Calles and Adolfo de la Huerta in Sonora. *Porfirista caciques* were replaced by revolutionary generals; and soon the *caudillos* in mufti who had led the conquest of the old order became themselves the chief obstacles to agrarian reform.

The scene for the 1920s was set, then: conflict among *caudillos* at the national level over the leadership of Mexico's future; conflict between national-state power and regional *caciquismo* over ultimate control of the Revolution; conflict also among *campesino* and state and dominant classes in civil society over control of political organization of the masses. The *campesinos*, with only the political power afforded them by their weapons, had to influence the agrarian reform in battle.

POSTREVOLUTIONARY POLITICS

In the years immediately following Madero's death, the liberal revolt he had led underwent broad transformations which gradually precluded the success of a pluralist order in postrevolutionary Mexico. Though the enduring traditions of 1824 and 1857 reappeared in Carranza's draft constitution (and, by and large, survived convention revisions), the epoch did not permit liberal tolerance or political pluralism to thrive.

An editorial in *Excelsior* (July 4, 1919) coldly stated some of the traditional problems of the Mexican polity:

> In Mexico militant political parties have never existed . . . first, because the triumphant party does not let its adversary live, but exterminates it; . . . second, because here opposition groups meet to conspire, to brew plots, to begin a revolution, but never to organize themselves peacefully within the law and develop a program.[44]

44. Cited in Córdova, *La ideológia de la Revolución mexicana*, p. 263.

Beyond this harsh assessment of Mexico's political condition, however, lay some inherent difficulties of the postrevolutionary search for order. As we shall see, Mexico has struggled throughout the twentieth century with issues stemming from populist promises to ensure an equitable distribution of wealth, as well as a growing capitalist economy.

Struggle Among Caudillos

Various regimes have maintained their legitimacy and strength through manipulating the *campesinos* and workers—mobilizing, then demobilizing, sectors of the working class for political advantage. The concept of institutionalizing those populist mobilizations is part of the legacy of the 1920s. And the continuing use of a cynical blend of legal and administrative manipulation and budgetary politics has enabled the Mexican populist regime to balance *caciques* against national leadership, to the advantage of centralized political control. This, too, originated as a response to the centrifugal forces that threatened the new populist state in the 1920s. Political pluralism—freely-contending independent parties and groups with different views—fell outside the demands of postrevolutionary political organization in the militant twenties. Within a decade of the formation of the PNR—the official institutionalized spokesman of the Revolution—pluralism withered in the face of the new, albeit limited, corporate political organization.[45]

The beginning of the postrevolutionary populist pact dates (at least formally) from the Constitution of 1917. This document declared the principles of the Revolution to be class conciliation, agrarian reform, worker rights, civil liberties, protection of private property, and administrative reform. A strong executive with extraordinary powers over a benevolent paternalistic state apparatus—a *caudillo*[46]—was needed to lead this political organization toward its goals.

The *caudillos* of the Mexican Revolution were many and varied—leaders like Zapata who had emerged from the resistance to Porfirian *caciques*; *hacendados* who took up the bourgeois revolutionary cause; as well as bandits and opportunists of every description. Their power was as unconditional as it was informal, for they most often filled a power vacuum left by *porfirista caciques* abandoning the field of battle.[47] But as national

45. Many parties surged during this period, but by the end of the decade most had been smothered through repression, internal conflict, regional isolation, etc. The political instability of the decade, characterized by brief tactical coalitions, electoral violence, and military domination, did not provide an auspicious climate for party development. See Wayne Cornelius, "Nation-Building, Participation, Distribution: The Politics of Social Reform under Cárdenas," in Gabriel Almond et al. (eds.), *Crisis, Choice, and Change: Historical Studies of Political Development*, p. 400.

46. *Caudillo* literally means commander, or leader, but has even broader connotations of power and authority than might be inferred in direct translation.

47. Luisa Paré, "Caciquismo y Estructura," p. 34.

leaders, the *caudillos* displayed the same regional, political, and personal differences that had characterized them in the states or regions they originally commanded. The first order of business for aspiring *caudillos* was to eliminate competing *caudillos*, and to mold the state according to the winner's personal vision. Territorial competition and personalistic rewards to the faithful were dim beacons for the anxious masses. Public policy naturally suffered from the resultant inconsistencies.

The first important national transition in the ascendance of *caudillo* populism was the overthrow and death of Carranza, First Chief of the Constitutionalist army.[48] Preceded by the entrapment and murder of Zapata in 1919, the conflict between Carranza and his best general, Álvaro Obregón Salido, was a bellwether of new directions for the postrevolutionary regime. Carranza, who never fully recognized the need for mass politics, contrasted sharply with General Obregón, who had maintained close hierarchical ties with the *campesinos* through the army.[49] Carranza's Plan of Guadalupe, in which he pledged to satisfy the needs of the masses through the constitution, was simply *maderismo* without Madero.[50] As José Vasconcelos later wrote of Carranza, "the Plan of Guadalupe meant only that the nation had found a chief, that the avenging revolution had been unified around a legitimate authority. The soul of the movement continued to be Madero."[51] The *campesinos* soon tired of Carranza's legalistic approach; they saw no material difference in their lives, and viewed Carranza as "twice a traitor:—traitor, because he has sold the fatherland; traitor, because he has sold it to the *hacendados*."[52] The solemn promise Carranza offered to the revolutionary veterans rang hollow alongside the competing promises of "land to the people."

Toward the working class, Carranza showed little sympathy. In response to a general strike of Federal District workers in July 1916, Carranza noted the small part of society comprised by workers. He cited the rights of other classes to be protected, and the necessity of avoiding "workers' tyranny," as well as "capitalist tyranny."[53] And, showing his

48. Of course, Villa's defeat by Obregón at the battle of Celaya in 1915 also represents a serious conflict among *caudillos*, but not of the governmental magnitude of the Obregón-Carranza duel, primarily because of the "fluid" condition of the national state at the time of the fall of the Convention government.

49. Córdova, *La ideología*, p. 195.

50. In a speech in Hermosillo, Sonora, on September 24, 1913, Carranza declared that the Mexican community "has lived falsely, famished and disgraced with a handful of laws that in no way favors the people." The historical task before the Mexican leadership was "to create a new constitution, the enactment of which benefits the masses." This abbreviated vision of revolutionary change does not depart from the liberal traditions of 1857. See Silva Hérzog, *Breve historia*, vol. II, pp. 59–64, for a full text of the speech.

51. José Vasconcelos, *Breve historia de México*, p. 486.

52. Córdova, p. 169.

53. "Decreto de Carranza contra los Trabajadores," August 1, 1916, reprinted in Silva Hérzog, *Breve historia*, vol. II, p. 299.

limited revolutionary legalism, he cited the 1862 Ley Juárez to justify the death penalty for "disrupters of the public order."

Another important aspect of Carranza's disregard for politically cultivating the masses surfaced in his attacks against the Church. After the liberal Reform of 1856–1859 and the consequent loss of power by the largely urban Church, the underprivileged countryside provided a new seedbed for clerical influence. During the *Porfiriato*, the rural church actually thrived, though not in secular wealth.[54] "Social Catholicism," which included civic action as well as tribute collection, and programs of literacy to complement the catechism, played a big part in the revival of Church fortunes among the populace during the *Porfiriato*.[55] During the 1912 crisis of Madero's revolutionary government, Church officials were asked to intervene on behalf of the Revolution. The Church hierarchy reluctantly responded, endorsing the legality of the Madero government, exposing some Catholic reactionaries conspiring against the Revolution, and spreading messages of support for Madero among the believers.[56] Relations between the Church and the revolutionary state stayed relatively positive until Carranza's defeat of Huerta in 1913. Then the Constitutionalists accused the Church of complicity with Huerta and the antirevolutionary cause.[57] Continuing the campaigns against Villa and Zapata, the Constitutionalists warred relentlessly against the Church also, destroying its property and effectively closing Church facilities.[58]

The anticlerical campaign of the *carrancista* forces became, like the purges of Villa and Zapata, a double-edged sword. Its limits became clear in the assassination of Zapata in 1919, and in the war against the clergy that endured from 1914 to 1920. Carranza's strategy seemed to be a unique denial of the importance of positive mass politics, combined with the systematic elimination of all rivals to his power over the masses. His intransigence toward the unions, the *campesinos*, and the clergy whittled away at the base of his personal authority as leader of the Revolution. His fall came, finally, as his last important base of support, the army, chose to fol-

54. Jean Meyer, *La Cristiada*, vol. II, *El conflicto*, pp. 44–45.

55. *Ibid.*, p. 48; also Robert E. Quirk, *The Mexican Revolution and the Catholic Church, 1910–1929*, p. 13.

56. Meyer, vol. II, p. 64. Quirk's account differs from Meyer's in portraying a more hostile relationship between *maderistas* and Church supporters. At what level this hostility took shape is not entirely clear, at least partly due to the aggregate form of clergy discussed by Quirk as against the multi-level hierarchy analyzed by Meyer. (See Quirk, pp. 25 and 36.)

57. There was some regional evidence supporting this charge, but nothing to confirm Carranza's allegation that the Church had participated in Madero's assassination. (See Meyer, vol. II, pp. 65–66.)

58. *Ibid.*, pp. 73–87; for a contrasting assessment, see Quirk, p. 43. Carranza's alleged neutrality toward the Church does not square with the unrelenting anticlerical violence that characterized his rule. In fairness to Carranza, however, that "neutrality" may have been strained severely by the conservative Catholic press and such affronts as the *Te Deum* sung for Huerta in Mexico City. (See Quirk, pp. 36–38.)

low General Álvaro Obregón, the hero of Celaya. The rise of Obregón in 1920 as the new champion of the masses properly begins the chronicle of populist politics in postrevolutionary Mexico.[59]

The Sonoran Dynasty Comes to Power

The advent of the now-famous strongmen from Sonora—Álvaro Obregón Salido, Plutarco Elías Calles, and Adolfo de la Huerta—signalled a change in mass politics that would eventuate in the institutionalization of *caudillo* leadership through the political party, the fragmentation of regional power-bases which competed with the national regime, and the end of violent overthrow as a means of presidential succession. By its very nature, however, the Sonoran dynasty of 1920–1934 would bear conflicting attitudes toward agrarian reform and the social obligations of the postrevolutionary regime. These conflicts manifested themselves in an array of national agrarian legislation which did little to affect the distribution of rural wealth in Mexico. But since legislation was a secondary front of the post-Carranza governments, let us first briefly examine some more pressing issues of the time.

The Sonoran dynasty falls into two deceptively neat periods: 1920–1924, Obregón's presidency; and 1924–1934, the *Maximato* of Plutarco Elías Calles. During those fifteen years, Mexico would not only endure the presidencies of three Sonorans,[60] but would experience major rebellions by Sonoran political and military figures, and the execution of Sonorans Arnulfo Gómez and Francisco Serrano for an attempted coup that died with them.[61] Sonoran *políticos* were definitely in the forefront of national politics.

The triumph of the *obregonista* rebellion in 1920 signalled the rise of the most advanced sector of the agricultural bourgeoisie to national power. Obregón represented some of the most progressive capitalist forces in Mexico; their ascendance began a new type of capitalist development impelled by agricultural production and facilitated by state intervention in the economy.[62] Obregón linked himself closely with "honest capital," envisioning a modern banking system; a fair labor code; a secure,

59. It was due to the overt repression of the *Zapatista* movement and the *campesino*-worker movements in general that Obregón decided to become a presidential candidate. He appealed to those who advocated concessions to the *campesinos* and workers to ensure the new order. (Jorge A. Calderón Salazar, *Algunos aspectos de la dinámica económica y social de México en el período 1920–1935*, p. 50.)

60. Obregón, Calles, and Abelardo Rodríguez (1932–1934). In addition, Adolfo de la Huerta was provisional president from May 24 to December 1, 1920, after he participated in the overthrow of Carranza.

61. The major rebellions were led by de la Huerta in 1923 and Escobar in 1929. More analysis of their importance will follow in this chapter. See William Weber Johnson, *Heroic Mexico*, chap. 45, for a good summary of the Gómez–Serrano affair.

62. Calderón Salazar, *Algunos aspectos*, p. 54.

tax-paying, small-producer class in the countryside; rationalization of petroleum exploitation; and a reduced role for the military.[63] In contrast to Carranza—who feared the banks as supporters of Huerta, and refused to author new banking codes[64]—Obregón pledged fiscal reform and a new, progressive image which would stimulate foreign investment while keeping national control over domestic wealth.[65] His supporters in Sonora included the same *hacendados* who had forwarded his nomination as municipal head of Huatabampo. Additionally, he counted on Calles and de la Huerta for support from merchants in Guaymas and the northeast. Unfortunately for many of his promoters, however, questions of political power and its transmission took precedence over those of economic development during the first half of the decade. The Obregón–Calles–de la Huerta struggle over national power and control of public policy culminated in bloodshed during the last half of Obregón's presidential term, in 1923 and 1924. Even afterwards, the main struggle between Obregón and Calles threatened the lives of their closest supporters. The Sonoran dynasty was built at the cost of many lives.[66]

Obregón rebelled against Carranza partly because of Carranza's callous attitude toward the populace—who, in great numbers, were living in squalor. The average daily wage for farm labor in Mexico as late as 1925 was 90 centavos, less than 40 cents U.S. Sonora, at 1.97 pesos—about 87 cents U.S.—shared with Yucatán the highest rural wage level in the country.[67] Of the nearly 69 percent of the population living in the countryside in 1921, only 53,908 people, or 0.54 percent, had benefitted from some 195 land-reform measures.[68] Agricultural production had declined 24 percent from 1910 to 1925 and lost another 7 percent before the great slump of 1929.[69]

In Sonora, the state which raised three of its favorite sons to national prominence in the 1920s, the situation was not much better. The National Agrarian Commission (CNA) had only restored two indigenous communities to their lands by 1920, and it had contributed no land reform in that

63. *Ibid.*, p. 56.
64. David H. Shelton, "The Banking System: Money and the Goal of Growth," p. 132.
65. Calderón Salazar, p. 55.
66. In the final, bitter twist to this bloodshed, Arnulfo Gómez, when captured in 1928 in rebellion against Calles, reportedly said: "He [Calles] cannot execute me, because he himself advised me to become a [presidential] candidate, to prevent the return of Obregón." Gómez was shot anyway, *by order of Obregón*. (Medina Ruiz, *Calles*, p. 104.) Some circumstantial evidence lends credence to this interpretation; see Lieuwen, *Mexican Militarism*, pp. 95–99.
67. Whetten, *Rural Mexico*, p. 261.
68. These measures included restitutions, *dotaciones* or grants, confirmations, and amplifications. (Mexico, Secretaría de Agricultura y Fomento, *Comisión Nacional Agraria, Estadística, 1915–1927*, p. 88.) Eyler Simpson, using data from the Agrarian Department, puts the figures at 190 cases affecting 48,382 people. (Simpson, *The Ejido: Mexico's Way Out*, p. 609.)
69. Data derived from Whetten, p. 255.

category since 1917. It had granted 21,694 hectares in answer to only four petitions from among 2,804 persons, but had not given definitive (permanent) possession to a single proprietor or ejidatario in its six years of existence in Sonora.[70] The Carranza reform, stopped in 1916, never accomplished anything of note in Sonora.

Finally, in November 1920, after the short interim presidency of Adolfo de la Huerta, Obregón ascended to the presidency of the Mexican Republic. It had been eight tempestuous years since Obregón had risen as municipal head of the Mayo valley community of Huatabampo to declare himself for Madero in the fight against Pascual Orozco.[71] At the head of 300 "irregulars" with virtually no firepower,[72] Obregón began what must have seemed an impossible quest to drive the orozquistas from Sonora. Only thirteen months later, his task accomplished, Obregón became brigadier general of the Constitutionalist army of Carranza and then chief of the Army of the Northwest, military commander of Sonora, Sinaloa, Chihuahua, Durango, and Baja California.[73] Defender of Carranza against Villa, conqueror of the villistas at Celaya, and finally, successful challenger for the presidency of Mexico, Obregón had compiled a long list of political obligations which permanently affected the structure of power in postrevolutionary Mexico. From his first campaign for the municipal presidency of Huatabampo, small-farmer Obregón counted on the support of a strange coalition of maternal family connections (the Salidos were among the most prominent porfirista families of southern Sonora), working-class and indigenous support, and the backing of various ascendant hacendados. This style of coalescing conflicting groups and artfully committing himself to contrary political positions, with his popularity as his main collateral, followed him throughout his career.

Obregón was the only major figure within the carrancista movement who did not abandon the Casa del Obrero Mundial (COM) after the general strike of 1916. Through his intervention, the COM had signed a pact with Carranza in 1915, which Obregón used to save their leadership from the harsh strike penalties Carranza demanded.[74] COM members had also been among his soldiers at Celaya, and in 1920 Obregón wished to repay the workers' loyalty with his own version of special presidential patronage.[75]

Obregón had also undertaken the burden of agrarian reform rejected by his predecessor. As a small proprietor of marginal lands in Huatabampo, Obregón had personally faced the problems of agricultural production

70. *Comisión Nacional Agraria*, p. 78.
71. Mario A. Mena, *Álvaro Obregón, historia militar y política, 1912–1929*, p. 15.
72. Various sources estimate his arsenal to have totalled from 2 to 14 rifles.
73. Mena, pp. 37–39.
74. *Ibid.*, p. 437; Córdova, *La ideología*, p. 214.
75. Mena, p. 75.

under the *Porfiriato*. As an innovative agricultural producer, an expert farm mechanic, and agricultural entrepreneur,[76] he chafed at the misuse and abandonment of cultivable land in his home state. Having attempted to negotiate a peaceful compromise reform with the Yaquis in 1915, after defeating Villa, his memories of the concentration of land in Sonora were not happy ones. The Yaquis, as always, had demanded absolute dominion of the valley and the expulsion of all white people. Obregón, in the heavy prose of his memoirs, recalls a microcosm of the Yaqui–Yori saga in the history of his state:

> To accede to them would have signified a retrograde complacency, which would detract from the tendencies of the Revolution, exchanging the well-done for the noxious, if, mistakenly, in the name of a just reparation owed to the Yaquis, the perpetuation of barbarity was sanctioned . . . and dominion was extended to them even where civilization had been implanted. Nevertheless, urged on by the greatest desires of arriving at a satisfactory agreement with the rebellious tribe, I tried a final conference with its delegates. . . .
>
> The night (December 20, 1915) when I received reports that the rebel Yaquis had attacked one of our garrisons on the railroad track to the south of Guaymas, I decided absolutely to abandon any conciliatory attitude toward the rebels, in view of the fact that they demonstrated themselves to be little disposed to enter into reasonable agreements, and only took advantage of the concessions that we had given them . . . to commit their accustomed depredations more easily, perhaps judging as weakness on our part that which was only a sincere desire to repair the injustices and spoliations on the part of dictatorial governments of which they had been victims in past epochs.[77]

On this pessimistic and bitter note, Obregón left Sonora to pursue the remnants of Pancho Villa's Northern Division. He left the Yaqui problem explicitly in the hands of the governor and military commander of Sonora, Plutarco Elías Calles.

Calles then proceeded to organize the registration of all *peones*, to record their movements, and to decide which of them made "common cause with the insurgents." He quickly obtained permission from Carranza to declare outside the law any Yaqui discovered on the state's roadways without a signed safe-conduct from his *patrón*. Within three months, Calles had engaged a full-scale campaign against the hapless Yaquis, driving them from their hideouts in the southern Sierra and sweeping them north and east to Ures and the furthest reaches of the mountains. Calles, like his predecessors, believed himself to be fighting "against the Yaqui rebels who for so many years have lived on pillage, committing nameless

76. In 1905, Obregón possessed a total of 230 hectares of mediocre land in the municipality of Huatabampo. In 1925, when he intervened to arrange the purchase of the Richardson Construction Co., he was described as the greatest entrepreneur in the valley. (Aguilar Camín, *La frontera nómada*, p. 426.)

77. Álvaro Obregón Salido, *Ocho mil kilómetros en campaña*, pp. 471–473.

crimes, holding back the progress of the state." He continued to fight this campaign throughout his term.[78]

As Obregón came to power, then, he faced a country in turmoil, still dominated by warlords like himself. Uncertain about the direction of agrarian reform, the extent of the government's obligation to fulfill populist provisions of the 1917 Constitution, and the military chieftains who would claim succession, the Sonoran *triumvirs* led by Obregón began to legislate new aspects of the Revolution and envision more structural aids for capitalist economic growth.

THE BIRTH OF EJIDAL LAW

Gradually, during the first ten years of the Revolution, a separation had occurred between advocates of small rural freeholdings and proponents of a system of ejidal land tenure. This ideological difference, of course, marked a main issue in Obregón's agrarian legislation, and he sided clearly with private property. His legislative efforts can be summarized briefly. His principal law, the *Ley de Ejidos* of December 28, 1920, created a legal maze more difficult and complicated than its predecessor. However, it began the codification of the Revolution's attitude toward the *ejido*.[79]

The CNA, created under the Law of January 6, 1915, itself began to play a contradictory role in agrarian reform. On the one hand, its Circular 40 imposed a limit on eligible *ejidos* by requiring them to demonstrate "political status" as communities, prior to receiving land. Though the circular received the praise of *agraristas* for its intent to expand *ejidos* onto *haciendas*, its true significance was in identifying the "political status" of a village with its eligibility for ejidal grants or restitutions. With that provision, all *peones acasillados* remained outside the agrarian reform, since their residence was *hacienda*-determined and they belonged to no politically organized *pueblo*. This severe limitation in the law remained until the Agrarian Code of 1934, affecting the majority of landless *campesinos*.[80]

On the other hand, *agrarista* influence was clear in the CNA's Circular 51, which proposed the collective exploitation of *ejidos*, their democratic

78. Aguilar Camín, pp. 441–443; Dabdoub, *Historia del Valle del Yaqui*, pp. 204–209; *Informe que rinde Calles, 1918*, p. 5. Neither of the partisan biographies of Calles (Rivera and Medina Ruiz) mentions the campaign of 1916–1919.

79. *Diario oficial de la Federación*, Jan. 8, 1921; see Jesús Silva Hérzog, *El agrarismo mexicano y la reforma agraria: exposición y crítica*, pp. 280–281, for analysis of the contradictory aspects of the law. Though the impact of mentioning the word *ejido* in a law may seem slight, it immediately drew fire from the *latifundistas*; see *El agrarismo*, p. 291, for an example.

80. For this circular and other CNA decrees, see Antonio Villarreal Muñoz, *Restitución y dotación de ejidos, el problema agrario en México: leyes, decretos, circulares, y disposiciones expedidas ultimamente en la materia*, pp. 93–173.

political organization, and the formation of cooperative societies for their management.[81] Though never implemented, this circular of October 11, 1922, showed agrarian sentiment to be very much alive in the Obregón government. It was not until 1925 that the government would respond to the circular with the Law of Ejidal Patrimony, which negated the intended effect of Circular 51.[82]

Obregón's Accomplishments

The best thing that can be said of the Obregón legislation of 1920–1924 is that it was a confused attempt to consolidate the chaotic Carranza reform and move forward. Obregón himself saw great potential in land reform, an opportunity to "conquer the respect of the masses" and discover the "secret of public tranquility" in "the patrimony of the rural classes."[83] But his attitude toward the *ejido* was not favorable—a product, perhaps, of entrepreneurial caution, political pressures, and his success as a small freeholder in Sonora. He favored private property, reduced dislocations in agricultural production, and incremental changes in general on questions of land tenure and exploitation.[84] Thus the vague, confused ejidal law of 1920 and its abrogation in December 1921 seem to indicate muddled conflicts within the Obregón camp, with *agraristas* opposing the defenders of cautious economic reconstruction of the agricultural sector.

But Obregón, as we have noted, was something of a master of coalition, sensing the direction and intensity of political currents with considerable accuracy. His reputation as leader of the only group capable of uniting the country[85] came at the price of coopting the bulk of *agrarista* leaders who survived Zapata. Díaz Soto y Gama's National Agrarian Party (PNA) and the newly-formed Leagues of Agrarian Communities of Veracruz (LCAEV) exemplify some of the rural pressure groups which caused occasional advance of the *agrarista* cause. *Agraristas* convened two Agrarian Congresses, in 1921 and 1923, during which the national representatives of *campesinos* revealed some aspects of the nature of rural struggle against the old order.[86] Partly due to the immediate debt he owed to the *zapatistas* for their crucial support in 1920, partly due to the bitter realities of land tenure in Sonora, and partly out of a keen sense of political alliances, Obregón stepped into the role of first agrarian reformer of the postrevolutionary period.

81. *Ibid.*; also Salomón Eckstein, *El ejido colectivo en México*, pp. 49–51.

82. *Ley reglamentaria sobre repartición de tierras ejidales y constitución del patrimonio parcelario ejidal, Diario Oficial*, Dec. 31, 1925. More will be said about this law later.

83. Obregón, *Discursos*, vol. II, p. 206.

84. Aguilera Gómez, *La reforma agraria*, pp. 130–131.

85. John Womack, Jr., *Zapata and the Mexican Revolution*, p. 366.

86. See Silva Hérzog, *El agrarismo*, pp. 302–311, for further treatment of these congresses.

Accomplishments in land-reform programs during his tenure were modest by comparison with those of later presidents, especially Cárdenas and Echeverría. But in the context of the limited postrevolutionary bureaucracy, and the entrenched legalism with which he approached the reform, Obregón accomplished some important standards for future official reform. The 1920 law and Circular 51 of the CNA were both halting but important steps toward the birth of the *ejido* as a revolutionary institution. His Decree of August 2, 1923, permitting provisional possession of unused national lands, also began a series of laws regarding the disposition of *baldíos*.[87] The first laws concerning agricultural credit, idle lands, and compensation for expropriation all originated with the Obregón administration.[88] Obregón is also hailed as the first *agrarista* president, by virtue of the land restitutions and grants authorized during his presidency.[89]

Unfortunately, this assessment does not stand up well under closer scrutiny. Of the 1.2 million hectares subject to reform from 1921 to 1924, less than half appear to have been cultivable. Though statistics are not available in aggregate form for Obregón's regime alone, the CNA statistics for 1915–1927 support this claim. During that period only 32.7 percent of land given out under the land-reform program was even arable; only 3.7 percent was irrigated.[90] The impressive figure of 1.2 million hectares granted under Obregón is, then, gravely misleading if the concept of agrarian reform involves giving out land which is suitable for cultivation. More specifically, in Sonora Obregón is credited with grants, restitutions, and confirmations totalling about 74,300 hectares, or 5.6 percent of all land granted nationally from 1920 to 1924 (see Table A1 in appendix).[91] However, only 6,568 hectares of that 74,300 (8.8 percent) was even susceptible to immediate cultivation (see Table A2 in appendix). Throughout the postrevolutionary period, as we shall see in future chapters, Mexican presidents have in varying degrees brandished impressive agrarian-reform figures which often misrepresent the amount of actual farmland involved.

Perhaps more important than the statistical aspect of Obregón's limited reforms was the regional configuration of the land-grants. Of the lands

87. *Diario Oficial*, Aug. 11, 1923.

88. The two most important are the *Ley sobre Bancos Refaccionarios de 29 de Septiembre de 1924* (*Diario Oficial*, Nov. 12, 1924); and *Ley de Tierras Ociosas de 23 de Junio de 1920* (*ibid.*, June 28, 1920). For a convenient summary of these laws, see Simpson, *The Ejido*, app. B, p. 729.

89. Almost all the standard surveys assign this role to Obregón. For two notable examples, see Silva Hérzog, *El agrarismo*, p. 280; and González Ramírez, *La revolución social*, p. 244.

90. Data elaborated from *Comisión Nacional Agraria*, p. 170.

91. 1920–1924 is used because of contradictory and partial totals in CNA data for 1921–1924; Obregón only presided over the reform during the latter dates. The trends, however, are unchanged.

included in the Sonoran reform under Obregón, only the *ejidos* of Moroncarit, La Misa, and Navojoa are in the rich coastal plain surrounding
the Yaqui valley.[92] The rest are fairly scattered in the northern and north-
central desert, which was largely uncultivable at the time. The one grant
in the Yaqui valley was Cajeme, named after the traditional Yaqui trading
center and the nineteenth-century rebel leader.[93] Cajeme was the first ejidal grant in the Yaqui river valley. But even though it represented a beginning of land restitution to the then-reduced Indians in the valley, the land
was not irrigated, a crucial shortcoming in an area known for capricious
variations in rainfall.[94] Further, the indigenous population of the valley
had diminished with the years of war, the advent of a migrant workforce,
plagues, and intermarriage. Nor should we slight the effects of the bias
against Yaqui landholding evident in such legislation as Calles' Law of
1918. Cajeme was more a symbol of reform than a precursor of further substantive reforms under Obregón.

Regarding the reform grants that actually did take place during this period, the cases that appear in Table A2 are the ones that were resolved
most easily, and therefore represented the most positive aspect of the
agrarian reform of that time. In contrast to these successful cases, many
petitioners experienced great difficulties in the bureaucratic process of
asking for land their families had possessed a century before. As an example, the *pueblo* of Banámichi appears in the summary statistics of the
CNA, but its "vital statistics" do not appear on the list of definitive possessions for the state of Sonora. Something went awry between the government's resolution and definitive tenure for the *campesino* beneficiaries.
As it happened, Banámichi had applied for a land-grant for 148 residents
who lacked land they could cultivate. On June 26, 1924, President Álvaro
Obregón dictated a presidential resolution granting the inhabitants of Banámichi almost 494 hectares *of land that did not exist.* Thus, the resolution could not possibly be executed. On March 22, 1926, the persistent
campesinos petitioned again for land for 177 residents, and on May 4 the
petition was inaugurated by the Local Agrarian Commission (CLA).[95] It
was not until August 24, 1933, that the Commission recommended a grant
of 1,805 hectares to the villagers, and the governor ordered the land

92. Moroncarit, in the Mayo valley, is located in the municipality of Huatabampo. Navojoa, also a Mayo valley *ejido*, is in the municipality of the same name, slightly north of the
city of Navojoa. La Misa is located in the valley of San José de Guaymas, in the municipality
of Guaymas.

93. Cajeme, meaning "he who does not drink," was the adopted name of José María
Leyva, a Yaqui political leader who fought from 1875–1887 against the *Yori* incursions into
the Yaqui valley. He was finally caught and executed at Tres Cruces in 1887 (see Chapter 3).

94. Mexico, Banco Nacional de Crédito Ejidal, S.A., *El sistema de producción colectiva
en los ejidos del Valle del Yaqui, Sonora*, p. 18.

95. The *Comisión Local Agraria* was the forerunner of the *Comisión Agraria Mixta*, the
agency at the state level that recommends grants and investigates controversies in land
tenure.

granted on October 8, 1933. After a study of the lands, however, the governor revised his resolution, conceding the village 1,916 hectares, of which 216 were irrigated—"sufficient" for 103 parcels and the rest for communal pasture-land. Some 74 individuals were left out of this final grant, consummated on March 11, 1935, by President Lázaro Cárdenas, *sixteen years after the initial petition was forwarded.*[96]

This trend of bureaucratic delay and incorrect handling of agrarian petitions was to continue throughout the 1920s. Another example comes from Tahuichopa, Arizpe, in the Sonora river valley, where 45 *campesinos* petitioned the governor for a land-grant in 1925. The recommendation of the Mixed Agrarian Commission (CAM) did not emerge until April 25, 1935—over ten years later. The governor immediately ordered execution of the grant, but he revoked his resolution after complaints from neighboring proprietors. Finally, in February 1938, President Cárdenas issued a presidential resolution granting the villagers 18,604 hectares. Of this generous grant, only 104 hectares were irrigated, and the rest were marginal cattle-lands, more desert than pasture.

The CLA was not the only agency guilty of unconscionable delays, but in Sonora it played an important part in the "counter-reform" of the 1920s.[97] The quality of land does not appear to have been the crucial factor in agrarian reform or denial thereof. Most of the land available in Sonora under the category of *baldíos*, or national lands not in use, was properly classified as desert land. Except possibly to Adolfo de la Huerta, who dreamt of cultivating spineless cactus on these lands, they were not considered premium investment opportunities for the anxious, progress-oriented *Sonorense* elite. More likely, the opposition to agrarian reform originated in a combination of bureaucratic bottlenecks, lack of revolutionary direction, hostility toward the underclasses, and the caste vestiges of Porfirian society.

So, regarding Obregón's reforms in Sonora, the "first steps" were wobbly ones, indicative of the many pressures he sought to balance in order to create the equilibrium necessary to the epoch. Nationally, the picture was no better. Though Obregón had, indeed, begun the agrarian reform, the character of social obligation—especially regarding the agrarian reform—had yet to be addressed. The state had still not taken meaningful action on the question of financing the reform, though this was partly due to continuing fiscal chaos. And the reform under Obregón never broke with the liberal insistence upon economic rationality as a guide for the land-grant

96. These data come from *Diario Oficial* and the files of Licenciado Leonel Arguelles Méndez, former *Asesor Jurídico* (Legal Advisor) for various Sonoran *ejidos*.

97. The CLA and CAM also delayed the petition of San Pedro de Aconchi, municipality of Aconchi, from April 1923 to September 1933. The *campesinos* petitioning this totally un-irrigated land did not gain definitive possession until May 1937. The *ejidatarios* had possessed the land being petitioned since 1715.

programs. This narrow view of "cost-effective" reforms resurged under Calles, and weighed down the reform until Cárdenas.

The Calles Presidency

In terms of agrarian-reform legislation, there is no easy division between the presidency of Álvaro Obregón and that of Plutarco Elías Calles. The continuation seen in the legislative efforts of 1925–1928 reflects both the limits of viewing politics from this single perspective and, conversely, the insights to be gained from analyzing presidential domination in the heyday of *caudillos*. If in examining the legislative record of the Calles presidency we overlook the dynamic political conflicts of the period, we can nevertheless see that Calles acted more as Obregón's subaltern than is generally realized. Calles continued the prolific, if confused, manufacture of agrarian laws, stacking one code on top of another until, by the end of the decade, the legislative aspect of agrarian reform was a jumbled mess.[98] Nevertheless, some important legislation was passed, probably at the urging of the retired Obregón.

One of the most revealing laws that emerged from the Calles administration was the Law of Ejidal Patrimony of December 29, 1925.[99] Engineered as a response to Circular 51 of the CNA, which had provided for communal exploitation of ejidal property, this law ordered the ejidal *comisarios* "to divide into lots the cultivated land of the *ejidos* . . . and to divide said lots in the most equitable manner agreeable to the majority of *ejidatarios*."[100] The Revolution still brooked no threats from its collectivist elements.

Despite the national chaos which plagued the Calles years—including the *cristero* revolt, several military pronouncements, and the ever-increasing militance of the Leagues of Agrarian Communities (LCA)—postrevolutionary ideology still foundered in elitist worries over indemnification of expropriated properties, establishing a new financial structure amenable to capitalist growth,[101] and exercising paternal control over mass political organization.

The most significant legislation of the Calles presidency was the Law of Agricultural Credit of March 2, 1926,[102] and the famous "Ley Bassols" of

98. Simpson, in *The Ejido*, lists some 52 laws, decrees, etc., from the Calles government. Many of them abrogated or reformed previous laws, but none of them fell under an organized agrarian code. The first agrarian code did not appear until 1934.

99. *Ley reglamentaria sobre repartición.*

100. *Ibid.*, chap. I, art. 5:III.

101. The problems of public finance and private capital formation had plagued the revolutionary leadership from the beginning. Although thorough banking reforms did not come until 1932, some early forays were made by Obregón and especially by Calles. For more information, see Shelton, "The Banking System," esp. pp. 134–140; Leopoldo Solís, *La realidad económica mexicana: retrovisión y perspectivas*, p. 107; and José Iturriaga de la Fuente, *La revolución hacendaria: la hacienda pública con el presidente Calles*, chap. 3ff.

102. *Ley de Crédito Agrícola de 2 de Marzo de 1926* (*Diario Oficial*, March 4, 1926).

April 26, 1927,[103] which called for "cleaning up" the agrarian-reform process and integrating it into a system of social justice *and* agricultural production.[104] This law, named after its author, Narciso Bassols, sought to clarify the constitutional status of the *ejido*, and in this sense it was productive, defining categories of eligible participants; by all accounts it offered a brilliant exposition of the points of law involved. But the Ley Bassols fell prey to the systematic deficiencies which characterized the legalistic approach of the revolutionary elite toward agrarian reform. By excluding *ranchos* (500 population or less with no political status) and *peones acasillados*,[105] it violated the eloquent prose of its author, who subsequently entreated opponents of the law: "*Toda la tierra; y pronto.*"[106] The curious difference between Bassols' commitment to radical *agrarismo* and the modest content of the law (made even more modest after several reforms) demonstrated the ideological indecision of the postrevolutionary regime—an indecision somewhat understandable in light of the social upheaval of the time and the conflicting class interests at stake.

The Law of Agricultural Credit was slightly more straightforward. Calles always felt that agrarian reform was a technical and economic problem, not a political one. With proper state control of the problem, an "integral solution" could be devised to modernize agriculture, control the *campesinos*, and stimulate industrial growth.[107] The Agricultural Credit Law of 1926 permitted the state to control the flow of public spending in the countryside in order to "foment, regulate, and maintain vigil over the constitution and over the functioning of regional and local agricultural credit societies"; and to make loans for agricultural purposes as well as for the "acquisition, division, and colonization of lands."[108] During this law's five years of operation, 39.5 million pesos were loaned. Only 6.6 million pesos went to some 18,590 small farmers in 338 cooperative societies; the rest, 83 percent of the total, went to 1,441 individuals, in keeping with the tradition set by the bank's predecessor, the venal *Caja de Préstamos para Obras de Irrigación y Fomento de la Agricultura* of Porfirio Díaz.[109]

Two other laws of the Calles era are relevant here. The Law of Agri-

103. *Ley de Dotaciones y Restituciones de Tierras y Aguas* . . . (ibid., April 27, 1927).
104. See his "La Nueva Ley Agraria," in Narciso Bassols, *Obras*, pp. 51–52.
105. Chap. I, art. 2.
106. Bassols, "Toda la tierra; y pronto," in *Obras*, p. 53.
107. Córdova, *La ideología*, pp. 332–333.
108. *Ley de Crédito Agrícola*, Title I, chap. I, art. 2. The language of Calles' annual report of 1925–1926 paraphrases this law. Calles said that he recognized the need to confront "the integral resolution of the problem, rationally organizing the development of cultivation and fomenting the exploitation of agricultural industries." (*Informes rendidos por el C. General Plutarco Elías Calles, Presidente Constitucional de los Estados Unidos Mexicanos, ante el H. Congreso de la Unión los días 1° de Septiembre de 1925 y 1° de Septiembre de 1926, y contestación de los CC. Presidentes del Citado Congreso*, p. 57.)
109. Simpson, "The Mexican Agrarian Reform," p. 143. The *Caja de Préstamos*, organized in 1908, loaned a total of 55 million pesos, of which 53 million went to 98 regime

cultural Credit was accompanied by the Ejidal Bank Law of March 16, 1926.[110] The separate promulgation of ejidal finance laws signalled the division in official attitudes toward private property and ejidal property. This law had two principal effects: the national control of campesino credit at the regional level, and the direction of agrarian reform according to national criteria of selection and funding, not through the more "spontaneous" process of pueblo-generated petitions for land.[111] As the credit requirements of the bank organized ejidatarios into "controllable" ejidal credit societies, much of the campesino-directed aspect of agrarian politics was left behind, to the distinct advantage of the state. In recent years the state has successfully manipulated credit societies to break the political and economic unity of the ejido.[112]

Finally, Calles also issued the first Law of Colonization on April 5, 1926.[113] Because the federal government had acquired some 36 million hectares during the Revolution, a colonization law reminiscent of the nineteenth century came to be viewed as a way of populating the frontier (over 23 million hectares of federal land was in the three states of Sonora, Baja California, and Chihuahua), removing the pressure for land reform against propietarios, and proving the value—through privately-held colonies—of private land tenure over ejidal usufruct.[114] As we shall see in Chapters 7 and 8, some of the self-financed colonists of Sonora became chief opponents of the ejidal system, evolved into absentee landlords, and overall represented little in the way of agrarian redistribution to the poor.[115]

Statistically, the effects of the Calles reforms again show the superficiality of reform efforts up to that time. Nationally, the Calles regime

---

favorites. The Banco de Crédito Agrícola of Calles' administration was financed largely (almost 40 percent of the assets) with doubtful assets from the failed Caja de Préstamos.

110. Ley de Bancos Ejidales de 16 de Marzo de 1926 (Diario Oficial, April 9, 1926).

111. On this latter point, see Jerjes Aguirre Avellaneda, La política ejidal en México, p. 69.

112. More on this in Chapters 6 and 7. Echeverría, explicitly recognizing that legally-contrived division, tried to unify the political and economic leadership of the ejido in the 1970s.

113. Ley Federal de Colonización de 5 de Abril de 1926 (Diario Oficial, May 11, 1926).

114. Aguilera Gómez, La reforma agraria, p. 132. Colonization now differed from that of the nineteenth century in the attempt to wrest control of the land from foreigners and colonize it with nationals. (See Informes rendidos por Calles, 1925–1926, p. 65.) Calles' greatest success in recapturing land from foreign companies came through Obregón's "private" negotiation for purchase of land in the Yaqui river valley from the Richardson Construction Co. In 1926, after financial reverses and repeated governmental threats to seize the lands for taxes, the Richardson Co. sold out to the Banco Nacional de Crédito Agrícola for $6,000,000 U.S. (See Dabdoub, Historia del Valle del Yaqui, pp. 326–328.) This purchase brought some 260,000 hectares of prime land under government domination and opened the way for colonization, which had been delayed by Richardson's speculation and poor investment record. (See Aguilar Camín, La frontera nómada, pp. 425–426.)

115. No colonies were, however, established in Sonora under the Law of 1926. (See Whetten, Rural Mexico, p. 638.)

distributed 3.25 million hectares, compared with 1.2 million during Obregón's tenure (Table A3 in the appendix). In Sonora, the pattern of granting useless land continued in the style established under Obregón. As Table A4 (in the appendix) shows, only 13.0 percent of total land granted was arable; a mere 5.3 percent was irrigated. A striking 87 percent was uncultivable "pasture-land," consistent with the 91-percent mark recorded under Obregón. Again, the *ejidos* granted stayed clear of the potentially prosperous Yaqui and Mayo valleys, for Obregón and Calles had other plans for this fertile bottomland. Before those plans were consummated, however, the violent Mexican political process swept away de la Huerta and Obregón, and left the future of agricultural development and agrarian reform in the hands of Calles.

FORGING THE POPULIST PACT

To focus exclusively on agrarian legislation in the 1920s would create a totally misleading image of postrevolutionary political culture and the forces struggling to form it. During the 1920s the Mexican populace witnessed the destruction of the Sonoran dynasty and the "gentleman's agreement" by which the presidency was to be passed alternately among Obregón, de la Huerta, and Calles.[116] The country, already racked by the bloody wars of 1910–1920, renewed its internal combat in the *cristero* rebellion of 1926. Francisco Villa, Felipe Carrillo Puerto, Primo Tapia, Arnulfo Gómez, Francisco Serrano, Lucio Blanco, and many other revolutionary partisans died at the hands of one government clique or another. And just as the calamitous decade closed, world depression gripped Mexico's already strained economy.

Calles was an intense, energetic figure who, despite his mercurial personality, inherited the task of attempting to create postrevolutionary order. A heavy drinker, he passed puritanical temperance and gaming laws as governor of Sonora. Defender of private property, he nevertheless attacked those *propietarios* who were "enemies of the cause."[117] Beginning as Obregón's reluctant subaltern, he later manipulated his own *peleles* in the presidency with equal disregard.[118] Called "bolshevik" by the Church and "friend" by international capital, Calles cast an eccentric shadow on the presidency. His aggressive attitudes toward the military,

116. Adolfo de la Huerta denied the existence of such a pact, but its terms generated much discussion in political circles before 1923. (See Huerta, *Memorias*, pp. 180–182.)

117. While proclaiming plans to "moralize" the populace of Sonora within the legal limits of the Revolution, Calles availed himself of the opportunity to dispossess political enemies through the agrarian reform. (Aguilar Camín, pp. 421 and 429.)

118. *Pelele* means "nincompoop" or "puppet," and refers here to the presidents—Emilio Portes Gil, Pascual Ortiz Rubio, and Abelardo Rodríguez—who were manipulated by Calles during the last half of the *Maximato* (1929–1934).

the *obregonistas*, the agrarian reform, and the Church helped turn the struggle for postrevolutionary order into a bloodbath.

Calles did not ascend without interference. Adolfo de la Huerta, the third member of the Sonoran triumvirate, sensed that his station in the Revolution had reached a peak. He had been interim governor of Sonora and provisional president of Mexico after the fall of Carranza; but if these morsels of power whetted his appetite, the banquet, nevertheless, was denied him. He opposed Calles in the rebellion of 1923 under the thin veneer of anti-imperialism and revolutionary morality, but survived only on the ambition of the generals supporting him and on his own personal sense of mission in trying to become president.[119] By rebelling, de la Huerta probably fulfilled his greatest revolutionary function; his defeat was more properly the defeat of the militaristic factions outside the control of the revolutionary state, and not incidentally beyond the control of de la Huerta himself. The 1923 rebellion involved 40 percent (23,224) of the federal army, not including 102 generals, few of whom had any allegiance to de la Huerta. Obregón's conquest of the rebel forces began a new era in state–military relations: professionalization of the army and the payment of *cañonazos* or "cannonballs" of thousands of pesos to ensure the subordination of the military to the civilian directors of postrevolutionary order.[120] The defeat of de la Huerta also guaranteed that Obregón's hand-picked successor would ascend to the presidency; the three voices vowing the "gentleman's agreement" had been reduced to a more manageable duet.[121]

Thanks partly to the verbal agreements between the United States and Mexico made at the 1922 Lamont–de la Huerta and 1923 Bucareli conferences, and partly to recognition of the Obregón regime by President Calvin Coolidge, Calles entered the presidency with a better international

119. De la Huerta himself treated the events of 1923–24 vaguely in his memoirs, claiming he declared himself in rebellion out of devotion to the democratic opposition, fear for his life, and opposition to the Bucareli talks over expropriations of foreign property and subsoil leases for foreign oil companies. (Huerta, *Memorias*, pp. 243–292.)

120. Lieuwen, *Mexican Militarism*, pp. 64–78. Professionalization, in the Mexican context, means integration into the institutionalized Revolution as much as the more conventional rationalizations of recruitment, promotion, training, etc. The military, as Lieuwen points out, was by no means "depoliticized," but it was no longer independent, either. Obregón supposedly said, "There is no general able to resist a *cañonazo* of 50,000 pesos." Those *cañonazos* continued throughout the Calles years, consuming an average 37.5 percent of the total budget from 1921 to 1928—as compared with an 18-percent yearly average under Cárdenas, only six years later. (See James W. Wilkie, *The Mexican Revolution: Federal Expenditure and Social Change Since 1920*, p. 102.) This corruption was so rampant that a popular anagram of the day changed the name of Álvaro Obregón to "*Vengo a robarlo*" ("I come to rob you").

121. Vasconcelos, bitter enemy of the Sonoran elite, noted that the de la Huerta rebellion was met with brutal repression designed "to impose General Calles on the presidency and assure by this his own return to power." (José Vasconcelos, *La Flama*, p. 13.)

image than he might have expected.[122] He soon developed good working relationships with the International Bankers' Committee on Mexico, and gradually renegotiated Mexico's external debt.[123] Calles achieved such repute among foreign businessmen that they proclaimed him "the bronze rock of order and peace," and "the best president of the country since Díaz."[124] By assuring United States assets in Mexico (which totalled over 1.25 billion pesos), Calles endeared himself to the north and secured his reign as no previous postrevolutionary president had. He was the first of the new order of *caudillos* who had the opportunity to concentrate almost exclusively on domestic politics and the reunification of the country.

Despite the *jefe máximo's* "conquest" of international capital and the more necessary subordination of much of the army to his power, his regime was plagued from the beginning by continuing church–state conflict and by Calles' own limits as leader of the *agrarista* faction of the Revolution. Though many of the agrarian *caudillos* were dead by 1925, the LCA strengthened the *campesinos* against landlord reaction to the still-puny agrarian reform. Rival political parties, among them the Communist Party and the PNA, incorporated *campesinos* into their ranks on a local level, rivalling the mastery of the state over mass politics. The Church, too, enlisted in the ranks for moderate agrarian reform. In 1921 the *Sindicato Agrario León XIII*, named after the reform Pope Leo XIII, who spurred the concept of "social Catholicism," called for the orderly and just "division (*fraccionamento*) of large rural property . . . [giving to all] access to landed property." Though the clergy's influence as a force for convincing *hacendados* to relinquish their land for the sake of Christian charity remained feeble, the Church proclaimed its devotion to the dictum of Leo XIII: "We must multiply in whatever way possible the number of property-owners."[125] Nevertheless, official hostility to the Church emphasized the role of the clergy in defending the *hacendados* and exploiting the *campesinos*. The Catholic Church and the state, already scarred by years of skirmishes and depredations on both sides, broke into a religious war in 1926, both using the many *campesinos* for their cannon fodder.

The relationship between the Church, the *cristeros*, and the *agraristas* is not easy to fathom. The *cristero* rebellion that racked Mexico from 1926 to 1929 was an extremely complex phenomenon that combined all of the elements of intrigue usually associated with the revolutionary governments of that period: class war between *hacendado* and peon; ideological

122. Ricardo J. Zevada, *Calles, El Presidente*, pp. 35–38.

123. Iturriaga de la Fuente, *La revolución hacendaria*, pp. 100–109.

124. Statements by Julio Janket, president of the German Chamber of Commerce in Mexico, and Dwight Morrow, U.S. Ambassador to Mexico; both cited in Jean Meyer, *La Cristiada*, vol. II, pp. 175 and 169.

125. *Estatutos del Sindicato León XIII, Sección Agrícola*; cited in Meyer, vol. II, pp. 221–223.

war between church and state; and, above all, a political war for control of the labor unions and *campesino* organizations of Mexico. None of the actors in the *cristero* rebellion—indeed, in the agrarian reform—fought to establish an independent peasantry with its own political and economic resources. The syndicates sponsored by the clergy challenged secular power in the name of humanitarianism, at the same time encouraging ostentatious acts of fealty which accelerated a confrontation between the "benevolent" clerical and secular patrons of the underclasses.[126] The PNA, Díaz Soto y Gama's semi-official agrarian party, was, according to one observer, "not a party of the *campesino* class, but a party of *agrarista* professionals that . . . [would] not hesitate to sell their political birthright for a plate of lentils."[127]

While the relations between various elite actors and the *campesinos* were difficult and complex, they did not reach the range and intensity of *campesinos'* feelings for each other. Most *agraristas* fought for the government, but unwillingly. They were variously approached with horror stories about clerical degeneracy, pleas for defense of the Revolution, and other emotional appeals. Often, however, the *agraristas* fought as an explicit obligation in return for their land. They came to be viewed by the *cristeros* as *campesinos* compromised rather than benefitted by the agrarian reform. The anti-*agraristas*, on the other hand, valued their independence from the corrupt machinations of the government. Other differences between *agraristas* and *cristeros* revolved around ejidal land tenure versus private property, expropriation of lands versus restitution of village lands, and so on.[128] The dominant thread in the venomous hatred between the two factions of *campesinos* was the attempt by both the government and the Church to destroy their organizational capacity, fractionate their class position, and create stability through the decimation of both *agrarista* and *cristero* ranks.

In the midst of the substantial turmoil created by the *cristero* war, the problem of presidential succession again reared its ugly head. Obregón's return from "retirement" caused great political debate in the capital. Obregón found himself opposed by the popular but lecherous Francisco Serrano, blocked by his ineligibility for office under Article 83 of the Constitution, and engaged in a battle for political power with the jealous incumbent Calles. In a rapid succession of events, Serrano rose against the government and was summarily executed on the road from Cuernavaca; Obregón triumphed in a farcical presidential election; and the newly-

---

126. As Quirk notes, apparently neither the Church nor the state considered collaboration to achieve their often quite similar goals of social reform. (Quirk, *The Mexican Revolution and the Catholic Church*, p. 26.)

127. *El Machete*, Sept. 27, 1927; cited in Meyer, vol. III. *Los Cristeros*, p. 62.

128. Meyer, vol. III, pp. 64–88. Often, the *agraristas* were persecuted by the *hacendados* and the government alike, somewhat confusing this facile picture of their connivance.

elected president was assassinated by a religious zealot in a San Angel restaurant. Emilio Portes Gil, first of the puppet presidents, was appointed until new elections could be held; Calles "retired" to manage national politics from backstage.

This chain of events resulted in transcendental changes in the structure of state power. The *obregonistas*, including the PNA, lost influence in favor of the Mexican Labor Party (PLM), and the official agrarian reform fell on hard times. Though the PLM and its leader Luis Morones had supported Calles, Obregón's assassination resulted in the purge of the Morones clique amid charges of conspiracy. The PLM subsequently died with the declining powers of Morones and formation of the new National Revolutionary Party (PNR) in 1928–29. The PLM was merely the last in a chain of parties to fall with their leaders.[129] The final blow to this system of "*partidos, partiditos, y partidillos*"[130] was struck by generals José Gonzalo Escobar, Jesús Aguirre, Fausto Topete, Román Yocupicio, and others. The Escobar rebellion of 1929, accompanied by the brutal massacre of some 300 *agrarista* radicals in Durango, revolted the nation and hastened the end of multi-party politics in Mexico.[131]

The Escobar rebellion spurred Calles to recognize the limits of *Callismo* as an institution. The PNR, designed to embody the principles of the Revolution, also opposed independent peasant organizations such as the National Campesino Leagues (LNC) and political parties such as Portes Gil's Frontier Socialist Party (PSF). The PNR sought to institutionalize *caudillismo*, not in the transient *persona* of a national leader, but in a political organ intimately tied to the revolutionary state. As Emilio Portes Gil stated:

> The PNR is a party of the state. The PNR is frankly a government party. . . . The revolution-made-government needs an organ of agitation and defense. . . . The PNR will go to the collectivities in order that they might organize themselves and make themselves cohesive with the program of the revolution and with the administrative program of the government. . . . We are not a class party, nor do we pretend to be. We will support . . . the interests of the proletarian classes of Mexico, workers and peasants; but we invite the rest of the collectivities to join us, given that the radical program of the revolution will be recognized by these groups.[132]

Over the next years of the *Maximato*, the PNR would fuse the populist pact; that is, the state would establish the basis of the pact in the institutionality of the regime.

129. Zevada, *Calles*, p. 76. Carrillo Puerto and the *Partido Socialista del Sureste* had died together in 1925.

130. Daniel Cosío Villegas, *El sistema político mexicano*, p. 45.

131. Romana Falcón, *El agrarismo en Veracruz*, p. 52. Escobar was made a division general after presiding over the execution of Arnulfo Gómez.

132. Cited in González Navarro, *Mexico: The Lopsided Revolution*, pp. 96–97.

But if the wild force of the abused *campesinos* had been corralled institutionally, it had not yet been subdued. The death of independent *agrarismo* was recorded by the "Stop Laws" of 1930, designed by Calles and executed by Ortiz Rubio. The CNA halted the division of lands among the *campesinos*, and Calles complained that "*agrarismo* as we have understood it and practiced it until now is a failure." The new policy was to stop the distribution of lands in favor of consolidating and helping small property-owners to produce.[133]

The *agrarismo* Calles referred to was, indeed, a failure: in 1930, 83.7 percent of the land was still monopolized by some 15,488 landholders, in plots over 1,000 hectares. Over 2.3 million *campesinos* still had no land. Of the 8.3 million hectares granted by 1930, only 1.9 million were cultivable; only 4,189 *ejidos* existed.[134] Only 6.4 million of a total 36.4 million pesos loaned by the National Agricultural Credit Bank had gone to local societies and cooperatives; the rest went to individual private landholders.[135] Only 38 *ejidos* existed in Sonora, accounting for 188,055 hectares of marginal land farmed by 4,071 *ejidatarios* and their families. *Latifundistas*—numbering only 919—controlled 89 percent of the land, in plots over 1,000 hectares.[136] After peaking in 1929 under Portes Gil, land distribution declined until the last year of Abelardo Rodríguez' rule.[137] Mexico was catalogued as "the most *latifundista* country in the world."[138] Agrarian reform had become a tool for manipulating the masses, not for attacking the relations of production that had provoked the Revolution in the first place.

This was not a stable condition, however. With the depression came labor and *campesino* violence: in 1929, 13,405 labor conflicts were recorded; in 1932, 36,781. It seemed that the entire capitalist system was in collapse, and the masses of workers and *campesinos* had no consolation but the words of Calles that Mexico suffered no more than other underdeveloped countries.[139] The depression brought further misery to the masses so necessary to the populist pact, and their violent reaction anticipated Cárdenas' attempts to channel the anger of the underclasses against the entrenched remnants of the old regime. Even former *cristeros*, in pronouncing against the injustice of the national government, took up the *agrarista* banner, exhorting their followers with a curious admixture of religious fervor, traditional *agrarismo*, anti-politics, and patriotism, in statements such as that of Enrique Rodríguez:

133. Aguilera Gómez, *La reforma agraria*, pp. 134–135.
134. Mexico, Secretaría de la Económia Nacional, Dirección General de Estadística, *Primer censo agrícola–ganadero, 1930*, vol. I. *Resumen general*, p. 20.
135. *Ibid.*, p. 23. This figure is consistent with Simpson's estimate. (*The Ejido*, p. 194.)
136. *Primer censo agrícola–ganadero, 1930*.
137. Mexico, Departamento de Asuntos Agrarios y Colonización, *Memorias de labores del 1° de Septiembre de 1968 al 31 de Agosto de 1969.*
138. Gilberto Loyo, "La concentración agraria en 28 paises."
139. Arnaldo Córdova, *La política de masas del cardenismo*, pp. 20–21.

The ideals of the *pueblos* . . . [in] the glorious Plan of Allala (*sic*) in us the people who feel the rigors of the government; because there is in us no dirty politics nor ambitions; we are sustained by dreams of rescuing the true rights of the *pueblos* and, although it is a little late, we struggle for religion as well as the rights of the fatherland to defend the true reason of the *pueblos*. *Agua, Tierra, Progreso, Justicia y Libertad, Viva Cristo Rey, Viva la Virgen de Guadalupe*.[140]

The inequities, cynicism, and carnage of the 1920s did signify progress in a limited sense, through the gradual consolidation of state power and the formation of modern political organisms to channel class conflict into controllable issues and against enemies of the Revolution. However, the state still had not established its base of legitimacy with either the rising bourgeoisie, caught in the throes of world depression, or the masses, who had received nothing new from the Revolution—nothing, in fact, but more war, death, hunger, and betrayal.

The task of the 1930s, in retrospect, was to consolidate the allegiances of the various parties to the populist pact and to organize their interests according to the program of the Revolution—that is, once the program was decided. *Cardenismo*, an open mobilization of the common people in response to the turbulence of the depression and inequities in the postrevolutionary social order, challenged the populace both to organize itself along class lines and to articulate its sectoral, regional, and class demands through political machinery designed by the state. It further sought to organize the working classes into meaningful units of production—*ejidos* in the countryside—both to feed the nation and to provide the foreign exchange necessary to develop national capital. Starting with a country in turmoil, Cárdenas in six years established the productive networks necessary to take advantage of the Second World War and its economic benefits for the Mexican growth program. It is to that six years that we now turn.

140. Jean Meyer, *La Cristiada*, vol. I, p. 378.

Chapter 5

Cardenismo: The Consolidation

of Revolutionary Populism

In the presidential campaign of 1934, Lázaro Cárdenas undertook a complete national tour, visiting all 28 states and travelling 27,609 kilometers by airplane, train, automobile, boat, and horseback.[1] After his election on July 1, 1934, he completed his pilgrimage, arriving at the Sonoran frontier—the edge of the Mexican Republic. The situation he encountered there was in many respects a desperate one.

The state of Sonora covered 182,553 square kilometers in surface area, but only slightly over 5,000 square kilometers fell under cultivation.[2] Only 3.6 percent of the land under cultivation belonged to *ejidos*, and, as we have seen, much of that land was marginal. Irrigation works, with the exception of certain portions of the former Richardson Concession, did not exist.[3] The population, overwhelmingly rural, still had not benefitted from land-reform measures. Farm labor, when paid in wage form, received 1.56 pesos daily in 1935, compared with 2.33 pesos in 1929. Including *ejidatarios*, only 3.3 percent of the Sonoran populace held any land. Of the 10,409 plots registered in Sonora, 5,577 (53.6 percent) were under 10 hectares (*minifundios*). Only 38 (0.4 percent) were *ejidos* of 50 hectares or more, and 919 private holdings (8.8 percent) exceeded 1,000 hectares.

1. Mexico, Secretaría de Prensa y Propaganda del Comité Ejecutivo Nacional del Partido Nacional Revolucionario, *La jira del General Lázaro Cárdenas*, p. 141.
2. Mexico, Secretaría de la Economía Nacional, Dirección General de Estadística, *Primer censo agr ícola–ganadero, 1930*, vol. I. *Resumen general*.
3. According to the 1933 governor's report, onl 5.2 percent of all land given under the agrarian reform through 1933 was irrigated. This figure is slightly higher than the 3.9 percent calculated for the 1920–1928 period. (Estado de Sonora, *Informe que rinde el C. Rodolfo Elías Calles, Gobernador Constitucional del Estado de Sonora, ante la XXXI legislatura del mismo, 1933*, p. 21.)

Despite the overwhelming preponderance of *minifundios*, they only controlled 0.3 percent of the agricultural land area surveyed, while the largest
latifundia controlled 89 percent.[4] As a former governor had attested in
1929, the state governments of Sonora had done virtually nothing during
the 1920s to alleviate the agrarian problems which continued to hinder
the reorganization of political and productive power.[5] To the newly-elec-
ted president, a veteran of the Sonoran campaign against Villa, the land
he returned to in 1934 must have appeared as poor and as undeveloped as
he had left it in 1918.[6]

Under the puppet presidents of the *Maximato*, the agrarian reform in
general had continued its downward spiral, and Sonora's poverty was
merely a reflection of national policy trends. The "Stop Laws" executed
by President Ortiz Rubio effectively halted the official agrarian reform in
1930–1931.[7] More important, there were few *independent* advocates of
the *agrarista* cause close to the centers of power in the capital. Despite
some regional anomalies like the Leagues of Agrarian Communities of the
State of Veracruz (LCAEV), the agrarian movement had begun to lose its
impetus in the seemingly eternal war of attrition against hostile governments and antagonistic classes. The *agrarista* cause during the *Maximato*
was being dissolved slowly by the regime's "transforming the agrarian
question into an agricultural one."[8]

Each dominant trend has its opposite, however, and *agrarismo* was by
no means totally moribund in 1934. As Calles and his minions were dismantling the official agrarian reform, the world depression and its catastrophic effects on the Mexican populace stimulated rebellion against the
conservative social policies of the 1930–1934 period. While revolutionary
generals enriched themselves with the spoils of power, the masses sank
further into poverty. *Campesinos* and workers were jobless and hungry;
the national government proposed to begin repaying the foreign debt. The
reaction of the surviving popular forces of the Revolution to the hardships
of the depression and the gross impropriety of national priorities intensified, despite the concerted efforts of the PNR and the state to dismantle
independent worker and *campesino* organizations. There was popular
discontent against Ortiz Rubio's insensitive anti-*agrarista* policies, but

---

4. *Primer censo agrícola–ganadero*, vol. I.

5. Estado de Sonora, *Informe que rinde el C. Francisco S. Elías, Gobernador Constitucional del Estado de Sonora, ante la legislatura del m smo, 1929*, p. 12.

6. In fact, Cárdenas made a note during this trip to establish agricultural zones for the
Yaqui Indians. He pointed out that "it is a strong race, a pure race that should fully expect its
revindication for the despoliation of its lands that past governments carried out." (Lázaro
Cárdenas, *Apuntes, 1913–1940*, p. 296.)

7. By the time of Ortiz Rubio's annual report of 1931, 12 states had initiated stop laws.
(*Excélsior*, July 23, 1931, p. 1.)

8. Romana Falcón, *El agrarismo en Veracruz: La etapa radical, 1928–1935*, p. 84. See
also Centro de Investigaciones Agrarias (CDIA), *Estructura agraria y desarrollo agrícola en
México*, pp. 600–601.

still the years 1931–1933 passed without significant gains in the redistribution of wealth in Mexico. *Agrarismo* was about to enter a new mode of
challenging conservative elements in the government and in civil society.
These transitional years were both coda to the chaos of the 1920s and prelude to the aggressive populism of Lázaro Cárdenas.

THE LEGACY OF THE MAXIMATO

As the puppet presidents who followed Calles continued their obei-
sance to the ex-president, they worried less about the condition of the
common people than about the structural incapacity of the Mexican capitalist economy to develop.[9] Virtually no new policies addressed the survival needs of the populace or mobilization of the economy during the
latter years of the *Maximato*. A planned nationalist renovation of domestic capital formation faltered with the arrival of U.S. Ambassador Dwight
Morrow and successive changes in the presidency. The economy came to
a standstill.[10] From 1928 to 1932, Mexico's export trade dropped from 285
million dollars U.S. to 97 million, a drop of two-thirds in the sector which
accounted for 20 percent of Gross Domestic Product. This decline was accompanied by an equivalent (68 percent) drop in imports.[11] Public income in the same period decreased by one-third, and public investment
fell 29 percent. The peso was devalued repeatedly as the country sank
deeper into depression.

Calles and his presidential henchmen did little to relieve the violent
tremors of the depression, and unemployment skyrocketed. In 1930, the
Bureau of Statistics estimated 89,590 Mexicans to be unemployed; by
1932 that number had grown to 339,378, not including the vast number of
women and children who had previously been important economic producers for their families. Cárdenas, in his campaign for the presidency,
made an explicit connection between the vast army of unemployed and
the enormous tracts of arable, uncultivated land in Mexico.[12] In the ejidal
census of 1935, some 48 percent of ejidal land—which represented only a
fraction of total arable land—went uncultivated.[13] Of the 103,107,013 hectares of private property under various forms of exploitation, only 5.2 mil-

9. Arnaldo Córdova, *La política de masas del Cardenismo*, p. 21.

10. Frank Brandenburg attributes the stall in Calles' development program largely to the
influence of U.S. Ambassador Dwight Morrow. (Brandenburg, *The Making of Modern Mexico*, p. 75.) Though his influence was great, Morrow's impact was also tempered by such
monumental conditions as the great depression, capital scarcity, a disorganized system of
production, and so on.

11. René Villarreal, *El desequilibrio externo en la industrialización de México, 1929–
1975*, p. 30.

12. Hilda Muñoz (ed.), *Lázaro Cárdenas: síntesis ideológica de su campaña presidencial*, pp. 64–65.

13. Mexico, Secretaría de la Economía Nacional, Dirección General de Estadística, *Primer censo ejidal, 1935*, p. 20.

lion hectares actually were cultivated in 1933, a mere 5.1 percent of the total. Land resources were clearly being misused and underused.

In addition to the imbalance between land available and land cultivated, there remained the continuing problem of distributing land to the masses who had been doubly dispossessed: first, pushed off their land under the old regime, and then cast off by the benumbed industrial sector that was producing at only half-speed during the depression. Calles, according to his political enemy and erstwhile follower Portes Gil, proposed to end the distribution of land to the *campesinos* in order to guarantee capitalist investment and consolidate the national economy in an orderly fashion.[14] Unfortunately, this policy—which in a sense foretold those of presidents Manuel Ávila Camacho and Miguel Alemán a decade later—was ill-timed and haphazardly planned. Not enough land had passed into *campesino* hands to establish the productive agricultural base from which the nation could industrialize. The arable land was only sporadically cultivated, as we have just seen. The social relations which could guarantee rationalization of the productive process in the *campo* did not exist, nor did the units of production which could form and train the *campesinos* in their productive niches. Infrastructure and heavy capital investments had not been forthcoming, which meant, simply, that the rural economy was not ready to produce a consistent, marketable surplus. Finally, despite the recent creation of the PNR, the revolutionary leadership still had to contend occasionally with independent *campesino* organizations whose plans and priorities often clashed with those of the government. Under these circumstances, the "Stop Laws," proposed by Calles for the sake of economic development, had precisely the opposite effect.

Nationally, from 1929 to 1934 the government granted a total of 4.4 million hectares to 302,299 beneficiaries. Though this total surpassed that of previous administrations, most of the period showed the uneven commitment of the Revolution to land reform. Calles' own record for land grants, in 1925, was exceeded in only one year, 1934; in that year, the last of the *Maximato*, the "Stop Laws" were repudiated and over one-third of all the lands given out under the *pelele* governments were distributed (see Table A5 in appendix).

The substantial increase in definitive ejidal possessions in 1934 mainly resulted, not from an aggressive land policy by Abelardo Rodríguez, but from repeal of the Law of Responsibilities—a law which mandated every Local Agrarian Commission to turn over all outstanding land petitions to the federal government within sixty days. This law had been designed explicitly to protect private-property owners from more radical local commissions.[15] The LCAEV, the most radical of the *campesino* organizations

14. Emilio Portes Gil, *Quince años de política mexicana*, 2nd ed., p. 407.
15. *Excelsior*, Sept. 20, 1932, p. 1.

still surviving at that time, and the "Úrsulo Galván" faction of the LNC—as distinguished from the PNR faction and the faction affiliated with the Mexican Communist Party (PCM)—both pressured the government to repeal the law, through the Agrarian Commission of the Chamber of Deputies.[16] The pressure worked, thanks partly to the substantial "left wing" in the Chamber, and Abelardo Rodríguez was forced to annul the Law of Responsibilities on October 1, 1932, by presidential decree.[17]

The fall of the Law of Responsibilities, an event not often noted in the agrarian annals of the period, throws some interesting sidelights on *cardenismo*. First and most obvious, because annulment of the law effectively transformed some 6,000 land petitions into definitive possessions by leaving their adjudication to the states,[18] the impressive land-distribution achievements of Abelardo Rodríguez appear to have been boosted substantially by an external *agrarista* impetus. The "left wing" of the legislature, author of the repeal, could be used selectively as a weapon for moderate agrarian change. Second, and far more important, the LNC "Úrsulo Galván," the prime mover behind the petition against the Law of Responsibilities, appeared momentarily as a *campesino* organization with substantial leftist inspiration, but with enough political flexibility to act as a catalyst for legislative change. The LNC in general rose temporarily in prominence from this point, while the radical, independent LCAEV of Veracruz Governor Adalberto Tejeda was subsequently destroyed.

The rise of the LNC "Úrsulo Galván" within "legitimate" congressional *agrarista* circles helped form an officially-sanctioned core group that could support a moderate *agrarista* like Cárdenas, as opposed to Manuel Pérez Treviño on the right and Adalberto Tejeda on the left.[19] Out of this nucleus grew the *Confederación Campesina Mexicana* (CCM), which lobbied militantly for the candidacy of Lázaro Cárdenas in 1933.[20] Though the LNC "Úrsulo Galván" itself refused to join the CCM, its protest was generally unheard, as many LNC members fled its ranks for the newly-formed, moderate CCM. The LNC "Úrsulo Galván," once favored over the more radical LCAEV, was itself now discarded as a used remnant of splintered leftist *campesino* sentiment. As usual, budding state organizations thrived on the left opposition's tendency to fractionate.

Given Cárdenas' popularity among the *campesinos*, and the destruction of independent alternatives, it is not difficult to see why the CCM was

16. *Ibid.*, Sept. 27 and 30, 1932, p. 1.
17. *Ibid.*, Oct. 3–4, 1932, p. 1; *Diario Oficial*, Nov. 22, 1932.
18. Falcón, *El agrarismo en Veracruz*, p. 102. Many of these petitions, perhaps the majority, came from *agrarista* states such as Veracruz, Michoacán, Tamaulipas, and San Luis Potosí.
19. Pérez Treviño was Calles' first Secretary of Agriculture and a pre-presidential candidate in 1933. He was unanimously regarded as a *veterano* against the *agrarista* cause.
20. The CCM was born on May 31, 1933, in San Luis Potosí, partly as a reaction to anticipated electoral competition on the left from Adalberto Tejeda and the highly organized LCAEV. (Moisés González Navarro, *La Confederación Nacional Campesina*, p. 136.)

able to dominate the politics of the countryside so readily.[21] During the years 1928–1935, the newspapers were filled with accounts of battles over land in the states of Veracruz, México, Puebla, Jalisco, Tlaxcala, Durango, Coahuila, Tamaulipas, Colima, Sinaloa, Guerrero, Chiapas, Yucatán, and Zapata's home state Morelos.[22] While the government extolled the virtues of the small proprietor,[23] "white guards" protecting the interests of *hacendados* and reactionary political leaders murdered *campesino* leaders, raided villages, and subverted the remnants of the agrarian-reform movement that did exist.[24] Rural leaders demanded more land division and protection from the "white guards." They accused *latifundistas* and government functionaries—including governors—of persecuting *campesinos*, paying daily wages as low as 30 centavos (8 cents U.S.), perpetuating debt peonage, and threatening reprisals against peons who petitioned land.[25] In light of the intensity of the conflict among *campesino*, state, and *latifundista*, and the appearance of the moderate *agrarista* Cárdenas on the presidential scene, the compromise association of state and *campesino* organizations seemed more reasonable.

Finally, after the long years of battle, *agrarista* groups had won two important legislative changes: repeal of the Law of Responsibilities, and the earlier (January 15, 1932) reform of Article 10 of the January 6, 1915, law, thus denying the right of *amparo* to landowners.[26] In light of their increasingly weak combat position vis-à-vis the government and private landholders, tremendous attrition in rebel *agrarista* ranks, and the need to subvert *callista* veterans' continuing shift to the right, the limited "inter-

21. Of course, another precondition for this dominance involved the destruction of *tejedismo*, which was abetted by the fractionation of the *agrarista* left. (See Falcón, pp. 95–164.)

22. For just a few examples, see *Excelsior*, Oct. 29, 1929, second section, p. 3; Feb. 19, 1930, p. 7; Feb. 20, 1930, p. 1; April 17, 1933, p. 1; Jan. 4, 1935, p. 1. Battles were especially frequent and bloody in the states of Veracruz, Mexico, and Puebla throughout the period.

23. The Secretary of Industry, Commerce, and Labor, Ing. Luis L. León, reiterated the government's pledge to the sanctity of private property by reasserting the tentative nature of the *ejido*. Among his remarks to an LNC Convention in 1930, León said: "Because the *campesinos* of Mexico did not know how to use the land, . . . the Law of January 6 [1915] and . . . article 27 . . . only ordered that the lands be given to the *pueblos* immediately, leaving for later the administration of the use of these lands." (*Excelsior*, Feb. 19, 1930, p. 1.) León was expelled from the country with Calles at the end of 1935.

24. In the first years of the Cárdenas regime, some 2,000 *agraristas* were killed in Veracruz alone. During three months of 1936, 500 persons were reported to have died for their *agrarista* affiliation. (CDIA, *Estructura agraria*, p. 603.)

25. Governor Alberto Terrones Benítez of Durango, for example, was accused of exterminating *campesinos* on the pretext of "eradicating sovietist organizations" in Durango. (*Excelsior*, Feb. 19 and 20, 1930, pp. 7 and 1, respectively.)

26. See *Excelsior*, Dec. 26, 1931, p. 1; Jan. 16, 1932, p. 3; Jan. 17, 1932, p. 1. *Amparo* in agrarian-reform matters amounts to an injunction preventing the agrarian proceeding from continuing. It was—and still is—used as a means of delaying, even halting, agrarian reform. Its temporary repeal in 1932 was perhaps the most critical prerequisite to speedy adjudication of lands under Cárdenas. (*Diario Oficial*, Jan. 15, 1932.) It reappeared under the "counter-reform" of Miguel Alemán.

est-group" successes of the LNC "Úrsulo Galván" appealed to the *campesino* leadership as a mode of future collaboration with a reformist state.

On the other hand, the tactical position of the state was also weak. The continuing demands of the populace were amplified by the hardships of the depression.[27] The conflict was escalating between *callista* veterans, who advocated ending agrarian reform and favoring private property, and the official *agrarista* left wing, which favored a more aggressive *campesino*-oriented agrarian reform based on the *ejido*. The governmental *agrarista* wing (basically, the left wing of the congress) realized that in order to disarm the independent left opposition, the state and the PNR would have to offer a credible facsimile of the left within their own organizations, controlled by the state. The goals of establishing "social peace" and controlling political mobilization were met by coopting agrarian leaders and issues and repressing the intractable elements of left opposition.

The coalition of the LNC's PNR faction and the moderate-left Leagues of Agrarian Communities (LCA) of San Luis Potosí, México, Tlaxcala, and Tamaulipas, combined with the new candidacy of the moderate *agrarista* Cárdenas, foretold a strategic political alliance that lasted throughout the tempestuous 1930s. Never before had a president garnered the unified, organized support of the *campesinos*; nor had a national leader been able to count on a massive, state-directed workforce dedicated to eradicating the persistent domination of regressive modes of economic and social organization—namely, the *hacienda*. Nor had the president of Mexico previously been able to exterminate the independent left by coopting their issues, their membership, their municipal bases of support, and even their socialism. *Cardenismo*—as we shall see in this chapter—embraced the opportunity to challenge the old guard on behalf of *agrarismo*[28] and to challenge capitalism and its depression on behalf of populist class cooperation. Both the challenge and the weapon—*cardenismo*—were unique products of the Mexican Revolution; the stakes included the survival of the postrevolutionary state.

THE STRUGGLE WITH CALLES

Cárdenas entered his presidential campaign with the endorsement of a weakened, but still dominant Calles, who apparently foresaw another pe-

---

27. Though many sources argue that the main effects of the depression had passed by 1935, the masses, as usual, did not experience any relief from rising aggregate indicators of economic health. Rural daily wages were as low as 15 centavos (4 cents U.S.) in 1935. (*Excelsior*, Jan. 27, 1935, p. 5.)

28. By mid-1933 even the government leadership was polarized over the question of land reform: *veteranos* vs. *agraristas*; private property vs. ejidal property; and *callistas* vs. the left wing of the PNR. (See Joe C. Ashby, *Organized Labor and the Mexican Revolution Under Lázaro Cárdenas*, p. 147.)

riod in which his statements would be associated so intimately with presidential power that they appeared in the daily press ahead of the opinions of the temporary occupant of "his" office. Calles, despite his basic limitations as a continuing beacon guiding revolutionary change, loomed over the entire stage of national politics in 1935. The *peleles* had provided the medium through which Calles had controlled the course of public policy, and Cárdenas originally gained Calles' blessing, undoubtedly with the understanding that as the new president he would continue that subservience.[29] But Cárdenas' sources of strength came from the very sectors Calles had neglected. The CCM turned out to be not only an effective campaign machine, but a social force to challenge the old party and state political leadership. Discounting, for a moment, its impact on the agrarian reform, the presence of the CCM in the political battle with Calles in 1935 helped Cárdenas immeasurably. Likewise, Cárdenas' collaboration with Lombardo Toledano and other radical labor leaders at the time conjured a popular hope of ending the corrupt, personalistic labor-bossism that had typified the Morones clique and the Regional Confederation of Mexican Workers (CROM) under Calles.

In his mid-1935 attack on the radical tendencies of the new regime, Calles loosed on himself the political wrath of the various groups that had backed Cárdenas' presidential campaign and program. The purge that followed resulted in the expulsion of the ex-president and his followers, and the end of *callismo* in Mexico. Responding to Calles' vituperative assault on the new administration, Cárdenas quickly mobilized the same agrarian forces that had helped proclaim his candidacy for office. On July 23, 1935, Tomás Garrido Canabal was deposed from the governorship of Tabasco, and his anti-*agrarista* proclivities received great publicity.[30] An old *callista* stalwart, Garrido Canabal had become an embarrassment because of his opposition to agrarian reform and his virulent attacks on the Church.[31] Shortly thereafter, following *campesino* demonstrations against government irregularities in agrarian-reform matters, the governor of Tamaulipas resigned and the governor of Colima was deposed.[32] By the end of

29. The Weyls contend that Cárdenas emerged at the end of May 1934 as a candidate of one of Calles' sons, and that the *Jefe Máximo* may not have initiated the action. Cárdenas himself states that Rodolfo Elías Calles had spoken with his father as early as April 19. By April 22, Cárdenas had state support from Sonora, Nuevo León, Tamaulipas, Nayarit, Sinaloa, Colima, and Jalisco, most of which were centers of Calles' power. If Calles was partially presented with a *fait accompli*, it was from the declarations of the LCA in support of Cárdenas on May 2, 1934. (Nathaniel and Sylvia Weyl, *The Reconquest of Mexico: The Years of Lázaro Cárdenas*, p. 108; Cárdenas, *Apuntes*, pp. 220–221; *Excelsior*, May 3, 1934, p. 1)

30. *Excelsior*, July 24, 1935, p. 1.

31. Garrido Canabal's confrontations with Rodulfo Brito Foucher and the *Camisas Doradas* (Gold Shirts) of the ARM (Acción Revolucionaria Mexicana) were the proximate cause for his downfall, but his political demise signalled the onset of the purge of Calles' supporters. (Brandenburg, *The Making of Modern Mexico*, pp. 76–83.)

32. *Excelsior*, July 27 and 29, 1935, both p. 1; Aug. 14, 1935, p. 1 (Tamaulipas); Aug. 22, 1935, p. 1 (Colima). In the cases of Tabasco and Colima, the action was taken by the *Comisión*

1935, the governors of Querétaro, Guerrero, Sonora, Sinaloa, Durango, Guanajuato, and Tlaxcala had been ousted, in that order.[33] In many of these states, *cardenista* LCA activity was at its most organized. Many of the deposed governors had fallen at the hands of the front rank of pro-Cárdenas *campesinos*. In each case, agrarian manipulation, loyalty to Calles, and sedition were charged. The first charge received the most publicity, but clearly the second carried the most weight.

Nationally, this prosecution of the governors of 10 states was accompanied by a purge of the Chamber of Deputies and the cabinet between September and December of 1935. The congress then expelled 17 deputies and 5 senators, all members of the *callista* opposition. These senators and deputies, ex-governors, and Calles himself were later expelled from the PNR for conspiracy against the government.[34] This purge of the governmental and party apparatus in 1935 marked the first phase of *cardenismo*: eradicating dangerous in-house opposition, strengthening the "left wing" of congress, and carefully cultivating revolutionary generals and *campesino* masses.

Sonora provides an interesting case during this period, because it presented a mosaic of the strengths and weaknesses of the early Cárdenas years. Before the Cárdenas–Calles split, Ramón Ramos, of the *latifundista* Ramos family, had been elected governor to replace Rodolfo Elías Calles, who had become Secretary of Communication and Public Works in the new cabinet.[35] Soon after the presidential schism, however, the Municipal Agrarian Committee of Navojoa asked Cárdenas to nullify Ramos' election, to promote free trade in seeds, and to remove anti-*agrarista* local authorities.[36] Ramos later suffered accusations of not being Sonoran by birth or by residence, but the PNR decided to approve the state elections anyway.[37] Protests against Ramos accelerated, however, now engineered by the *Centro Director Unificador Popular de Sonora* (CDUPS) and the *Comité pro-Dignificación de Sonora* (CPDS), two shadow organizations of unclear lineage[38] which charged that Ramos was associated with the Calles and Villarreal (the recently-deposed governor of Tamaulipas) "impositionists."[39] The CDUPS charged Ramos with arresting his political oppo-

Permanente of the *Cámara de Diputados*, a standing commission designed to help ensure constitutional rule in the states.

33. *Excelsior*, Sept. 30, Nov. 6, and Dec. 17 and 18, 1935, all p. 1.

34. *Ibid.*, Sept. 13 and Dec. 15 and 19, 1935, all p. 1.

35. Rodolfo Elías Calles was removed from the cabinet as a part of the reorganization which followed Cárdenas' split with Calles.

36. *Excelsior*, July 11, 1935, p. 1.

37. *Ibid.*, Aug. 22, 1935, p. 1.

38. These two organizations probably emerged from the tradition of creating fictitious committees as a means of entering the political fray momentarily. Mostly single-issue associations, their presence suggests the absence of strong class organizations, which generally had better access to the loci of power.

39. *Excelsior*, Aug. 27, 1935, p. 1. The charge of "impositionism" is a recurrent theme in Sonoran politics, as we will see in Chapter 6.

nents and, despite the support of ex-Governor Rodolfo Elías Calles (or perhaps because of it), Ramos' inauguration day dawned with a throng
chanting "death to Ramos" in the Plaza of Zaragoza in Hermosillo.[40]

Despite popular opposition, Ramos appeared securely entrenched until
an October uprising by the cristero-linked Popular Liberation Army (EPL)
under the quixotic Luis Ibarra, a veteran of the Cristiada in Jalisco. The
military situation in Sonora quickly deteriorated as cristero rebels took
over several municipalities. The federal army, with reinforcements from
Jalisco and Chihuahua, attacked the hostage municipalities and finally
routed the rebel forces.[41] At that point, rebel leader and Sonoran cattleman Pablo Rebeil claimed that "Sonora is loyal to President Cárdenas, and
our conflict has been of a local nature. If Governor Ramón Ramos resigns,
there will be peace."[42] A month after federal occupation of the state,
Ramos was ousted, and peace returned briefly.

The Ramos case was but a prelude to the conflict that characterized
Sonoran government for years after the Cárdenas epoch. While Cárdenas
and his followers were mainly interested in the destruction of Calles'
allies in government positions, local agricultural groups—ironically,
groups organized by Rodolfo Elías Calles—prosecuted the case against
Ramos over questions of municipal autonomy and the marketing of seeds.
Similarly, the EPL sought to pressure the state government into passive
acceptance of illegal clerical activity in Sonora. The cristero revival of
1935 extended to 15 states—but in Sonora it evoked bitter memories of Indian wars, since the soldiers of the EPL included 400 Mayos.[43]

40. Excelsior, Sept. 2, 1935, p. 1.
41. The municipios of Altar, Magdalena, Montezuma, Santa Ana, and Sahuaripa all were
affected. (Ibid., Oct. 8–Nov. 10, 1935.)
42. Ibid., Oct. 26, 1935, p. 1.
43. Jean Meyer, La Cristiada, vol. I. La guerra de los Cristeros, pp. 375–386. Himself an
anti-cleric, Cárdenas nevertheless mollified the growing rift between the faithful and the
state by deposing Garrido Canabal and by coopting much of the agrarista sentiment which
pervaded cristero ranks. As Meyer notes, cristeros and agraristas shared the common concerns of local autonomy and land to the campesinado. If these traditional forces were never
the vanguard of socialized property, neither were they the intransigent enemy of land reform. Though Cárdenas never attempted to reconcile church–state differences, he ensured
the gradual "localization" of the conflict by separating cristero ranks from their clerical men-
tors and by drawing off much of the membership with his progressive agrarismo. By challenging the radical right as a political movement instead of a religious crusade, Cárdenas
recreated the modus vivendi between church and state; though his "socialist education"
programs brought bitter reaction at the parish level, the Church hierarchy generally steered
away from major confrontations with the government. The "localization" of this conflict
proved crucial in states such as Sonora, where unification of the opposition was difficult at
best.
  As for the secular right, it was driven underground after the bloody battle between the
ARM and the police in the zócalo of Mexico City in 1935. The only real survivor of that
secular right is the COPARMEX (Confederación Patronal de la República Mexicana, or Employers Federation of the Mexican Republic), which exists today. (See Hugh G. Campbell, La
derecha radical en México, 1929–1949; also Chapter 7 of this study.)

The confusion of individual goals among participants in the 1935 assault against Ramos laid much of the groundwork for the polarization of state politics in the next decade. Indians, clerics, *agraristas*, landowner associations, and union organizers all participated in a form of destructive pluralism, confusing national issues of agrarian and economic organization with local matters, and reducing all governmental options to the eventual downfall of Ramos. Municipal and village governments became the relevant levels at which Sonoran state authority could be challenged. The Agrarian Committee of Navojoa was a municipal organization, itself protesting a *callista* municipal government; the Catholic rebels seized municipalities as their most audacious defiance of state authority; and peace was reassured in the state only when the army finally controlled the rebel municipalities. This early lesson was not lost on Cárdenas. In Sonora, as in other states with minimal party organizations, the political organization of the countryside would have to supplant these atomized local interest-group and class conflicts in order to connect the political populism of Cárdenas with the economic organization and growth of the state. That movement began in Sonora in 1937, under the new governor Román Yocupicio.

THE CÁRDENAS PLAN

By the end of 1935, then, with the creation of the CCM and the ascendance of Cárdenas, the *campesinos'* position as organized workers and land-petitioners had greatly strengthened since 1930. Landowners, employers, and local officials notwithstanding, the common people had finally institutionalized their entry into the postrevolutionary regime. The terms of the populist pact were set.

Relevant questions about the Cárdenas government now centered on the goals of the regime, the direction of the popular mobilization that was so evidently taking place. What were Cárdenas' economic-development goals to challenge the devastation wrought by the great depression? Where did the roots of the popular mobilization lie? The First Six-Year Plan of the PNR afforded a general set of goals to which the Cárdenas administration committed itself: division of large landholdings, redistribution of the rural population, and internal colonization. But the Plan was vague, prepared without any technical planning methods, and only demanded from Cárdenas a basic adherence to constitutional principles.[44]

The specific logic of Cárdenas' development plans came from a conjunction of economic necessity, political cunning, and a firm understanding of Mexican realities in 1935. Allying his regime with the cause of the

44. Miguel S. Wionczek, "Incomplete Formal Planning: Mexico," pp. 152–154.

workers and *campesinos* of Mexico was not only the "revolutionary re-sponsibility"[45] of the political leadership, but the political means of his independence from Calles and prior forms of political domination. Re-structuring the agricultural economy and providing a state-directed pro-gram for capital growth, infrastructure investment, and future monetary and fiscal stability were necessary for the survival of the state, no matter what its momentary political affiliations. Choosing to strengthen the state as the arbiter of class conflict in civil society—mediator and protector for the working class and *campesinos*, capitalist promotor for the bourgeoi-sie—derived not only from the exigencies of a society notorious for the weakness of its civil institutions, but also from the expedience of the growing power that would accrue to the state through fulfilling such a role. To succeed, the *cardenista* program had to be politically dominant, socially responsible to the underclasses, and economically rewarding to the investors in the national economy.

The mode of achieving the *cardenista* program of economic expansion, social justice, and political organization under a unified revolutionary party rested with the state-dominated sectoral organization of all pro-ducers and the encouragement of "corporative contention, from which justice and improvement for all men must emerge."[46] In the industrial sector, the Confederation of Mexican Workers (CTM) was organized as an agent of class struggle against exploitation by the bourgeoisie. Likewise, the organization of employers into industrial chambers and chambers of commerce represented a parallel aspect of the populist political pact.[47] In the countryside, which is the concern of this study, the populist pact in-cluded the formation of the National Campesino Confederation (CNC), which declared its principles to be:

> ... defense of the interests of the *campesino* within a frank spirit of class struggle, acceptance of the cooperation of the state in the creation of this or-ganism, defense of the thesis that the land belongs to those who work it, in-cluding ... *peones acasillados*, sharecroppers, small farmers, and the rest of the organized workers of the *campo*. ... That the *ejido* be converted into the pivot of agricultural policy, and the division of *latifundios* [be undertaken] for their collective cultivation by organized *campesinos*. ... In other words, "the socialization of the land."[48]

45. "Discurso de protesta como candidato presidencial," December 5, 1933, reprinted in Muñoz, *Lázaro Cárdenas*, p. 19.
46. Mexico, Secretaría de Prensa ... del PNR, *La jira del General Lázaro Cárdenas*, p. 32.
47. Both CONCAMIN (*Confederación de Cámaras Industriales*, or Federation of Indus-trial Chambers) and CONCANACO (*Confederación de Cámaras Nacionales de Comercio*, or Federation of National Chambers of Commerce) had existed since 1917. (Juan Felipe Leal, *México: estado, burocracia y sindicatos*, p. 85.) Cárdenas asserted that both employer and worker organizations had equal rights to be represented in relations between state and civil society. (*Apuntes*, p. 344.) But at the same time, he proclaimed that "the government is the arbiter and regulator of social life."
48. *Excelsior*, Sept. 8, 1935, p. 1.

This "socialization of the land," however, had to take place within a framework of capitalist growth and expansion. Aside from being an explicit part of the populist pact, the entire structure of the postrevolutionary economy was designed for capitalist development. The Law of January 6, 1915; the Constitution of 1917; the creation of the Bank of Mexico in 1925; the National Agricultural Credit Bank in 1926; the *Nacional Financiera* (national investment finance bank) in 1933—all pointed toward accumulation under a capitalist mode of production.[49] Combined with the increasing role of state investment in the economy as a capitalist promotor, the existence of the populist state depended on capitalist expansion and development. The essence of Cárdenas' "cooperativist" alternative to capitalism and communism consisted of a state-dominated economy which incorporated both principles of capitalist growth and socialist redistribution of value. To Cárdenas, the Plan of the PNR came to mean that the state should intervene "to organize all of the aspects of the *campesino* sector, to enable it economically to assure the greater agricultural production of the country."[50] The first order of business in achieving this goal was to reestablish the right of the revolutionary state to "regiment social life, . . . to intervene in the social relations of production . . . in the name of the masses."[51]

Once translated from the sometimes demagogic tone which characterized the period, the *cardenista* program presented an awesome challenge fraught with conflict and risk. The program began with dismantling *callismo* both at the national level and in the states, as we have seen. It followed with state-induced mass mobilization and education of the *campesinos* and the working class against reactionary vestiges of prior forms of land tenure and exploitation and regressive pockets of counterrevolutionary industrialists. Finally, the Cárdenas plan demanded the creation of a durable system of public finance and investment, and an infrastructure base promoting nationalist capitalist development. The program had the potential both to reinforce the social reforms begun under state tutelage and, by expanding economic growth under capitalism, eventually to increase bourgeois participation in the domination of civil society.

THE CÁRDENAS AGRARIAN REFORM

In order to understand the Cárdenas program more fully, we must first understand its primary aspect: the agrarian reform. Agrarian reform under Cárdenas involved at least four aspects: the reform as an organizational (and, therefore, a political) weapon; as a mode of bringing "social justice"

49. Octavio Ianni, *El estado capitalista en la época de Cárdenas*, p. 123.
50. "Plan sexenal del PNR, 1934–1940" (Mexico: 1934), p. 33; cited in Córdova, *La política de masas del Cardenismo*, p. 49.
51. Córdova, pp. 46–47.

to the *campo* through land redistribution; as a method of organizing the postrevolutionary means and relations of production; and as a midwife for the birth of industrial capitalism in Mexico. Each of these aspects in the Sonoran agrarian reform of the 1930s had its limitations and contradictions, creating many of the political and economic problems confronted in succeeding decades.

The Ejido

The institution that joined these facets of the Cárdenas program together was the *ejido*, the primary tool for dealing with two-thirds of the working population of Mexico.[52] The *campesinos* were also organized through various presidential programs of rural education, the land-reform mobilizations of the CTM and CCM, and the frequent ad-hoc defensive reactions to hostile *latifundistas* persecuting *campesinos* who legitimately solicited land under the provisions of the 1934 Agrarian Code. But clearly the main organizational instrument of the agrarian reform under Cárdenas was the *ejido*. With its roots in traditional, indigenous communal agriculture, the *ejido* in its postrevolutionary incarnation deserves our attention as a weapon in the political arsenal of the new populism.

As we have seen, the *ejido* had an uncertain future under the Carranza, Obregón, and Calles governments. Seen as an adjunct to private property, the *ejido* had been used mainly as a "first step" to the parcelization of large landholdings. Originally, before the Revolution, *ejidos* were the "common land of a village or town."[53] The *fundo legal*, or basic unit of land belonging to a *pueblo* under Spanish law, dates from an Ordinance of May 26, 1567, and forms the core of ejidal property. The *fundo legal* plus the ejidal commons constitute, then and now, the basic dimensions of the *ejido*.[54] During the first years of the agrarian reform, the ejidal form of land tenure was kept as a mode of perpetuating subsistence agriculture while the productive network underwent reorganization. But Cárdenas held a new vision of the *ejido*, a vision much more closely integrated with his national hopes for economic and social organization:

> The ejidal institution today has a double responsibility: as a social system, inasmuch as it frees the country worker from the exploitation of which he was the object in both the feudal and the individual [land-tenure] systems; and as a system of agricultural production, inasmuch as the responsibility of feeding the country weighs upon the *ejido*.[55]

52. 67.7% of the working population came from the agricultural sector in 1930, 63.3% in 1940. (Ianni, *El estado capitalista*, pp. 58–59.)

53. Francois Chevalier, *Land and Society in Colonial Mexico: The Great Hacienda*, p. 322.

54. Antonio Villarreal Muñoz, *Restitución y dotación de ejidos, el problema agrario en México*, p. 15.

55. Excerpted from a speech in Torreón, Coahuila, Nov. 30, 1936; in Lázaro Cárdenas, *Ideario político*, p. 130.

Instead of rigidly separating government policies of land redistribution, agricultural credit, *campesino* mobilization, rural education, and political indoctrination, Cárdenas combined the several missions of his populist state and channeled them into the *ejido*.[56]

The *ejido* represented, in the 1930s, a unique mode of integrating the rural population politically and economically, while still maintaining substantial central control over the institution itself. Prior to the Agrarian Code of 1934, as we have seen, there had been no attempt to unify the legislation pertaining to agriculture. Before the extension of the PNR, the CNC, and the CTM, the *campesinos* had been dependent upon infrequent government initiative for authoritative adjudication of their lands. That initiative, on the rare occasions when it surfaced, scarcely challenged the *hacendado*; neither did it enable the *campesino* to produce. Codification of the reform laws in 1934 was the first step in changing the mode of *campesino* dependency—at least temporarily.

Under the Agrarian Code of 1934, to petition land as a "nucleus of population" (as opposed to the exceedingly restrictive political unit, the *pueblo*), twenty or more *campesinos*, each eligible for a land grant, had to submit an application. To be eligible, one had to be male, over sixteen years of age, and Mexican by birth; to reside in the "nucleus of population" for six months prior to application; to work the land personally, as an occupation; and not possess individual capital in industry or commerce of more than 2,500 pesos.[57] *Peones acasillados*, the bulk of the agrarian population in central and southern Mexico, and an important factor in the north as well, were not permitted to form "nuclei of ejidal population" on their own, though they were permitted for the first time to be included in initial agrarian proceedings of nuclei in their areas.[58] *Acasillados* later received full rights under the agrarian reform, in a significant amendment to the Agrarian Code in 1937. In addition to permitting all of the rural population to participate in the fruits of the new *agrarismo*, Cárdenas in this 1937 amendment expanded the land subject to expropriation by decreeing that all properties of a single owner be considered as one plot for purposes of land division. The 1937 reform also restricted exemptions from land limits imposed by the agrarian-reform law (150 hectares irrigated, 300 hectares seasonal land), thus depriving *latifundistas* of another shelter from the land reform.[59]

56. The government had already recognized the need to reorganize credit as an integral part of the reform; the agricultural banks later assumed a larger role in the general political and formative aspects of the reform. CDIA, *Estructura agraria*, p. 761.

57. *Código Agrario de los Estados Unidos Mexicanos*, April 9, 1934, Title III, chap. 3, art. 44; in *Diario Oficial*, April 12, 1934.

58. *Código Agrario*, Title III, chap. 2, art. 42; chap. 3, art. 45. *Peones acasillados* were defined as "those workers of agricultural estates *fincas agrícolas*] who, occupying houses on the same [*fincas*] without rent, depend economically on the salary they receive for their services." Obviously, rent-free residence was the key factor in this definition.

59. *Decreto que reforma varios artículos del Código Agrario de los Estados Unidos Mexicanos, de 9 de Agosto de 1937*; in *Diario Oficial*, Aug. 12, 1937.

The Agrarian Code also recommended the procedures for petitioning ejidal grants and for the adjudication of land. Briefly, these procedures included: an initial agrarian census of all prospective members of the ejidal nucleus and the land in question; a ruling by the local Mixed Agrarian Commission (CAM) on the merits of the application; a governor's ruling on the application; an Agrarian Department study and subsequent presidential resolution; and the execution and publication of the presidential resolution by state authorities.[60]

The Cárdenas plan insisted on organizing *ejidos* on a collective basis, which varied by region and *ejido* according to productivity, extension, crops cultivated, and many other factors. The "collective *ejidos*," as Eckstein reminds us, were an invention of the Cárdenas epoch, and were generally not really collective, but cooperative.[61] Part of the distinction between "cooperative" and "collective" rested on the concept that the land in *ejidos* was always in usufruct, belonging ultimately to "the nation" and used in good faith by the community that worked it; it was only in a limited sense the collective property of the community or ejidal nucleus. In contrast with traditional communal property—whose use was justified for a politically-established pueblo, an individual, or a family unit by virtue of prior patrimony—the *ejido*, collective or individual, enjoyed use of the land only as a permanent ward of the state. Agrarian rights (*derechos agrarios*) could be rescinded for any number of reasons, as we have seen, and ownership of the land would revert to the *ejido* or to the state.[62] Thus the *ejido* in its postrevolutionary form differed from traditional communal land tenure, as the modern *ejido* was an invention of the postrevolutionary state. Its future has always been dependent on the indulgence of the state.

But the real separation between the cooperative *ejidos* of the 1930s and collective agriculture in general came in their organization, division of labor, and marketing. Only at the limits of ejidal cooperativism, in the cases referred to as *colectiva* by the Ejidal Bank (see note 61), did the collective *ejido* really operate collectively.

Probably the most collective aspect of the collective *ejidos* came in the area of credit. The Law of Agricultural Credit of 1934 signified a stronger role for the state in advancing credit to private property-holders, thereby increasing the role of the bank as a social institution with broader con-

60. *Código Agrario*, Title IV, chaps. 1–3, arts. 62–82.
61. Salomón Eckstein, *El ejido colectivo en México*, p. 1. The Ejidal Bank distinguishes among four degrees or modalities of collectivization: *de parcelas*—cultivable land is parcelled and worked individually, with some cooperation in some services, such as acquisitions, sales, etc.; *semicolectiva vertical*—part of the cultivation is done individually and part is shared, but the parcels remain individual; *semicolectiva horizontal*—part is cultivated individually and part is shared, but the land is divided into collective and individual sections; *colectiva*—where all credit operates in common, and all land is worked in the same manner. (CDIA, *Estructura agraria*, p. 490.)
62. *Código agrario*, Title VIII, chap. 4, arts. 140–142.

cerns than merely recovering loans and charging interest. It set up a network of regional banks, local credit societies, and auxiliary institutions that served the purpose of extending and controlling credit to the countryside.[63] In 1935 the government set about reforming the new law to include a system which provided for ejidal credit exclusively. Since *ejidatarios* were not proprietors per se, but usufructuaries, different rules had to be devised to allow extension of credit without property or machinery as collateral. A national system of agricultural credit emerged from the 1935 law, forming the National Bank of Ejidal Credit.[64] The "collective" aspect of ejidal credit becomes obvious in interpreting the conditions for local ejidal credit societies. Societies were required under the law to accept "unlimited responsibility," whereas private farmers had the option of "limited," "supplemental," or "unlimited" responsibility.[65] Translated, this means simply that *ejidatario* members of a credit society were forced to accept unlimited responsibility for the credit allowed to the society as a unit. That is, if twenty members (then the legal minimum to constitute a credit society) borrowed conjointly and applied their individual shares to their own ejidal parcels, even if only one *ejidatario* brought in a crop he was responsible for the debt of the entire credit society. Obviously, in a period of heavy borrowing and marginal profits, one bad crop had the potential of wiping out an entire society or mortgaging their future crops and machinery interminably. Private credit societies, not an option for *ejidatarios*, could assume "limited responsibility"—responsibility for their own share of the society's debt—or "supplemental responsibility"— a limited share of the society's debt beyond one's own personal portion. These prejudicial distinctions have operated to the permanent disadvantage of the ejidal credit society, have caused dissension within the *ejido*, and have functioned as a weapon for enhancing state-bank control over *ejidos*.[66]

Employing the Political Weapon

The success of Cárdenas' new *agrarismo* depended on a number of elements, including even the self-defense militias formed to fight the ubiquitous "white guards." Tight control over state and local party machines was necessary to provide ideological discipline at the local government

63. *Ley de Crédito Agrícola de 7 de Febrero de 1934;* in *Diario Oficial,* Feb. 9, 1934.

64. *Diario Oficial,* Dec. 20, 1935. The local ejidal credit societies, mainstay of the ejidal credit system, had already been organized formally under the 1926 *Ley de Crédito Agrícola* (Title I, chap. 3, art. 4; in *Diario Oficial,* March 4, 1926).

65. *Ley de Crédito Agrícola, 1934,* Title I, chap. 3, art. 44. This was amended in the *Ley de Crédito Agrícola de 1955* (see Chapter 7).

66. Many other structural weaknesses in ejidal credit appear as a result of dependence on the bank to liquidate the crop at the end of the season, the inability of many *ejidos* to meet their credit obligations, and the extreme power of the bank to deny credit to *ejidos* who disagree on policy questions. Some of these problems will reappear in the exposition of the Sonoran case.

level, as well as to encourage the worker and *campesino* organizations struggling for reform against a hostile set of privileged classes and groups. Aware of the difficulty in executing his sweeping reform measures without such weapons, Cárdenas in 1936 and 1937 began to use the national state to create an organized, mobilized, state-guided class equilibrium.[67] The party (PNR), the CTM and the CNC, and the *ejido* were the main agents advancing the egalitarian political goals of the land reform.

In Sonora, with its weak party organization and the conspicuous lack of local party control over government action, the burden of *cardenismo* fell squarely on the collective *ejidos* of the southern Yaqui and Mayo river valleys, and to the CTM under Vicente Lombardo Toledano and his Sonoran compatriots. Their emergence in 1937 and 1938 complicated an already-volatile political polarization in Sonora, keyed by a conflict between the policies of Román Yocupicio and those of Lázaro Cárdenas.

Remembering that the Ramos controversy lay buried in a very shallow grave, it is not surprising that the next gubernatorial election—in 1936—found Sonora brimming with political intrigue and scandal. In September, 2,000 federal troops entered the small towns of Navojoa and Huatabampo, in the heart of the Mayo valley, to preempt possible violence over the election of a governor to replace General Jesús Gutiérrez Cázares, the interim successor to Ramón Ramos. The candidates were General Ignacio Otero Pablos, endorsed by the PNR; Colonel Leobardo Tellechea; and General Román Yocupicio, a pure Mayo. The two main contestants were clearly Otero and Yocupicio—the former because of his PNR endorsement, and the latter because of his ability to mobilize militant "action groups" of Yaquis and Mayos on behalf of his right-wing candidacy.[68] Though Otero carried the imprimatur of the PNR—usually tantamount to election—his election campaign seemed to create as many enemies as allies, and Yocupicio became Sonora's new governor on January 4, 1937.[69]

67. This equilibrium, given the polarization of rich and poor in Mexico, obviously meant long years of favoring the underclasses. The equilibrium did not signify a quiescent balance, but a broader conception of equity and distribution as well. As Cárdenas explained: "The policy of the government is directed toward maintaining equilibrium among the factors that intervene in production, which are labor and capital. In order that [this] equilibrium be stable, it is necessary that it rest on a wide base of social justice and an elevated spirit of equity that must preside over worker–employer relations." (Speech to workers of the Huasteca Petroleum Company; cited in *Excelsior*, Feb. 27, 1936, p. 1.)

68. At one point, 300 Yaqui partisans of Yocupicio threatened Otero's supporters in Nogales, apparently suspecting PNR vote-counting methods. The Yaquis beat their drums ominously outside the town hall, and the election officials took the hint: Yocupicio won handily. (*Excelsior*, Sept. 28, 1936, p. 1.)

69. The *Sindicato Feminil de Oficios Varios* of Hermosillo, an adherent of the PNR, protested to Cárdenas that Otero was throwing *mezcal* (cactus-liquor) parties for the Indians in an attempt to garner more votes. Whether this was a legitimate complaint or conservative antipathy toward Otero's apparent worker-and-*campesino* sympathies is unclear. (*Excelsior*, Sept. 20, 1936, p. 1.) When Otero lost the election, he protested to Yocupicio that, as the official PNR candidate, he should be governor. Yocupicio reminded him of this lack of mass support, and Otero retired.

Román Yocupicio became possibly the biggest issue in the politics of the Sonoran agrarian reform from 1937 to 1939. Born in Masiaca, Navojoa, he had supported the Revolution, fought against de la Huerta in 1923, and then turned to join José Gonzalo Escobar in the ill-fated uprising of 1929.[70] As an *escobarista*, he had no reason to expect to be allowed a future in Mexican politics—but by mobilizing the feared Indians of southern Sonora, he strong-armed his way into office against the anemic PNR in remote Sonora. His political affections were suspect from the start; barely a month after assuming office, the Permanent Commission of the Chamber of Deputies charged Yocupicio with opposing *campesino* organization in Sonora and violating the constitution in the matter of religious cults.[71] At the same time, the CTM petitioned the Permanent Commission to get rid of Yocupicio for arbitrary actions against the workers of the state. The Federation of Workers of Southern Sonora (FTSS) charged that Yocupicio overthrew the municipal authorities of Ciudad Obregón because of their CTM affiliation.[72] He was further accused of assassinating the state delegate of the Agrarian Department. The Yocupicio calling-card was, purportedly, "Death to Cárdenas, long live Franco and Mola."[73]

Though it is sometimes difficult to assess the charges against Yocupicio, it is abundantly clear that he opposed the Cárdenas rural education and land-reform programs, and that his administration attempted to eliminate the CTM from the governing councils of Ciudad Obregón. Since 1935, groups of workers and *campesinos* had attempted to influence decision-making in the key city of Ciudad Obregón, heir to Cócorit as the hub of the Yaqui valley. In March 1937, General Francisco Urbalejo, head of the municipal council of Ciudad Obregón, resigned or was fired over differences with Yocupicio. Yocupicio's replacement candidate was shot by the chief of police, after assaulting the mayor, Felipe Ruiz, with a pistol. The CTM forced the next two municipal heads to resign, and so it went until the end of Yocupicio's reign in Sonora.[74]

The presence of Yocupicio in the state government of Sonora takes on more importance in light of his ability to mobilize some of the populace viewed by Cárdenas as targets of the new populist reforms. The national state had to tolerate Yocupicio as a potentially dangerous adversary who could be dealt with more easily in office, through political in-fighting

70. Roderic A. Camp, *Mexican Political Biographies, 1935–1975*, p. 337.
71. *Excelsior*, Feb. 24, 1937, p. 1.
72. *Ibid.*, Feb. 25, 1937. p. 1.
73. General Emilio Mola was righthand to Spain's Generalissimo Francisco Franco until his death in 1937. In fact, Yocupicio was suspected of collaborating with Nazi spies through the German consulate in Sonora, and receiving arms and money from Japanese agents. (See Campbell, *La derecha radical*, p. 67.)
74. Unfortunately, Sonoran historians tend to gloss over the Yocupicio period, and much more work remains to be done to complete this fascinating story of state government from 1937 to 1939. See Claudio Dabdoub, *Historia del Valle del Yaqui*, pp. 346–347, for brief accounts of some of the municipal disputes in Ciudad Obregón.

and compromise. The *ejidos* proposed for the Yaqui and Mayo valleys could provide a counterweight to Yocupicio's municipal dominance in Ciudad Obregón, Navojoa, and Huatabampo. Collectivist *ejidatarios* represented a potentially effective parry to Yocupicio's *latifundista* clientele. And with careful management, the agrarian-reform programs of irrigation and credit could be lent to the mutual advantage of power at the national level and individual pecuniary interests at the local level in Sonora. In any event, the competition between the national government and Yocupicio over the allegiance of the previously-spurned Yaqui and Mayo indigenous populations provided one of the great political ironies of the late 1930s. It also stimulated the agrarian reform, the availability of ejidal credit, the opening of more arable land in the valleys, and even the repatriation of 1,800 Arizona Yaquis who had fled the ravages of previous regimes in Sonora.[75]

The standoff between the Yocupicio and Cárdenas administrations, a political expression of opposing class interests, intensified during 1937, much as the belligerents in a siege settle down for a long, painful battle. In June a rash of incidents, including the kidnap of the CTM delegate in Sonora and the arrest of delegates to the constituent congress of the Regional Federation of Workers and *Campesinos* (FROC),[76] rekindled the investigation of Yocupicio by the Permanent Commission, spurred by the threat of a general work stoppage by the CTM. Amid raucous demonstrations against his administration,[77] Yocupicio continued to arrest labor leaders, harass *campesino* organizations at all levels, and even fire members of the state Supreme Court for not imprisoning CTM municipal leaders from Ciudad Obregón.[78]

Finally, in the fall of 1937, the serious confrontation between state and national governments was resolved. On September 5, the Permanent Commission officially charged Yocupicio with "fomenting the creation of groups of doubtful revolutionary orientation" and dividing workers and *campesinos* to the point of armed conflict. It was affirmed in the Commission report that Yocupicio had, indeed, supported fascist groups and ha-

75. The repatriation, of course, created substantial political capital for Yocupicio, who proclaimed his devotion to making the Yaqui valley a paradise in his lifetime. (Speech before the Chamber of Deputies; cited in *Excelsior*, March 30, 1937, p. 1.)

76. Among the luminaries arrested or harassed by Yocupicio were Fidel Velázquez, member of the executive council of the CTM, and Alejandro Carrillo Marcor, *lombardista* nominee for the Chamber of Deputies from the third district (Navojoa) of Sonora. Velázquez succeeded Lombardo Toledano as secretary-general of the CTM in 1940, a post he still held in 1980. Carrillo, though he did not become the deputy from the third district in 1937, has held many prestigious electoral and party positions, and went on to become governor of Sonora in the crisis of 1975 (see Chapter 7).

77. Toward the end of June, some 2,000 demonstrated against Yocupicio in Navojoa. (*Excelsior*, June 24, 1937, p. 1.)

78. *Ibid.*, July 9, 1937, p. 1.

rassed the CTM.[79] In a time when political candidates were purged from the PNR for launching their campaigns as independents, and opposition governors were regularly deposed by the Permanent Commission, it seemed certain that Yocupicio was headed for political extinction. But instead, Yocupicio again showed his remarkable ability to survive. When the presidential Yaqui Zone Commission travelled to Sonora to reconnoiter land-reform possibilities, Yocupicio called the landowners of the Yaqui valley together to oppose rumored land invasions. Always regarded as a spokesman for *latifundista* interests in the state, Yocupicio openly proclaimed himself the defender of property in Sonora and the brave opponent of anarchic invasions.[80] Sonoran politics had been polarized by class. In October, Yocupicio accompanied Gabino Vázquez, head of the Agrarian Department, to Mexico City for a confidential meeting with Cárdenas. But instead of the expected fall of Yocupicio, the two executives announced the compromise division of lands in the Yaqui valley.[81]

Before analyzing the distributive aspect of the land division in Sonora, it is instructive to examine the conflict between Yocupicio and Cárdenas as an instance in which the official agrarian reform was used as a political weapon. Remembering the painful tradition of indigenous warfare in Sonora and the weakness of governmental organization evident in the Ramos purge of 1935 and the 1936 elections, Yocupicio would seem to have had a definite superiority in local power. Able and willing to mobilize large numbers of faithful Yaquis and Mayos against political opponents, Yocupicio also reaped the benefits of strong support from local leaders and agricultural and cattle interests in the state. Against this impressive coterie, the revolutionary government offered a party organization too weak to elect its own candidate governor, nascent CTM and CNC class representation that could not even muster organized land invasions like those that had characterized much of the rest of the nation, and a record, antedating Cárdenas, of pillage and trickery against the indigenous populations of Sonora. Still, the national government could effect a neutralization of hostility between itself and the Yocupicio opposition by virtue of its ultimate power to remove the governor from office and its superior capacity to deal rewards to the *campesinos*. In fact, this became the basis for agreement by which Yocupicio remained in office, the *ejido* advanced in the Yaqui and Mayo valleys, and the landowners of the valleys received substantial pre-

79. *Ibid.*, Sept. 6, 1937, p. 1.

80. *Ibid.*, Sept. 13, 1937, p. 1. In July 1938, even after the consummation of many of the reform grants, the Office of the Prosecutor for Indigenous Communities of Sonora sounded an ominous warning against land invasions by future *ejidatarios*. (*El Imparcial*, July 21, 1938, p. 1. González Navarro, *La CNC*, p. 153, also cites Yocupicio's defense of private property-holders.)

81. *Excelsior*, Oct. 29, 1937, p. 1.

miums as well. To understand this phase of the ejidal program, we must examine the agrarian reform in terms of its redistributive aspect.

Agrarian Reform as Social Justice

If 1936 was to be the year of agrarian-worker populism, Cárdenas had started a month early. On the heels of his calmly executed victory over Calles, Cárdenas distributed nearly 700,000 hectares to 42,368 *ejidatarios* in December 1935 alone—6 percent of all land distributed since 1915. In the six years of his government, he distributed over 20 million hectares, as shown in Table 4. Before the end of 1937, Cárdenas initiated sweeping land-distribution measures in Coahuila, Durango, Querétaro, Baja California, Yucatán, and Campeche. To complete the reform of the principal productive regions of the country, he announced on October 28, 1937, the division of the rich lands of the Yaqui river valley.

In 1935, after having been notified that *campesino* land petitioners had begun to increase, the Confederation of Agricultural Associations of Sonora (CAAES), defending the private property-holders and colonists of the Yaqui valley, requested an investigation of the Richardson Concession. The immunity (*inafectabilidad*) guaranteed the landowners in presidential decrees of 1926 and 1928 was proffered as one part of the defense against land division in the valley.[82] However, the landowners offered to withdraw "some land" from cultivation to provide irrigation to ejidal plots, and to make available cleared, irrigated land for the formation of ejidal districts. At the time, only 85 proprietors owned 68 percent of the irrigated land in the valley,[83] and they were attempting to keep ejidal encroachment restricted to the north bank of the river, away from the principal canals of the modern valley.

Instead of the expected response, however, the government commission recommended constituting two ejidal districts, as the landowners had suggested, but both would lie in the heart of the valley: Quechehueca along the principal canal, and the other, larger district also in the fertile north-central valley. While the government had always pledged security to legally-constituted private property, the concentration of resources in the Yaqui valley obviously did not fall within government definitions of

82. The Richardson Concession, bought by the government for 6 million dollars in negotiations led by Álvaro Obregón in 1926, had been offered by the *Banco Nacional de Crédito Agrícola* to colonists for purchase since 1928. (Mexico, Banco Nacional de Crédito Ejidal, *El sistema de producción colectiva en los ejidos del Valle del Yaqui, Sonora*, pp. 19–20.) With purchase came a guarantee of ownership against any claims of the agrarian-reform program (*inafectabilidad eterna*). From property belonging to the former Richardson Concession, several colonies still exist, including Colonia Militar, Colonia Jecopaco, Altos de Jecopaco, Tovarito, Marté R. Gómez, Agua Blanca, and Villa Juárez; also *ejidos* Quechehueca, Pueblo Yaqui, Esperanza, Providencia, Campo 5, Morelos (1 and 2), Campo 60 (F. J. Mina), Campo 77 (Independencia), Campos 47, 104, and 16, and Campo 43 (La Noria).

83. *Ibid.*

Table 4

Land Distribution under Cárdenas,
1935-1940[a]

YEAR	AREA (hectares)	BENEFICIARIES
1935	1,923,456	110,286
1936	3,985,700	183,194
1937	5,811,893	199,347
1938	3,486,211	119,845
1939	2,218,207	95,678
1940	2,681,577	54,659
Totals	20,107,044	763,009

[a]SOURCE: Mexico, Departamento de Asuntos Agrarios y Colonización, *Memorias de labores del 1º de septiembre de 1968 al 31 de agosto de 1969*. These figures are very close to other estimates.

small property. The landowners then began to complain, with Yocupicio as their principal ally, that the inviolability of the colonies of the Richardson Concession required that the proposed ejidal districts be rejected, as locations for two topographically united ejidal districts could not be found without rupturing the unity of the Yaqui valley forever. In addition to these complaints, the CAAES decried the lack of water in the valley, and worried aloud about the collective nature of the *ejidos* proposed.[84]

Finally, in May of 1938, after assurances that the landowners of the valley would receive 30,000 hectares of pasture-land in return for the 16,000 hectares of irrigated land expropriated,[85] and after repeated assurances of the general security of private property,[86] 13 ejidal grants reached the Yaqui valley (see Table A6 in the appendix)—not in districts, but sprinkled throughout the area, breaking the unity of the valley so jealously guarded by the CAAES.

That Yocupicio opposed the Yaqui valley grants is clear, both from his public statements and from his defense of the colonists and landowners of the valley. Though in the last instance he supported the actions of the national government in the valley, he did not effectively prosecute land reform in other areas of the state, notably the Mayo valley whence he

84. *Ibid.*, p. 21.
85. *Excelsior*, Dec. 7, 1937, p. 1. Later, with the completion of irrigation projects in the valley, this land was irrigated also.
86. *Ibid.*, April 12, 1938, p. 1; *El Imparcial*, April 13, p. 1.

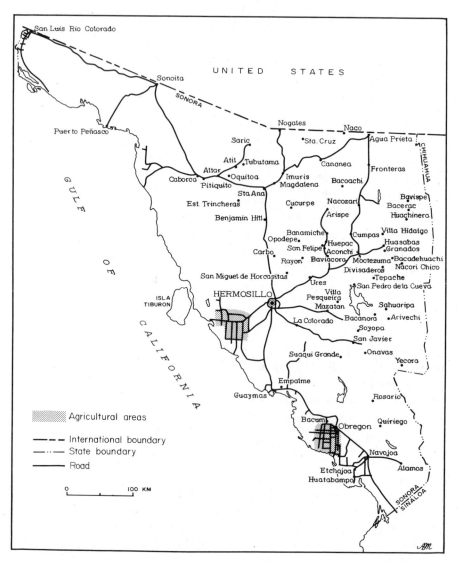

Sonoran Municipalities

came. Not until mid-1938 did Yocupicio begin the agrarian proceedings necessary to grant some 24 Mayo valley *ejidos* to resident petitioners,[87] in concert with the Yaqui valley grants being executed simultaneously.[88]

Though Yocupicio did finally undertake the agrarian reform in the Mayo valley, it resulted in many acts of violence, much as his other

87. Estado de Sonora, *Memoria de la gestión gubernamental del C. General Román Yocupicio En el estado de Sonora, 1937–1939*, pp. 177–178.

88. *El Imparcial*, June 5, 1938, p. 1.

agrarian acts had previously. In October 1938, government officials "kidnapped" or "arrested" (depending on the version) Jacinto López, Maximiliano López, and Aurelio García, along with other CTM leaders involved in ejidal elections in the Mayo valley town of Navojoa. Amid charges of "impositionism," Lombardo Toledano accused Yocupicio of carrying out a purge of CTM workers in the Mayo valley, beating women and laying siege to strikers all over the state.[89] A rebellion against government persecution of *comisariados ejidales* (political leaders in the ejidal system) followed in the Mayo and Yaqui valleys. The uprising was minimized, especially in the local press, but it was important enough to warrant a sudden visit from Secretary of Defense Manuel Ávila Camacho,[90] who proclaimed the problem to be "political, not military," though he admitted to having disarmed some Yaquis.[91] While Ávila Camacho publicly explained the matter as a standard conflict among parties to the 1940 election campaign, he still replaced the chief of military operations, an opponent of Yocupicio and an apparent rebel sympathizer.[92]

Jacinto López, secretary-general of the Federation of Sonoran Workers (FTS), a CTM affiliate of recent vintage, alleged that Yocupicio had opposed the collective *ejidos* of the Yaqui and Mayo river valleys and the work of the Ejidal Bank.[93] Ironically, the collective *ejidos* of the Yaqui valley were originally designed as an institution under state tutelage that would redistribute land, destroy antirevolutionary local authority, and allay the fears of large landholders and investors that the parcelization of the valley through the agrarian reform meant destruction of the natural productive potential of the area forever.[94] In fact, Yocupicio and the landowners of the valley forced the parcelization of the valley through their ultimate refusal of the ejidal-districts proposal. The resulting land reform left private landholders and *ejidatarios* side by side, to the distinct disadvantage of the *ejidos* in terms of future competition for the scarce resources of the valley.

Regarding land reform outside the Yaqui valley, the two points of focus are the Mayo valley land-division of 1938 and the land distribution to the Sierra *pueblos* in the eastern part of the state. According to his own reports, Yocupicio claimed to have initiated distribution of the lands in his native Mayo valley through the scheme presented in Table A7 (in appen-

---

89. *Ibid.*, Oct. 14–15, 1938, p. 1; *Excelsior*, Oct. 15.
90. *Excelsior*, Oct. 16, 1938, p. 1.   91. *Ibid.*, Oct. 29, 1938, p. 1.
92. *Ibid.*, Nov. 2, 1938, p. 1.
93. Earlier, Yocupicio had, in fact, announced that he was exploring the possibility of using the affected *latifundistas* of the state as a credit source for *ejidos*, since the *Banco Ejidal* was incapable of providing them with credit. Actually, as we shall see, the bank paid substantial credit attention to the *ejidatarios* of the Yaqui valley, and their main obstacle to receiving it was often governmental delay in giving them definitive possession of their lands.
94. Cynthia Hewitt de Alcántara, *Modernizing Mexican Agriculture: Socioeconomic Implications of Technological Change, 1940–1970*, p. 182.

dix). Though land reform in the Mayo valley benefitted hundreds of *campesinos* in Etchojoa and Huatabampo, it must be noted that virtually all of the agrarian grants appeared in 1938, and no Mayo valley grants surfaced in Yocupicio's earlier reports.[95] This implies strongly that the same pressure by Cárdenas served to divide the lands of both the Yaqui and the Mayo valleys, against the will of Yocupicio. Even so, only two ejidal grants occurred in the municipality of Navojoa, and with good reason: Yocupicio himself owned at least 6,000 hectares of Navojoa, which could only be jeopardized by ejidal grants in the area.[96] Nevertheless, 1938 land-reform measures affecting some 46,403 hectares eventually benefitted nearly 4,000 *ejidatarios*, though they had to wait some time to possess their land. The Yaqui and the Mayo valleys were, then, the most successful aspect of the Cárdenas reform plan in Sonora. Other communities were not so favored.

The Underside of the Reform: The Sierra

Sonora, like other states in Mexico, varies regionally, from the rich valleys of the Mayo and Yaqui rivers to their headwaters at the foot of the Sierra Madre Occidental. The area at the Sierra's hem, where damp Pacific winds collide with the mountains to provide rain to the Yaqui river, receives substantial rainfall, but it is surrounded on all sides by semi-arid and arid regions.[97] The municipalities that cluster around the tributaries of the important rivers of Sonora—the Concepción, the Mayo, the Sonora, and the Yaqui—are themselves starved for water.[98] In the Sierra of Sonora we can find the same disequilibrium that has plagued regional development schemes throughout much of Mexico. In addition to the dualism between private property and ejidal property, which is the constant shadow of agricultural development and agrarian reform in Mexico, public policy toward Sonoran development in the 1930s sustained the economic polarization between the rich alluvial valleys of the Yaqui, Mayo, Sonora, and Concepción and the harsh desert of the Sierra Madre Occidental to the east. Isolated by mountains without roads, ignored for their combative pallor compared with the ferocious Yaqui, the farmers of the Sierra received lands without water or credit under Cárdenas.[99] Of the 169 *ejidos* that constituted the Sierra region of Sonora in 1975, 57 received their land

95. The adjudication of the Mayo valley had been delayed since 1932, despite its status as a chief priority of state government. *Informe que rinde el C. Rodolfo Elías Calles, 1933*, p. 11.

96. Finally, at the end of 1956, Yocupicio's land was "affected" by the agrarian reform; 3,488 hectares formed the new community "General de División Francisco R. Serrano," populated by 171 *campesinos*. (*El Imparcial*, Nov. 1, 1956, p. 1; *Diario Oficial*, Oct. 25, 1956.)

97. Ángel Bassols Batalla, *El Noroeste de México*, p. 13.

98. Roger Dunbier, *The Sonoran Desert: Its Geography, Economy and People*, pp. 206–211.

99. In 1979 it remained a fact that post-Cárdenas regimes had not seen fit to change (see Chapter 6).

grants before 1940.[100] Some 413,000 hectares fell under those presidential resolutions, but only 474 hectares were irrigated. By comparison, the Yaqui river valley redistribution of 1937–1938 included 17,000 hectares of irrigated land and 36,000 hectares of pasture-land that was later susceptible to cultivation with increased irrigation works.

The Cárdenas program made no provisions for organizing, modernizing, or providing credit or irrigation to these marginal *ejidos*. Irrigation works in Sonora under Cárdenas consisted almost exclusively of the construction of the Álvaro Obregón dam on the upper channel of the Yaqui river. The Cárdenas program of small irrigation works in 1939 included projects in 19 states, but none in Sonora.[101] Though credit and infrastructure growth blossomed in the fertile river valleys of the coast, as late as 1968 only about 7,700 hectares of irrigated land had been added to the 50 eastern municipalities of Sonora, an area almost twice as large as the 29 Sierra municipalities surveyed in the land-reform statistics cited in Table A8 (in appendix).[102] In the 29 municipalities cited, the problem is the same now as it was under the Cárdenas development plan: the Sierra Madre Occidental ranges throughout the eastern part of the state, cutting deep arroyos and irregular, enclosed valleys. Though the land that is level is perfectly susceptible to cultivation, the costs to supply the necessary water and land-improvement measures would be prohibitive. Because the farmers of the Sierra held little political threat (or promise) for the national and state governments in 1938, because they hinted of no vast agricultural wealth for the flagging economy, and because they did not yield to the cost-effective criteria of credit sources, they were effectively ignored. The *ejidos* of the Sonoran Sierra clarify the meaning of regional marginality and unbalanced growth.

The duality of the Sonoran agrarian reform under Cárdenas becomes even more striking when considered in terms of its credit policies. The Cárdenas government nationally distributed ejidal credit in the amounts shown in Table 5. The direction of credit flows, however, depended on the organization of the local ejidal credit societies. This dependence of credit on local administrative and political organization resulted in a sub-

100. The Sierra region includes the municipios of Álamos, Arivechi, Bacadehuachi, Bacanora, Bacerac, Bavispe, La Colorada, Cumpas, Divisaderos, Fronteras, Granados, Huachinera, Huasabas, Mazatlán, Moctezuma, Nácori Chico, Nacozari, Onavas, Quiriego, Rosario, Sahuaripa, San Javier, San Pedro de la Cueva, Soyopa, Suaqui Grande, Tepache, Villa Hidalgo, Villa Pesqueira, and Yécora. Bassols Batalla uses basically the same classification, excluding La Colorada, Fronteras, Nacozari, Onavas, and Villa Hidalgo, and adding Baviácora, Banámichi, Oputo, Ures, Aconchi, Huépac, San Felipe, and Tepupa. (The first list is from the Departamento de Asuntos Rurales del Estado de Sonora. Bassols Batalla's is from *El Noroeste de México*, pp. 378–379.)

101. *Excelsior*, Jan. 4, 1939, p. 1.

102. See Dunbier, *The Sonoran Desert*, p. 206. In the 29 municipalities cited, the Sonora Departamento de Asuntos Rurales shows, as of 1975, 12,852 hectares irrigated, including private properties as well as *ejidos*. The ratio of irrigated land to wasteland is 6.1 percent in the state outside the Sierra, where it is 1.1 percent (see Chapters 6 and 7).

Table 5
Loans Made by the Banco Ejidal,
1936-1940[a]
(pesos)

YEAR	AMOUNT[b]
1936	23,278,000
1937	82,880,000
1938	63,442,000
1939	61,177,000
1940	59,149,000
Total	289,926,000

[a]SOURCE: Nathan L. Whetten, p. 194.
These data agree with CDIA figures in
*Estructura agraria y desarrollo agrícola
en México*, p. 784.
[b]In 1974 pesos.

stantial bias toward the highly organized, economically productive areas which were the primary concern of the Cárdenas land reform. In the Laguna, the most important economic region in Mexico during the first two decades of the Revolution, nearly 300 local credit societies had been formed by the end of 1938.[103] In Yucatán, a total of 333 local societies was reached, including some 46,000 *ejidatario* members within the bank's purview.[104] In the Yaqui valley, 13 (Eckstein says 14) local credit societies were formed as the lands of the valley were divided in 1937–1938. There is no doubt that the bulk of credit went to the Laguna, Yucatán, Mexicali, Michoacán, and the Yaqui valley. To the collective *ejidos* of the Laguna went virtually all of the ejidal credit for 1936.[105] Throughout the Cárdenas years, the Ejidal Bank mainly attended to the Laguna, the Yaqui valley, and the other rich and select areas mentioned above.[106]

While the National Bank of Ejidal Credit in Sonora very generously dispensed credit to the collectives of the Yaqui river valley (see Table 6), the lands outside the valley did not receive the same attention. The Sierra, for instance, received virtually no attention from the government. It is true that much of the Sierra could never be brought under agricultural pro-

103. Eckstein, in *El ejido colectivo*, p. 139, puts the number at 273; Silvia Gómez Tagle, in *Organización de la sociedades de crédito ejidal de La Laguna*, p. 7, puts it at 284; Cárdenas, in his *Informe presidencial* of 1938 (*Excelsior*, Sept. 2, 1938), uses a figure of 288.
104. Cárdenas, *Informe presidencial*.
105. Eckstein, p. 140.
106. Even now, the Laguna, Yaqui valley, and Yucatán generally account for 50 percent of the Bank's operations. (CDIA, *Estructura agraria*, p. 776.)

Table 6

Credit Granted by Banco Ejidal to
Collective Ejidos in the
Yaqui Valley, 1937-1940[a]

(pesos)

YEAR	AMOUNT
1937	315,913
1938	1,338,481
1939	3,075,262
1940	3,199,584
Total	7,929,240

[a]SOURCE: Mexico, Banco Nacional de
Crédito Ejidal, *El Sistema de producción
colectiva en los ejidos del Valle del
Yaqui, Sonora*, Table 7A.

duction within the means of the Mexican state. It was necessary for the success of the irrigation and growth projects in the coastal valleys to minimize diversion of the headwaters of the Sonoran rivers—that is, to discourage the development of more marginal lands in eastern Sonora in favor of more productive development of the rich coastal bottomlands. This, in part, explains the lack of credit to the Sierra *ejidos*, and the decision not to extend the small irrigation program to the Sonoran Sierra where it would result in less water for the prestigious projects of the late 1930s, the dams of the Yaqui river.

Despite a tone of equality of distribution in the agrarian reform, it seems that, in the face of scarce resources, the poorest of the *campesinos* often found their petitions delayed or ignored. Cárdenas asserted that

the program of Revolutionary action . . . makes land available to the *campesinos* . . . in sufficient quantity, not only to resolve the economic problem of each family . . . but in order to augment agricultural production with respect to what was produced or could be produced under a system of land absorption into the hands of a few.

The Revolution desires that the products of every *ejido* go to the consumer markets in order to help the entire Republic achieve a higher standard of life. But, in order to do this, it is indispensable to help the *campesino* with the construction of dams and other irrigation works and with the introduction of more modern systems of cultivation.[107]

107. Mexico, Departamento Agrario, *Ideario agrarista del general de división Lázaro Cárdenas, presidente constitucional de los Estados Unidos Mexicanos*, pp. 71–72.

With statements like these, he committed his government to a genuine social obligation to every *campesino*. But the execution of that promise, as in years past, was often unfulfilled. In a recent study of agrarian-reform petitions and their execution carried out under CDIA auspices, it was found that delays between application and final adjudication of lands averaged almost five years in the Bajío, three years in the Laguna, over four years in Tlaxcala, and about seven and one-half years in Michoacán.[108] In Sonora such delays were common, as we saw briefly in Chapter 4.

As a further example of those delays, Table A9 (in appendix) shows the disposition of ejidal lands which were processed beginning in 1934 under Rodolfo Elías Calles. The 1934 provisional possessions show that a significant portion of the nearly-four-year lag between initiation and definitive possession originated with the national government. The time lost in bureaucratic handling occurred mostly between the dates when the governor granted provisional possession to the *ejido* and sent the relevant documents to the Agrarian Department for final adjudication. Once a presidential resolution was dictated, final possession of the land proceeded quickly—for the most part within a few months. This manifests the already well-known reticence of the *pelele* regimes at the national level to effect a positive and expeditious agrarian reform—the effects, no doubt, of earlier policy changes like the "Stop Laws" and the polarization of *veterano* and *agrarista* sentiment within the government.

In the 1937 and 1938 provisional possessions (Table A10 in appendix), a different pattern emerges. The lag between the governor's resolution and provisional possession and the appearance of a presidential resolution confirming the adjudication (lag A) was nonexistent in the Yaqui valley, and averaged only one year in the Mayo valley and less in the Sierra. After the dictation of the presidential resolution, however, the lag increased in the Sierra and the Mayo valley, producing a total average delay in processing (lag B) of three years in the Mayo and over four years in the Sierra—roughly the same lag experienced under the pre-Cárdenas regime of Rodolfo Elías Calles. In contrast, in the Yaqui valley, where national attention focused on the restitution of lands to the residents, and the presidential commission presided over the execution as well as the adjudication of grants, the entire process took less than one year.

The disparity in the handling of petitions from different areas of the state reflected the privileged status enjoyed by the residents of the Yaqui valley, and the general hostility with which the Sonoran state authorities approached the agrarian-reform question under Yocupicio's leadership. It also affords us an early glimpse at the inequities and imbalances in the agrarian reform which still pervade Sonoran agriculture more than forty

108. CDIA, *Estructura agraria*, pp. 534–535.

years later. More important, though, the prejudicial execution of the Cárdenas agrarian reform manifests the increasing power of the national state over *campesino* organizations, the economic component of "social obligation," and the fragility of the populist state's commitment to continued aggressive land redistribution. The year 1938 was both the zenith of Sonoran agrarian reform and the beginning of its descent in favor of local agri-capitalist accumulation and political domination by the national state.

THE END OF AGRARISMO

By the time of his 1939 trip to Sonora to inspect the agrarian work of his administration, Cárdenas' land-reform program was already winding to a halt.[109] The economic crisis of 1938, in addition to the generally perceived anticapitalist slant of Cárdenas' reformist government, provoked a flight of domestic capital abroad and a declining level of direct foreign investment as well.[110] Public-sector income could not, at the end of the Cárdenas regime, sustain the spending necessary for economic growth. Domestic capital was in short supply, and the government debt was not being sold successfully to the public.[111] The 1938 oil expropriation further frightened Mexican capitalists, who conjured visions of the collapse of the peso and paralysis of the economy to the point of national bankruptcy. The oil companies themselves speculated that Abelardo Rodríguez, Joaquín Amaro, Manuel Ávila Camacho, and Román Yocupicio would join the rebel forces of Saturnino Cedillo against Cárdenas.[112]

The 1938 crisis, and its political effect of raising the spectre of organized rightist opposition to Cárdenas and his successor, accelerated a shift in *agrarismo* that had been forthcoming since Cárdenas had announced—before the oil expropriation—that the end of his term would bring the land-grant program to a halt.[113] In March 1938 the populist president declared that the main geographical areas subject to land reform had already been investigated and divided. He restored to local governors the power to initially determine the validity of land petitions, as well as the power to decide when and where agrarian centers should be armed for self-defense. Along with repeated assurances of the security of small property, Cárdenas declared the new goals of the agrarian reform to be in-

109. The contention that land division fell sharply after 1937 does not stand up, however, due to lags in administration and adjudication of already-committed grants. In that respect, Albert L. Michaels' critique of the crisis of *cardenismo* is inaccurate. (Michaels, "The Crisis of Cardenismo," esp. p. 64.)

110. The index of direct U.S. investment in Mexico declined by 48 percent during the period 1929–1940, 18 percent after 1936. (James W. Wilkie, *The Mexican Revolution*, p. 265.)

111. David H. Shelton, "The Banking System: Money and the Goal of Growth," pp. 148–149.

112. Lorenzo Meyer, *México y los Estados Unidos en el conflicto petrolero (1917–1942)*, pp. 349–352.

113. *Excelsior*, Jan. 11, 1938, p. 1.

creased production, conservation of the sources of agricultural wealth, and finally, redistribution.[114] Yocupicio's voice was among the first to declare support for Cárdenas' new orientation.[115]

This monumental change in approach to redistribution was reflected in the change in agrarian policy announced by the *cardenista* secretary of agriculture. The "national interest," according to the ministry, dictated

> that it be considered of urgent national necessity to terminate the grants and extensions (*ampliaciones*) of lands, in order to establish full confidence throughout the country in the rights of [land] tenure . . . in the *ejido* as well as in [the lands] that our own agrarian laws judge to be *inafectable*.[116]

The proposed 1939 Ministry of Agriculture and Development budget included only 3.5 million pesos for the Division of Ejidal Organization, compared with 35 million for irrigation works.[117] The heyday of *campesino*-oriented land reform had come to an end.

Accompanying this landmark turnabout was the reorganization of the PNR. Cárdenas exploited the 1937 rift between the powerful CTM and the PCM over state–party relations[118] by proposing a new "popular front" strategy that would, remarkably, exclude the PCM from the coalition. The reorganization centered around a sectoral approach to party representation: worker, *campesino*, military, and popular sectors subsumed under the corporate umbrella of the state party. While the influence of the PCM among some workers and *campesinos* was substantial, eliminating the Communists from the official political coalition assured that the *campesinos* would remain closer to state tutelage and control. It also assured a sectoral division of the working class—which meant, in effect, less real power for the CTM and Vicente Lombardo Toledano. The CTM agreed to this final blow against the original concept of the popular front partly because of Lombardo's tight control over the organization, plus general nationalist discontent with the PCM, and the continuing need for access to the national center of power through the party.[119]

The CNC, of course, had always been a state-controlled organization. The key to the agrarian reform had been the organization of the *campesinos* under state domination, and the reorganization of the PNR (now the

114. *Ibid.*, March 29, 1938, p. 1.
115. *Ibid.*, April 2, 1938, p. 1.
116. Mexico, Secretaría de Agricultura y Fomento, *Sugestiones presentados por la Secretaría de Agricultura y Fomento a la Secretaría de Gobernación para la formulación del Segundo Plan Sexenal que se someterá a la consideración de la convención plenaria del PRM*, p. 100.
117. *Ibid.*, p. 117. The entire ministry budget totalled only 55 million pesos, so irrigation was obviously the key priority. This followed extrabudgetary expenditures in 1938 of 24.7 million pesos for dams and irrigation canals. (*Informe que rinde el C. General Lázaro Cárdenas, 1939.*)
118. Ashby, *Organized Labor and the Mexican Revolution*, p. 84.
119. Arturo Anguiano, *El estado y la política obrera del cardenismo*, pp. 128–139; Ashby, p. 88.

Party of the Mexican Revolution, or PRM) institutionalized that state control over the masses of *campesinos*. As contrasted with the independent organization under the PCM of the *campesinos* in the Laguna in 1936, the PRM now stood as the single voice of the organized *pueblo*. The future of national agrarian reform, just as in the days of Calles, again rested with state initiative. Class struggle in civil society gave way to corporate representation in a state-dominated economy. The common people, now treated as corporate sectors, depended more than ever on the benevolent state for their due.

With the corporate renovation of the party, the consolidation of state populism was complete.[120] The agrarian-reform mobilization was being dismantled, partly for economic reasons, partly because of the danger of mass mobilizations and independent class conflict. The state, having ensured its position as "regulator of social life," as Cárdenas had put it in his famous Fourteen Points of 1936, now turned to other aspects of its battle for continued legitimacy. The venerable issues of administrative rationality, fiscal stability, economic growth, industrialization, and a stable currency resumed the prominence they had lost temporarily in the froth of agrarian populism. Though manufacturing survived the Revolution in relative health, the private sector in agriculture and extractive industries had deteriorated.[121] Public-investment spending expanded under Cárdenas, and it was necessary to stimulate return on that investment. In sum, agrarian populism had come to the point of giving way to a new development emphasis.

A LAST LOOK AT SONORA

In mid-1939, Cárdenas again journeyed through the north and northwest, spending over a month in Sonora. On May 22, 1939, he entered the state from the east, passing through the Cañon del Púlpito, deep in the Sierra. The scene there was replete with the symbols of his regime. To celebrate Cárdenas' return to his former battleground, Yocupicio mustered a column of cavalry to line the path of the presidential caravan arriving from Chihuahua. Yocupicio and Anselmo Macías Valenzuela announced the president's arrival, and the three generals—Macías, Cárdenas, and Yocupicio—greeted each other in the middle of the canyon.[122] With this impressive entourage of state dignitaries and armed cowboys, *campesinos*, and ranchers, Cárdenas began his tour of Sonora. Skipping from the mines of Nacozari to the Yaqui and Mayo valleys, he dispensed gifts in all sizes: the return of an old church to the faithful of Nacozari, a mill and a

120. Arnaldo Córdova, *La formación del poder político en México*, p. 39.

121. Clark Reynolds, *The Mexican Economy: Twentieth-Century Structure and Growth*, pp. 163–166.

122. Alberto Calzadíaz Barrera, *Dos gigantes: Sonora y Chihuahua*, vol. I, p. 118.

truck to Pilares, a university for the capital, and assurances of perpetual protection and aid to the Yaquis.[123] He exhorted the *campesinos* in Sonora to continue their struggle for land, and promised them assistance from the National Mortgage Bank for construction of small irrigation projects.[124]

On arrival in the Yaqui valley, Cárdenas dispensed resolutions which promised developmental aid to the heads of the eight *pueblos* of the Yaquis, and rights to half the water from the new dam (then still in construction) "La Angostura." Highways, schools, warehouses, producer cooperatives, irrigation pumps and canals, and other projects were specifically promised to the Yaquis.[125] In his final attention to the Yaqui Indians, Cárdenas committed the state to eliminating the grinding poverty of the residents, which continued despite the land reform of 1937–1938.[126] The future of that commitment after 1940, however, rested in other hands.

The trip to Sonora ended the Cárdenas initiative in the northwest, and before the dust settled on the new arrangement between landowners and *ejidatarios*, the struggle between collectivists and individualists began, not surprisingly, in the Yaqui valley.[127] The clash was joined by conflicts between the CTM, the CROM, and the CNC over *campesino* representation and the control over various *ejidos*, as we will see in Chapter 6. Meanwhile, the radical right was arming itself for the 1940 elections. To try to deflate the growing forces of the right against land reform, redistribution, and the worker-and-*campesino* emphasis in the Cárdenas phase of Mexican populism, Cárdenas defended his revolution to the nation, finally, as a moderate one—an assessment with which the now-defunct LCAEV and LNC "Úrsulo Galván" would have agreed.

> More than political reforms, what really defines a regime . . . is its economic and social organization; and the Mexican government has not collectivized the means or instruments of production, nor monopolized foreign commerce converting the state into an owner of factories, houses, lands, and warehouses. . . . There is no communist government in Mexico. Our Constitution is democratic and liberal, with some moderate hints of socialism in its precepts that govern territorial property, principally for reasons of restitution, and in the mandates that refer to relations between capital and labor, that are

123. *Ibid.*, p. 119. Cárdenas was struck by the poverty of the Yaqui valley but, strangely, did not comment on his trip through the Sierra except to note arrivals, departures, and other minutiae. (*Apuntes*, pp. 422–428.) The university story appeared in *Excelsior*, May 29, 1939, p. 1.

124. *Excelsior*, May 28 and 30, 1939, both p. 1.

125. For the text of the resolution, see Dabdoub, *Historia del Valle del Yaqui*, pp. 231–235; also *Excelsior*, June 13–16, 1939, all p. 1.

126. The intensity of that poverty is graphically apparent in Rosalio Moisés et al., *The Tall Candle: The Personal Chronicle of a Yaqui Indian*, esp. Chaps. 11 and 12. It goes without saying that such poverty was endemic throughout the state and not exclusive to the Yaqui valley.

127. *El Imparcial*, April 7, 1940, p. 1.

not . . . more radical than those of other democratic countries, and even some of those that maintain monarchic institutions.[128]

But it was too late to save the gains of 1935—1940 by invoking the old ghosts of liberal constitutionalism. The political polarization of hostile groups and classes, and the fragmentation of organizations sympathetic to the agrarian reform, sprang partly from the sectoral reorganization of the party and its effects on working class and *campesino* solidarity, and partly from the questionable compromise settlement that counterposed private farmer and *ejidatario* in the Yaqui valley. Dependent on a benevolent state attitude, and now disarmed by state governors, the *ejidatarios* waited for the new regime to reveal its complexion. They did not have to wait long.

128. "Mensaje al país pronunciado ante el Congreso del estado de Guerrero, Chilpancingo, Feb. 20, 1940," in Mexico, Departamento Agrario, *Ideario político*, pp. 68–69.

Part III

The Crisis of Mexican Populism: Capitalist Accumulation or Agrarian Redistribution?

By the end of the Cárdenas epoch, the terms of the organization of Mexican society were set. The state now extended beyond the realm of simple government operations by virtue of its participation in mixed and public enterprises, as well as by the intimate relationship between government and political party. During the early 1930s, while *cardenismo* was still gaining support and power through a popular alliance with the *campesinos* and working class, the problem of political authority revolved around "social obligation" to the *campesinos*. Fortunately for Cárdenas, this obligation roughly coincided with the desire of the bourgeoisie to rid the countryside of inefficient latifundia in order to replace them with capitalist farms which could generate foreign exchange for the national economy. For different reasons, and with widely varying degrees of intensity, the weak national bourgeoisie encouraged the growth of a paternalistic state predicated upon future capitalist growth with continued popular support based on agrarian populism.

The populist pact of the 1930s was necessarily temporary, however. As we have seen, redistribution in the form of land grants and credit depended directly upon the economic viability and political sensitivity of

129

the region. The agrarian reform was tied, from the first, to the logic of capitalist accumulation, which fostered the parallel growth of private and public farms, individualist and collectivist ideologies. The seed of *agrarista*-versus-capitalist conflict germinated in the period of World War II. As we shall see in Chapters 6 and 7, the conflict has continued in some form until today.

The components which fed the growth of this eventual conflict between economic growth and agrarian populism were many and complex: the United States market, hungry for imports to nourish the burgeoning war effort; import-substitution industrialization, which was based on agricultural export but also drained capital away from production of primary goods; Mexico's geographic proximity to the United States, resulting in unique cultural influences and political pressures on Mexican society; and the ever-present shortages of primary needs for agriculture, sparking battles over land, water, labor, and surplus value.

Most important, however, was the direction in which the national economy was led over the three decades of the "economic miracle." The state's authority to impose redistributive policies on rural property-holders was a direct result of the bourgeoisie's dependence on the state to guarantee "social peace" and the capital for private investment. But over the years of the miracle, as the bourgeoisie gained economic strength and political organization, they exerted their influence to reduce the range of independent state power and to impose their own vision of progress on Mexican society. Perhaps the greatest indicator of their success in this respect is the low tax-rate in Mexico, which reflects the policies of presidents sympathetic to the national bourgeoisie.

On the other hand, the power of the Mexican state was further diminished as a result of its increasing neglect of the popular aspect of the populist pact. The state exhorted workers to cooperate with capital for the sake of aggregate growth, but failed to address the ever-widening gap among income groups, or the problems of underemployment and unemployment. While the state provided an expensive infrastructure for rural development in export crops, the marginal *campesinos*, permanent wards of the state, received little to improve their lot. The pattern of Mexican growth under the "miracle" ensured the growth and security of national capital, but deteriorating economic and political conditions for the common people—both of which contributed to the relative decline of state power.

In the context of these long-term problems, and in the aftermath of the violent rebellions of the 1960s over the inadequacy of revolutionary ideology and dependent capitalist growth, Luis Echeverría came to power in 1970. Pushed to the left by a combination of popular pressures, personal vision, and international *tercermundismo* ("third-worldism"), Echeverría pledged to recover the populist pact from domination by the bourgeoisie.

A president of unusual personal style in an era of administrators and technocrats, Echeverría was an anomaly who disrupted the terms of order in modern Mexico, to the delight of some *campesinos* and the chagrin of the national bourgeoisie. But, as we shall see in Chapter 7, he was attempting a political power-play of great magnitude with a state apparatus already weakened by the bourgeoisie and by the legitimation crisis of the 1960s. The president, trying to carve out a new populist pact, was using the same tools others had employed to repress and control the masses. The combination of systemic political cynicism, bureaucratic stagnation, personal inconsistency, and structural contradictions may have proved fatal to Mexican *agrarismo*, at least for the foreseeable future.

Chapter 6

Economic Growth
and Populist Decline, 1940–1970

Cárdenas' presidency represented a watershed in postrevolutionary Mexican society, not only because of the economic growth that followed, but also because of the level of political achievement it attained. The Mexican state in 1940, after thirty years of revolution and rebellion, fully asserted its dominance as the authoritative apparatus guiding political society. Competing parties had been destroyed, for the most part, and the Party of the Mexican Revolution (PRM) in its reorganized form controlled Mexican politics as never before.[1] By the close of the Cárdenas epoch, national and local politics had become synchronized to a much greater degree than had been possible during such stormy conflicts as that between Cárdenas and Yocupicio. This synchronization gradually increased in the 1940s and 1950s, at the expense of dissenters—*campesinos*, rival *políticos*, and intractable working-class organizations which were excluded from the plans of the developmentalist regimes of the time. In an institutional sense, the problem of forming the Mexican national state had been resolved.

In the economy, the state exercised more authority by virtue of increased levels of public investment in infrastructure; protectionist policies which benefitted domestic industries; state access to foreign loans; and state capacity to formulate economic-development plans that substituted for the chronic weakness of the bourgeoisie in civil society. Shaken

---

1. By 1940 the PRM existed in its mature form—which survives today, minus formal military representation. In 1946 the party name was changed to *Partido Revolucionario Institucional*, and "PRI" has since become the best-known logo in the country. See José Ángel Conchello et al., *Los partidos políticos de México*, pp. 353ff., for a brief historical sketch and relevant documents. Also Vicente Fuentes Díaz, *Los partidos políticos en México*, pp. 222ff.

by the economic crisis of 1938 and willing to coalesce with a more sympathetic state-development orientation, many progressive capitalists of the 1930s actively joined in official plans for priorities in the 1940s.[2]

The story of the "economic miracle" which transpired over the period from 1940 to 1970 has been recounted elsewhere.[3] While this study does not pretend to be a history of the Mexican economy—perhaps the most sophisticated in Latin America—we must examine some highlights of postwar economic growth in order to establish certain key relationships and trends in the tense dialectic between state and civil society. To understand the "take-off" of the Mexican economy, we must look at the effects of World War II on Mexico's production. To clarify points of contact between state and class, we must know some of the main lines of public policy toward capital formation, public finance, development of the internal market, and the role of foreign capital in domestic growth. To see the general direction of the national economy, we must sketch the role of agriculture in generating foreign exchange for import-substitution industrialization (ISI).[4] And finally, to understand the agrarian-reform policies of the post-Cárdenas period, we must try to interpret the effects of the "miracle" on the *ejido*; the structural deficiencies of the pattern of aggregate economic growth; and the inevitable consequences for state–*campesino* relations.

WARTIME BOOM AND STRUCTURAL GROWTH

While Mexico remained militarily on the fringes of the Second World War, its economy received a great, sustained boost which really initiated the miracle of aggregate growth. Both agriculture and domestic industry benefitted from the rapid expansion of exports to the United States. War shortages in the United States raised commodity prices and assured Mexican producers a high rate of return on primary goods. After a slow 1.11-percent growth of GDP in 1940–1941, the economy showed an average 7.08-percent growth-rate over the next four war years.[5] By increasing ex-

---

2. David H. Shelton, "The Banking System: Money and the Goal of Growth," p. 156.
3. The most accessible and complete survey of this period is Clark Reynolds, *The Mexican Economy: Twentieth Century Structure and Growth*. Other key presentations of the aggregate growth of the Mexican economy during this period (i.e., the "economic miracle") include: Dwight S. Brothers and Leopoldo Solís M., *Mexican Financial Development*; Roger D. Hansen, *The Politics of Mexican Development*; Timothy King, *Mexico: Industrialization and Trade Policies Since 1940*; Sanford A. Mosk, *Industrial Revolution in Mexico*; Leopoldo Solís, *La realidad económica mexicana: retrovisión y perspectivas*; Raymond Vernon (ed.), *Public Policy and Private Enterprise in Mexico*; and René Villarreal, *El desequilibrio externo en la industrialización de México, 1929–1975*.
4. Import-substitution industrialization, simply put, is the process by which an economy substitutes new domestically produced goods for those previously imported.
5. Villarreal, *El desequilibrio externo*, p. 59.

port and import duties, the government supplemented its general revenues destined for infrastructure investment. Such direct investment by
the government, plus public enterprise investment, reached 40 percent of
total domestic capital during the war years.[6]

As in other countries of Latin America, the war boom inaugurated a period of "inward development" based on expansion of commercial agriculture, protection of the internal market, transfer of capital from the export
sector to the domestic sector, and creation of a fundamental infrastructure
to support import-substitution.[7] Key goals in the government's plans for
ISI included: increasing agricultural exports, and devising mechanisms to
transfer capital from agriculture to industry; financing ISI through foreign
borrowing in the face of traditionally low tax revenues, reduced even more
by postwar protectionism;[8] and controlling the foreign debt and balance-
of-payments disequilibrium generated by ISI. Generally, the economic miracle of the Mexican economy also combined the organizational virtues of
state control over labor unions and a large reserve army of labor receiving
low wages during the 1940s—which, in turn, kept the profit share of national income high. Favorable tax and tariff policies kept producer costs
low.[9] Heavy industry, benefitting not only from generous state policy but
also from the war boom, expanded rapidly. New export opportunities
stimulated production in textiles, iron and steel, cement, and pulp and
paper, while chemicals and fertilizer were numbered among the ISI industries. Increased domestic demand, partly due to the lack of foreign
supplies, spurred the industrial economy. Because of high rates of postwar inflation, investment borrowing sustained a negligible rate of interest, which further fueled the miracle.[10]

Throughout the first phase of ISI, from 1939 through 1958,[11] wages lag-
ged behind prices, while the condition of labor improved mainly through
shifts in sector of employment. The economy gained from external trade,
improved technology, a shift to commercial agriculture, and an expanded
internal market.[12] Each of these aspects of the growth economy bore costs,
however, as we shall see later with respect to the transfer of capital away
from the agricultural sector.

6. *Ibid.*, p. 67.
7. Fernando H. Cardoso and Enzo Faletto, *Dependencia y desarrollo en América Latina*,
p. 104.
8. Brothers and Solís, *Mexican Financial Development*, p. 52. Mexico's tax revenues
average 8–12 percent compared with 20–30 percent in advanced industrial countries.
9. Reynolds, *The Mexican Economy*, pp. 190–191; Villarreal, *passim*.
10. Reynolds, pp. 22–23 and 86. Inflation was at an annual rate of 8.4 percent from 1941
to 1947. (Solís, *La realidad*, p. 110.)
11. This convenient demarcation is borrowed from Villarreal (p. 7), who divides ISI into
two phases: goods for final consumption, 1939–1958; and intermediate and capital goods,
1959–1975.
12. Reynolds, pp. 38 and 83.

Of course, this growth-oriented "developmentalist populism" did not spring full-blown on the Mexican scene. As we have seen, Cárdenas geared his administration's public-policy plans toward increased agricultural production, public support for large infrastructure works (i.e., capital formation), and the gradual growth of domestic industry. When Treasury Secretary Eduardo Suárez confessed in 1941 that the economy would have to diversify and expand for Mexican society to advance, he simply reiterated the policy orientation of the late Cárdenas regime in its concern for the development of private industry to offset excessive export-dependency.[13] The Cárdenas regime, despite its preoccupation with the "social obligation" of the Revolution to redistribute national resources to the underclasses, nevertheless influenced the economic miracle in many more conventional ways. Government spending on public works during the 1930s resulted in increased industrial production and effective demand in the 1940s.[14] Likewise, the Cárdenas regime was no enemy of the manufacturer. During the Cárdenas *sexenio*, domestic manufacturing was the liveliest sector of economic activity, growing at an average yearly rate of 21.3 percent from 1935 to 1941, and representing, in 1940, nearly one-fourth of Mexico's national income (see Table A11 in appendix). ISI in the 1940s was, in a real sense, a logical epilogue to the policies initiated under Cárdenas.

Nacional Financiera also took hold in the Cárdenas period and began, on a small scale, to promote industrial development in 1936 and 1937. By 1940 it was the key factor in the securities market, making industrial loans and generally coordinating the awakening economy.[15] Tariff protection, dating from 1930, and tax exemptions for industrial development, a policy since 1926, both blossomed under Cárdenas, helping the economy shrug off the limitations of a dependent commercial enclave. By 1945 the annual report of *Nacional Financiera*, divulging the pro-business inclinations of the Ávila Camacho regime, declared the economic policy goals which dominated Mexican development over the next twenty years:

> The progress of the Mexican economy should not be based on the export of a relatively small number of articles, essentially mineral and agricultural raw materials, . . . but rather should rest on a change in its structure . . . [toward] the export not only of raw materials, but also of certain manufactured products or of raw materials with some degree of processing, and in which imports consist preferably of capital goods.[16]

13. Shelton, "The Banking System," pp. 149–150. Some continuity of regimes with regard to finance and industrial policy is shown by the fact that Suárez, the *cardenista* Secretary of Treasury and Public Credit, and *Nacional Financiera* (National Finance Investment Bank) Director Antonio Espinosa de los Monteros both remained in their key posts until 1945.

14. Mosk, *Industrial Revolution*, pp. 59–60; Reynolds, p. 167.

15. Reynolds, p. 191.

16. Mexico, Nacional Financiera, *Informe anual, 1945*, pp. 31–32.

Portents of Populist Decline

Meanwhile, besides encouraging aggregate economic growth in the industrial sector, *cardenista* populism had ensured that the state would still be obliged to attend, at least formally, to the "social obligation" of the Revolution, including agrarian reform and worker rights under Articles 27 and 123 of the Constitution of 1917. Because the surplus-value and productivity gains of the wartime economy came from the declining worker-share of income, shifts by the rural population to more lucrative occupational sectors, and the increased proletarianization of the agrarian sector, the goals of developmental populism gave rise to many rural political tensions which eluded easy remedy.

The limited official redistribution model, in the context of postwar Mexican development, seemed to consist of appropriating domestic savings generated by agricultural export and channelling them to some rising public social expenses, generally centered in urban locales—ignoring or giving short shrift to the rural poor. The obvious deficiencies in such a model for a traditionally rural society resulted in serious political conflicts in the countryside. Other tensions resulted from a simultaneous decline in importance of the program of ejidal grants and credit. After 1939, the ideology of the agrarian reform had returned to the "integral reform," based on accelerating supplies of labor, credit, and technology to the private smallholder. The collective *ejidos* subsequently fell under ideological attack from the right as "unproductive" and "communistic" units of production not suitable for the Mexican economic environment.[17] The general anti-Communist, antifascist fervor of the war period added impetus to the private sector's war on the *ejido*, which frequently appeared to be a vendetta of the ascending business community against the noxious reminders of the worker–*campesino* populism of Lázaro Cárdenas, Graciano Sánchez, and Vicente Lombardo Toledano. During the entire period between 1941 and 1945, both *Excelsior* and *El Imparcial* gave the impression of a country unified behind the war-production effort and the boom that resulted from the conflict between Axis and Allies in distant theatres. Labor and *campesino* leaders, even Lombardo himself, pledged fealty to the national-unity program of the government and vowed to delay strikes and other worker mobilizations until after the war, for the sake of "The Fatherland."[18] When the war ended, and interclass conflict resumed its previous prominence in civil society, the working class suffered from the organizational demobilization and "decommunization" which had weakened it politically during the war-production period.

The postwar assault on the agrarian reform could not have been achieved without prior reduction of the CNC and CTM to simple puppet

17. CDIA, *Estructura agraria y desarrollo agrícola en México*, p. 40.
18. E.g., *Excelsior*, June 6, 13, and 18, 1942, all p. 1.

organizations for the control and demobilization of the working class and *campesinos*, in stark contrast to the more aggressive roles they had commanded in the 1930s. In the years following its organization as the rural complement to the urban industrial CTM, the CNC had initiated a feud with the CTM over political control of the *ejidatarios* and the substantial fruits of the official agrarian reform. Sensing the pro-individualist shift in presidential politics, and using its substantial arsenal of anti-*lombardista* invective, the CNC during the 1940s took an increasingly individualist position toward land tenure and exploitation, even joining with private property-owners in some states to pressure the regime for stabilization of land tenure.[19] With the formation of the National Confederation of Popular Organizations (CNOP) in 1943 as an arm of the PRI's popular sector, the CNC found itself in the impossible position (in Mexico, at least) of defending the rights of agricultural workers and *ejidatarios* while belonging to an organization (CNOP) made up of landed proprietors and petty bourgeoisie.[20] In 1942, two years after Lombardo's retirement from the CTM, the CNC underwent a substantial metamorphosis that resulted in a decade of conflict. Graciano Sánchez, the veteran *cardenista* so intimately associated with the official collectivist aspirations of the ejidal program under CNC auspices, was felled by an internal coup in the CNC and replaced by individualist Gabriel Leyva Velázquez.[21]

With the fall of Graciano Sánchez and the *cardenista* wing of the CNC, the waning influence of Lombardo Toledano and the radical faction of the CTM, and the change in affections of the government toward the *ejido*, the official proponents of agrarian policy found little "in-house" resistance to a procapitalist agricultural-development bias. The consequent anti-*campesino* shift in agrarian politics in the 1940s has been known ever since as the "counter-reform."[22] Its dimensions had lasting impact on the *ejidos* of Sonora and the political future of the national state as well.

The Impact on Sonora

In Sonora, as in much of the rest of the nation, the political battles of the counter-reform often took the guise of vendettas against Lombardo Toledano—who was, after 1945, routinely excoriated as a dupe of Moscow. In 1948, a campaign began to ensure that, in the words of the head of the

19. Moisés González Navarro, *La Confederación Nacional Campesina: un grupo de presión en la reforma agraria mexicana*, p. 177.

20. CNC cooperatives formed part of the CNOP, along with associations of small property-holders, merchants, small factory-owners, the *Confederación Nacional de Trabajadores Intelectuales*, youth, women, artisans, and the *Federación de Trabajadores No Asalariados*. The CNOP has opposed taxation and ejidal credit, and has advocated the cause of private property over that of ejidal reform. (Gerret Huizer, *La lucha campesina en México*, pp. 76–77.)

21. González Navarro, pp. 169–170; *Excelsior*, June 21, 1942, second section, p. 11.

22. Manuel Aguilera Gómez, *La reforma agraria en el desarrollo económico de México*, pp. 144ff.; Jerjes Aguirre Avellaneda, *La política ejidal en México*, pp. 83ff.

Agrarian Department, "Communist poison is extirpated from agrarian politics."[23] Lombardo's old nemesis Luis Morones charged him with being "the representative of Communism in Mexico," and the CTM and PRI vowed to purge their ranks of *lombardistas* in order to "decommunize" their respective organizations.[24]

Though the rhetoric at the national level seemed overinflated, it resounded throughout the countryside, reaching Sonora at a particularly inopportune time, at least as far as the *ejido* was concerned. The battle against Lombardo and the newly-formed leftist Popular Party was carried on in the *ejidos* of the Yaqui and Mayo river valleys, again disrupting the progress made in the area's farm production. In February 1948 the battle flared into large-scale violence, as three *ejidatarios* from "Francisco J. Mina" were killed and five were wounded at the hands of "individualists" responding to the anti-collectivist incitement of the state delegate from the Agrarian Department. After federal troops intervened to control the situation, it became clear that the struggle involved members of the CNC against *lombardistas*.[25] Though a subsequent referendum on collective versus individual exploitation in the Yaqui valley favored collectivism by a slight margin, the movement was, in fact, dying at the hands of the official power arrayed against the collectivist CTM renegades.[26] Barely five months later, the perpetrators of the "Francisco J. Mina" killings were released from jail without sentences.[27]

Further blows to the collectivist cause occurred in 1949 and 1950, all but eliminating independent leftist *agrarismo* as an overt political force in Sonora until 1958. The first blow came in the hotly contested gubernatorial election in July of 1949. It appeared that Jacinto López, veteran Sonoran CTM organizer and founding father of the Popular Socialist Party (PPS), had defeated the PRI candidate. All of the candidates for governor—Jacinto López, Armando Velderráin Almada, and the eventual winner, Ignacio Soto—of course declared themselves victorious.[28] López, anticipating PRI intervention, called the election "a scandalous fraud,"[29] and the PPS complained of hired thugs harassing PPS supporters on or-

23. *Excelsior*, April 24, 1948, p. 1. Communism, Lombardo, and the collective *ejido* were often invoked interchangeably, although the PCM had only sporadic influence in the countryside. In Sonora, the PCM had little sway in CTM–*ejido* politics.

24. *Ibid.*, April 1–5, 1948, p. 1.

25. *El Imparcial*, Feb. 17–March 2, 1948, all p. 1. At the time of the attacks, *lombardistas* controlled the *Unión de Sociedades Colectivas de Crédito Ejidal*, exercising great influence in ejidal politics in the Yaqui valley.

26. The most prominent individualist *ejidos* included: El Yaqui, Primero de Mayo, Nueva Casa de Teras, and 31 de Octubre; collectivists included: Cajeme, Francisco I. Madero, Francisco J. Mina, Cuauhtemoc, Quechehueca, Morelos, and Guadalupe Victoria. *Ejidos* such as Providencia, Robles Castillo, and Progreso were more or less evenly divided. The referendum results were: *colectivo*, 872; *individual*, 849. (*El Imparcial*, March 29, 1948.)

27. *Ibid.*, August 4, 1948, p. 1.

28. *Excelsior*, July 5, 6, and 7, 1949, pp. 4, 8, and 1, respectively.

29. *Ibid.*, July 7, 1949.

ders from PRI candidates.[30] Velderráin, in announcing his victory in an advertisement in *Excelsior*, warned President Alemán against the "crude [*burda*] imposition of a candidate such as Ignacio Soto, who only obtained 10 percent of the vote."[31] The PRI, through energetic publicity engineered by the young Luis Echeverría Álvarez, refused to acknowledge the issue in the press and, instead, touted computer verification of federal district electoral results and the virtues of electoral democracy.[32] President Alemán, obviously unwilling to admit an electoral subversion of PRI dominance, mobilized troops to impose his party's candidate, Ignacio Soto. The president—as López expected—also took advantage of the opportunity to break up centers of PPS sentiment, i.e., the collective *ejidos*. A campaign against the PPS in Sonora began; before it ended, federal troops even occupied one of the collectives (Pueblo Yaqui) to ensure the battle victory of individualists who had surrounded a collectivist minority in the machinery yard.[33]

A subsequent critical incident, in 1950, was the proclamation that the Ejidal Bank had pursued, and would continue to pursue, a policy of economic discrimination to drive the collectivists from the valley. In the unusually frank words of *El Imparcial*, itself no friend of the collective:

> In the beginning of the agrarian land division in the Yaqui valley, that is, in the epoch of President Cárdenas, the so-called *ejidos colectivos* emerged, . . . which survived thanks to the efforts of the Ejidal Bank; but, because a great deal of demagogy surrounded the matter [the land division], the *ejidos* wasted no time in entering political life under the protection, in those days, of the CTM of Vicente Lombardo Toledano.
>
> If, on the one hand, the *ejidos* of the Yaqui valley gave the region its economic life, at the same time they made themselves intolerable with their constant aggression and arrogance toward the State Administration, fed first by the CTM of Lombardo, and later by the so-called *Partido Popular*, also of Lombardo.
>
> The situation created in the Yaqui valley by those leaders was not only intolerable for the state administration, but the problem even reached the federal government, and . . . the Government of the Republic decided finally to end this state of affairs by using . . . a powerful weapon: economics.

30. *Ibid.*, July 2, 1949.
31. *Ibid.*, July 6, 1949.
32. Echeverría was the PRI's Director of Press and Propaganda at the time.
33. Cynthia Hewitt de Alcántara, *Modernizing Mexican Agriculture; Socioeconomic Implications of Technological Change, 1940–1970*, p. 194. An interesting sidelight to this story is the failure of the PPS to record this moment in its greatest electoral campaign. None of the standard works on political parties in Mexico (see note 1) refer to the incident. Robert Paul Millon's sympathetic biography of Lombardo, *Vicente Lombardo Toledano: Mexican Marxist*, does not mention it either. Aside from Hewitt's interviews and reportage in the *Diario del Yaqui*, Ciudad Obregón's most prominent daily, the only mention made of this interesting episode is in Francisco Gómez-Jara, *El movimiento campesino en México*, p. 164. Perhaps the incident is not mentioned because of factional problems plaguing the PPS at the time; whatever the reasons, the subject certainly invites more investigation.

> Thus, the Ejidal Bank entered the game to reorganize not only the Ejidal Union, but the credit societies that depend on it, liquidating once and for all everything that smells of the *Partido Popular* in order to give entry . . . to the flag of the CNC, an adherent . . . of the PRI.[34]

This and other indications of government hostility to the collective *ejido* and its supporters did not in themselves transcend the ordinary rough style of politics which has characterized Sonora specifically and the Mexican Revolution generally for decades. But the intervention in the 1949 election in Sonora came at a time when Lombardo Toledano and his colleagues were divided over the question of whether even to participate in electoral politics. When the moderate *agraristas* subsequently left the PPS, the already-weakened *agrarista* forces were further fractionated politically. At the same time, the PPS and the General Union of Mexican Workers and *campesinos* (UGOCM), a PPS derivative, were in effect excluded from electoral politics unless they lost. This prejudice, along with the anti-collectivist policy of the Ejidal Bank, dried up the greatest political asset of the nonrevolutionary independent *agraristas*—the prospect of gaining a share of the system's rewards.

Of course, the fact that the Ejidal Bank was discriminating against the collective *ejidos* could have surprised no one familiar with the new tone of the agrarian reform. *Ejidatarios* had long complained of corruption in the bank's handling of ejidal produce,[35] and the Union of Local Credit Societies of the Yaqui valley—a collectivist organization—had been embattled against the individualists since 1948.[36] Data from the Ejidal Bank show that credit to the ejidal sector stagnated after 1937 relative to agricultural credit to private farms, achieving an average annual growth-rate of 2.6 percent over the 1940–1950 decade, and a dismal 5.4-percent average annual growth-rate over the entire 1940–1970 period. Meanwhile, agricultural credit from the official bank serving the private sector showed a different, more positive trend, averaging a 25-percent annual growth-rate from 1940 to 1970. Private agricultural credit also grew, averaging a growth-rate of 11.7 percent annually over the period 1943–1969 (see Table A11 in appendix). Only after 1965 did private sources begin to withdraw credit from agriculture.

In Sonora, official credit followed the irrigation districts, as did the rest of the benefits of the northwest development plan. Private credit societies sprang up on the Hermosillo coast, in the Guaymas valley, and in the northern irrigation district (no. 37) which included Caborca, Altar, Pitiquito, Trincheras, and Oquitoa.[37] Meanwhile, the eastern half of Sonora,

34. *El Imparcial*, June 21, 1950, p. 1.
35. E.g., *El Imparcial*, Oct. 27, 1947; Aug. 20, 1948; Dec. 22, 1948.
36. Ibid., March 2, 1948, p. 1.
37. Hewitt, *Modernizing Mexican Agriculture*, pp. 147–148. By 1949, some 40 private credit societies formed a National Association of Credit Unions to inveigh against land re-

along with much of the rest of the nation, languished without the benefit of official credit resources. While privileged areas such as the Laguna, the Yaqui valley, and the Yucatán peninsula regularly absorbed half the loans of the Ejidal Bank, only 13 percent of all *ejidatarios* could expect to receive official credit in a given year.[38]

The PPS and UGOCM in Sonora were unable to sustain their non-revolutionary left *agrarismo* for the same reasons that others had failed before them: they were totally excluded from the system of rewards available through the regime, while their leaders were being offered lucrative and prestigious inducements to prostrate themselves before the government. As the rebels reeled from the penalties of opposition to the PRI, Maximiliano López, a charismatic leader from Ciudad Obregón, former anti-*yocupicista*, member of the PPS, and UGOCM founder, tried to remobilize the *campesinos* for a new wave of land invasions. On November 26, 1953, he was shot and killed as he opened the door of his home.[39] The message to the *agraristas* was clear, and agrarian politics entered a period of relative quiescence.

AGRICULTURAL PRODUCTION, AGRARIAN REFORM, AND THE ECONOMIC MIRACLE

During the Cárdenas years, the *campesino*-oriented agrarian reform had dominated state policy toward the agricultural sector, and it was not until 1939 and 1940 that the government turned its attention more fully to the goal of increasing agricultural production per se. As Table A12 shows, agriculture during the transitional years of the economy was able, along with manufacturing and cattle-raising, to sustain its proportion of national production. By 1945 these three activities comprised over 40 percent of national income. The main sources of agricultural growth were in the export crops: rice, wheat, sugar, coffee, barley, cotton, garbanzos, and sesame. Meanwhile other primary goods, notably petroleum and mining, stagnated and were unable to meet the expanding economy's needs for foreign exchange. The agricultural sector became the primary aspect of the "engine of growth" for the national economy by generating foreign exchange to pay for ISI.

A number of factors influenced the continuation and acceleration of agricultural-development programs as a key tenet of developmental populism. Of course, there was a certain logic inherent in the structure of the economy, since nearly 65 percent of the population was rural in 1940.[40]

---

form, for agricultural price guarantees, and for more official credit to the private sector. (See also *El Imparcial*, Dec. 10, 1949, p. 1.)

38. CDIA, *Estructura agraria*, p. 776.
39. *El Imparcial*, Nov. 27, 1953, p. 1.
40. CDIA, *Estructura agraria*, p. 380.

This logic was buttressed by intensive attempts under Cárdenas to orga- nize the *campesinos* and to make them productive members of the devel- oping economy. The impetus given to agriculture during the 1930s, and its status as chief support of the national economy, encouraged the state to continue to favor farmers through infrastructure and credit (generally with political considerations in mind, of course). Looking further to the future, economists of the period also realized that plans for rural develop- ment benefitted national growth plans in other ways. The industrial work- force was too small to provide an effective mass market for domestically produced goods; the proletarianization of the subsistence-farm sector and the commercialization of farm output provided a natural source, not only of cheap labor, but of potential domestic-market expansion.[41] And in view of industry's chronic inability to absorb all of the migrating workforce from the countryside, commercial agriculture could (and did) increase its share of rural wage-employment.[42]

Less direct political pressures and circumstances impinged upon the agricultural policy decisions of the 1940s as well. After the Cárdenas pe- riod, both Manuel Ávila Camacho and his successor, Miguel Alemán, be- lieved that the second phase of the agrarian reform—its "technification" for greater production—had to be undertaken at the cost of continued *campesino*-oriented reforms in land tenure.[43] The new Agrarian Code of 1942 heralded the change in mass politics in the countryside, emphasiz- ing "order in the *campo*, . . . which can only be achieved by stopping the excessive and unconscionable ejidalist policy and by guaranteeing to pri- vate individuals the proprietorship of their lands."[44] Ávila Camacho, the new president, further changed the revolutionary government's claim to populist legitimacy when he restated an age-old canon of capitalist development:

> The businessman needs to count on the stimulus that his foresight, con- stant effort, and bravery in challenging risks is going to meet with institu- tional guarantees. For his part, the worker will with simple clarity reach the conviction that production benefits not only the businesses and the homes of the workers, but the health of the entire republic.[45]

The new, modified Agrarian Code symbolized the state's changing emphasis favoring private landholding in agricultural production. It was the first legislative pillar of the counter-reform and, along with the Law of Agricultural Credit of 1955, represented the most important legislative

41. Mosk, *Industrial Revolution*, p. 204.
42. Reynolds, *The Mexican Economy*, p. 42.
43. González Navarro, *La CNC*, pp. 191 and 194; *Excelsior*, Aug. 29, 1946; Mexico, Con- greso, *Diario de los debates*, XLI (Oct. 18, 1946): 3–5.
44. Aguilera Gómez, *La reforma agraria*, p. 145.
45. Mexico, *Cámara de Diputados, Los presidentes ante la nación, 1821–1966*, vol. IV, pp. 149–150.

change in agrarian reform since Cárdenas' 1934 Agrarian Code. Like the other parts of the official agrarian-reform apparatus, the new code favored private property and export agriculture over the ejidal sector and subsistence *minifundios*. Plantations of key export items such as henequen, rubber, coconut, grapes, olives, vanilla, and quinine were declared immune from official land limitations up to 300 hectares.[46] Similarly, cattle ranches under the new law were exempt from land limits previously imposed, "up to the limit of land area indispensable for maintaining 200 head of cattle."[47] Certificates of immunity for a period of 25 years were routinely granted under the new code; during this time the land named in the concession was not subject to any action under the agrarian-reform laws.[48] Cattle-raising *ejidatarios*, in contrast, had to provide at least half the cattle necessary to cover whatever land area they wished to petition—which, of course, effectively excluded the landless *campesinos* from early participation in cattle-raising enterprises altogether.[49]

In addition, the new code placed great emphasis on entitlement of each *ejidatario*, which effectively parcelled the *ejido*, ostensibly in order to "render the security of [the land's] possession to each *ejidatario*."[50] This new emphasis reinforced the individualistic turn the official agrarian reform was assuming, abetting a political and credit campaign favoring smallholders that was already taking place in the *campo*. While the battle raged against the PPS, the UGOCM, and the collective *ejidos*, the government ostentatiously presented a large number of *ejidatarios* with "Certificates of Agrarian Rights." On a single day in 1949, 1,200 certificates were dispensed to 27 *ejidos* in Sonora.[51] Less than two months later, some 1,543 certificates were announced on two different occasions, involving the same *ejidos* as the first wave.[52] Since the census figure for these *ejidos* totalled only 1,171, the second and third reportings were probably a repetition, or at most an update, of the first.

The new Law of Agricultural Credit of December 31, 1942, further enhanced the individualist cause by reducing collective ejidal exploitation to a mere alternative under the law, rather than the officially preferred mode of agrarian organization, and by dropping the requirement that *ejidos* use medium- and long-term infrastructure credit communally.[53]

46. *Código Agrario de los Estados Unidos Mexicanos*, Book Two, Title II, chap. 8, arts. 104–114; in *Diario Oficial*, April 27, 1943.

47. *Ibid.*

48. *Ibid.*, Book Four, Title III, chap. 2.

49. *Ibid.*, Book Three, Title I, chap. 1.

50. Aguirre Avellaneda, *La política ejidal*, p. 79.

51. *El Imparcial*, Sept. 23, 1949, p. 1.

52. *Ibid.*, Nov. 5 and 7, 1949, both p. 1. The Nov. 5 story cites 1,543 certificates; the Nov. 7, 1,546.

53. *Diario Oficial*, March 27, 1943. This particularly damaged the Yaqui valley collectivists who had operated under the Presidential Accord of March 9, 1941, which recognized the priority of collective cultivation in the valley. (*El Imparcial*, Feb. 17, 1948, p. 1.)

Later, in 1947, ejidal-credit organizations were subsumed under the control of the Ejidal Bank, which assumed full authority for the capitalization, development, marketing, and credit functions of the *ejido*, at the expense of the local societies.[54]

The impact of the new legislation was not felt fully until Miguel Alemán became president, at the end of 1946. His regime combined a counter-reform orientation with an open-door policy toward foreign capital; tighter control of the CTM and CNC; and high-cost federal capitalization of some areas of agricultural production, at the conscious neglect of other, less productive areas. As the budget data for the agricultural and irrigation projects show (see Table A13 in appendix), Alemán initiated a period of heavy government spending in agriculture that continued for roughly 25 years. His policy orientation toward agricultural development and agrarian reform put technical and managerial expertise and heavy public investment into the private sector, at the expense of the *ejidatarios* who had been beneficiaries of the *cardenista* agrarian reform.

Increased public investment in agriculture was not, however, unique to the Alemán government. Cárdenas had appropriated an average of 8.4 million pesos annually to the Agrarian Department, 7.1 percent of total public expenditure. Ávila Camacho had continued to spend heavily in the agricultural sector, averaging 10.1 million pesos yearly, or 7.3 percent of total public expenditure.[55] What separated Alemán from his predecessors was the degree to which he shunted federal spending away from the *ejido* to the private holding; the increased emphasis on large-scale irrigation projects (and corresponding neglect of small irrigation works); the initiation of seed- and yield-improvement centers, later recognized as the foci of the "green revolution"; and the general emphasis on export agriculture, at the expense of domestically consumed foodstuffs. Alemán set the tone for an agrarian policy that lasted until the time of Echeverría (1970–1976). It is therefore worthwhile for us to examine each of the aspects mentioned above in the context of Sonoran development, as Sonora was one of the prime recipients of credit and technology under the counter-reform.

SONORA IN THE POSTWAR PERIOD

Sonora in the first half of the 1940s did not yet reflect the dramatic new agrarian policies of Ávila Camacho, though the stage was being set for future combat in the postwar period, pitting CTM against CNC, individualists against collectivists, and the official, agrarian-reform-turned-capitalist, against the anti-official, left *agrarismo*. In the Yaqui valley in 1940–1945, farm organization and production had improved rapidly, both in the

54. Aguirre Avellaneda, pp. 80–81.
55. CDIA, *Estructura agraria*, appendix IX–5; James W. Wilkie, *The Mexican Revolution: Federal Expenditure and Social Change Since 1910*, p. 130.

Table 7

Average Yearly Rice and Wheat Yields
in the Yaqui River Valley,
1938-1943[a]
(kg/hectare)

CROP	ALL FARMS	EJIDOS
Wheat	774	823
Rice	1,636	1,688

[a]SOURCE: Mexico, Banco Nacional de Crédito Ejidal, S.A., *El sistema de producción colectiva en los ejidos del valle del Yaqui, Sonora*, p. 38.

ejidal sector and among small property-holders. The 1938–1943 yields in valuable crops such as wheat and rice were larger, and productivity was comparable across land-tenure sectors, as is shown in Table 7.

In the Mayo valley, as we saw in the last chapter, most of the definitive ejidal possessions were not complete until 1941 and 1942. Since irrigation works had for the most part not been completed, organization and exploitation of the land were still relatively primitive.[56] The rest of the state was similar, generally involved in the mundane politics of local land exploitation, organizing in the CNC and CTM according to allegiances forged in the 1930s, and gearing up for the political struggle over the remains of collectivism in the state.

The actual process of redistributing land in Sonora had slowed to a crawl. After execution of the Mayo valley grants that had been forced upon Yocupicio by Cárdenas, little was done toward continuing the land distribution which had reached its peak in 1937 and 1938. The Sonoran decline in ejidal land reform followed a national trend. While from 1930 to 1940 ejidal grants surged, the trend was reversed in striking fashion during the 1940–1950 period (see Table 8). The number of new ejidal grants slowed, and the proportion of land held by *ejidos* relative to private properties over five hectares stagnated nationwide, and actually declined in Sonora. From 1940 to 1950 only 43 *ejidos* were created, compared with 187 in the previous decade. There was a similar trend in the private realm, where *minifundios* of five hectares or less declined relative to larger private holdings. By 1950, as Table 9 shows, the ratio of *minifundios* to larger private holdings had been cut to half its 1940 level, both in number and in area. Locally, in Sonora, the trend away from ejidal grants

56. The creation of the Río Mayo Irrigation District did not take place until 1951. (*Diario Oficial*, July 26, 1951; *El Imparcial*, Aug. 6, 1951.)

Table 8

Ejidal Growth in Mexico, 1930-1950[a]

(hectares)

YEAR	NATIONAL		SONORA	
	NUMBER	AREA	NUMBER	AREA
1930	4,189	8,344,651	38	188,055
1940	14,680	28,922,808	225	938,905
1950	17,579	38,893,899	268	1,367,337

[a]SOURCE: México, Secretaía de la Economía Nacional, Dirección General de Estadística, *Censos agrícolas-ganaderos y ejidales*, 1930, 1940, 1950.

Table 9

Private Land Tenure Trends, 1930-1950[a]

	1930		1940		1950	
	NUMBER	AREA[b]	NUMBER	AREA[b]	NUMBER	AREA[b]
National						
1. ≤5 hectares	576,547	889	928,593	1,157	889,393	1,363
2. >5 hectares	277,473	122,361	290,336	98,669	360,798	105,260
3. 1:2[c]	2.08	.0007	3.20	.0117	2.47	.013
Sonora						
1. ≤5 hectares	6,880	13	7,784	18	5,532	14
2. >5 hectares	6,130	6,421	5,931	5,642	8,485	8,393
3. 1:2	1.12	.0019	1.31	.0031	0.65	.0017

[a]SOURCE: *Censos agrícolas-ganaderos y ejidales*, 1930, 1940, 1950.
[b]Area given in thousand hectares.
[c]Ratio of *minifundios* to private holdings over 5 hectares.

continued throughout the decade of the 1950s. The number of ejidal grants fell to a sexennial average of 38 from 1940 to 1964 (see chart). Only during the last years of Díaz Ordaz' presidency did the land reform regain some prominence, and then only by wholesale grants of worthless, arid land in answer to *campesino* unrest, as we shall see.

The real agrarian action was taking place in the acceleration of certificates of immunity for cattle-raising issued by the national government.[57]

57. Between 1938 and 1950, Sonoran landowners benefitted from 41 certificates of immunity, covering 598,460 hectares. (*Diario Oficial de la Federación*.)

EJIDAL GRANTS IN SONORA, 1940-1970[a]

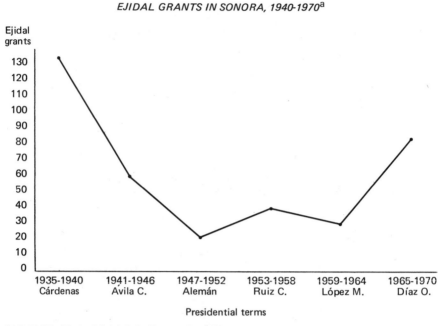

The agrarian-reform bureaucracy busied itself expediting 25-year certificates barring land-reform petitions in much of the state. Despite the fact
that the new Agrarian Code stipulated that the land-reform needs of the
local populace must be met before immunity could be granted,[58] a raft of
such certificates were circulated. In terms of cattle production, they seem
to have had the desired effect, although data from individual concessions
are not available. After 1945, cattle production remained the most stable
agricultural enterprise, and it provided a mainstay of foreign exchange for
the economy even after agricultural production declined, starting in the
1960s.[59] But the undeniable cost of immunity was a regressive land-tenure
policy which manifested itself in *campesino* rebellion, beginning in the
late 1950s, as we shall see.

Land Tenure in Sonora, 1940–1970

A direct indictment of the counter-reform's approach to land-tenure
questions comes from the results of the combined policies toward ejidal

58. *Código Agrario*, Book Two, Title II, chap. 8. That Sonora did not qualify under this
criterion is clear from the fact that over 50 percent of Sonoran land in 1950 lay in plots of
more than 5,000 hectares (see Table 10).

59. Cattle production averaged a 4.4-percent annual increase from 1940 to 1970, while
other agricultural production increased at an annual rate of 4.8 percent. After 1960, agricultural growth began a gradual downturn, while cattle-raising stabilized at a high rate of
growth (see Table A19 in appendix).

Table 10
Private Land Tenure in Sonora, 1940-1970[a]

YEAR	PERCENTAGE OF POPULATION		PERCENTAGE OF LAND	PERCENTAGE OF LAND IN PLOTS OF >5,000 HECTARES
1940	Bottom	72.6 own	0.77	
	Top	5.9 own	85.15	60.0
	Smallholder[b]	17.0 own	1.68	
1950	Bottom	65.0 own	1.06	
	Top	9.2 own	85.45	56.19
	Smallholder	25.2 own	1.95	
1960	Bottom	60.4 own	0.86	
	Top	12.1 own	87.17	53.27
	Smallholder	24.3 own	1.35	
1970	Bottom	52.1 own	0.89	
	Top	16.0 own	84.12	41.79
	Smallholder	27.3 own	1.65	

[a]SOURCE: *Censos agrícolas-ganaderos y ejidales*, 1940, 1950, 1960, 1970.
[b]Smallholder here refers to the much-touted *parvifundio* of 10-100 hectares.

reform, national irrigation districts, and colonization. As Table 10 shows, the basic structure of private land tenure in Sonora did not change after 1940. Though the data indicate some slight attenuation in land concentration over the thirty years between Cárdenas and Echeverría, the fact that in 1970 over 40 percent of rural land still lay in plots of over 5,000 hectares clearly shows the impact of the counter-reform.

The single most promising aspect of private land tenure—the increase of *parvifundios*, or smallholdings between 10 and 100 hectares—is to some degree a superficial reform. In fact, most of the improvement noticeable in the aggregate data of Table 10 resulted from new colonization projects on the Hermosillo coast, in the Guaymas valley, and in Caborca, Pitiquito, and Altar, along with continued colonization of the Yaqui valley.[60] These colonies, later to become national irrigation districts as well, became centers of agricultural production because of the wide-scale use of irrigation pumps, which tapped subterranean water reserves. In keeping with Alemán's agricultural-production priorities, the exploitation of underground water reserves accompanied the development of high-yield

60. The Hermosillo coast was the first of the new colonization efforts, beginning at the end of 1949; Guaymas followed in 1951. All colonists had to be self-financing, which eliminated the redistributive aspect of the agrarian reform almost entirely.

Table 11

Value of On-Site Irrigation Works,

1940 and 1970[a]

(thousands of pesos)

YEAR	NATIONAL	SONORA	SONORA'S PERCENTAGE OF NATIONAL VALUE
1940	101,446	6,200	6.1
1970	2,327,435	413,833	17.8

[a]SOURCE: Censos agrícolas-ganaderos y ejidales, 1940, 1970.

seeds, increases in fertilizer production, the mechanization of agriculture, increases in credit to the private sector, and extensions of the government price-support program.[61] Due to this set of policies implemented by Alemán, and continued more or less without interruption until the 1970s, Sonoran agricultural production underwent a profound transformation, resulting in a mixed record of successes and failures—a record that accentuated both the productive possibilities of Mexican agriculture and the limits of the dualistic approach under which one part of the state thrived while another stagnated.

The irrigation districts—both the ancient river valleys and the new colonies—became the focus of the development plans of the 1950s and 1960s. Just as credit followed the irrigation districts, so did capitalization. The value of machinery and irrigation infrastructure climbed rapidly in Sonora (see Tables 11 and 12). Excluding the major dams and canals, which generated the main expenditures of the postwar period,[62] in-situ irrigation works grew to a value of over 400 million pesos by 1970. Of that value, only 1,912,000 pesos (0.5 percent) went to irrigation units of less than five hectares, and 35,124,000 pesos (8.5 percent) was the total allocated to ejidal plots. Of the 311 million pesos invested in pumping stations, about 284 million went to plots over five hectares, 1.5 million to minifundios, and 26 million to the entire ejidal sector.[63] The highly-touted irrigation districts produced an ever-increasing proportion of national agricultural production until, by 1960, they yielded a full 40

61. For an article outlining the Alemán irrigation policy, see Adolfo Orive Alba, "Programa de irrigación del C. Presidente Miguel Alemán." Under Alemán, over 14.5 million pesos went to the Altar, Caborca, and Pitiquito irrigation projects alone, and another 9.6 million pesos to the Río Sonora. (Mexico, SRH, Informe anual, 1953.)

62. As a single example, the Álvaro Obregón dam on the Yaqui river cost 149 million pesos in only three years. Of the roughly 55,000 hectares opened up by the La Angostura dam on the upper Yaqui in 1941, all of it went to the private sector. (SRH, Informe anual, 1953–1955; Hewitt, Modernizing Mexican Agriculture, p. 145.)

63. Censo agrícola–ganadero y ejidal, 1970.

Table 12

Mechanization of Irrigation Districts in Various

Geographic Zones of Mexico, 1964[a]

ZONE	PERCENTAGE OF MECHANIZATION		
	TOTAL	PARTIAL	NOT MECHANIZED
Northwest	65.81	32.57	1.62
North	31.57	53.60	14.83
Northeast	37.61	30.74	31.65
Center	13.63	43.93	42.44
South	16.54	7.14	76.32

[a]SOURCE: José María Dorronsoro, "La mecanización de la agricultura en los distritos de riego en México," p. 109.

percent of the national crop value.[64] In Sonora, vanguard of large-scale irrigation, 70 percent of state production came from irrigation districts.[65]

By these impressive production gains, it is apparent in retrospect that the Sonoran economy at the end of World War II had been in bud, merely marking time until sufficient water resources could lend impetus to the development plans of regional farmers and politicians. The gradual development of major irrigation works under Alemán brought about the flowering of Sonora's agricultural-export economy, which dominated local affairs throughout the 1960s. By 1950, the "Mocuzari" dam on the Mayo river permitted irrigation of part of the Mayo valley, turning the rich coastal soil into first-class farmland for which battles would later be fought. By 1952, there were dams on the rivers Altar, Bavispe, and Yaqui, with others planned for the Yaqui and Mayo valleys.[66] Between 1947 and 1952, 21,380 hectares of newly irrigated land were opened up as a result of federal spending under the Alemán government; additionally, many older irrigation works in the state were improved, serving 7,940 hectares (see Table A14 in appendix).

In 1945 the Hermosillo coast was opened to large-scale well-drilling to exploit the underground water reserves of the region. By 1950 there were 258, and by 1955 a total of 484 wells had been dug in one of the most impressive colonization efforts ever attempted by the Mexican government. Some 110,000 hectares of formerly arid land were irrigated by pumps that

64. Aguilera Gómez, *La reforma agraria*, p. 246.

65. The Sonoran statistic represents the 1958–1959 irrigation-district crop value (1,082,340 pesos) as a percentage of the state production total (1,542,800 pesos). (Taken from SRH, *Informe anual*, 1969, and *Censo agrícola–ganadero y ejidal*, 1960, respectively.)

66. SRH, *Informe anual*, 1971–1972, app. 2.

extracted 900 million cubic meters of underground water annually.[67] Colonies in the Guaymas valley added some 40,000 hectares through pump irrigation.[68] Colonization, the will-o'-the-wisp that had eluded Mexican governments since Iturbide, gained new adherents in the small property-holders of the Yaqui valley, the political elites of Hermosillo, and the commercial leaders of Guaymas. Colonization by private small-holders did much in the 1950s and 1960s to divert the agrarian reform from campesinos to an agricultural bourgeoisie which produced under highly capitalized, technologically sophisticated conditions.[69] As we shall see in Chapter 7, this new class of colonists and private landowners used a wide variety of ruses in the 1970s to avoid the constraints of the laws against land concentration.

Mechanization in the irrigated zones proceeded apace. American machine companies had for some time tested new models of agricultural machinery in Sonora before marketing them in the United States, and the Alemán government and its successors encouraged the capitalization of agriculture in general.[70] The northwest, including Sonora, rapidly out-stripped the rest of the nation in mechanizing agricultural production, which even extended to the richer ejidos[71] (see Table 12). By 1970, the capitalization of agriculture in Sonora had produced a remarkable dual-ism, characterized by a few highly technological, costly irrigation dis-tricts producing crops for export, and the rest of the state remaining rela-tively valueless, producing at best for self-consumption (see Tables A15 and A16 in appendix).

Table 13 shows to some degree the dualism which characterized Sono-ran agriculture by 1970. Land value in both the ejidal and minifundio sec-tors remained far below that of the larger private holdings, as did on-site irrigation and general capitalization of holdings. But to look merely at the capital invested in various holdings does not fully disclose the polariza-

67. Ángel Jiménez Villalobos, "Condiciones de las aguas subterraneas en el Distrito de Riego #51, Costa de Hermosillo, Sonora," p. 65. Later data cite 498 wells and 118,066 hec-tares harvested, with 855,732 cubic meters of water. (CDIA, Empleo, desempleo y subempleo en el sector agropecuario, vol. II, p. 172.)

68. Sonora, Informe rendido ante la XXXIX legislatura constitucional del estado . . . del 1° de Septiembre de 1950 al 31 de Agosto de 1951, p. 34. If this report is correct, the vast majority of the pumps installed were financed by the colonos themselves. The program of pequeña irrigación in Sonora was virtually nonexistent, and only 11 wells had been drilled under the program by 1953. More on this later.

69. The number of colonists in Sonora is unclear. The Censo agrícola—ganadero y ejidal consistently underestimates the number, arriving at a statewide total of 243 colonos. The SRH estimated 765 colonists working land on the Hermosillo Coast alone in 1975. (Censo, 1970; SRH, Informe anual, 1976.)

70. Hewitt, Modernizing Mexican Agriculture, p. 142.

71. In the northwest—which includes Baja California, Sonora, and Sinaloa—59 percent of the ejidal sector was totally mechanized, compared with 74 percent of the private sector. (José María Dorronsoro, "La mecanización de la agricultura en los distritos de riego en Méx-ico," p. 109.)

Table 13

Land Tenure and Capital Invested, Sonora, 1970[a]

PLOT (hectares)	NUMBER OF PLOTS	LAND VALUE PER HECTARE (pesos)	IN SITU IRRIGATION (pesos)	MACHINERY (pesos)	OTHER (pesos)
>5	9,910	82.81	376,797	1,339,096	943,286
≤5	3,120	3.23	1,912	172,662	25,382
Ejidos	417	0.52	35,124	93,617	33,319

[a]SOURCE: *Censo agrícola-ganadero y ejidal*, 1970.

tion of farm life in Sonora. Not only do the farms within the irrigation districts dominate export-crop production, they are also responsible for the bulk of domestically consumed foodstuffs and seed production for corn and vegetables (see Tables A15 and A16 in appendix). The Sierra and other marginal areas of Sonora produce little for themselves and even less for the market. While in other regions of Mexico undercapitalized smallholdings may generate a surplus in domestic comestibles, in Sonora—a land without water—the poor small farm generally does not produce.

To counter the polarization of productive power that so obviously divided Sonora at the end of the Cárdenas epoch, the governments of the 1940s proposed a national program of small irrigation, a network of canals and pumps to be built and maintained by the federal government with some state cooperation.[72] This program, now called "irrigation for rural development," systematically ignored Sonora's eastern proprietors, both *minifundistas* and *ejidatarios*, as Table 14 implies. While thousands of hectares of land in other areas of Mexico received some slight attention from the small-irrigation program, only about 5,700 hectares of Sonoran land received any benefits from the program, much of it in the irrigation districts themselves. The remainder of irrigation improvements at the local *minifundio* level came from self-financed projects—which, in most cases, meant that they did not occur in areas not producing a cash surplus and without credit available, i.e., the Sierra and the northern desert.[73]

The result of this policy becomes apparent, not in the aggregate data of the decennial census, but in the more revealing data of disaggregated regional capital investment (see Table A17 in appendix). The Sierra and other municipalities outside the irrigation districts derive virtually none of their capital investment from on-site irrigation works, even in the municipalities that lie in the river valleys supplying water to the irrigation

72. Orive Alba, "Programa de irrigación," p. 23.
73. In the 1960 *Censo agrícola–ganadero y ejidal*, a sum of 514 million pesos is listed as the credit outlay for Sonora. Of that amount, 80 percent went to plots over five hectares and the other 20 percent to *ejidos*. *Minifundios* received no credit.

Table 14

Land Irrigated Through Pequeña Irrigación Program,
1937-1970[a]

YEARS	(1) NATIONAL (hectares)	(2) SONORA (hectares)	PERCENTAGE (2/1)
1937-1940	5,031	0	0.0
1941-1946	37,044	540	1.5
1947-1952	146,442	481	0.3
1953-1958	147,993	2,415	1.6
1959-1964	109,698	2,260	2.1
1965-1970	85,108	0	0.0

[a]SOURCE: México, Secretaría de Recursos Hidráulicos, *Informes Anuales*, 1947-1971.

districts.[74] *Minifundios* and *ejidos*, with rare exceptions, have less in the way of on-site irrigation as a percentage of total capital investment, even though their level of investment is much lower than the large landholdings. Finally, a correspondingly dismal assessment of land values in areas outside federal irrigation districts is compounded further by the capital bias against *minifundios* and *ejidos*. In view of such data, it is a wonder that *ejidatarios* and smallholders in the Sierra and desert produce as much of the Sonoran agricultural product as they presently manage. The *minifundio* survives in Sonora, as is again apparent from capital-investment statistics, by using its marginal resources to the fullest extent, leaving no land of any value unworked—in sharp contrast to the larger landholders and *ejidatarios*.

Despite their tenacity, and largely due to the factors just mentioned, many *ejidatarios* and *minifundistas* have been forced to rent their lands to cattlemen or large landholders, perpetuating the cycle that began with the settlement of Sonora. Resultant shifts in the workforce have benefitted the large farmer and the industrialist, who need the army of wage-labor available and idle for the two-crop harvests that have characterized Sonora for much of the postwar period. During the period 1940–1970, the proportion of the population economically active in agriculture, cattle-raising, forestry, hunting, and fishing sank from 53.7 to 38.5 percent, despite

74. Some *municipios* influenced by headwaters of the major Sonoran rivers include: Río San Miguel: Cucurpe, Opodepe, Rayón, Horcasitas; upper Río Sonora: Bacoachi, Arizpe, Banámichi, Huepac, San Felipe, Aconchi, Baviácora, Ures; Río Moctezuma: Cumpas, San Pedro, Suaqui, Villa Pesqueira; Río Bavispe: Fronteras, Agua Prieta, Huachinera, Bacerac, Bavispe, Oputo, Huasabas. By and large, their proportion of irrigation is the same as less privileged areas, and the share allocated to *minifundios* seems unchanged.

a 3.8-percent birthrate in Sonora and an annual migration rate to the northwest of 4.9 percent.[75]

In summary, land, capital, and irrigation infrastructure formed the basis for a pattern of concentration of resources during the counter-reform years of 1940–1970. As the tables on irrigation and property (Tables A16, A17, and A18 in appendix) show, Sonora in 1970 bore the scars of thirty years of programs dedicated to the eradication of the *minifundio*, regional isolation of the *ejido*, and cost–benefit criteria within the land-reform bureaucracy that effectively negated the promise of "social obligation" to the countryside under the Revolution. The 14 Sonoran municipalities within the official national irrigation districts blossomed until the mid-1960s under the same policies that impoverished the 55 municipalities of the Sierra and desert regions of the state. The dualism of the counter-reform is painfully evident in these data.

The Resurgence of Mass Agrarismo

It is of course difficult to pinpoint a resurgence of *campesino* unrest in a state characterized by institutionalized combat over land, credit, and water among the competing forces of government, landowner, and landless *campesino*. Certainly *agrarismo* was dealt a severe blow with the assassination of Maximiliano "Machi" López in 1953—a blow compounded by internal strife between Lombardo and other leaders of the PPS and UGOCM. But despite these grave handicaps, a seed of *agrarismo* remained alive in the local land-tenure struggles of the Yaqui and Mayo valleys. During the three decades of the counter-reform (1940–1970), *agrarismo* in Sonora became identified with the locally famous struggles over Bacame, Sibolibampo, Capetamaya, and San Ignacio Río Muerto.

In the conflict between *ejidatarios* of Bacame, Etchojoa, and the proprietors of Sibolibampo—primarily Epifanio Salido—the Agrarian Department's unwillingness or inability to act decisively over a point of agrarian law resulted in more than twenty years of strife, sometimes bloody, always deadly serious.[76] Sibolibampo had been granted a 25-year certificate of immunity for cattle-raising in 1946. Shortly thereafter, however, due to improved postwar irrigation works, the land became agri-

75. Birthrate from Mexico, Secretaría de Industria y Comercio, *Anuario estadístico*, 1970–1971; migration rate from CDIA, *Empleo, disempleo y subempleo*, p. 378. PEA (population economically active) statistics from Nacional Financiera, *Sonora: fideicomiso para la promoción de conjuntos, parques y ciudades industriales*, 1971.

76. Details of this summary come from 1977 interviews with legal advisers to Bacame and other Mayo valley *ejidos*, and *ejidatarios* from Bacame, including the *comisario ejidal* (head of the political organization of the *ejido*) and two *socios delegados* of ejidal-credit societies in Bacame. Other sources are *El Imparcial*, Aug. 2, 1961; Oct. 20, 1962; Nov. 15, 1963; and Nov. 26, 1971; and a paper entitled "Recorrido al sur de Sonora," prepared by a former PRI youth-sector president during the election campaign travels of Carlos Armando Biébrich in 1973.

culturally valuable and changed classification. The Salidos subdivided and sold tracts of the land without Agrarian Department authorization, violating the conditions of the plot's immunity. *Ejidatarios* from Bacame petitioned the Agrarian Department that Sibolibampo had become an agricultural *latifundio* (4,600 hectares of irrigated farmland). Petitioners from two other potential "new centers of agrarian population," Machi López and Victoria del Yaqui, also challenged the Salido family *latifundio*. Even after responding to some *campesino* petitions,[77] and after the expiration of the certificate of immunity (which was respected, even in its owner's violation of the law), Sibolibampo in 1973 still monopolized 2,600 hectares of prime agricultural land. In 1975 conflict again quickened, adding measurably to the crisis of southern Sonora in the last years of *echeverrismo*.

Capetamaya, another conflict which later dominated the 1975–1976 invasions of the Mayo river valleys, also had its roots in the years of the counter-reform. After some twenty years of petitions and resolutions, the Agrarian Department in 1960 announced the grant of 1,630 hectares of irrigated land to the new *ejido* Antonio Rosales.[78] Shortly thereafter, however, the courts granted injunctions to the owners of the petitioned lands and ultimately decided the grant was invalid because the landowners were "small property-owners." The Agrarian Department offered the *campesinos* land in Guaymas, but this was refused. The petitions stayed in the courts while the *campesinos* repeatedly invaded the land, were jailed, relocated, and threatened. In 1975 and 1976, Capetamaya was invaded and cleared by soldiers at least seven times.

San Ignacio Río Muerto, which in 1975 became the bloody symbol of the crisis in Sonoran agrarian politics, also petitioned land under the counter-reform.[79] In fact, according to one recent account, the lands petitioned were adjudicated in 1954 by Governor Ignacio Soto, but the company *Irrigadora del Yaqui* had subdivided the land, causing the proceeding to bog down until the 1975 invasions.[80] As we shall see in Chapter 7, even the post-massacre land division in San Ignacio had its own peculiar ironies.

As important as these conflicts were to the survival of *agrarismo* in Sonora during the counter-reform, the outstanding invasion of the period

77. The *ejido* Augustín Melgar was created from 1,000 hectares of Sibolibampo in 1961. (*El Imparcial*, Aug. 2, 1961; *Diario Oficial*, July 28, 1961.) In response to a 1958 petition against Sibolibampo, however, the petitioners were granted 2,110 hectares from the estate of José María Maytorena and his widow in Guaymas, not Etchojoa. (*Diario Oficial*, Oct. 18, 1962; *El Imparcial*, Oct. 20, 1962.)

78. The land granted came from the minors Luis Mario and Mario Antonio Morales Salido and from José María Zaragoza. (*El Imparcial*, April 15, 1964, and Oct. 16, 1964; *Diario Oficial*, April 29, 1960, and April 9, 1964.)

79. *El Imparcial*, Oct. 25, 1958; Sept. 7, 1967.

80. Carlos Moncada, *Años de violencia en Sonora, 1955–1976*, p. 117.

took place in Cananea. In 1957, agrarian leaders of the PPS and UGOCM, under the guidance of Jacinto López, began to threaten invasions of various latifundia in Los Mochis, Sinaloa, unless the government rectified the land concentration that characterized that one-time haven of the United Sugar Company.[81] Subsequently, López and the UGOCM invaded the *latifundio* belonging to the Greene family's Cananea Cattle Company.[82] Though the UGOCM invaders were expelled by federal soldiers, and López was jailed,[83] a new wave of *campesino* militance surged. New land invasions in the Yaqui and Mayo valleys spurred the national government to move quickly to resolve the Cananea issue.[84] On February 8, 1959, Adolfo López Mateos arrived in Sonora to create seven collective cattle *ejidos* with a total area of 261,653 hectares. Jacinto López was released from jail, but few of the UGOCM petitioners received land under the grant. The CNC, always looking for new adherents, submitted its own list of petitioners, which was considered the official ejidal census, preempting the UGOCM's list which dated from 1953.[85] Once again, the CNC "carpetbagged" at the expense of the UGOCM.

Despite this distressing conclusion to the expropriation at Cananea, the UGOCM continued to agitate in the northwest. As soon as Jacinto López was released from his six-month stay in jail, he returned to land invasions in Sonora. In 1959 and 1960, the UGOCM invaded landholdings in Tubutama, Huatabampo, San Luis Río Colorado, and elsewhere, often encountering violent resistance by affiliates of either the CTM or the CNC.[86] Additionally, the left was beginning to fractionate again; Lombardo and Jacinto López disagreed over the merit of land invasions (among other things); Lázaro Cárdenas endorsed the new National Liberation Movement (MLN), which vied for *campesino* affiliation; and the Independent Campesino Confederation (CCI) sprang up in Baja California in 1963 un-

81. The UGOCM held a convention in Sinaloa in 1957, at which they issued this warning along with a more general promise of invasions in the states of Sonora and Baja California. (Huizer, *La lucha campesina*, p. 93.)

82. The Cananea Cattle Co., founded May 10, 1901, was the personal company of the legendary entrepreneur and copper magnate William C. Greene. (C. L. Sonnichsen, *Colonel Greene and the Copper Skyrocket*, pp. 232–248; see also Chapter 3 of this study.)

83. *El Imparcial*, Feb. 12, 15, and 25, 1958.

84. Actually, newspaper articles appeared in early 1957 indicating that the Cananea *latifundio* was to be nationalized. (*El Imparcial*, Feb. 6, 1957.) The governor's resolution ordering its acquisition is cited in Sonora, *Informe de gobierno del C. Álvaro Obregón, Gobernador Constitucional del Estado de Sonora, 1957–1958*. The speed with which the process was completed, and the publicity it received, indicate the impact of the invasions.

85. For more details of the Cananea expropriation, see: Ángel Bassols Batalla, *El noroeste de México*, pp. 548–551; Huizer, *La lucha campesina*, pp. 93–96; CDIA, *Estructura agraria*, pp. 504–509; Gómez-Jara, *El movimiento campesino*, p. 165; Moncada, *Años de violencia*, pp. 164–168; and Salomón Eckstein, *El ejido colectivo en México*, pp. 165–168.

86. *El Imparcial*, Nov. 17, 1959; Jan. 5 and 29, Feb. 15, April 13, and Dec. 6, 1960. The CTM, despite its problems in the 1940s, still controlled 194 agricultural-ejidal organisms in Sonora in 1968—over two-thirds of its national total. (Gómez-Jara, p. 259.)

der its charismatic leader Alfonso Garzón Santibañez. To this divided left fell the task of uniting the *campesinos* against a hostile federal and state government slowly nearing the brink of institutional political crisis.

CRACKS IN THE MIRACLE

As *campesino* unrest began to rebuild following the expropriation of Cananea and the advent of multiple representatives of anti-official *agrarismo*, the miracle of the Mexican economy, which had borne the weight of postwar legitimation, began to show strain. At the national level, the 1960s opened with the exposure of two frightful structural realities of the Mexican economy which had lain hidden during the aggregate growth of the 1940s and 1950s. As would soon become apparent under Díaz Ordaz (1964–1970), the agricultural sector was suffering from a process of "de-capitalization," and ISI was generating an impressive foreign debt and balance-of-payments problem. Related fiscal crisis, inflation, and unemployment tested the resilience of the national economy.

Over the entire 1940–1970 period, the agricultural sector provided the national economy with much of its dynamic, even after industrial production assumed a greater proportion of GDP. Export crops, especially coffee and cotton, generated much fiscal revenue for the tax-shy Mexican government. Though much of this revenue was returned to agriculture in the form of public infrastructure investment,[87] such public works were also key elements in sustaining the economy at large. After 1954, given the relative decrease in its importance to GDP, public investment in agriculture stagnated for a decade.[88] This became obvious in the production decline of the mid-1960s. In 1970, exports of agricultural and cattle products registered their first decennial decline as a proportion of GDP since the war boom.[89] The aggregate statistics actually underestimate this decline, as cattle exports buoyed up a sagging agricultural sector (see Table A19 in appendix).[90]

Another indicator of the decrease in capital investment in agriculture is the discrepancy between capital generated by agriculture to the banking system and capital allocated to agriculture through the banking system. In a 1967 study, Leopoldo Solís showed that the agricultural sector provided

87. CDIA, *Estructura agraria*, pp. 137–139. The fiscal balance in favor of agriculture added some 3 billion pesos to the agricultural and cattle-raising sector over the postwar decades 1940–1960.

88. *Ibid.*, Table II-20, p. 180.

89. *Ibid.*, Table II-10, p. 166.

90. From 1960 to 1970, animal exports increased to 4.4 percent of GDP (from 408 to 634 million pesos), while agricultural exports dropped from 22.1 to 15.3 percent of GDP (from 3,282 to 3,699 million pesos). (*Ibid.*, Table II-12, p. 169; see also Table A19 in the appendix and note 59 of this chapter.)

the banking system with about 19.4 percent of its total resources from 1942 to 1962. But the banks returned only an average of about 12.2 percent of their total resources to agriculture during this period, resulting in an estimated net loss of capital to farmers of nearly 2.5 billion pesos.[91]

During the 1950s, low agricultural prices resulted in a further loss of capital to this sector. Because agricultural prices were lower than the general price index in many years, the *Centro de Investigaciones Agrarias* estimated that an additional 3.6 billion pesos was lost to agriculture from 1940 to 1960.[92] Lower rural wages (averaging 15–25 percent lower than the urban minimum), private speculation and loan-sharking, and other subtle mechanisms within the economy contributed to a net decapitalization of Mexican agriculture totalling an estimated 3.1 billion pesos, including the beneficial effects of public investment in infrastructure.[93]

In itself, this decline in capitalization of the agricultural sector was not disastrous. But in the context of the Mexican postwar developmental model, the results of capital transfers away from agriculture combined with other equally important national trends to strip the economic miracle of some of its spectacular veneer, revealing cracks in the structure of postwar economic growth. We have mentioned a few of those national trends: the polarization of farm life, to the benefit of the agricultural bourgeoisie and at the expense of the *minifundista* and *ejidatario*; proletarianization of the *campesino*, in a system characterized by unequal income distribution between city and country; and agricultural-credit policies clearly favoring the private agricultural-export sector. Possibly even more important, however, were the problems generated by the model of ISI, the resultant foreign debt, and the recruitment of capital-intensive multinational corporations to propel the industrial economy.

While the Mexican state had dominated the domestic economy's advance in the first phase of ISI (1939–1958), state-led ISI had failed to solve the growing problems of underemployment, unemployment, and urbanization which attended the structural transformation of the traditional agrarian economy. ISI in Mexico was typically capital-intensive because it cheapened the relative cost of capital with respect to labor, especially in the post-1958 era of concentration on intermediate and capital goods.[94] Additionally, the open doors to foreign capital sharpened the tendency toward capital-intensive technology. The result in terms of unemploy-

91. Leopoldo Solís, "Hacia un análisis general a largo plazo del desarrollo económico de México," p. 63; cited in CDIA, *Estructura agraria*, Table II-21, p. 181.

92. CDIA, *Estructura agraria*, p. 141; Table II-22, p. 182.

93. Ibid., p. 143.

94. Villarreal, *El desequilibrio externo*, pp. 69 and 92–93. Overvaluation of the peso during this period also encouraged imports of capital, subsidizing foreign capital rather than domestic labor and capital. See also Rafael Izquierdo, "Protectionism in Mexico," pp. 270–271.

ment indicates that up to 27 percent of the work force was *officially* unemployed by 1970, with another 21.5 percent underemployed.[95]

In the period from 1959 to 1970, the expensive ISI program concentrated on intermediate and capital goods. Combined with increased imports of luxury consumer goods, a decline in agricultural revenue, and perhaps most important, the growing needs of domestic industry for capital (and incapacity to finance it), this resulted in greater demand for foreign capital and a skyrocketing foreign debt. Public foreign debt in the 1960s increasingly became not only the principal means of compensating for the mounting rents to foreign investment capital,[96] but also a key source of finance for social capital expenditures (irrigation, electrification, etc.) and public enterprises. Gradually, as public investment continued to rise and taxation remained unchanged, foreign debt became the mechanism by which the gap between public expenditure and public saving was closed.[97] Like the decapitalization of agriculture, it appeared in the late 1960s as a newly-evident structural condition of the Mexican economy; it would loom large in the political crisis of the 1970s.

CRACKS IN THE SONORAN EARTH

As if foreign debt and domestic unemployment did not bode ill enough for the Mexican political economy in the 1960s, new problems appeared in Sonora which exacerbated the tensions threatening to disrupt the forced harmony in this key export region of Mexico. During the counter-reform, as already noted, many *minifundistas* lost their lands and were forced onto the migratory farm-labor circuit, sustained by the two-season economy which the sunny, warm climate of the northwestern Pacific coast afforded Sonora.[98] Even in the richer areas—mainly the Yaqui and Mayo valleys, as far as the *minifundio* was concerned—the *minifundistas* failed, not because of inefficiency (see Table A17 in appendix), but because of the combined hardships imposed by capital shortage, water monopolies, underemployment, and—to a certain extent—economies of scale. According to a study made jointly by the agriculture and treasury departments and the Bank of Mexico, the northern Pacific region had

---

95. Villarreal, p. 90.

96. Foreign investment from 1959 to 1970 represents a net charge against the Mexican balance of payments. Rents on direct foreign investment exceeded the amount of that investment by 145 million dollars in 1970, and by 1,123 million in the years 1959–1970. (Nacional Financiera, *Informe anual*, 1959–1970; also Villarreal, p. 114.)

97. Rosario Green, *El endeudamiento público externo de México 1940–1973*, p. 125. Taxes remained constant at around 11 percent of GNP. (Manuel Aguilera Gómez, *La desnacionalización de la economía mexicana*, p. 69.)

98. Rodolfo Stavenhagen, "Aspectos sociales de la estructura agraria en México," p. 17. Nationally, farm labor was forced to urban centers, where the service sector continued to absorb those who could not find industrial jobs. (David Barkin, "Mexico's Albatross: The United States Economy," p. 77.)

Table 15

Percentage of the Labor Force

in Agriculture and Livestock, 1965[a]

(percent)

CLASSIFICATION	NATIONAL	NORTH PACIFIC[b]
Wage-earners	24.1	46.1
In ejidos	8.6	13.4
In private holdings	15.5	32.7
Not wage-earners	75.9	53.9
Ejidatarios	36.5	33.0
Propietarios	39.4	20.9
>5 hectares	12.6	15.4
≤5 hectares	26.8	5.5

[a]Secretaría de Agricultura y Ganadería, Secretaría de Hacienda y Crédito Público, and Banco de México, S.A., *Projections of Supply and Demand for Agricultural Products in Mexico to 1970 and 1975.*

[b]The northern Pacific region includes Baja California, Sonora, and Sinaloa.

the highest proportion of wage-labor in Mexican agriculture in 1965 (Table 15).

In addition, *ejidos* with small plot sizes, which under the counter-reform could not perform as the cooperative enterprises they had once been, began to rent their land on a large scale. *Ejidatarios* were forced into an already overcrowded urban workforce and into the crime of renting ejidal lands. *Rentismo* became so common that even the richer valleys of Sonora showed a startling rate of alienation of ejidal property.[99] The center of ejidal production in the late Cárdenas years had been gradually transformed into a nest of land speculators and *latifundistas* misappropriating ejidal lands, as Table 16 shows.

These trends, which jeopardized the *ejido* and the *minifundio*, were compounded in the 1960s by another crippling revelation: the decline in water reserves in Sonora. The overexploitation of subterranean water reserves, like the decapitalization of agriculture and the structural problems of ISI, had been recognized since the 1950s. In fact, Governor Álvaro Obregón had ordered the study and conservation of geo-hydrological resources in 1958.[100] Moreover, the Ministry of Water Resources (SRH) in a 1960 study had noted the limited resources, not only of the areas pri-

99. By the mid-1960s, about 80 percent of Yaqui valley *ejidatarios* had abandoned their lands to rental and wage labor. (Hewitt, *Modernizing Mexican Agriculture*, p. 213.)

100. SRH, Distrito de Riego no. 51, Costa de Hermosillo, Sonora, "Document 51-498" (Aug. 22, 1958).

Table 16

Ejidal Rentismo in Irrigation Districts 38 and 41,
Mayo and Yaqui Valleys, 1973-1974 Season[a]

MUNICI-PALITY	TOTAL EJIDAL GRANT (hectares)	(1) TOTAL AREA IRRIGATED (hectares)	(2) AREA RENTED (hectares)	PER-CENTAGE (2/1)
Bácum	22,490	14,318	3,102	21.7
Cajeme	67,092	39,326	7,555	19.2
Etchojoa	45,266	30,438	11,263	37.0
Guaymas	3,096	1,830	145	7.9
Huatabampo	41,264	17,244	7,132	41.4
Navojoa	54,709	10,409	2,907	27.9
				Average
Totals	233,917	113,565	32,104	28.3

[a]SOURCE: Sonora, Departamento de Asuntos Rurales.

marily served by pump (Altar, Hermosillo coast, Guaymas valley), but also of the limits to water in the Yaqui valley, claiming that only 43 of the 200 wells in the valley were cost-efficient.[101] The SRH subsequently issued a regulation on May 14, 1963, banning new wells without permits and limiting water extraction by pump.[102] Nevertheless, water reserves continued to decline at critical rates. In Guaymas, extractions in 1967–1970 exceeded recovery of the water table by a factor of two.[103] By 1976, the pump-irrigation centers of the state were extracting two and a half times the volume recovered, resulting in salination of the reserves, lower crop yields, higher pumping costs, and related difficulties.[104]

To make matters worse, pump irrigation began to play a more important role in Sonoran agriculture, even outside the primary pump-irrigation areas. As Table A20 (in appendix) shows, the storage dams on the principal rivers of Sonora have only held their full capacity for short peri-

101. Vicente Vargas Alcántara, "Perforación de pozos profundos para explotación de aguas subterraneas," pp. 102–103.

102. Jiménez Villalobos, "Condiciones de las aguas subterraneas," p. 65.

103. SRH, Subsecretaría de Construcción, Dirección General de Grande Irrigación y Control de Ríos, Dirección de Estudios Específicos, *Estudio para el mejoramiento integral e incremento de la productividad en los Distritos de Riego del Río Fuerte, Río Mayo, Río Yaqui, y Colonias Yaquis*, pp. 35–36.

104. José Luis Jardines Moreno, "Los Distritos de Riego por bombeo del centro y norte de Sonora." This decline was confirmed in personal interviews conducted in April and May 1977 with Ing. Jardines Moreno, former director of the *Plan Hidráulico del Noroeste* (PLHINO) and current promotion and program subdirector of the SRH, and with Ing. Eduardo Ruiz Castro, director of SARH in northern Sonora.

Table 17

Area Irrigated, By Land Type,

Sonora, 1973[a]

AREA	EJIDAL (hectares)	PRIVATE (hectares)
Pump irrigation	35,742	219,618
Guaymas valley	4,719	17,000
Hermosillo coast	1,684	121,000
Caborca region	3,000	45,000
San Luis Río Colorado	1,339	21,618
San Miguel, Sonora, Sanjón rivers	25,000	15,000
Gravity irrigation	119,203	207,543
Mayo valley	42,760	50,527
Yaqui valley	74,086	142,372
Cuauhtemoc dam (Altar)	757	2,244
A. I. Rodriguez (Hermosillo)	1,600	12,400

[a]SOURCE: Secretaría de la Reforma Agraria, "Plan Nacional Agrícola: Sonora."

ods of time since their construction (mainly in 1966–1968), despite the increasing demand for water in the lower river valleys of the coast. With the critical lack of seasonal rainfall in most of Sonora, the hotly contested struggle for pumping permits became a virtual war, fought on the battlefields of political corruption and influence. More water was taken from the ejidal sector and from the headwater municipalities of the Sierra[105] (Table 17). The private sector continued to monopolize high-cost pump irrigation, and the future of the two-crop season was called into question.

Responses to the Agricultural Crisis

The private landholders responded to this problem not only with renewed interest in complete control of on-site irrigation (which, as the tables on capital investment show, they already largely had), but with a continuation of the wasteful land- and water-management practices that had earned them the nickname of "the mining farmers."[106] Pumping lim-

105. As an example of both tendencies, an SRH study of an area on the Sonora river feeding the A. I. Rodríguez dam showed that in the five municipalities along the river (Baviácora, Aconchi, San Felipe de Jesús, Huepac, and Banámichi), private property in 1972 controlled 85 percent of agricultural land as against 63 percent of wasteland. (SRH, "Estudio agrícola–ganadero de un area del río Sonora." See Table A18 in the appendix for a further breakdown of ejidal and private property and water control.)

106. Hewitt, *Modernizing Mexican Agriculture*, p. 122.

its were continually violated, and private farmers ran their pumps constantly to extend their domains. In the Yaqui and Mayo valleys, the control of water was tied to the control of more land, since water rights were vested in the plots to which they pertained. The land conflict resurged—partly as a function of water scarcity, partly due to the mismanagement and ambition of the large landholders. The new *latifundistas* managed to force the sale of lands owned by *minifundistas* and older, marginal colonists from the Cárdenas days, and Sonora's rural tensions increased. Water and soil management followed the decadent profligacy which characterized the life-styles of the millionaire colonists of the Hermosillo coast and the "nylon farmers" of the southern river valleys. Hewitt estimates that by 1971 about 80 percent of the large agricultural enterprises on the Hermosillo coast were operating at a deficit, and the situation approached crisis in the Yaqui valley as well.[107] Agricultural profit, like water, ran through the fingers of the agricultural bourgeoisie of the northwest, not stopping long enough to replenish its source, the earth. Numerous government sources noted the waste of expensive pump irrigation, overconsumption, lack of reinvestment in the land, monocultivation, and so on.[108] The government's irritation with the subsidized waste of the rich Sonoran farmers came to a head in 1975, as we shall see in Chapter 7.

The immediate government response to the increasing difficulties with water management came in several forms. Besides the ordinance against excessive pumping and other measures within the SRH, the federal government secured over 300 million pesos in two loans from the Inter-American Development Bank for the *Plan Hidráulico del Noroeste* (PLHINO).[109] This irrigation plan, which has subsequently become most elusive and vague, was designed to extend 370,000 hectares of irrigated land to the northwest from excess water resources in Nayarit, of which 52,000 hectares were to benefit Sonora. The 5.4-billion-peso price-tag would provide a combined hydroelectric, flood-control, and irrigation network involving 18 rivers and arroyos and 19 dams from Nayarit to Sonora.[110] The Ministry of Agrarian Reform (SRA) felt that the "hope that PLHINO will solve the water problem keeps the farmer alert, and he does not become discouraged, [because he can] think of the general benefits [PLHINO] can bring our economy and his own agricultural sector."[111]

Another manner in which the government responded to the water shortage was to grant virtually no useful lands to new ejidal centers. Díaz Ordaz, who claimed great feats as an *agrarista* president, in fact primarily

107. *Ibid.*, pp. 163–164 and 178.
108. See esp. Jardines Moreno, "Los Distritos de Riego," p. 17.
109. *El Imparcial*, Dec. 20, 1966, p. 1.
110. SRH, "Plan Hidráulico del Noroeste." Also *El Imparcial*, Dec. 10, 1965, p. 1, which states that 1,250,000 hectares were to be added to the northwest irrigation system.
111. SRA, "Plan Nacional Agrícola: Sonora."

gave worthless lands to the ejidal sector. Of 84 ejidal grants made by Díaz Ordaz from 1965 to 1970, only 13 were in the Yaqui and Mayo valleys, where they stood a chance of benefitting from irrigation. Another 27 were in pump-irrigation areas where no new permits were issued to *ejidatarios* (who could not afford the expense, anyway), and the remainder fell among the desert expanses of Álamos and other arid municipalities.[112] There was little "social obligation" evident in these marginal grants.

By the time Luis Echeverría came to power in December 1970, the ejidal and *minifundio* sectors of Sonoran agriculture were in dire straits, and the politics of social control in Sonora reflected the resulting hostility.

Faustino Félix Serna and the "Revolution of 1967"

Amid the continued, but sporadic, land invasions gradually accelerating in the northwest, the general political unrest that characterized the 1960s came to Sonora.[113] Class and university conflict was combined in a teachers' strike and a typically intense gubernatorial election campaign in 1967. Before the conflict ended, at least five persons died from gunshot, and many more were teargassed, stoned and beaten; the cry of "impositionism"—a relic of the nationally-imposed elections of Ramos, Yocupicio, Macías, and Soto—suddenly rang out again; the candidate chosen by the future president Luis Echeverría went down to defeat; and the *campesino* and worker organizations of Sonora were again split.

During December 1966 and the first two months of 1967, three candidates appeared for governor of Sonora: cattleman Enrique Cubillas, former assistant federal prosecutor Fausto Acosta Roma, and Yaqui valley politician Faustino Félix Serna. Acosta Roma allegedly had the approval of then-Secretary of Government Luis Echeverría Álvarez, a rapidly-rising star in Díaz Ordaz' political retinue. Faustino Félix Serna, on the other hand, had the organizational backing of the CTM and CNC leadership. Cubillas, the cattlemen's candidate, was regionally isolated and counted on little support in the populous southern part of the state.

It soon became obvious, through carefully staged rallies of disorderly militants, that Faustino had garnered much support in contrast to his rather lackluster opponents, and that the election would break down to a struggle between Faustino's followers and the amorphous but determined opposition to this much-feared former municipal head of Cajeme. Cubillas and Acosta Roma both disappeared from the race, and Leandro Soto

112. Data taken from *Diario Oficial*, 1965–1970.
113. Useful studies of some of the more illustrious examples of political unrest in Mexico can be found in Evelyn P. Stevens, *Protest and Response in Mexico*; Kenneth F. Johnson, *Mexican Democracy: A Critical View*; and Judith A. Hellman, *Mexico in Crisis*. Information on the Sonoran events comes from *El Imparcial*, Feb.–June 1967, and from interviews with three former student leaders of the University of Sonora Student Federation (FEUS), and with participants in the defense of the *preparatoria* in Navojoa. See also Moncada, *Años de violencia*, chap. 3.

Galindo took up what now became an anti-*felicista* crusade. Faustino, however, was prepared with greater weaponry than his opponents, and gained the endorsement of the PRI.

In March the Student Anti-Impositionist Front (FEAI), organized as the principal opposition to Faustino, clashed several times with his permanent force of vigilantes, nicknamed the *ola verde* (green wave).[114] The struggle extended even to the secondary and preparatory schools of the Yaqui and Mayo valleys, where the student movement fought pitched battles with armed thugs from the *ola verde*.[115] The Sonoran gubernatorial election became transformed into a conflict of the PRI and Faustino against students and anti-government dissidents, backed by a substantial number of the Sonoran electorate. After much violence, and a declaration by Echeverría himself that Faustino was the candidate of the party regardless of FEAI and FEUS (University of Sonora Student Federation) opposition,[116] the awesome PRI–Faustino alliance went forward to victory. A teachers' strike which closed schools from Caborca to Navojoa was crushed by the *ola verde*. The university and *preparatorias* were occupied by federal soldiers, and many student leaders were forced into hiding in distant redoubts.

The issues which generated these clashes between students and *felicistas* are sometimes difficult to determine, but it is clear that the university-led forces had substantial popular support. The Sonoran populace, in times of accelerating political struggle and socioeconomic inequality, has often raised banners of anti-imposition, university autonomy, and land reform, all of which appeared in the "revolution of 1967." To a degree the spring 1967 events appear as part of the nationwide political discontent among the young, combined with the increasing anxiety and militance of the *campesinos* of Sonora. Faustino, as the opposition knew, was a hardliner who in his *sexenio* would do little to improve the deteriorating lot of the *ejidatarios* and *campesinos* of Sonora. In his final gubernatorial report, usually reserved for reviewing the successes of the outgoing admin-

114. The *ola verde* was so named for the green hatbands its members wore. Hundreds of them—reminiscent of the right-wing "action groups" of Rodolfo Elías Calles, Ramón Ramos, and Román Yocupicio in the 1930s—camped out in the streets of Hermosillo during the "revolution."

115. In Navojoa, the preparatory school was attacked in April by riflemen of the *ola verde*, who besieged a school-building full of teen-agers until repelled by *ejidatarios* and other parents from nearby areas. The newspapers and Moncada's treatment of the "revolution" ignore the action outside Hermosillo, the formal seat of power. Small local papers provided some spotty coverage of the events in the south, but my main source of information has been direct interviews with *ejidatario* and student leaders from the Navojoa *preparatoria*.

116. After Faustino's selection as candidate of the party's *campesino*, worker, and popular sectors (March 21, 1967), and his nomination as official PRI candidate (March 26, 1967), this allegiance was really not seriously doubted. Possibly Faustino's strongest trump in this regard was his ability to mobilize the *ola verde* against opposition (remember Yocupicio's militia). (*El Imparcial*, March 22 and 27 and April 18, 1967.)

istration, Faustino devoted less than two pages to "agrarian action," relegating land grants to one paragraph.[117] Landowner, *cacique*, and veteran old-style politician, Faustino exemplified political power during the reign of Gustavo Díaz Ordaz. Echeverría, in the next Sonoran campaign in 1973, tried to separate himself from the legacy of both Díaz Ordaz and Félix Serna.

PRELUDE TO POPULISM: THE MIRACLE IN CRISIS

During the hectic years 1965–1970, the postwar development model began to break down, as we have seen, under the pressures of escalating foreign debt, stagnating agricultural production, increasing foreign corporate presence in the Mexican economy, and a host of other pressures which revealed the continuing inadequacy of the counter-reform. By 1970, as we have seen in this chapter, Mexico—and especially Sonora—was faced with the contradictory problems of a capitalist agricultural sector that was not producing at a level commensurate with public investment, and an ejidal and *minifundio* sector that had been excluded from production by years of harassment and neglect. Cheap wage-labor, lured from the wastelands of eastern Sonora to the valleys of the coast, migrated slowly and began to petition land as "new centers of ejidal population" under the agrarian code. Though ignored at first, their growing militance in the 1960s necessitated state response in the 1970s.

Clearly the Mexican political system, probing for new ways to ensure political legitimacy and economic growth, needed to address the "social obligation" promises of the Mexican revolution, always mentioned in campaign speeches, but long-forgotten in the realm of public policy. Echeverría, distant, enigmatic, and hounded by the massacre of Tlatelolco, came in 1970 to lead the official populist revival. His six years in office were the most electric since the Cárdenas epoch, as we shall see.

117. Sonora, *Informe del gobierno del C. Faustino Félix Serna, 1973*.

Chapter 7

Echeverría: Populist Revival
and the Crisis of Legitimation

Echeverría's advent heralded major policy changes which addressed not only the problems of the agrarian reform, but the larger concerns of the national economy and revolutionary ideology. Echeverría, from the time of his "unveiling" (*destape*) as the PRI's presidential candidate in the fall of 1969, undertook his image-building campaign with unexpected fervor. A stern, introspective man, Echeverría missed few opportunities to pontificate about the great destiny of Mexican society or to scold prodigal businessmen and "enemies of the Revolution." The campaign of 1970 momentarily restored luster to the tarnished demagogy which had come to symbolize the failed promises of the counter-reform in crisis. While other presidents since Cárdenas had yielded the sceptre of personalism to the growing bureaucratic state apparatus, Echeverría promised not to rest "one single day of the *sexenio* from the task of promoting the betterment of the *campesinos* and of rural life."[1] Whereas the counter-reform had concentrated the resources of rural development in a few areas, and had excluded most *ejidatarios* and *minifundistas*, Echeverría averred that "every [rural] population center must be able to dispose of adequate resources in order to convert its labor into well-being."[2] In contrast to the conservative, pro-business inclinations of his predecessor Gustavo Díaz Ordaz, Echeverría vowed to bring to Mexico an "*agrarista* and *obrerista* government."[3]

Echeverría's personal style contributed greatly to the substance of his

1. Mexico, Presidente de la República, "Discurso de toma de posesión del Presidente de México," Dec. 1, 1970; reprinted in Mexico, Banco Nacional de Comercio Exterior, *México: la política económica del nuevo gobierno* (Mexico: 1971), pp. 175–189.
2. *Ibid.*
3. *El Imparcial*, Sept. 25, 1970, p. 1.

regime. His demagogic exhortations to the masses, his constant presence "before the entire nation," and his intense feeling of personal mission led Daniel Cosío Villegas, the dean of Mexican historians, to describe him as a man driven by a physiological necessity to talk: a man who impressed one as "dead when found alone, and alive, even exalted, when he has before him an auditorium [full of people]."[4] The new president's personal energy and optimism regarding the possibilities of the Mexican political economy initially surprised and excited even the most jaded bureaucrats when he exhorted them to

> Go to the *campo*, . . . to that part of the *campo* which has the greatest need, the deserts! Let us take off our ties, go to the *campo* in jackets, stretch out our hands to the *campesinos*, and thus return each Monday reassured of serving in our offices better.[5]

At times, Echeverría's optimism and indefatigable rhetoric tested the limits of Mexican reality, as we shall see in this chapter.

Whatever value may be assigned to Echeverría's personal idiosyncrasies—which were constantly examined and conjured with in Mexican political circles during his term of office—Echeverría and the populist resurgence of his presidency must be assessed in terms of the many policy initiatives his government attempted, and their results in the context of the realities of contemporary Mexican political economy.

As we saw in Chapter 6, the Mexican economy in 1970 faced a declining output from the primary-goods sector, especially crop-raising and mining. The vaunted stability of the Mexican peso, while still featured as a prime asset of the economic miracle, was beginning to feel the pressure of inflation. Balance-of-payments deficits, fed by a snowballing foreign debt, threatened to undermine Mexico's credit position, while unemployment, structural inadequacies in industry, and ISI expenses called for more public investment than ever before. The "social peace," which had survived the regional and sectoral disequilibria of the counter-reform years, had begun to crumble in the late 1960s. The conjuncture of Mexican political unrest, economic dislocations, and socioeconomic polarization called for a man of action in the office of the presidency. The term "man of action" fit the self-description of Luis Echeverría Álvarez.

ECHEVERRÍA'S STRATEGY FOR 1970–1976

The new president immediately began to legislate major changes in the national area. Echeverría's government professed very early to include

---

4. Daniel Cosío Villegas, *El estilo personal de governar*, p. 33.

5. Mexico, Presidente de la República, "Exposición del Presidente de México en la primera sesión del Consejo Directivo de la Comisión Nacional de las Zonas Áridas," Dec. 17, 1970; reprinted in Banco Nacional de Comercio Exterior, p. 214. Merilee S. Grindle, in *Bureaucrats, Politicians, and Peasants in Mexico*, chap. 4, discusses the various responses to

among its goals the following measures: fiscal reform as a redistributive mechanism; pilot programs to alleviate the misery of arid zones and indigenous communities; modernization of the agricultural sector through land reform, greater productivity, rural industry, and self-finance; channeling health, community development, social security, and housing funds to the poorest rural and urban areas; achievement of a new balance of regional development among sectors and classes; decentralization of industry; and a reform of national education to benefit the working classes.[6] From the new wave of social and economic legislation Echeverría promoted, two measures survived as the foundation of the all-important official agrarian reform in the 1970s: the federal Agrarian Reform Law of March 22, 1971, and the federal Water Law of December 30, 1971.[7] Later, in 1976, they were joined by a new Rural Credit Law. These were the cornerstones of substantial changes in the agrarian law of Mexico, as well as important subsidiary measures to the more general plans of the Echeverría government. But the agrarian-reform programs, support for workers against industry, and attempted fiscal reforms also engendered a battle with the conservative Mexican bourgeoisie that would not end until Echeverría left office.

State Populism Versus Domestic Capital: The First Skirmishes

Echeverría's populist programs began with his first act as president: creation of the National Commission for Arid Zones, only a few hours after he took office in December 1970. He followed that modest proposal for redressing regional imbalances with far more controversial proposals that, in the context of the political turmoil of the 1970–1971 period, induced confrontation between the state, as class conciliator, and bourgeois civil society. Most prominent among these proposals was the fiscal-reform bill he recommended in early 1971.

In 1970, even before taking office, Echeverría had formed an advisory commission to suggest a program for fiscal reform. This commission circumvented the normal channels for fiscal policy—the Secretary of the Treasury and Public Credit and the Bank of Mexico—with the prior assent of the leading national capitalist organizations.[8] Echeverría's early interest in genuine fiscal reform was stimulated by the conflict between his avowed commitment to heavy public spending for social expenses and redistributive social capital investment and, on the other hand, the growing fiscal debt of the Mexican state. Among the specifics of the commission's

Echeverría's programs and the degrees of technical competence, political resistance or support, and personal enthusiasm they generated.

6. Banco Nacional de Comercio Exterior, pp. 70–71.

7. The Agrarian Reform Law appeared in *Diario Oficial* on May 1, 1971; the Water Law on Jan. 11, 1972.

8. See John F. H. Purcell and Susan Kaufman Purcell, "El estado y la empresa privada"; and Carlos Arriola, "Los grupos empresariales frente al estado mexicano, 1973–1975."

fiscal-reform proposal were: elimination of bearer bonds and stocks, which made tax evasion such a simple matter; taxation of capital gains at the same rate as salaries; creation of a national property tax; strict restriction of business expense write-offs; and a progressive increase in personal taxes.[9]

From the outset, however, the leading representatives of the private sector opposed the fiscal reform, and it never survived its initial bureaucratic dissection within the Treasury and the organized business community. The reform endured only in pieces, minus its most important feature, the elimination of bearer bonds; the result was a modest increase in federal taxation.[10] A more important, negative result was the hostile reaction of COPARMEX, the rightist spokesman for Mexican capital. The day after the fiscal reform was introduced, COPARMEX threatened to "interrupt the dialogue between government and private initiative," since the reform had not been cleared first with the private sector. This comment on the "rules for reform" was only the first indication of the weakness of the state vis-à-vis dominant forces in civil society.[11] Echeverría responded by scolding the businessmen for thinking only of themselves and ignoring the commonweal, and relations between COPARMEX and the president began to cool.[12]

A related confrontation between the populist renaissance and organized capital arose from the fight against inflation. In late 1972 and throughout 1973, inflation swelled to dangerous levels and showed no signs of abating. Wholesale prices in the capital increased by 20 percent during the year beginning in October 1972.[13] The organized working class, through the Labor Congress (*Congreso de Trabajo*), demanded price controls and government protection from the ravages of inflation, and the national government proposed an inflation-fighting campaign based on price controls and increased state participation in the marketing of goods and services. This proposal was rejected outright by the business community. While the rhetoric by all parties to the issue—labor, capital, and the state—escalated, relations between Echeverría and the conservative bourgeoisie deteriorated rapidly; the *New York Times* reported that Mexican industrialists viewed Echeverría as a revolutionary agitator.[14] Finally, Echeverría supported the workers' position, calling for a program of price controls and profit ceilings.[15] Even as private business asserted that exces-

9. Purcell and Purcell, p. 231.

10. Banco Nacional de Comercio Exterior, *Mexico, 1976: Facts, Figures, Trends*, p. 251.

11. "Censura la confederación patronal la iniciativa de reformas fiscales," *El Día*, Dec. 17, 1970; cited in Soledad Loaeza, "La política de rumor: México, Noviembre–Diciembre 1976," p. 133.

12. *Excelsior*, Jan. 29, 1971, p. 1.

13. Arriola, "Los Grupos Empresariales," p. 44.

14. *New York Times*, Nov. 7, 1973, second section, p. 4; reprinted in *Excelsior*, Nov. 8, 1973, p. 1.

15. Arriola, p. 46.

sive government spending was the key cause of inflation, Echeverría parried by proclaiming the new populism, a direct reversal of Ávila Camacho's counsel to the Mexican working class about its dependence on capital.

> A business movement . . . in a mixed economy like ours should know that its own security, its own stability, depends on its cooperation in an authentic growth in the acquisitive capacity of the great majority. The month of September [1973] will be one of readjustment . . . to benefit all Mexicans, the political stability of the country, social tranquility with a spirit of progress for the masses, because that was what the Mexican Revolution meant.[16]

Amid the storm that followed Echeverría's statement of support for the working class, Eugenio Garza Sada, elder of the conservative "Monterrey Group" of Mexican businessmen, was killed in an attempted kidnapping, allegedly by left-wing terrorists. The Monterrey Group blamed Echeverría for the assassination at Garza Sada's funeral.[17]

Echeverría's attacks on the private sector, which increased in number and venom in the latter years of his sexenio, represented a single aspect of his new conception of Mexican revolutionary populism. Through his programs of fiscal reform, worker support, and agrarian redistribution, Echeverría intended to create a new engine of growth for the Mexican economic miracle—a policy path suggested by some economists for many years, but never attended to during the rapid growth years of the counterreform: "expansion of the consumer market through a concerted policy of housing, employment, just salaries, and rational and equitable redistribution among regions and social groups."[18]

The purpose of the new populism, as one might infer from past popular mobilizations in Mexico, was not exclusively to secure potential benefits for the underclasses. It was an attempt also to strengthen the state, to arrest the decline of state power before local and foreign capital which had begun in the 1940s.[19] Faced with attacks by the conservative bourgeoisie so early in the sexenio, Echeverría expanded his populist commitment,

16. Echeverría, speech to the National Council of the CTM, Aug. 30, 1973; reprinted in *El Día*, Aug. 31, 1973, p. 10.

17. Irma Salinas, a member of the Sada family, recently tried to publish a book in which she claimed that the family itself ordered the assassination of don Eugenio. The book, branded "libelous" by the government, was seized days before publication and banned from further release. (Marlise Simons, "Behind the Scandal Rocking Mexican Politics," *San Francisco Chronicle*, April 19, 1978, p. A3.)

The funeral oration included the following remarks by Ricardo Margáin Zozaya, president of the advisory council of the Monterrey Group: "It is only possible to act with impunity when respect for authority is gone; when the state does not maintain public order; when the most negative ideologies are not only given free rein, but are permitted to harvest their negative fruits of hate, destruction, and death." The orator went on to accuse the government of supporting Marxist ideas and attacking the private sector. (Arriola, p. 48.)

18. Arriola, p. 50.

19. Julio Labastida M. del Campo, "Nacionalismo reformista en México," p. 37.

seeking the support of the army and the masses in a "Popular Alliance" which would exclude the businessman, politically.[20] The linchpin of the popular alliance was the rural sector, and the new agrarian-reform and water laws pointed up the desire to reclaim for the state its dominant role in the Mexican populist equation.

The Legal Basis of the Populist Revival

During Díaz Ordaz' presidency the results of the counter-reform became somewhat clearer, at least with respect to the decay of the *ejido* and the *minifundio* and the corollary decline in agricultural production in the late 1960s. Echeverría, facing the task of allying himself with the common people against the unregenerate bourgeoisie, immediately proposed changes in the Agrarian Code which had been in force since 1942. The new law attempted to balance the economic and political power of the highly productive cattle-raising sector against the pressures arising from demands by the *campesinos*, whose support was so necessary to the strength of the state.[21] The right of *amparo*, guaranteeing a powerful legal weapon against action under the agrarian reform, was continued.[22] This concession to farmers and cattlemen remained, despite the opposition of the CNC and the new head of the Agrarian Department, Augusto Gómez Villaneuva. Likewise, the law maintained the dimensions of "immune" (*inafectable*) land, and extended to cattlemen for the first time the right to grow forage on their immune lands.[23]

But major changes in the law affected the status of the *ejido* within the revived agrarian reform. It outlawed the common practice of "concentration of advantage" (*concentración de provecho*), by which the use of more than one plot fell to one owner through registering small children as farmers, obtaining *prestanombres*, and other shady mechanisms for avoiding the intent of the reform.[24] Moreover, the law presented a new "integral" vision of the *ejido* as a combination of the ejidal farm proper with a local credit society and a social nucleus for community action. The obvious benefit of strengthening the *ejido* and making it cost-effective would accrue to an interventionist state based on protection of the rural populace.

The law touched a nerve among sensitive rural interests, and opposition sprang up in many quarters of national politics. The congressional session which finally approved the new law was described by *Excelsior* as replete with "shouting, insults, hissing, booing," and similar gestures of high emotion. One PRI deputy even brandished a gun during heated debate.[25]

20. Arriola, p. 50.
21. Manuel Aguilera Gómez, "Balance de la Nueva Ley de Reforma Agraria," p. 62.
22. *Ley Federal de Reforma Agraria*, March 22, 1971, Book Four, Title II, chap. 3, art. 219.
23. *Ibid.*, chap. 8, arts. 249 and 258.
24. *Ibid.*, chap. 3, art. 210.
25. *Excelsior*, Feb. 20, 1971, p. 1.

The new Agrarian Code took on added importance in the context of the early confrontations with the Mexican bourgeoisie. After the law established the individual or collective exploitation of the *ejido* as a matter of democratic choice within an *ejido*,[26] the government in 1973 moved to ensure "that the complete collectivization of the *ejido*, small property, and communal holdings in the whole country will be held up as a goal." The Echeverría government claimed the future to be "large land-holdings without *latifundistas*,"[27] and 1973 to be the "year of the *campesinos*."[28] The state then embraced an ambitious program of collectivization, which ended up claiming far more than it accomplished.

The new federal Water Law, partner of the Agrarian Reform Law of 1971, proposed a future dominated by government participation in the allocation of resources and property within federal irrigation districts, at least partly in order to "satisfy agrarian necessities."[29] Basically, the law was more a reassertion of Article 27 of the 1917 Constitution regarding national domain over water rights than a revolutionary attitude toward the disposition of national waters. The new law did, however, limit new water grants to small property of twenty hectares or less;[30] it further limited the private ownership of land in new irrigation districts to twenty irrigated hectares.[31] Combined with an ambitious program of federal irrigation projects for the 1970s, it promised to reassert the government's role in productive agriculture in Mexico. Given the overpowering importance of federal irrigation districts to national agricultural production, the Water Law and the 1971 Agrarian Reform Law provided a legislative basis for the nation to seize substantial control of the most important agricultural resources of the country.[32] First, of course, the government would have to confront yet another sector of national capitalists: the powerful agricultural bourgeoisie.

The first two years of Echeverría's term were devoted to establishing the legislative base for the *agrarista* revival. The promised land grants, credit, and water really did not start to flow to the rural populace until 1973, the "year of the *campesinos*" (see Tables A21–A23 in the appendix). The massacre of students on the feast of Corpus Christi in 1971, the acceleration of radical adventurism on the left, and the establishment of a Third World leadership role for Mexico all for a time upstaged the coming

---

26. *Ley Federal de Reforma Agraria*, Book Three, chap. 1, arts. 130–131.
27. "Crédito condicional al campo," *Análisis Político*, 2; no. 7 (Feb. 19, 1973): 5.
28. *El Imparcial*, Dec. 20, 1972, p. 1.
29. *Ley Federal de Aguas*, Dec. 30, 1971, Title II, chap. 3, sec. 2, art. 50.
30. *Ibid.*, Title III, chap. 2, art. 124.
31. *Ibid.*, Title II, chap. 3, sec. 2, art. 52.
32. The *Plan Nacional Hidráulico* envisioned an expenditure of 76.7 billion pesos over the years 1970–2000, with 25 percent going to the Pacific northwest, 10 percent to the north, 27 percent to the center-Pacific region, and 38 percent to the Gulf-southeast region. The enormous plan envisaged reaching 4.4 million hectares in all. (Fernando J. González Villarreal, "Plan Nacional Hidráulico.")

of the new *agrarismo*. When, in 1973, the program finally began, it began slowly, as we shall see in the case of Sonora.

SONORA, 1973: THE GREENING OF THE PRI

As has been the case throughout its history, political events in Sonora during the 1970s reflected some of the major issues confronting Mexico at the national level. Perhaps nowhere was this truer than in the gubernatorial campaign and election of Carlos Armando Biébrich in 1973. Sonora under Echeverría gained status as a repository of populist symbols, from the agrarian reform to the call to youth to participate in the "democratic opening" of the PRI. Sonora, equated with revolutionary spirit by the new president, contained remnants of the battles of the 1960s which had harassed conservative authoritarian rule. Sonora, home of Obregón and Calles, and beneficiary of the economic miracle, represented both the successes of official agrarian reform and the tenacity of *latifundismo*. Sonora in the 1970s was a window into the heart of the populist resurgence in Mexico.

In the midst of Echeverría's presidential campaign—even as the president-to-be toured Quechehueca, the model of collective *ejidos* in the state—invaders led by Humberto Serrano occupied Capetamaya in another attempt to wrest control of the land from José María Zaragoza.[33] During the first months of Echeverría's *sexenio*, the CNC and UGOCM began another fight amongst themselves for ejidal grants and water rights.[34] The CNC, meanwhile, reasserted the claim that 80 percent of all ejidal land in southern Sonora—some 116,000 hectares—was in the hands of renters, and that 80,000 *campesinos* were waiting for land in Sonora alone.[35]

In 1972 the UGOCM asked the federal government to reduce the legal limit on small property to conform to the Water Law, which mandated a limit of twenty hectares.[36] And the *campesinos* and their organizations pressed for a more expeditious and complete agrarian reform, at least partly based on the publication in *Excelsior* of a widely circulated list of *latifundistas* in Sonora. This list, first published in 1970, indicated that 800,000 hectares in Sonora and Sinaloa were in the hands of only 114 family groups, in lots of up to 27,000 hectares. The list amounted to a virtual "Who's Who in Sonora": the Esquer family, Próspero Ibarra and brothers, descendants of Álvaro Obregón, Plutarco Elías Calles, and others of simi-

33. *El Imparcial*, Oct. 21, 1970, p. 1. Humberto Serrano later became a leading member of the Pact of Ocampo.

34. *Ibid.*, Feb. 26, 1971, and Aug. 13, 1971, both p. 1.

35. *Ibid.*, June 29 and July 13, 1971, both p. 1. The CNC estimate was confirmed by a later SRA estimate of 100,000 hectares rented. (*Ibid.*, Feb. 21, 1973, p. 1.)

36. *Ibid.*, March 4, 1972. Eventually, the Secretary of Water Resources and the Secretary of Agrarian Reform both supported the proposal, along with complete nationalization of the irrigation districts.

lar stature.[37] Sonora, presidentially anointed heartbeat of the Revolution, needed drastic change.

The first opportunity to move toward that change presented itself in 1973, in the campaign for the governorship of Sonora. Until Faustino Félix Serna left office, no real change in Sonoran land tenure was possible, and his *ola verde* guaranteed that the national government would not attempt to depose him. But clearly Echeverría regarded Faustino as a member of the "old guard" from which the president was trying to separate himself. In 1973, when Faustino proposed Alfredo Robinson Bours, of a *latifundista* family, as his successor, Echeverría countered with his own nomination: Carlos Armando Biébrich.

Biébrich, mentioned in our introductory chapter as a symbol of youth, represented an important cog in the populist machinery of Luis Echeverría. His connection with the highly political students of Sonora through his presidency of the Sonoran PRI youth group made him the consummate "youth candidate" for governor. Echeverría—perhaps because of the militance of the students in 1970, perhaps because of his role in the repressive regime of Díaz Ordaz—had claimed his nomination as PRI presidential candidate in the name of "an entire generation of youth." He restated the mandate of the young in a visit to the northwest in the first months of his regime, lauding "this generation, in whose name we have arrived at the presidency."[38] Likewise, in his highly publicized "political reform" program, Echeverría reduced the voting age to 18 and the ages of eligibility for federal deputy and senator to 21 and 30, respectively.[39] So Biébrich's candidacy, in addition to its defiance of Faustino and the southern *latifundistas*, fit nicely into Echeverría's bid for youth support in the hinterland.

Biébrich, with his young, photogenic family, embraced the power of Echeverría, if not the programs of populist restoration. Suddenly political seers and rumor-mongers began talking of Biébrich as presidential material, a star of the future. It is tempting to speculate—as many have in Sonora—that Biébrich's belief in his close ties to Echeverría contributed to his inattention to land reform and his eventual downfall.[40]

In any event, Biébrich's victory did not eventuate in an improvement in agrarian action, as had been hoped by Echeverría and his advisers. Shortly after his accession in September 1973, Biébrich ordered the occupation of the University of Sonora (on October 20), defending a rightist

37. *Excelsior*, Jan. 17, 1970, p. 1.
38. Cosío Villegas, *El estilo personal de gobernor*, p. 20.
39. Rafael Segovia, "La Reforma Política: el ejecutivo federal, el PRI, y las elecciones de 1973," p. 53.
40. This reflects the opinion of many politically knowledgeable people in Sonora, including bureaucrats, U.S. consular officials, and student leaders with whom interviews were conducted. This explanation is partial, however, and must be placed in the context of the events of 1975, which will be treated shortly.

rector against the opposition of the student federation (FEUS) and the left wing of the faculty.[41] While Biébrich verbally supported "total social assistance to the *campesino* in Sonora,"[42] his single annual report contained nothing about the agrarian-reform programs he allegedly had undertaken.[43] Additionally, Biébrich began to point up some of the contradictions inherent in Echeverría's plan to decentralize government powers while maintaining strong control over government policy directions. Biébrich attempted to maintain a neutral affection for all the traditional sources of political power in the state: northern cattlemen, southern *latifundistas*, and politicos from Hermosillo. Echeverría, meanwhile, wanted to push forward a program of agrarian reform which would impinge upon the privileges of these same groups.

Despite Biébrich's inaction, however, Echeverría began some small moves to rectify the corrupted land-tenure situation in Sonora. In 1973, reports indicated that 42,000 hectares of irrigated ejidal land in the Yaqui and Mayo valleys alone had been rented to private landholders.[44] The Echeverría government, realizing the structural factors which had led to this condition, began to buy back those lands for their rightful owners and *ejidatario* users.[45] Echeverría renewed the program of rural education, expanding the number of agricultural schools from 52 to 850 nationally during his term. The proportion of public spending devoted to agriculture under Echeverría exceeded that of any president since Alemán.[46] Public credit in agriculture quintupled from 1970 to 1976 (see Table A23 in appendix). CONASUPO, the national purveyor of basic foodstuffs, expanded its budget from 4 million to 32 million pesos from 1970 to 1975, and extended its retail facilities and rural warehouses by similar proportions.[47] But due to the lag in maturation of agricultural investments, plus continuing climate problems, a reduction in the amount of land farmed with seasonal rainfall, and an end to productivity increases, the much-hoped-for agricultural turnaround did not materialize. Clearly the new regime had to do more to stimulate agricultural production and populist mobilization.

At the same time that agricultural production continued its decline,

41. Rubén Jiménez Ricárdez, "Movimiento campesino en Sonora," p. 75.
42. *El Imparcial*, May 3, 1974, p. 1.
43. Estado de Sonora, *Informe de gobierno del C. Carlos Armando Biébrich, 1974*.
44. Jiménez Ricárdez, p. 68.
45. Ing. Sergio Reyes Osorio, a senior member of the CDIA investigative team and Subsecretary of Organization in the SRA during 1976, contends that the government bought back 34,000 hectares in the Yaqui and Mayo valleys during 1973. (Figure cited in a presentation given at El Colegio de México, May 26, 1977.) The state government achieved this goal through the Commission for the Organization and Agrarian Development of the South of Sonora. The existence of this state commission has been cited as the origin of political enmity between Agrarian Department head Gómez Villanueva and Biébrich. (Jesús Blancornelas, *Biébrich, crónica de una infamia*, p. 24.)
46. Grindle, *Bureaucrats, Politicians, and Peasants*, pp. 104–105.
47. Purcell and Purcell, "El estado y la empresa privada," pp. 233–234; Grindle, *passim*.

Table 18

Value of Agricultural Production
in Irrigated Areas of Sonora,
1969-1970[a]

REGION	VALUE OF PRODUCTION (pesos)
Colonias Yaqui	45,191,600
Hermosillo coast	660,434,100
Guaymas valley	79,599,100
Altar, Pitiquito, Caborca	218,446,900
Mayo valley	366,712,700
Yaqui valley	1,164,046,500

[a]SOURCE: CDIA, *Empleo, desempleo y subempleo en el sector agropecuario*, vol. II, table 37, p. 163.

water-resource problems became more severe. During the droughts of the 1970s, PLHINO became the official panacea for all the hydrological damages and imbalances wreaked in Sonora since the counter-reform began. During Echeverría's first years, the Secretary of Water Resources publicized PLHINO regularly, but gave little substance to the publicity. Maps of the project and figures relating to the amounts invested were routinely paraded in the newspapers, and it seemed that PLHINO would arrive in southern Sonora at any time.[48] The optimism—and level of conflict—was so high that parties within Sonora began lobbying for PLHINO's benefits, trying to save their two-season cultivation. The CNC agreed with Water Resources that PLHINO should reach the Hermosillo coast, since only 105 of 564 wells there were available to *ejidatarios* and colonists.[49] Water Resources, in an apparent attempt to fend off the request, promised to study the matter.[50] A short time later, coincident with Echeverría's first Christmas trip to southern Sonora, Water Resources announced that PLHINO would extend only to Sahuaral, Etchojoa, in the Mayo valley.[51] Ten days later it was announced that 143,132 hectares of new land would be opened to irrigated cultivation in the Yaqui and Mayo valleys as a result of PLHINO, and construction would begin in a matter of weeks.[52] In the next year, though no physical evidence of the benefits of PLHINO could be found in the state, the press dutifully reported its "rapid advance";[53] a

48. E.g., *El Imparcial*, March 4, 1971; March 5 and April 6, 1972.
49. *Ibid.*, Jan. 27 and Sept. 20, 1973. Only 9 of 498 wells listed by the SRH were for ejidal benefit. (CDIA, *Empleo, desempleo, y subempleo en el sector agropecuario*, p. 172.)
50. *El Imparcial*, Oct. 21, 1973, p. 1.   51. *Ibid.*, Dec. 4, 1973, p. 1.
52. *Ibid.*, Dec. 14 and 24, 1973, both p. 1.   53. *Ibid.*, Oct. 9, 1974, p. 1.

Table 19

Value of Production by Land Tenure,
Irrigated Areas of Sonora, 1969-1970[a]

REGION	EJIDOS (pesos)	PRIVATE PROPERTY (pesos)
Colonias Yaqui	45,192,000	––
Hermosillo coast	4,914,000	655,520,000
Guaymas valley	11,345,000	68,254,000
Altar, Pitiquito, Caborca	7,283,000	211,184,000
Mayo valley	155,792,000	210,921,000
Yaqui valley	427,566,000	736,940,000

[a]SOURCE: CDIA, *Empleo, desempleo, y subempleo en el sector agropecuario*, table 38, p. 164.

conference was held at the University of Sonora on "Advances in Construction of PLHINO in Sonora."[54]

During 1974, the agrarian mobilization at the national level began to heighten *campesino* expectations and capitalist alarm in Sonora. Echeverría ordered the purchase of 70,000 private hectares to create collective *ejidos*; 50,000 hectares in the Yaqui, Mayo, Guaymas, and Sahuaripa regions were ordered cleared for ejidal grants;[55] and Water Resources requested federal control of all wells on the Hermosillo coast.[56] As we have seen in Chapter 6, and as Tables 18 and 19 illustrate, the Echeverría government was tampering with the most valuable agricultural land in the state, and thereby creating enmity from the most powerful of the country's agricultural bourgeoisie.

The Agrarian Department, under the leadership of Gómez Villanueva, also began a scheme at this time to return Tiburón Island to the Seri Indians of Sonora. The Seri, persecuted by colonial and Mexican governments alike, had become in the 1950s and 1960s the object of much anthropological curiosity. Likewise, their fierce independence made them a perfect symbol of the new wave of *indigenismo* that was blossoming in intellectual and political circles. As a bonus, the Seri lured a number of American tourists to their picturesque coastal fishing villages, where they sold ironwood carvings and bright woven baskets. Finally, the island was agriculturally worthless, and therefore expendable. Gómez Villanueva recommended the return of the Seri home as a benefit not only to the Seri, but to the struggling populist revival in Sonora. To this end Echeverría, on February 10, 1975, signed legislation restoring Tiburón Island to the Seri and creating the

54. *Ibid.*, Nov. 6, 1974, p. 1.   55. *Ibid.*, Oct. 23 and 26, 1974.
56. *Ibid.*, Nov. 22, 1974, p. 10.

Commission for the Development of the Seri Tribe of the State of Sonora. The purpose of the legislation and the commission was to guarantee tourist development of Tiburón on behalf of the Seri.[57] This provoked conflict between Gómez Villanueva and Biébrich, because Biébrich allegedly had entered negotiations with representatives of Howard Hughes for the private exploitation of Tiburón as a tourist resort catering to the American hunting and fishing trade.[58] In any event, Tiburón was legally returned to the Seri with much fanfare, and Biébrich presided over the commission governing their development.[59]

At the same time that Biébrich and the national agrarian-reform team had this falling-out over Tiburón, Echeverría began to press harder to speed up reforms in Sonoran land tenure. In March 1975 Gómez Villanueva, now head of the newly-formed Secretariat of Agrarian Reform (SRA), which supplanted the old Agrarian Department, made a blanket promise to the *campesinos* that all of their land-tenure problems in the south of Sonora would be resolved during the Echeverría term;[60] land tenure in Sonora would be investigated regardless of existing certificates of immunity.[61] The CNOP and the National Federation of Small Property (CNPP) reacted by calling for an end to demagogy and a new concentration on agricultural production instead of threats to private property.[62] The CNPP, as expected, was rapidly becoming one of the centers of local bourgeois opposition to Echeverría in Sonora. Echeverría opened the official land investigation anyway, in June 1975, and a team of investigators entered the field shortly thereafter.[63]

57. 'Decreto que crea la Comisión de Desarrollo de la Tribu Seri del Estado de Sonora."

58. As might be expected, there is no way to confirm or refute this allegation definitively. It is a product of the "informed rumor mill" which plays such an important role in the closed system of Mexican political infighting. (See Evelyn P. Stevens, *Protest and Response in Mexico*, and Loaeza, "La Política del Rumor," for discussions of the importance of rumors as a source of information.) An important confirmation of the alleged Seri conflict came out recently in a book that appears to be a semi-official account of the Sonoran crisis of 1975 and 1976; Mario Sevilla Mascareñas, in *Aquí, Sonora, S.O.S.* (p. 53), alleges that Biébrich reacted to the SRA proposal to return Tiburón to the Seri by exclaiming:

Return Isla Tiburón to the Seri? Why? What would be the purpose? They're illiterate Indians, vice-ridden and indolent! It would be a grave error to miss the opportunity to attract investment of national and foreign capital to exploit the island touristically. Forget it!

Though the quote seems suspiciously like a script, the story of Biébrich's attitude toward the Seri restitution probably was not made up out of whole cloth. A version much more favorable to Biébrich, though still noting his opposition to the return of Tiburón to the Seri, appears in Blancornelas, *Biébrich*, pp. 58ff.

59. *El Imparcial*, Feb. 11 and March 4, 1975, both p. 1. In March 1977, over two years after the presidential resolution, the Seri still had not received their island from the government, because it had been declared a natural preserve and refuge for forest fauna. ("Isla Tiburón, vedada a los Seris.")

60. *El Imparcial*, March 5, 1975, p. 1.   61. *Ibid.*, March 7, 1975, p. 9A.

62. *Ibid.*, April 15, 1975, p. 1.   63. *Ibid.*, June 16, 1975, p. 1.

But the weapon of land-tenure investigation had a double edge, and in 1975 the damage done to illegal landholdings in Sonora mainly affected *campesinos* and *ejidatarios*. While the Echeverría regime recognized that ejidal rentals and abandonment were structurally induced by the biases of the counter-reform (as can be seen from the repurchase of rented land in 1973), the SRA land investigators did not display such understanding toward the *ejidatarios* themselves. In a nationwide purge, the government "cleansed" 15,000 *ejidos* of their old vices and made them newly eligible for official credit and resources. In this "cleansing," some 125,000 *ejidatarios* were deprived of their agrarian rights for abandoning, renting, or not working their land.[64] The effect of the agrarian-reform initiative often was to penalize the victims of the previous system. As a result, the conflict between private property and *ejidatario* or *campesino* claimants heightened and threatened to exceed the boundaries set by officially controlled rural political organizations.

THE LIMITS OF ECHEVERRISMO, 1970–1975

The simplest single reduction which exposes the limits of Echeverría's populist strategy for the countryside lies in its essential premise of balancing the power of the bourgeoisie against the pressure of the mobilized *campesinos* and working class. It was a traditional strategy, similar to that employed forty years earlier by Cárdenas in the first great land-reform epoch. Cárdenas also had sought to balance the power of the privileged classes by expanding the state-supervised mobilization of the lower classes. It was a classic strategy intended to play one class against the other. But by 1970 the advance of Mexican society had changed the relative power of all of the factors in the populist equation.

In 1975 the agricultural bourgeoisie, while economically declining and politically inferior to the industrial bourgeoisie, were much better organized than the *latifundistas* of 1936–1938. Moreover, they were able to count on substantial (though not total) support from the powerful industrial capitalists led by the Monterrey Group, whose antagonism toward Echeverría overshadowed sectoral and political differences separating the bourgeoisie as a class. The working class and *campesinos* tired of the slow, government-manipulated machinery of the CNC, CCI, and UGOCM, and other participants in rural politics.[65] Because the CCI and UGOCM had lapsed into a coopted format—the Pact of Ocampo—and the formerly

64. *Ibid.*, July 28, 1975, p. 1. A report in August raised the number of *ejidatarios* purged after 1970 to 157,000. (*Ibid.*, Aug. 31, 1975, p. 1.)

65. Quite often, the member organizations of the Pact of Ocampo delayed or halted land invasions and failed to press the agrarian-reform petitions of their constituents. ("Agrarismo y política.")

independent rural unions had turned to arguing over the crumbs doled out to the rural sector by the state, *campesinos* strained to form new organizations to vie for land reform independently. So on both counts—the growing economic and organizational strength of the bourgeoisie, and the increasing dissatisfaction of *campesinos* with the gap between official rhetoric and concrete results—the third partner in the populist pact, the state, lost power and control over the direction of Mexican civil society. As Echeverría continued to promise substantive agrarian reform, the tensions heightened.

In fact, the Echeverría government, though committed in its way to a new agrarian reform, never intended to foment independent class organizations among the *campesinos* and workers in civil society. Like the Cárdenas regime, the *echeverristas* had to control the *campesino* mobilization in order to attain the goals of the national state. Although Echeverría sporadically supported independent challenges to the CTM as a means of defying the industrial bourgeoisie, we shall see that in Sonora the government continued its cynical manipulation of *campesinos* through the Pact of Ocampo. The scene in the Sonoran land reform of the 1970s closely resembled the former modes of rural domination, emphasizing violence, cooptation, and the monopoly of material rewards by the state.

The Fruits of Agrarian Policies

The collectivization of ejidal property and the occasional references to nationalizing irrigation districts and small property further increased tensions in the Mexican countryside. As we saw in Chapter 6, the post-Cárdenas years brought a concerted campaign against collective land tenure and exploitation. With the conservative bourgeois leadership already proclaiming Echeverría to be a leftist sympathizer, the collectivization program fueled rumors of the "communization" of the countryside. On the other hand, public policy toward collectivization was inconsistent and often superficial. The SRA's campaign to educate *ejidatarios* to the virtues of collectivization was spotty and frequently ineffective. The goals of the regime were optimistic in the extreme: the SRA projected the organization of 7,000 collective *ejidos* by 1975.[66] One source contends that only 633 presidential resolutions ever appeared collectivizing *ejidos*, and those emerged from the last two weeks of the Echeverría *sexenio*.[67] While the government claimed responsibility for the creation of thousands of collectivized *ejidos*, critics contended that the reform program was ill-considered, bureaucratically immobilized, and structurally superficial. The

---

66. Arturo Warman, "La colectivización en el campo: una crítica," p. 48.
67. "El gobierno define: colectivizar, única salida agraria." Actually, Echeverría collectivized 634 *ejidos* on November 30, 1976, the day before he left office. (*Diario Oficial,* Nov. 30, 1976.)

bank continued to dominate the ejidal economy, and credit still went to those *ejidos* producing cash crops and crops for export. The disjuncture between *ejidatarios* and rural workers still blocked achievement of the stated goals of equity in the country.[68] Unemployment, underemployment, insufficient crop and credit diversification, and official corruption added to the woes of the collectivization program.[69]

With respect to the problems of rural workers, the Echeverría regime faced one of the key contradictions of the revolutionary land-reform program writ large: the conflict between the development of highly productive agricultural capitalism, based on cheap rural labor, and the stated commitment to sustain and expand an independent peasantry made up of elements of that rural working class. While the proletarianization of rural residents served the growth of the industrial labor supply, the industrial sector could not absorb rural labor as quickly as it became available. While the agrarian reform relieved some of this pressure on the cities and on the social order, agricultural capitalism was based on the same discrimination between proprietor and wage laborer.[70] This disjuncture created the very class tensions allegedly mollified by the populist state. It further created class divisions between *ejidatarios* and rural workers, many of whom were of similar origins. And finally, it created a system of rural violence over private property and revolutionary ideology, in which rural worker and populist state both lost to capitalist accumulation.

In addition to the limited program of collectivization and the contradictions of rural labor and property, the state found itself faced with contradictory goals in the rural environs, due to its weak fiscal position and growing foreign debt. The development of tourism, a leading producer of foreign exchange, frequently conflicted with the goals of agrarian reform and distributive justice. One example already mentioned involved Tiburón Island and the Seri Indians. Other examples proved equally scandalous. Echeverría had proposed that, under the new agrarian reform, *ejidatarios* "not only dedicate themselves to agriculture, but also to cattle businesses, industry, commerce, hunting, and tourism."[71] In Nayarit, Guerrero, Baja California, and Yucatán, *ejidatarios* were urged to turn their attention to the cultivation of tourism instead of more traditional crops.[72] Echeverría, in cooperation with the new National Fund for Ejidal Growth (FONAFE), formed the ill-famed Bahía de Banderas Commission

68. Warman, "La colectivización"; Francisco J. Guerrero, "La colectivización capitalista del campo y otros límites del reformismo," p. 80.

69. "El ejido colectivo."

70. This was especially true after 1972, when farmers turned from labor-intensive cotton production to mechanized crops after the collapse of international cotton prices. The labor effects of this change were especially severe in Sonora.

71. Cited in Cosío Villegas, *El estilo personal de gobernar*, p. 59.

72. *Ibid.*, pp. 59–63.

to preside over the transformation of 140 kilometers of Nayarit's coastline into tourist resorts. In one of the biggest scandals in current Mexican history, the project failed, the director fled to the United States, and the *campesino* industries and fishing cooperatives formed by FONAFE passed out of existence.[73] The ejidal union "Bahía de Banderas," made up of seven *ejidos*, told of the extortion and pressure by the state and federal governments to give up their lands to tourist-resort developers and government functionaries. Though the Echeverría government ostensibly countered those tactics with FONAFE and the Bahía de Banderas Commission, the fact remained that the *ejidatarios* were not substantially better off after a grandiose, 500-million-peso fraud. The expectation that poor, mostly illiterate *ejidatarios* would have been able to manage the new tourist and ejidal enterprise was only the beginning of a series of contradictions that caused analysts to wonder at the exotic solutions Echeverría sought for problems of agrarian reform in potential tourist areas.

Other examples abound which demonstrate the difficulty attending the populist resurgence in the context of an economy in fiscal trouble. Echeverría faced the problem of maintaining agricultural production for export, which generated crucial foreign exchange for the Mexican economy. The hub of export agriculture lay in Sonora and Sinaloa, also the chosen foci for the second great land-reform attempt of the Mexican Revolution. The threat by bourgeois partisans to withdraw their land from cultivation, though an unlikely reality, could cause major tremors in national politics. As we shall see, its effects on the money market were startling.

Deficit spending, at least partly a product of the failed fiscal reform, contributed to the inflationary spiral which had begun in late 1972.[74] In turn, inflation and foreign debt undermined the spending capacity of the state, overvalued the peso, and slowed the real growth of the GDP to 2.2 percent by 1976.[75]

Bottlenecks in official credit, corruption in the distribution of improved seeds and fertilizers, the lack of water for new land entering cultivation, and general bureaucratic obesity all chipped away at the possibilities for the genuine transfer of agricultural resources to the *campesinos*. The propensity of landowners and political *caciques* to protect their lands with hired guns was another unspoken restraint on Echeverría's grandiose reform. And finally, it must be remembered that the *echeverrista* reformers

---

73. Alfredo Ríos Camarena, director of the Bahía de Banderas Commission, was extradited from the United States, and has implicated many government officials in the scandal, including the former head of the CNC and SRA, Augusto Gómez Villanueva. (Miguel López Saucedo, "Ineficiencia y pillaje en Bahía de Banderas"; and Rodolfo Guzmán, "Gómez Villanueva en el escenario de Bahía de Banderas.")

74. The inflation rate of wholesale prices in 1970 was 2.7 percent; in 1976 the rate was 45.9 percent. ("Desequilibrios económicos del sexenio anterior.")

75. *Ibid.*

themselves were born and bred in the Mexican system of authoritarian politics. As the drama of agrarian confrontation heated up in 1975 and 1976, all of the cynicism and violence which were the regime's ultimate political weapons boiled to the surface.

The Challenge of The CCE

Another basic economic constraint hindering Echeverría's populist plans was the increasing national foreign debt, which was related to the agricultural decline of 1965–1976. In a complex web of relationships, it became apparent during the latter years of Echeverría's term that the continued capacity of the Mexican government to secure foreign loans was tied intimately to its ability to sustain a positive investment climate for foreign capital.[76] This security for capital, more a product of subjective perception than of structural analysis of the Mexican economy, in turn revolved around the evaluation of the domestic political climate by such leading capitalist organs as the American Chamber of Commerce in Mexico and the newly-formed Enterprise Coordinating Council (CCE).[77] The "spectre of Communism," which appeared so regularly to the Mexican investor, caused a decline in private investment of 20 percent from 1971 to 1974. In 1973 alone, 10 million pesos left the Mexican economy as a result of the growing conflict between populist state and bourgeois civil society.[78] In 1976, the crisis of capital flight worsened.

The benediction of the bourgeoisie, which proved so necessary to the survival of the Mexican economy, was tied to a demand for the abandonment of official agrarian-reform plans. The CCE viewed private property as a "natural right," which the state could regulate to an extent, but never destroy. Not surprisingly, private enterprise represented to the members of the CCE "the basic cell of the economy, and one of the most peculiar and valuable manifestations of the creative capacity of man and expression of the spiritual wealth of those who contribute to realizing, sustaining, and improving it."[79] Agricultural small property was nothing less than the "spinal column of the agricultural economy," against which po-

76. The importance of this relationship became clearest, perhaps, in 1976 and 1977, after massive capital flight had crippled the national economy. An economic evaluation of Lloyd's Bank International which affirmed the long-term investment security of the Mexican economy carried a great deal of weight in the repatriation of capital in the first months of 1977, as did support from the World Bank and International Monetary Fund. (*Excelsior*, May 21, June 17, and July 9, 1977.)

77. The CCE was formed in May 1975 with constituents from CONCAMIN, CONCANA-CO, COPARMEX, the Mexican Bankers Association, Mexican Council of Businessmen, and Mexican Association of Insurance Institutions. For a treatment of the influence of the American Chamber of Commerce on the domestic economy, see Angela M. Delli Sante, "The Private Sector, Business Organizations and International Influence: Mexico, a Case Study.")

78. *Excelsior*, March 3, 1974.

79. CCE Declaration of Principles, printed in *Excelsior*, May 8, 1975, p. 16.

litical aggression could not be tolerated. In a word, the CCE challenged the expanded right of eminent domain claimed by the Mexican state after the Revolution.

Perhaps even more important to the struggle between state and bourgeoisie, the CCE challenged the right of the state to govern education in civil society. It claimed the "right and obligation" of parents to educate their children, limiting the state to a role of providing a "climate of liberty that might facilitate the participation of the private sector in the programming and realization of educative tasks." Education was viewed as a factor contributing to economic progress through the formation of an educated skill-pool for the economy.

The CCE, then, in the name of the Mexican bourgeoisie of the 1970s, threw down the gauntlet before Echeverría and the revived populist state. At its base, the duel was over agrarian reform, worker independence, fiscal reform, and other immediate issues of the political economy. In its most expansive implications, the struggle was over the authority of the state to control the burgeoning hegemony of the dominant class in civil society. The battleground upon which the two forces faced each other was the agrarian reform in Sonora.

CONFRONTATION IN SONORA, 1975–1976

Shortly after Echeverría's return to Sonora for Christmas 1974, it became apparent that land conflict in the state was quickening. Conflicts among *ejidatarios* over the limited land available to them intensified. In a series of events indicating the heightened state of agrarian tensions, state and class organizations maneuvered to stake their claims to a part of Sonoran agrarian politics. In one case, affiliates of the CTM opposed members of the CNC over the same *ejido*, a patch of 620 hectares of waterless pasture-land.[80] Biébrich finally announced an investigation into land tenure and water monopolies in Guaymas and Empalme.[81] A number of new and established *ejidos* conflicted with small property-owners over the new presidential grants in Álamos, the Guaymas valley, the Mayo valley, and other parts of the state.[82] Mass unemployment began to haunt the machine-cultivated fields of the Yaqui and Mayo valleys, and *campesino* unrest threatened to exceed the limits imposed on it by state authority.

In October, the leading Hermosillo newspaper drily acknowledged that the schism between the private proprietors of the Yaqui valley and the SRA had intensified.[83] *El Imparcial*'s analysis presaged the greatest agrarian conflict in Sonora for nearly forty years.

80. I refer to the case of "El Henequén," Cajeme, granted in *Diario Oficial*, July 9, 1971. (*El Imparcial*, Feb. 23, 1975, p. 1.)

81. *El Imparcial*, March 6, 1975, p. 1.   82. *Ibid.*, July 31, 1975, p. 1.

83. *Ibid.*, Oct. 9–10, 1975, p. 1.

San Ignacio Río Muerto and Its Aftermath

The sun rose on October 20, 1975, on a large land invasion in the northern Yaqui valley, about a twenty-minute drive from Ciudad Obregón. The plots invaded, Blocks 717 and 719, included 100-hectare plots belonging to Erich Dengel Hilton, nine-year-old son of Miguel Dengel; Luis Ramírez Figueroa; and the widowed Señora Rosalía Toledo de Parada, all of locally-known, large landowning families.[84] The Federation of Small Property-Owners (FPP) of Sonora called immediately for government action against the invaders.[85] Many conservative newspapers also joined the call for state action against the invaders. In *El Imparcial*, a columnist wrote on October 23:

> The situation in the Yaqui valley, and in the entire southern part of the state, is becoming icier [*más álgida*] by the day. . . . The law states clearly that a violation is being committed—a grave violation—and the authorities have no alternative but to act, as a consequence. . . . [If not], they would be giving open authorization to anarchy, violations, disorder, and chaos.[86]

Biébrich gave notice that the invasion must end within 48 hours.[87] The invaders, in turn, sent a letter to Echeverría, recounting the antecedents of their 21-year struggle for the land, adjudicated in 1954 but delayed until now by various legal maneuvers. The executive committee of San Ignacio, which had reinitiated the petition for Plot 717 in 1970, had been blacklisted by farmers employing *campesinos* in the area. As a result of continuing frustration in their quest for land, 400 invaders made their way through the night to occupy the land they called "El Chaparral," in the area of San Ignacio Río Muerto, on October 20.[88]

At dawn on October 23 a party of State Judicial Police, backed by members of the 18th Federal Cavalry Regiment, opened fire on a group of invaders led by Juan de Dios Terán, a local schoolteacher. Witnesses and partisans of the invasion claimed, with obvious grounds, that the purpose of the shooting was to eliminate the *agrarista* leadership of San Ignacio. Some asserted that Juan de Dios Terán was first wounded, then executed with a shot to the head; Benjamín Robles, another leader, bled to death after being refused medical attention.[89] Officially, 7 died (Jiménez and the *Proceso* report cited below say 10); 20 to 30 more were wounded, and many others were arrested as they were thrown off the land by the police and armed vigilante "white guards" in the employ of private landholders. The Secretary of Agrarian Reform, now Félix Barra García, and all of

84. *Ibid.*, Oct. 21, 1975, p. 1.   85. *Ibid.*, Oct. 22, 1975, p. 1.
86. *Ibid.*, Oct. 23, 1975, p. 4.
87. Sevilla Mascareñas, *Aquí, Sonora, S.O.S.*, p. 54.
88. Jiménez Ricárdez, "Movimiento campesino," pp. 70 and 72.
89. *Ibid.*, p. 73. This is also the version given by Sevilla Mascareñas, p. 63, and in "Cosechas de violencia," *Proceso*, 2 (Nov. 13, 1976): 13. See also *El Imparcial*, Oct. 24, 1975, p. 1; and *Excelsior*, Oct. 24, 1975, p. 1.

the leaders of the Pact of Ocampo immediately flew to Sonora and demanded the resignation of Biébrich and the arrest of State Police Chief Francisco Arellano Noblecía. While Biébrich met to conciliate the hostile agrarian leadership in the Hotel Valle Grande in Ciudad Obregón, 10,000 campesinos marched against him.[90] On October 25, forced by the Echeverría administration and the campesinos, Biébrich resigned.[91] Arellano Noblecía fled the state and is still a fugitive, widely rumored to be a member of the presidential guard. Alejandro Carrillo Marcor, a former partisan of Lombardo Toledano in the CTM struggles of the late 1930s, was appointed governor of Sonora.

There are several contending interpretations of the origins and meaning of the massacre at San Ignacio Río Muerto, and none of them shed particularly favorable light on the Echeverría government. The most common interpretation is based on Biébrich's enmity with Gómez Villanueva and Celestino Salcedo Monteón.[92] The Tiburón Island dispute, according to this interpretation, was only part of the general disaffection felt by the "left wing" of Echeverría's cabinet at Biébrich's inattention to agrarian-reform matters. Further, when Biébrich supported Mario Moya Palencia as a presidential pre-candidate, the same people on the left of the PRI were annoyed by his opposition to their pre-candidate, José López Portillo. Moya Palencia, then Secretary of Government, was ultimately rejected for his sympathy with the industrial bourgeoisie, and Gómez Villanueva began to plot political revenge against his partisans, especially Biébrich. Since the program of Echeverría's government centered around land reform—a land reform that was conspicuously stalled in Sonora—Gómez Villanueva and Salcedo Monteón of the CNC encouraged land invasions in the already tense Yaqui valley. Given the state of alarm among private landholders and their influence with Biébrich, some confrontation appeared likely. The massacre at San Ignacio Río Muerto, whether accidental or planned, provided the vehicle whereby Biébrich's enemies could safely demand his removal by Echeverría, the governor's former benefactor.

Whether Biébrich actually ordered the shooting—or, alternatively, the judicial police acted in concert with paid "white guards" for landlords in the area—is unclear. It is certainly within the realm of possibility that

90. Sevilla Mascareñas maintains (p. 55) that Biébrich mocked the righteous indignation of Celestino Salcedo Monteón, secretary-general of the CNC and head of the Pact of Ocampo.

91. El Imparcial, Oct. 26, 1975, p. 1.

92. Adherents to this interpretation—with small personal variations—include Jiménez Ricárdez, various U.S. consular officials in Hermosillo, and the leaders of the Independent Campesino Front (FCI) which arose out of subsequent invasions in the spring of 1976. Rosa Delia Amaya, legal advisor to the petitioners at San Ignacio, also apparently held this view, according to friends. Since she died mysteriously in an accident during the 1976 invasions, her opinion must be recorded indirectly. Two extended interviews were conducted on March 26 and April 1, 1977, with Carlos Ferra and Anita López de Ferra (daughter of "Machi" López), legal advisors of the FCI.

Arellano Noblecía—a man given to violent performance of his duties, as former students at the University of Sonora can attest[93]—acted irresponsibly on his own authority or on private commission. The FCI contends that the entire massacre was staged to depose Biébrich and rid the Yaqui valley of independent leadership. According to the FCI and the version told to other *agraristas* by Rosa Delia Amaya before her death, the secretary-general of the *ejido* San Ignacio Río Muerto, Alejo Cárdenas, left the invasion surreptitiously the night before the massacre took place. Cárdenas was suspected as a government provocateur, though the role he might have played is still not clear.

The leading opponent of this interpretation is Mario Sevilla Mascareñas. His interpretation of the October events lays the blame exclusively with Biébrich, whom he paints as a latter-day *cacique*, sneering at the great mission of the Mexican Revolution. Ultimately, this interpretation rightly castigates the political insensitivity of the Biébrich government to the needs of Sonora's *campesinos*, but it does so in the name of *echeverrismo*, which proved itself equally unable to serve the *campesinos* in 1976. That the Biébrich affair transcended mere personal political callousness and the massacre at San Ignacio became apparent in the elimination of virtually every high official in Biébrich's entourage, including the secretary-general of the Sonora Campesino Leagues and the state PRI chief. The scale of the reaction to the San Ignacio treachery demands a wider explanation than that offered by Sevilla.

Following the political tidal wave that swept Sonora after October 23, the national government sought to defuse the potential violence generated by the San Ignacio killings. Almost immediately after the new governor's inauguration, Agrarian Reform Secretary Félix Barra García announced that shortly the *campesinos* of San Ignacio would receive ejidal grants. The SRA also promised further attacks against Sonoran *latifundismo*.[94] In the heat of the aftermath of the San Ignacio massacre, the Echeverría agrarian reform had finally gained its needed impetus. A rash of invasions throughout the month of November ensured that the government could not deny its obligation to the *campesinos*.[95]

On November 28 and 29, 1975, Echeverría granted 4,387 hectares of irrigated land to 433 *campesinos* from San Ignacio Río Muerto. As the first irrigated ejidal grant of importance since the formation of the Pact of Ocampo, San Ignacio and its neighboring plot San Isidro held special importance for the government-dominated *campesino* unions. In typical fashion, all of the signatory unions to the Pact of Ocampo demanded to be included in the ejidal census of San Ignacio and San Isidro. As a result, in

93. Arellano was the chief of police when his forces occupied the University of Sonora at Biébrich's behest in October 1973.

94. *Excelsior*, Oct. 26, 1975, p. 1; *El Imparcial*, Oct. 29, 1975, p. 1.

95. *El Imparcial*, Nov. 4 and 21–25, 1975, all p. 1.

a scene reminiscent of Cananea in 1958, outsiders who were not a part of the original census were included in the final grant and, in a final bitter twist, five widows of fallen invaders killed at San Ignacio were excluded.

Despite the episodic character of the San Ignacio grant and the need to reduce tensions in the Sonoran countryside, the agricultural bourgeoisie went on the offensive. On November 30, a group encompassing most of the southern Sonoran agricultural bourgeoisie—and extending as far north as Tijuana and Nogales, and as far south as Tepic, Nayarit—called for a halt in agricultural production and related activities.[96] The president of the Employers Central of the Yaqui valley claimed that the government "is taking a turn toward Communism. You now realize that they [the functionaries] want to eliminate agricultural property, and later commerce."[97] The CCE chimed in by seconding the stoppage to protest "the unjust aggression of the authorities against small private property, action that is oriented toward its extinction through the pulverization of the land."[98]

In Navojoa and Ciudad Obregón, a parade of agricultural machinery stopped on the main thoroughfares, and the stalled tractors driven in from the fields formed a blockade on the principal arteries of the agricultural heartland of Sonora.[99] The picture of stalled John Deere tractors appeared in newspapers throughout the country, and the stoppage achieved its dramatic effect. Nevertheless, the appearance of crisis in southern Sonora was belied by the fact that the agricultural bourgeoisie, just in from the fall wheat planting, did not at that time need the machinery in the field. Also unstated in the stagy drama unfolding in Ciudad Obregón were the regional and sectoral disagreements between the agricultural *dons* of southern Sonora and the industrial bourgeoisie of the region. The CCE, hostile to Echeverría and his threats against property, supported the stoppage by the "mining farmers" who were being attacked by the land reform. But the CCE also encouraged negotiations which ended in the creation of a Tripartite Agrarian Commission (CAT) and the end of the stoppage.[100] Additionally, the agricultural strike against the regime failed

96. *El Imparcial*, Dec. 1, 1975, p. 1. Affiliates of the stoppage included members of the *Centro Patronal del Valle del Yaqui*; *Centro Patronal del Valle del Mayo*; Hermosillo and Ciudad Obregón delegations of CANACINTRA (National Chamber of Industries of Transformation); CONCANACO delegates from Ciudad Obregón, Guaymas, Navojoa, Nogales, San Luis Río Colorado, Culiacán, Los Mochis, La Paz, Mexicali, Tepic, Tijuana, Mazatlán, Guasave, and Guamuchil. (Carlos Moncada, *Años de violencia en Sonora, 1955–1976*, p. 173.)

97. *Excelsior*, Dec. 2, 1975, p. 1.

98. Arriola, "Los grupos empresariales," p. 65.

99. *El Imparcial*, Dec. 2, 1975, p. 2.

100. Arriola, p. 65. *Campesinos*, ever wary of new government commissions, nicknamed the CAT "*Comision Tripa Hartita*," or the commission full of tripe. (*El Imparcial*, Dec. 4, 1975, p. 1.) The Tripartite Commission did not appear to favor *campesinos*, as they were outmanned by partisans of the right and had only officialist representatives to plead their case. In Sonora the Commission consisted of: SRA delegate Ricardo Martínez Wilson; CNC delegate Ignacio Martínez Tadeo; Jaime Miranda Peláez, president of the CNPP; Hector

to take into account the fact that the rest of the state of Sonora was in relative calm, with the notable exceptions of Sibolibampo and Capetamaya, where hostilities continued.

With the lifting of the agricultural work stoppage, which the Sonoran governor had denounced at the outset as a "masquerade,"[101] agrarian activity again died down in Sonora. The Pact of Ocampo was not utilized in pursuing threats against *latifundistas*, even though national agrarian officials formally took an *agrarista* posture. As a result of this official reticence, a group of militant *campesinos* in the Yaqui valley broke out of the Pact of Ocampo and started Sonoran *agrarismo* and the Echeverría government toward a final showdown in 1976. The power of that confrontation left Sonora still stricken well into the *sexenio* of José López Portillo.

The April Invasions: Limits to Independent Agrarismo

It has long been a commonplace of Mexican politics that the national state ensures its survival with a crafty blend of political cooptation and violence. If the occasional populist mobilizations depart from the "normal" routine of PRI politics and state domination in their intensity and redistributive promise, both Echeverría and Cárdenas ultimately refused independence to working-class and *campesino* organizations when state control was threatened. Whereas the bourgeoisie has gained tremendous power in both political and civil society through the "economic miracle," the underclasses have gained power only in sporadic rebellion against the terms of the revolutionary populist pact. The state, as promotor of capitalist accumulation and suppressor of underclass organizations in civil society, can no longer function as the "neutral" arbiter of multi-class coalition. A later case illustrating these assertions revolved around the formation of the Independent Campesino Front (FCI) in April 1976, and the state's response to the maverick organization.

On April 3, 1976, a group of Yaqui valley *campesinos*, some of whom formerly participated in the UGOCM, invaded Block 407 in the heart of the valley. This block was chosen for its strategic importance, as this was to be a siege, not a momentary occupation. Bounded on all four sides by large poplar trees, Block 407 stood as a solitary fortress surrounded by the otherwise-level cropland of the central valley. Unique in its natural protection, this block, called "San Pedro," also became famous for its occupants, the founders of the FCI.

The day after its occupation, and after initial negotiations failed, Sonora SRA official Ricardo Martínez Wilson entered the occupied land with two agronomists to inform the invaders that military action might be

---

Acedo Valenzuela, president of the UGRS; and Alberto Zazueta Nieblas, executive director of the Departamento de Asuntos Rurales de Sonora. (See also *El gobierno mexicano*, 61 [December 1975]: 37.)

101. Moncada, *Años de violencia*, p. 173.

taken if they did not abandon the block. As the federal army surrounded the invasion, the leaders declared the visiting officials hostages, as insurance against military assault.[102] On April 8, after personal assurances of protection from Governor Carrillo, the FCI released the hostages unharmed.[103] On April 28 they peacefully left Block 407, having given birth to the FCI.

Rather suddenly, invasion activity heightened in the Yaqui and Mayo valleys and other parts of the state. Echeverría, again travelling to Ciudad Obregón, told a rally of 50,000 campesinos that "the law is the way," and that the SRA would stay in Sonora as long as necessary to protect the interests of the campesinos.[104] But suddenly the president who had taken on the mantle of Zapata and Cárdenas refused to support or defend land invasions, declaring himself an advocate of "neither invasions nor latifundios. . . . I have requested that all of the governors impede all invasions, with the cooperation of the Secretary of National Defense; I am responsible for that policy."[105] Almost immediately, in Chiapas, the federal army intervened in a land controversy in the municipality named "Venustiano Carranza." Five agraristas, all Tzotzil Indians, fell dead at the hands of the military on May 12, manifesting Echeverría's attitude toward land invasions.[106]

At the same time, the SRA and the Sonoran government agreed with an old UGOCM proposal—newly restated by 10,000 campesinos in Ciudad Obregón—that the upper limit on irrigated private property should be reduced to twenty hectares.[107] In another conciliatory move, the SRA announced that 30,000 hectares might be opened to ejidal petitioners in the Yaqui valley, if only the water could be found to irrigate it.[108] This trial balloon soon became official proclamation when, on May 14, the SRA announced that 7,000 campesinos would be given 35,000 hectares of Yaqui valley land by November in an extension of Irrigation District 41.

In the extension of District 41, both left and right partisans within the Echeverría regime found an agreeable solution to the tar-baby they had found in southern Sonora. To the official agrarian-reform organizations and the Pact of Ocampo, the extension of District 41 meant strengthening

102. El Imparcial, April 6–9, 1976; interviews with Carlos Ferra.

103. Ferra (and other sources, not partisans of the FCI) claims that Alejo Cárdenas, secretary-general of San Ignacio Río Muerto and suspected provocateur in the October 1975 massacre, also played the role of government agent at Block 407. Cárdenas was the leader of a faction within the invasion who wanted to hang the hostages in full view of the army. Other leaders, uninterested in personal acts of vengeance against the hostages (and probably aware of the consequences), prevailed. Cárdenas disappeared from the invasion shortly thereafter. He disappeared from San Ignacio in the spring of 1977 during a wave of pistolerismo carried out by "white guards." (El Imparcial, March 8, 1977, p. 1.)

104. El Imparcial, April 20, 1976, p. 1.

105. "Invasiones agrarias y rigidez política."

106. "El ejército en Chiapas."   107. El Imparcial, April 10–11, 1976, p. 1.

108. Ibid., May 4, 1976, p. 1D.

their increasingly eroding position among Sonoran *campesinos*. Part of the District 41 plan was to demand that all prospective *ejidatarios* petitioning within the extension be made to clear the land for survey and planting. In the steaming heat of the Sonoran summer, which daily exceeded 100 degrees Fahrenheit, thousands of *campesinos* left land invasions elsewhere to clear the new land, thereby undercutting FCI efforts to organize the *campesinos* outside of the Pact of Ocampo. Another aspect of the District 41 extension benefitted the Pact members as well. The "volunteer" labor to clear the land was put squarely in the hands of the CNC, CCI, and UGOCM, who declared that participants would have to work the land under the aegis of one of the above organizations in order to prove their status as *campesinos* under the agrarian-reform law.[109] Again, by controlling the material rewards available through the agrarian legal-bureaucratic system, the official *agrarista* organizations of the state maintained their domination in the countryside.

At the same time, both the advocates of collectivization and the defenders of small private property found merit in the District 41 extension. The plan stipulated that all new *ejidos* created in the area would be collective, not individual. Many old collectivists were lured by this proposal, despite the mammoth problems that confronted any new *ejidos* to be created in the area. Small proprietors, meanwhile, pushed in favor of the extension, even offering to trade their worthless land for inclusion in the new district plan. And this they did, signing contracts with the SRA to donate their pasture-land for "public use" in return for small plots in the extension area.

To the *ejidos* that already existed at the margin of the District 41 area, the extension represented a menace, dividing them against themselves and diverting their attention from more important matters. Bacame, for instance, which was still locked in a struggle over Sibolibampo, opposed the extension of District 41 because it jeopardized the political and economic well-being of the *ejido*. One faction wanted to petition for an expansion (*ampliación*) of Bacame, petitioning new land from the District 41 area. But the mainstream of political power opposed the expansion, because the plots in the added area of District 41 were to be only five hectares, too small to survive as a unit of production. The *ejidatarios* of Bacame (and Buaysiacobe) had twenty hectares of irrigated land each, not an excessive amount, but enough to survive at a modest standard of living. Such successful *ejidos* feared that including five-hectare ejidal plots within their *ejidos* and credit societies would eventually cause conflict over the unequal division of lands, as well as bringing economic disaster to those with the twenty-hectare units.[110] These *ejidos* demanded that the

---

109. *Ley Federal de Reforma Agraria*, Book Four, Title II, chap. 2, art. 200.

110. Remember that each member of an ejidal credit society has expanded responsibility for his fellow members' debts. In a mixed-credit society, with some members farming twenty

land in the Yaqui valley (Sibolibampo, for example) be divided first, before the District 41 plan was put into effect. Despite the merit of their position, such demands put a heavy strain on marginal *ejidos* which stood to benefit from new water rights.

Finally, with all of the ejidal division and political conflict caused by the District 41 proposal, two small but important items almost escaped notice. First, Article 27 of the Constitution and Article 220 of the federal Agrarian Reform Law of 1971 state that the minimum ejidal grant per *ejidatario* must be ten, not five, hectares of irrigated land.[111] And second, as is shown in Table A20, it had been some time since any dam in the Yaqui valley had stood at capacity. Echeverría, in his attempt to control events in Sonora, violated his own Agrarian Code and proposed to extend a water district already plagued by drought and perennial water-storage shortages. Under pressure, the underside of Mexican agrarian politics was resurfacing.

While the District 41 maneuver began to have its disarming effect on the invading *campesinos*, tensions in the Yaqui and Mayo valleys still remained at a high pitch. In June, 200 small proprietors invaded *ejidos* in various parts of the state.[112] The federal army, still in the field, invaded a number of *ejidos* "in search of arms for Block 407."[113] And while many adamant *ejidatarios* refused the extension of District 41, the SRA promised that within ninety days the government would expropriate 20,000 to 40,000 hectares in the Yaqui and Mayo valleys.[114]

On July 1, partisans of the newly-formed FCI stormed Blocks 407, 509, and 609, and were quickly surrounded by the army. While the army fought to dislodge the invaders,[115] all of the aspects of recent issues seemed to come together in a cacophonous clash of forces in the Sonoran fields. In a simultaneous rush to action, the SRH announced a grant of 130 million pesos for District 41; the SRA published the expropriation of 800 certificates of immunity; and 8.6 million pesos were offered to former owners of expropriated land in San Ignacio Río Muerto, in order to stave off rising bourgeois enmity. While the CNPP armed itself for a defense of private property, the official agrarian reform organizations—CNC, CCI, and UGOCM—took a more militant stance toward land invasions. The battle in the Yaqui and Mayo valleys was also a battle for clientele, and the birth of the FCI drove official agrarian politics a significant step to the left.

In October the redistributive promises of the past summer seemed to

hectares successfully and others succumbing with only five hectares, the economic burden would be too heavy for the *ejido* to bear.

111. *Ley Federal de Reforma Agraria*, Book Four, Title II, chap. 4, art. 220.
112. *El Imparcial*, June 5, 1976, p. 1.   113. *Ibid.*, June 12, 1976, p. 1.
114. *Ibid.*, June 18, 1976, p. 1D.
115. *Ibid.*, July 2–3, 1976, pp. 1–2. Blocks 509 and 609 were vacated on July 6, but a reported 600–700 invaders stayed in 407 until July 23. (*Ibid.*, July 7, 21–22, and 24, 1976, all p. 1.)

fade while winter planting took place. The *campesinos*, still waiting for land, again threatened to renew invasions. As had become custom in past months, Block 407 led the way, and other invasions followed suit. Capetamaya, symbol of *campesino* militance in the Mayo valley, was occupied and cleared repeatedly. Finally, in a scene reminiscent of the nineteenth-century wars pitting Indians against Porfirian *latifundistas*, the Mayos began on October 31 to beat their drums continuously as a warning that land invasions would intensify if no agrarian action took place before November 10.[116] While the SRA scrambled to expedite the 34,000 hectares officials wanted to grant to *ejidatarios*, the difference between official *agrarismo* and the FCI became clear in the Yaqui. On November 10, as the ultimatum expired, the FCI invaded six plots of land, including, of course, the famous Block 407. Meanwhile, partisans of the Pact of Ocampo organizations merely carried out symbolic invasions, marching to the margin of a *latifundio* and camping in front of it.[117] On November 13, six more *latifundios* fell to the FCI. The *campesino* mobilization had peaked.

ECONOMIC DECLINE AND CLASS POLARIZATION, FALL 1976

As the conflict between the populist state and the bourgeoisie heightened, so did the structural crisis of the Mexican economy. The public foreign debt climbed to 40.4 billion pesos by 1975, with a total public debt of over 216.7 billion pesos.[118] Real growth in the GDP had slowed by 1976 to 2.2 percent, which meant a decline of 1.2 percent in GDP per capita for that year.[119] The official rate of inflation for 1976 was 22.2 percent, compared with 10.5 percent the year before.[120] Mexico's crucial foreign-trade balance had declined over the *sexenio* as well, at least partly due to the world recession of 1974–1975. While exports increased during 1970–1976, inflation continued to hamper efforts to diversify foreign markets for Mexican manufactures, and the domestic economy suffered as a result. Likewise, reliance on primary goods for 79 percent of exports, and on the United States for two-thirds of total trade, made the Mexican economy vulnerable to sudden dislocations, as the 1974–1975 recession showed.[121]

During this period of economic difficulties, a common rumor held that the peso was about to be devalued for the first time since the spring of 1954. With capital and intermediate goods assuming an ever-larger role in the structure of Mexican imports, a favorable balance of trade was crucial to a stable economy and manageable foreign debt. According to René Vil-

---

116. *Ibid.*, Oct. 31, 1976, p. 1.

117. *Ibid.*, Nov. 10–14, 1976, all p. 1.

118. Banco Nacional de Comercio Exterior, *Mexico, 1976*, p. 262.

119. "Desequilibrios económicos del sexenio anterior."

120. *Business Trends: The Mexican Economy, 1976*, p. 80. The *Proceso* article cited above gives a figure of 45.9-percent increase in the wholesale price index for 1976.

121. *Business Trends*, p. 114.

larreal, the peso had been seriously overvalued since 1960, and by 1975 was overvalued by 32.2 percent.[122] In order to improve the competitive position of Mexico's exports internationally, and to stimulate domestic investment at the same time, many economists advocated the politically and symbolically unpopular move of devaluation. After much indecision and the further decline of the peso in 1976, Echeverría "floated" the peso on the eve of his final presidential report to the nation.[123]

But more than economic problems affected the devaluation, and the final quarter of 1976 became a test of strength between bourgeoisie and populist state, personified in Luis Echeverría. Since the failure of the fiscal reform and the resignation of Treasury Secretary Hugo Margáin in 1972, relations had worsened between state and bourgeoisie. Speculation and capital flight in 1973, the 1974–1975 recession, and the controversy surrounding Echeverría's social policies compounded the difficulties. In 1976, after the first devaluation, some of the bourgeoisie took advantage of the economic situation to enrich themselves through speculation, simultaneously striking a blow at the Echeverría administration. One businessman remarked that "the next cabinet better be staffed by experienced and reasonable politicians . . . to return the confidence that Alejo, Muñoz Ledo, and Gómez Villanueva made us lose."[124]

When agrarian instability continued after the peso had stabilized, speculators again spurred a massive capital flight on the occasion of the first parity quotation since September 1. On October 26, the newly-fixed peso (at 19.70/19.90) began to sink on the international market to a level of 26.24/26.50, due mainly to large-scale currency speculation. By November 23, the Treasury and the Bank of Mexico effectively closed their foreign currency dealings, due to the excessive dollar demand. In a two-day period preceding the announcement to halt the dollar trade, an estimated 1.2 billion dollars had left the country.[125] Domestic capital quickly withdrew from investment in the national economy, and growth in capital formation had to come primarily from foreign sources. Due largely to capital flight during August and September 1976, the movement of capital out of Mexico accelerated to 2.2 billion dollars in 1976, compared with 406 million in 1975 and 339 million in 1973, the other years characterized by massive capital flight.[126] The national economy was being devastated by monetary instability which far exceeded the severity of the structural economic crisis.[127]

122. Capital and intermediate goods amounted to 91 percent of total imports in 1969. (Villarreal, El desequilibrio externo, Table 63 and p. 202.)

123. Excelsior, Sept. 1, 1976, p. 1.

124. "Tiempo de la reconstrucción económica."

125. "Candado a la fuga de dólares."

126. Banco de México, Informe Anual, 1973, 1975, 1976.

127. The capital flight did not respond to conventional signs of international confidence in the peso. In addition to the continued presence of foreign capital in Mexico, the International Monetary Fund on Oct. 27, 1976, approved 837 million dollars in special drawing

In the midst of this brew of economic and political turmoil, another assault on Echeverría began. From the early days of September, rumors had circulated to the effect that a coup was imminent, that Echeverría, or the army, or "the Communists," were preparing to take over the government in a grand *golpe de estado*.[128] Despite the continuing failure of this *golpe* to appear on various rumored occasions, the popular attitude carried the stories faithfully, according to the old dictum, "If you hear the river running, it's because it's carrying water."[129]

Echeverría lashed out at the Monterrey Group as the focus of capital flight and rumor-mongering. In October he scolded "the powerful rich of Monterrey, who say they are Christians and beat their breasts, but refuse to help their fellow humans, and although they create industries, they lack social sensitivity, which converts them into . . . reactionaries and enemies of the people."[130] Rumors continued to build, alleging a future of frozen bank accounts, rationing, and the nationalization of the banking system. In turn, bank accounts closed, hoarding began, and the tempo of impending confrontation accelerated.

THE LAST GASP OF AGRARIAN POPULISM:
SONORA, NOVEMBER 1976

It was in the context of this heated political polarization that events again focused on Sonora. As we have seen, Sonora's agrarian struggles were not born in 1976, but had existed since time immemorial. They took on added importance during the Echeverría *sexenio*, however, due partly to Echeverría's proselytizing and the statements of his ministers. In the summer 1976 confrontation between state and bourgeoisie, the Secretary of Agrarian Reform pointed his finger at "the nylon farmers . . . and industrialists of Monterrey who have participated in a failed attempt to destabilize the political structure of the country."[131] Political forces around the country, with the exception of the extreme right, accused "the forces aligned with the CCE, the bankers, . . . the *latifundistas*, almost crazy with rage, . . . the American Chamber of Commerce, . . . and the CIA" of propitiating the campaign of rumors flooding the country.[132]

As might be expected, a curious blend of circumstance and logic dictated that Sonora be the focus for Echeverría's last stab against the bourgeoisie. Andrés Marcelo Sada, president of COPARMEX, was alleged to be

rights for Mexico after the new peso parity was declared. The U.S. Federal Reserve authorized 600 million dollars on a short line of credit to stop the flight of capital. But the trend continued, and capital did not begin to return until after Echeverría left office. (Banco de México, *Informe Anual*, 1976.)

128. Sara Moirón, "A falta de información, el rumor."
129. "Si el río suena es que agua lleva"; quoted in Loaeza, "La política del rumor," p. 139.
130. *Excelsior*, Oct. 16, 1976, p. 1.   131. *Ibid.*, June 19, 1976, p. 1.
132. *Ibid.*, Nov. 23, 1976, p. 1.

the chief author of many of the rumors of an impending coup. He and his organization, which represented the vestiges of the secular right dating from the 1930s, had led the 1975 industrial stoppage in Sonora. The logical theatre for a show of strength against COPARMEX was in Sonora, where they had fought even the moderate land reforms of the past year. Sonora also demanded agrarian action because of the recent appearance of the FCI and the continuing fear that *campesino* organization, so crucial to Echeverría's strength, might slip from the grasp of the wavering populist state. In November the Sonoran land invasions continued, and the FCI held numerous properties throughout the central Yaqui valley.[133]

It is important to cite the outstanding characteristics of Sonora as a battleground, mainly because the agrarian struggle was not unique to Sonora. Simultaneous confrontations were unfolding in Sinaloa, Chiapas, the Federal District, Veracruz, Oaxaca, and Yucatán. But Sonora held a special place because of the importance of its land and Echeverría's determination.

On November 18 and 19, 1976, *Diario Oficial* published 87 presidential resolutions for the Yaqui and Mayo valleys, dividing 37,131 hectares of irrigated land and 61,655 hectares of pasture-land among 8,944 *campesinos* belonging to 156 *ejidos*. In one fell swoop, Echeverría had divided more irrigated land in southern Sonora than any president since Cárdenas. In addition, the president announced the transformation to collective exploitation of 634 *ejidos* nationally, of which 22 were from Sonora, 19 of them within federal irrigation districts.[134] The land came from 67 individual family groups, not counting extended kinship. Of those groups, fully 39 had member landowners under the age of eighteen, and 18 listed landowners ten or younger. Carlos Calderoni Obregón was the youngest "farmer" expropriated, at age one.[135]

The Rural Bank and SRH pledged credit to the newly-created *ejidos* immediately. The reaction of the agricultural bourgeoisie was equally swift and equally predictable. The second annual agricultural work stoppage was declared on November 23, and again tractors sat idle in the streets of Ciudad Obregón and Navojoa.[136] *El Imparcial*, which had stood against Echeverría throughout the troubled *sexenio*, ran a poem by their agri-

133. The FCI invaded at least 12 properties on November 9 and 13: Block 1302, belonging to Alberto Fernández; 809, Francisco Bórquez; 512, Sergio Esquer; 407, Bórquez family; 510, Victor Sánchez; 1812, Laborín family; 913, 915, 917, Benjamín Castelo family; 611, Señora Marcela Becerril; 1414, various sons of Rosalía Toledo de Parada; 2412, Muñoz family. (*El Imparcial*, Nov. 10–14, 1976, all p. 1.)

134. *Diario Oficial*, Nov. 19, 1976.

135. This is undoubtedly an underestimate of the number of juvenile farmers expropriated, since the published list contained only 391 ages for 560 landowners. (*El Imparcial*, Nov. 23, 1976, p. 7A.)

136. *Excelsior*, Nov. 23, 1976, p. 17A; Nov. 24, p. 20A; Nov. 25, pp. 10A and 13A; Nov. 26, p. 1.

cultural correspondent entitled "Individualism and Collectivism," which compared Echeverría's collectivization with Stalin's.[137]

Simultaneously, Echeverría's agrarian-reform team launched a final assault to destroy the campaign of rumors against the regime. Celestino Salcedo Monteón, secretary-general of the CNC, lashed out at Andrés Marcelo Sada, head of COPARMEX, as "manipulator of . . . [COPARMEX], which he has purchased in order to unleash his insane appetites and personal vanities, which are at the service of the darkest and most antipatriotic interests of reaction." A PRI senator further identified the campaign against Sada as a more general strike against the bourgeois enemies of *echeverrismo*:

> Not only has he been characterized as being the principal promotor . . . of the campaign of anti-patriotic rumors, but also he and his closest relatives, friends, and associates are mentioned in Texas, Florida, and other places as being among the distinguished Mexican businessmen who have taken and continue to take large quantities of money out of the country for the last two or three years.[138]

While Sada lamented the "disappearance of private initiative in [the state's] search for a socialist or communist state,"[139] Fidel Velázquez, leader of the CTM, identified Sada as "one of the greatest enemies of the regime." Sada, symbol of conservative bourgeois sentiment and outstanding culprit in the hostile actions of Mexican capital, was charged with sabotage and treason on the floor of the Chamber of Deputies and Senate.[140]

In the midst of the agricultural work stoppage, the rumor campaign against Echeverría, the impending presidential succession, and the ejidal grants of November 18 and 19, the *campesino* rebellion in Sonora continued. The FCI and the Pact of Ocampo organizations carried out 14 more invasions on November 24, enveloping land belonging to a handful of the many *latifundistas* still operating in the Yaqui and Mayo valleys. Four properties belonging to the family of Elías Calles fell to invaders; ten more belonging to the Zaragoza, Barcenas, Santini, and other families also were occupied.[141] Capetamaya was invaded again. Over 385,000 hectares in Durango and over 20,000 hectares in Sinaloa succumbed to *campesino* uprisings in the last two weeks of the Echeverría presidency.[142]

On November 30, his last day in office, Echeverría granted some 491,738 hectares to *ejidatarios* nationally. He ended his term of office by granting

137. R. Valenzuela G., "Individualismo y Colectivismo," in *El Imparcial*, Nov. 23, 1976, p. 5A.

138. *Excelsior*, Nov. 25, 1976, p. 1.   139. *Ibid.*, Nov. 24, 1976, p. 1.

140. *Ibid.*, Nov. 26, 1976, p. 1.   141. *El Imparcial*, Nov. 25, 1976, p. 1.

142. *Ibid.*, Nov. 29, 1976, p. 1; *Excelsior*, Nov. 18, p. 1; Nov. 28, p. 1; Dec. 1, p. 4A.

the controversial extension of District 41 in the Yaqui valley.[143] As Luis Echeverría Álvarez rode in José López Portillo's inaugural parade down Mexico City's broad Paseo de la Reforma to the presidential palace, it seemed he had struck the last blow in a memorable six years which shook the foundations of political order and contributed to the temporary collapse of capitalist growth in Mexico for the first time since 1938. But while Echeverría had to govern by *sexenio*, the national bourgeoisie by no means ceded its power on December 1. In López Portillo they had an ally upon whom they could count for "just recompense" for lands expropriated and the restoration of order in the countryside.

EPILOGUE: DISMANTLING ECHEVERRISMO, 1977

When López Portillo donned the presidential sash on December 1, capitalists around the country breathed an almost audible sigh of relief. Echeverría was finally gone, and the country could return to normal. The metaphor of the pendulum emerged again; everyone seemed sure there would be a swing to the right in presidential politics. During the first part of the new administration, many changes occurred, further besmirching the image of Echeverría and laying waste to the reforms of 1975 and 1976.

First, on December 7, 1976, a district judge declared the expropriations of November 18 and 19 unconstitutional, null and void. Immediately an outcry was heard from every quarter: COPARMEX and the Farmers Association of Southern Sonora saluted the great jurisprudential independence of the judge; the Pact of Ocampo declared him partisan and incompetent.[144] Ten days after the judicial decree, the new Secretary of Agrarian Reform, Jorge Rojo Lugo, declared the expropriations legal and promised that the new regime "will not take one step backward" in the agrarian-reform process.[145] Then for eight months the government negotiated with the ex-landowners of the Yaqui and Mayo valleys over the price of indemnification through which the *latifundistas* would give up their already-expropriated land. Finally, in August 1977, the *latifundistas* received their original demand of 680 million pesos for 17,000 hectares. The other 20,000 hectares of the original expropriation were not indemnified.

Invasions continued throughout the early months of López Portillo's presidency, however, and the agrarian-reform process seemed not to have come very far, despite the image of radical transformation under Echeverría. While the Pact of Ocampo promised its faithful collaboration with the government,[146] and even echoed the private sector's complaint of insecurity in land tenure,[147] invasions by independent *campesino* groups

143. *Diario Oficial*, Nov. 30, 1976; *El Imparcial*, Dec. 1.
144. *Excelsior*, Dec. 11 and 15–17, 1976, p. 1.
145. *Ibid.*, Dec. 17, 1976, p. 11. 146. *Ibid.*, Dec. 8, 1976, p. 1.
147. *Ibid.*, May 28, 1977, p. 23A.

swept the nation. The CNPP declared that 800 properties in Nayarit and Jalisco alone had been invaded since López Portillo had assumed office. The CNPP, joined by other capitalist organizations such as CONCAMIN, CCE, UGRS, and CAAES, demanded an end to *campesino* unrest as a condition for their participation in the new president's "Alliance for Production."[148] *Campesinos* in San Luis Potosí, Sonora, Chiapas, Veracruz, Coahuila, Durango, Morelos, Nayarit, Oaxaca, Sinaloa, Querétaro, and Jalisco continued their rebellion, despite Pact of Ocampo disapproval.[149] Violence dominated at least four of the states.

To stop the progression of events that seemed to be leading to another outbreak of political violence and antipathy at the national level, López Portillo used a combination as old as Mexico: *pan y palo,* bread and stick. He increased the credit available to agriculture and continued the agrarian proceedings in Sonora. At the same time, he tacitly endorsed a new law in Querétaro condemning the instigators of land invasions to forty years in prison.[150] While the SRA under López Portillo carried out the organization of the new collective *ejidos* created on November 18 and 19, 1976, agrarian-reform officials simultaneously purged Sonoran *ejidos* of 2,400 *campesinos* who had violated their status by taking jobs outside agriculture or by moving from their municipality of residence.[151]

While López Portillo claimed to assign a very high value to agrarian reform, differences with the Echeverría regime appeared very early in 1977. The completion of agrarian reform was seen primarily as an aid to the new "Alliance for Production," not as a permanent redistributive program.[152] This reorientation of rhetoric agreed with the claims of the CAAES and the CNPP that the land-reform initiative of 1976 would cause irreparable harm to agricultural production in the Yaqui and Mayo valleys.[153] In fact, the new tone of the official agrarian reform and the pronouncements of the agricultural bourgeoisie were both based on the supposition that the new *ejidos* would not produce as well as private holdings. Actually, however, in a study of 62 *ejidos* in the southern valleys of Sonora, the Rural Bank found the opposite. Although the scarcity of water dictated that mostly wheat be planted, with less soya, sesame, sorghum, safflower, and cotton, 29,845 hectares (of almost 33,000 hectares irrigated) were planted immediately. The average wheat yield (4,684 kg/hectares) exceeded the total average yield of the Yaqui valley (4,300 kg/hectares)

148. *Excelsior,* March 23, April 15 and 20, and May 6, 1977, all p. 1; *El Imparcial,* April 14, 1977, p. 1. CAAES, *Confederación de Asociaciones Agrícolas del Estado de Sonora,* is the largest agricultural proprietors' organization in the state. UGRS, *Unión de Ganaderos Regionales de Sonora,* is the cattlemen's equivalent.

149. *Excelsior,* May 10, 1977, pp. 20–21A; May 18, p. 5A; May 24, pp. 18A and 32A; May 26, p. 23A; May 27, p. 30A; May 28, p. 28A; June 2, p. 28A; July 12, p. 31A; July 16, p. 27A.

150. *Ibid.,* April 21–26, 1977.

151. *El Imparcial,* March 14, 1977, p. 1; March 18, p. 1; March 27, p. 7.

152. *Ibid.,* March 25, 1977, p. 1.

153. *Excelsior,* May 2, 1977, p. 14A.

and the total average for southern Sonora (3,500 kg/hectares). Value of production in these new *ejidos* exceeded 468 million pesos in the first year.[154]

Despite the promising results of the first crop year in the new *ejidos*, the federal government was not anxious to publicize its support for them. Water continued to be a problem, and government support prices were too low to ensure a decent profit margin for *ejidatarios*. Enemies of the ejidal system even blamed the new *ejidos* for the appearance of *chahuixtle*, a form of wheat rust.

López Portillo's failure to intervene on behalf of the *campesinos*, in the style of a guardian of the populist revival, is crucial to our understanding the new low-profile posture of the national state, in sharp contrast with the Echeverría presidency. The law against invasions in Querétaro was unopposed by the new regime, despite some complaints from the CNC and other *campesino* organizations. An illegal production tax on Sonoran *ejidos* went unprotested at the national level, despite its crushing impact on the new *ejidos*.[155] But the new regime had to court the national bourgeoisie in order to further the Alliance for Production.

Sensing that the regime favored a quick, permanent resolution of agrarian matters and a new posture of high productivity and fiscal austerity, the CCE began to suggest patterns for future state–bourgeois relations. The Monterrey Group promised to return the capital which had fled under Echeverría. They felt "sure that we have a future full of great accomplishments. The only thing lacking is that we dedicate ourselves to work instead of making politics *a la mexicana*."[156] COPARMEX and the other affiliates of the Monterrey Group warned the state not to engage in economic tasks, however, and to leave the economy to them and to the superior efficiency of the market.[157] The bourgeoisie would reinvest only on its own terms. The Alliance for Production, and ultimately presidential politics, depended on their good will.

Mexican politics as it entered 1977 had come full circle in forty years. The state, formerly the dominant partner in the populist pact, now was forced to cede power to the dominant forces in civil society, which would dictate the major economic and social policies of the new *sexenio*. The victims of the changing face of power will be those who have depended on benevolent state tutelage under the agrarian reform: the *campesinos*.

154. Untitled memorandum from *Banco Rural*, Ciudad Obregón, covering the 1976–1977 crop year.

155. In the spring of 1977, a 3-percent production tax was imposed on *ejidos* by the Sonoran state legislature, in direct contravention of the federal Agrarian Reform Law, art. 106, which reads: "In no case may ejidal agricultural production be taxed." See also *El Imparcial*, April 12, 13, 14 and 24, 1977, and *Excelsior*, April 26, 1977, p. 31A.

156. *Excelsior*, March 4, 1977, p. 1.

157. *Ibid.*, June 5, 1977, p. 5A; June 23, p. 17A.

Chapter 8

Toward a Theory of Mexican Populism

In order to explain the complex relationship among this study's themes of legitimacy, economic domination, political hegemony, and state authority, we must develop a more sophisticated notion of the relations between state and civil society. The Mexican state, as must be obvious from the foregoing chapters, cannot be neatly fitted into predetermined, often "economistic," categories. To comprehend expressly political and occasionally anti-bourgeois aspects of Mexican ideology such as the land reform of 1976 in Sonora, we must develop a new mode of understanding a political system based on class conflict in civil society and class conciliation in political society. When conceived in these terms, the Mexican state can (as it does in reality) conflict with its own reason for existence, in the short run; it can oppose its need to maintain authority as a capitalist promoter (through stimuli to productivity and participation in national economic growth) with its need to fulfill the revolutionary promises of social obligation (through land redistribution and political rhetoric against the bourgeoisie), designed to preserve its image as the primary arbiter of the collective national well-being.

In the course of seeking the specific social relations which explain these general propositions, we must keep in mind certain crucial historical peculiarities of Mexican development. These include Mexico's traditional problems of administrative unification, and the resultant political strength of the bureaucracy in the twentieth century; fiscal inadequacy, which exacerbates problems of increasing social capital-investment costs and social expenses;[1] and geographic proximity to the United States,

---

1. Charles A. Hale, *Mexican Liberalism in the Age of Mora*, *passim*; Manuel A. Villa,

which has prompted special problems of dependency, unique changes in the structure of imports and consumption, and a constant polemic of populist nationalism in Mexican politics. These constant elements in Mexico's political economy underlie a *continuous* aspect of twentieth-century public policy in Mexico. The concrete developmental demands which the Mexican state has faced in various stages of its consolidation continue to refute the simplistic assumption that the state directly reflects the collective wishes of the bourgeoisie. In fact, Mexican political history supports a contrary proposition, that—in Stavenhagen's words—the modern state *created* the bourgeoisie and the working class *as classes*.[2] This difference also strengthens the argument for a new explanation of the interaction between state and civil society.

So, our mode of exposing the "real" crisis of the modern Mexican state—albeit only partially—includes, in addition to the basic stuff of agrarian reform and legitimacy in Sonora, the greater issues of state coherence which are necessary for the survival of the regime. Certain problems plaguing advanced capitalist regimes are even more acute in dependent Mexico. To the descriptions of Jurgen Habermas and James O'Connor, which recount the contradictions of advanced capitalist economies,[3] we may add a specific analysis of Mexican economic instability, fiscal crisis, historic political weakness, and international dependence.

FROM THE PORFIRIATO TO 1940

A basic problem of Mexican civil society, as we have seen, has been that it suffers from the lack of a dominant progressive class to lead national development. Throughout the nineteenth century—as we saw more specifically in Chapters 2 and 3—Mexico's nascent bourgeoisie struggled to replace the stunted, moribund colonial social formation. From Mora to Porfirio Díaz (1821–1910), in addition to the primary task of nation-

---

"Las bases del estado mexicano y su problemática actual," p. 444; and Benjamín Retchkimán K., "La política fiscal mexicana," *Problemas del Desarrollo*, p. 94.

2. Rodolfo Stavenhagen, "Reflexiones sobre el proceso político actual," p. 19. Only when we speak of politically organized classes' expressing a set of goals does the term "class" take on its special political meaning. The Mexican bourgeoisie of the nineteenth century existed as a limited economic force, but failed to congeal as a positive social and political force in the same sense that elements of the Mexican bourgeoisie of the 1970s have. Part of the explicit mission of the postrevolutionary state has been to nurture the political and economic development of that class.

Stavenhagen's general line of argument seems to parallel that of Gramsci on political will formation: the specific objective reality of state–class relations depends, not only on structural considerations, but also on the continuing and unpredictable conflict among classes in civil society. This differs from the general tone of most structuralist thought. (Antonio Gramsci, *Selections from the Prison Notebooks*, pp. 139ff.)

3. Jurgen Habermas, *Legitimation Crisis*, *passim*; James O'Connor, *The Fiscal Crisis of the State*, p. 9 and *passim*. Also see Retchkimán, "La política fiscal," for a sketchy but interesting application to the present situation in Mexico.

building, the political leadership sought to guide economic development and state-building, but with mixed results. Even conceding the aggregate economic gains of the late *Porfiriato* (1890–1910), economic and political progress over the long run were highly questionable. Though Porfirio Díaz' dictatorship provided administrative authority and structural growth for the first time since independence, its foundation was so fragile that it quickly plummeted from boom to depression and from order to revolution, even after two decades of successful aggregate economic growth. The key to regime survival and legitimacy, it appears, was far more elusive than Díaz realized.

Without joining the historiographical battle that has raged over the decay of the *Porfiriato*, we can at least observe some crucial points at which the old order stagnated. The state did not properly execute the functions it needed to fulfill as a capitalist state in the liberal mold of the reform Constitution. In particular, small groups of entrepreneurs, government officials, and foreign concessionaires dominated the national economy. The Porfirian state permitted no genuine structural expansion of this ruling group. Porfirian positivism, as heir to the failed liberalism of the postcolonial period, *contradicted a basic goal necessary to its political survival: the expansion of the dominant class and its political base.* To expand the market and to build a strong structure of productive and educative relationships in civil society, the Mexican state in the growth years of the late *Porfiriato* needed to provide an integrating mechanism for the eager middle-sized progressive *hacendado*. Its failure to do so created the conditions for rebellion by the spurned elites. Related economic instability resulted from archaic forms of production and exploitation. Goods and services, produced in wildly mixed relations of production, could find no uniform, well-extended, "neutral" market.

The Porfirian regime not only lacked the means of regulating production and the expansion of the dominant class. Perhaps more important, in light of the *campesino* support given the Madero rebellion, was that *the Díaz government was totally incapable of supporting those classes which produced value in the society.* Instead, in order to ensure economic "progress," the regime revived the land question—formally depoliticized by the reform Constitution—to seduce regime favorites, concessionaires, and reactionary *hacendados. Property became a force against production in many cases, a bribe unrelated to its usual economic role as capital.*

Due to a permanent structural weakness of Mexico's economy, *development financing had to come from outside the country, as did infrastructure development.*[4] As a result of such financing—and the added effects of

4. Fernando Rosenzweig, "El desarrollo económico de México de 1877 a 1911," pp. 431–435; Villa, "Las bases del estado mexicano," p. 429; David H. Shelton, "The Banking System: Money and the Goal of Growth," p. 130.

the shortcomings noted above—the economic fluctuations that distorted most capitalist economies in the 1870–1910 period virtually destroyed the Porfirian economy.

Perhaps the most noteworthy lapse on the part of the Porfirian state was *its incapacity to propel capitalism beyond a certain limited level.* The importance of the free circulation of capital and labor becomes clear when we realize the preeminence of two preliminary goals of capitalist development prior to industrialization: the concentration of capital for investment (including landed property, of course) and the guarantee of a ready supply of labor.[5] The Díaz regime was able to ensure dispossession through concentration, but with two important qualifications: the bourgeoisie could not absorb the newly-created labor force, because of its limited productive structure (related to denial of its entry into the middle sector); and the possessors of national wealth did not necessarily constitute a producer class, since many represented vestiges of precapitalist Mexico—traditional *latifundistas.*

A more basic debility of dependent Mexico in the nineteenth and early twentieth century underlies these specific weaknesses of the *Porfiriato.* Mexico strove toward bourgeois developmental goals without a developed social class to lead civil society, to organize productive growth, to control capital investment and formation, and so on. The state, distorted by an infinitesimal domestic market, no domestic savings, lack of an investment ethic, etc., was forced to legitimate those undertakings generally resolved by the market and a well-developed civil society (mainly aggregate economic growth, infrastructure development, intersectoral expansion, and the concentration of capital). This meant that the state, without a developed class structure in civil society, made these growth matters its own political business. Once accumulation became a central matter, legitimacy became the stake.[6] The Porfirian state, in the absence of private order and growth in civil society, had to become civil society itself, in a sense. The state, not the market, became the symbol of order. Accumulation entered the political realm as the state assumed leadership of the growth economy. The *Porfiriato* was doomed in some measure because the state undertook capitalist development as a project before the necessary classes existed as genuine social forces in civil society.[7] This anomaly of the *Porfiriato* later haunted Mexico's postrevolutionary search for political identity, and predetermined to a certain extent the range of possible choices for future development.

5. Maurice Dobb, *Studies in the Development of Capitalism*, p. 185. This process is simply that of creating a class of the dispossessed.

6. This class weakness marks a chief difference between outcomes of primitive accumulation in Western Europe (as described by Dobb) and the unique compromise arrived at after the overthrow of the old regime in Mexico.

7. Juan Felipe Leal, *México: estado, burocracia y sindicatos*, p. 9; Nicos Poulantzas, *Poder político y clases sociales en el estado capitalista*, pp. 89–90.

The Class Aspect of Postrevolutionary Organization

The weakness of classes in the formation of postrevolutionary Mexico makes the analysis of change in the social structure more difficult. As in other bourgeois revolutions, the various elements of the Mexican Revolution found themselves locked in struggle with each other over the creation of the new society.[8] But true to the uniqueness of the Mexican conflict, no class or class faction had sufficient power to impose its will and its own version of progress and domination. Equally, the most radical factions lacked a national plan and organizational coherence. Nationalist Mexico in 1920 needed a life-sustaining coalition among the various parties to the revolutionary conflict, above all the bourgeoisie. Excessive political pressures from the United States over the formation of the new state constrained the already-limited political power of the tiny national agro-commercial bourgeoisie. The class most able to determine Mexican progress in a postrevolutionary capitalist economy had to soften its nationalist policy goals in the shadow of a hostile, anti-national neighbor to the north.[9] Embracing capitalism, rejecting the United States, and assuming a mantle of social responsibility to the underclasses, the revolutionary leadership lurched toward the populist compromise.

The difficulty in maintaining political legitimacy in postrevolutionary Mexican society resulted mainly from its class aspect. The capitalist state had to guarantee the rules of capitalist society: free circulation of capital and wage-labor, guarantees for private property, unlimited private accumulation, and stimulation of the market as the focus of civil society. But the state, due to Mexico's nineteenth-century dependent heritage, itself had to resolve weaknesses in the market structure and enter the market as a capitalist through state industries and social capital investment. In short, the Mexican state found a wide range of possible roles extending beyond, and confusing the boundaries of, the realm of exclusively political activity.

A general relationship between the Mexican state and the bourgeoisie

8. As Dobb says (p. 172): "While . . . [the] revolution requires the impetus of its most radical elements to carry through its emancipating mission to the end, the movement is destined to shed large sections of the bourgeoisie as soon as these radical elements appear, precisely because the latter represent the small man or the dispossessed whose very claims call into question the rights of large-scale property."

9. As an example of that hostility, Fiorello La Guardia, in 1919, offered "help" in a very strange way. "Yes, I would go down with beans in one hand and offer help to the Mexican people," volunteered La Guardia, "but I would be sure to have hand grenades in the other, and God help them in case they do not accept our well-intended and sincere friendship." President Woodrow Wilson stated the U.S. position more delicately, but with equally unambiguous meaning: "The United States government intends . . . to exert every influence it can exert to secure Mexico a better government under which all contracts and business concessions will be safer than they have been." (Both cited in Robert Freeman Smith, *The United States and Revolutionary Nationalism in Mexico, 1916–1932*, pp. 90 and 34, respectively.)

which guarantees the state's political legitimacy presents one aspect of a continuing process which links legitimacy and economic growth. The greater the strength of the economically dominant class, the sharper the *formal* political boundaries between state and civil society, between purely political legitimation and social and economic domination by a class or class coalition. Civil society, as the realm of private production and depoliticized "rights"—including the right of accumulation—commands many of the institutions of order in society, removing power over the daily routine of society from the public/political realm. In contrast to the Mexican state's near-total responsibility for order in the immediate postrevolutionary period, for instance, its authority has diminished since 1940, to the benefit of the dominant forces in civil society.

If we can speak in general terms of the attrition of state responsibility for civil order, which generally accrues to the benefit of the growing power of the bourgeoisie, what of the phase of Mexican development in which the state initially had to nurture an infant class of native bourgeoisie who held no real claim to economic domination or control over civil society? Before we posit the diminution of state power before the advance of civil society, we must remember the political arrangements made by the state during the epoch in which the market was so weak that the very system of capitalist accumulation was called into question—the period in which the state guaranteed Mexican capitalism's survival. How did the postrevolutionary state manage a class coalition and "populist pact" based on interclass cooperation, and at the same time guarantee the future of a fledgling productive structure based on class domination? And what were the consequences of the political promises made in the postrevolutionary years (1920–1940) for the future legitimation problems of the Mexican regime in the "development decades" (1940–1970)?

The weak and undirected classes of Mexican civil society struggled during the initial formation of the postrevolutionary Mexican state, radical and conservative elements each trying to impress its stamp on society through the new state. The market, which played a central role in the legitimation of class relations in civil society, was fragile, manipulated by foreign interests, and capital-starved. The political leadership clearly favored a mercantilist form of economic development under the watchful eye of the state. The bourgeoisie, weak but well-represented in political society, agreed, as long as the government operated in its interest.

The underclasses, mainly *campesinos*, still remained marginal to the macro-political equation. Nevertheless, if they lacked the ability to guide the political direction of the country, they still provided the real fighting strength of the postrevolutionary regime. Throughout the 1920s, the state concerned itself—albeit in a halting, uncertain manner—with including them in the postrevolutionary development plan. To guarantee the social peace needed for capitalist accumulation, the state had to appear to benefit the *campesinos* materially. By challenging *caciques* and by employing a vague *agrarista* tone, the state promised to dispense political power through its institutions on behalf of the masses.[10] This strategy demanded not only a coherent ideology, but a wider conception of political legitimacy. The *campesinos*, comprising almost 70 percent of the population, were after all the physical resource upon which the social peace had to be built.

Mexico in the 1920s faced a twofold problem, then, the solution of which would determine the political survival of the regime. To guarantee its future and the future of the nascent capitalist economy which complemented it, the state had to act as a sort of "class surrogate," integrating the forces of production toward the goal of capitalist accumulation and growth. This regency was clearly based on the extraction of surplus value from a wage-earning class. On the other hand, this already-complicated task would not suffice. The masses who had participated in the revolutionary war had to be included. The contradictory political goal of class conciliation formed the ideological backdrop for capitalist accumulation based on domination of one class by another. Let us briefly examine why this came to be the choice for postrevolutionary Mexico.

Since the Mexican bourgeoisie lacked political control in 1917, the state—acting as the primary agent of the mode of production, in order to maintain its legitimacy and survive—either had to coopt or suppress other independent social movements which challenged the authority of civil society. On one hand, this task was lightened by the weakness of other classes (and the weakness of the leading class, as well). Blanket repression was unsuitable as an alternative in the postrevolutionary period of state formation, if for no other reason than the peculiar circumstances the state then faced: it had an extremely weak class base; the *Porfiriato* had fallen at least partly due to its repressive tendencies; and the federal army was made up largely of contingents from the working class and rural poor. In addition, the Mexican state (qua capitalist promoter) in the 1920s had to rely on popular support for productive reasons as well as reasons of coercive power. The Mexican state, in short, simply did not have the coherence or the physical capacity to suppress by itself all the popular revolts of the postrevolutionary period. Thus, instead of consolidating the Revolution exclusively around the strongest sectors of bourgeois support, the Mexican state had to cement together a weak coalition, including the underclasses, with the *promises* of social reform under revolutionary auspices. The promises included capitalist growth to the bourgeoisie and distributive equity to the workers and *campesinos*. While capitalist growth

10. Arnaldo Córdova, *La ideología de la Revolución mexicana*, pp. 19 and 247.

included future bourgeois hegemony, equity for the deprived classes required continuing social obligations administered by the state.[11]

But why was the social peace bought with such volatile concessions as property and redistribution of wealth? Here it becomes apparent that populism concerned itself with economic progress as well as demands for distribution of wealth. In institutionalized form (Articles 27 and 123 of the Constitution of 1917, plus various statutory reforms), the property question became paramount after the Revolution. If the new state did not address the problem of land tenure as well as other aspects of capital formation, the traditionally agrarian economy would have no secure foundation (see Chapter 4). Without a labor pact, industrial development had no chance. Without a meaningful stance toward the ownership of property, the state would again fall prey to regional division, *caciquismo*, and possibly more civil war. Foreign capital might never return; invasion from the north was believed possible.

Resolving the property question, however, carried with it all the contradictions of Mexican society. The populist solution could not uncouple property from the political realm.[12] As the single most coherent apparatus available to Mexican society in the formative years following the Revolution, the state encumbered itself with the role of balancing the social demands of the *campesinos* and the accumulation demands of the bourgeoisie. The populist solution demanded both "free-market" economic principles and interventionist strategies of redistribution. The basic contradiction—which has surfaced in the 1970s in more antagonistic forms between *campesino* and capitalist—emerged from the Mexican Revolution as a product of class weakness, capital scarcity, *campesino* and worker demands, and the specific foreign influences which conditioned Mexican society. The state undertook its search for legitimacy through a political coalition cemented by ambitious projects of social obligation. The bourgeoisie sought the promise of future class domination through the mediation of a strong state, expecting—and by and large receiving—

11. This two-stage conceptualization owes much to Habermas' distinction between social integration and system integration. (Habermas, *Legitimation Crisis*, p. 4.) In this divided loyalty, though it is clearly weighted toward the bourgeoisie, the state begins to exist on a wider, more demanding base of popular support. Complicated by its familiar bureaucratic tendencies to perpetuate existing roles, the state's own survival may frequently appear at odds with bourgeois economic rationality. This was especially true of the postrevolutionary period in Mexico. The word "promise" was frequently used by constitutionalists when referring to the agrarian reform. (See Chapter 4.)

12. Property was part of the political realm in the sense that the regulation of values in civil society (among which property was a leader) was incomplete. The state, a profoundly political organism, made adjustments in that structural weakness. (Roger Bartra, *Estructura agraria y clases sociales en México*.) See Francisco J. Guerrero, "La colectivización capitalista del campo y otros límites del reformismo," pp. 74ff. for an application of Bartra's conclusion that the state had two basic choices: the populist or the "classical" solution. Bartra and Guerrero both rightly conclude that the classical solution was in fact no real alternative.

favor as the heir to the temporary regency of the class surrogate. The *campesinos*, in contrast, depended on the veracity of the populist promise for mere survival.

What had been accomplished up to this point, then, was a renewable lease on political legitimacy—renewable, that is, *if* the political promises were fulfilled. But in promises like these resides the germ of state–class conflict.

Postrevolutionary Legitimation

How, then, has the Mexican state ensured legitimation of the postrevolutionary regime? It has attempted a peculiar combination of mass mobilization and social peace achieved through obligation, and a simultaneous attack on the problems of economic growth and the expansion of the bourgeoisie. But what, specifically, is the populist pact? Briefly, it originated as a coalition of antipathetic forces, which "balance each other in a catastrophic manner; that is to say, they balance each other in such a way that a continuation of the conflict can only terminate in their mutual destruction."[13] This "Caesarist" coalition described here by Antonio Gramsci, though not written about Mexico, has two fundamental characteristics in its Mexican application: the forces (classes) in balance are incurably opposed (in the historical sense);[14] and the coalition can in some instances resolve that opposition through the neutralization/statization of the class bases of the conflict. *That was, in fact, the mission of the Mexican revolutionary state before 1940: to guarantee both capitalist expansion and worker–campesino power, mediated by state intervention in both spheres.* After the boom of World War II, control was tightened over the working class and less attention given to state-obligation functions (see Chapter 6).

If, like Philippe Schmitter,[15] we consider corporate organization partially as a response to the failure of the pluralist model of capitalist society, the political strategy of class conciliation becomes more reasonable and obvious. In fact, as already stated, the Mexican coalition represented the single cement of the new social formation after the Revolution. Also, the eventual political restructuring of class conflict through reorganization of the political party, in 1938, represented the crowning attempt of the state to control the direction and intensity of class and sectoral demands. The formative days of the populist political solution are further

---

13. Gramsci, *Selections*, p. 219.

14. "Incurable opposition in the historical sense" simply means that class interests of individual members of the coalition are opposed *in the long run*; obviously they cannot be incurably opposed at every juncture, or no voluntary coalition would be possible. Only through analysis of the entire postrevolutionary period does one achieve a sense of this incurable opposition, the elements of which were structurally present in some form from the beginning.

15. Philippe Schmitter, "Still the Century of Corporatism?" p. 108.

clarified by the realization that, in those heady days of the postrevolutionary epoch (1920–1940), the "historical opposition" of the parties to the
basis of the coalition was not always obvious. The limited, weak articula-
tion of class goals, as opposed to personal goals, strengthened the state, as
well as lending it time to organize before class antagonism congealed at
an organized, systemic level.[16]

As Arnaldo Córdova convincingly argues, the Mexican Revolution itself stopped short of its declared goals of social renewal. Rather than
fulfilling those aims for which the common people struggled, revolutionary leaders turned against its rebellious regional vanguards. Mexican
populism, the political brake applied to the social rebellion, was born in
the fight of Carranza and Obregón against Zapata and Villa. By "giving the
centavo to earn the *peso*," the new state maintained a certain amount of
control over the political shape of the new pact. The personalism which
characterized much of the postcolonial epoch was to give way to a limited
institutional social guarantee for all the classes molding the new society.[17] By the end of the Cárdenas era, the political party held the chief
role in managing the institutionalization of this multi-class guarantee (see
Chapter 5).

What were the dimensions of this multi-class coalition which headed
the new state's claims to legitimacy? They were precisely the terms of legitimation spelled out in the promise of social obligation to the masses
and the guarantee of future domination to the bourgeoisie. The state had
to become the guarantor of capitalist growth, as Cárdenas said.[18] This began a permanent link between the economic capacity of the state and the
efficacy of populist politics: the state's political legitimacy, at least in this
respect, was tied to the business cycle and the mercurial fluctuations
characteristic of the Mexican economy.[19] The crux of populist capitalism
combined the unlikely twin goals of national capital growth and the si-

16. True, there was open class struggle during the Cárdenas era, but even that statement
must be qualified. First, as Ashby shows, *cardenista* labor organization was paternalist from
the outset. (Joe C. Ashby, *Organized Labor and the Mexican Revolution Under Lázaro Cárdenas*, p. 52.) Second, the struggle was mostly between incipient class organizations and
regressive pockets of pre-capitalist or anti-revolutionary resistance. When capitalist–worker
struggle occurred, the result quite often benefitted state-dominated political organization
and the rationalization of production.

17. Córdova, *La formación del poder político en México*, pp. 22–23 and 32.

18. "The function of the Mexican state is not limited to that of a simple guardian, provided with tribunals to discern individual justice under the law, neither is this state recognized as titular head of the economy, but instead . . . the state . . . [is] the regulator of the
great economic phenomena which are registered under our mode of production and of the
distribution of wealth." (From a speech made by Cárdenas on March 28, 1934, in Villaher-
mosa, Tabasco; reprinted in Mexico, Secretaría de Prensa y Propaganda del Comité Execu-
tívo del PNR, *La gira del General Lázaro Cárdenas*, p. 48; also in Hilda Muñoz (ed.), *Lázaro
Cárdenas: síntesis ideológica de su campaña presidencial*, p. 37.)

19. Manuel Aguilera Gómez, *La desnacionalización de la economía Mexicana*, pp. 70
and 72.

multaneous satisfaction of popular demands emanating from the mass explosions of 1910–1940.[20] By tracing throughout this study some specific public-policy problems confronting the nascent coalition, we have seen reasons for directing the political economy along certain developmental paths. We have also seen some of the inherent weaknesses in such strategies.

POPULISM AND ECONOMIC GROWTH

We should be extremely cautious with the investments that imperialist Wall Street interests are trying to realize in our territory, and give all manner of assistance to . . . capital that wishes to come from our neighboring country to cooperate with us in the development and exploitation of our natural resources, so that we can become better known by honest capital . . . which will always be our ally . . . when the Wall Street interests try to distort the truth to provoke conflict and international crises between . . . both countries, as has occurred on repeated occasions.[21]

Obregón was not as naive as one might think after reading this statement. The distinction he made between "honest capital" and "imperialist Wall Street" makes more political sense when read in the light of the populist developmental task of the 1920s and 1930s. But to understand Obregón's remarks, we must cut a little deeper to divine the particular requisites for this developmental populism. In economic terms, fortifying the domestic market involved at least the following: (1) making capital available to be reinvested domestically; (2) generating foreign exchange to finance industrialization programs; (3) incorporating the workforce through some limited form of distribution; (4) generating some entrepreneurial capacity; (5) assuring a minimum of efficiency and responsibility in public administration; (6) conciliating conflicting interests through coherent political leadership.[22]

Each of these requirements for development naturally had its associated difficulties. Mainly, in the Mexican case, as Obregón realized, foreign capital was required as a source of domestic investment. A productive agricultural economy had to generate foreign exchange destined for industrial purchases. The state had to protect some of the interests of the working class and guarantee a broad-based system of rewards. Each of these facets, as we saw in Chapter 4, had political ramifications for Mexican populism, especially for the agrarian reform. The economic dilemma—how to create conditions for bourgeois growth and eventual control of the national economy, under the weighty influence of uncontrolled external

20. Córdova, La ideología, p. 314.
21. Álvaro Obregón Salido, Discursos, vol. II, pp. 74–75; Córdova, La ideología, p. 299.
22. Fernando H. Cardoso and Enzo Faletto, Dependencia y desarrollo en América Latina, p. 106.

forces—diminished for a time in the era of Dollar Diplomacy, only to surface again in the wake of the world depression.[23]

The Populist State's Political Problems

The fundamental political task associated with dependent economic
development in the populist mode is that of convincing the masses of
their equality in relation to the other components of the productive system. As we have seen, the Mexican state chose to accomplish this through
a revolutionary ideology promising state obligation to the masses, headed
by agrarian reform and worker rights. Among the several problems of this
task were: shunting class conflict to controlled political organizations;
abolishing structural inequality under the law; and ability to mobilize or
demobilize the working class for political or production purposes. By
controlling the extent of worker organization and capitalist redistribution, the state by definition became paternalistic. It recognized inequality between capitalist and worker in production, but at the same time
declared their political and social relations equal, through its intervention. Workers and capitalists alike improved their situation through
association with the state, and secondarily through "free-enterprise"
mechanisms.[24]

The populist state became paternalistic in another sense: it played a
definite educative or formative role in the political realm, particularly due
to the absence of a strong civil society. Through mass education—not necessarily formal—the state performed the service of adapting the population to the necessities of continuous development of the productive apparatus. In its most fundamental sense, it solved the problem of "turning
necessity and coercion into freedom."[25] As we saw in Chapter 7, the CCE
appeared ready in the mid-1970s to limit that formative role of the state.

It may appear that the state just described assumed the countenance of
Leviathan, manipulating the masses, repressing class conflict, destroying
class alignments. But this is only a partial picture. The populist state itself
relied on the support of the masses, the confidence of the bourgeoisie, and
the will of the international investor.[26] After all, the balance maintained

23. Robert Freeman Smith, "The Morrow Mission and The International Committee of
Bankers on Mexico," pp. 150, 155, and 159; also Córdova, La ideología, p. 299.
24. Córdova, La ideología, pp. 234–235. Córdova illustrates the problem of attempting to
equalize classes through labor legislation in Mexico. If we think of classes in civil society,
they are obviously unequal; if we think of them as political equals (in other than a purely
electoral sense), the paternalistic state must intervene on behalf of the presently weaker class
in civil society, which violates the traditional formal boundaries between state and civil society. If left alone, conciliation between antagonistic classes is unlikely; if social equality is
enforced, the relations of production are altered, to the detriment of capitalist growth and
accumulation.
25. Gramsci, Selections, p. 242.
26. Again, Cárdenas clears up the class balance as he perceived it: "The conservatives of
Mexico, enemies of the social program of the Revolution, would like the policy of the gov-

by the Mexican populist state has been a function of the equal political strength of classes as well as of state intervention in the economy. But in reality, the basic economic inequality which inheres in capitalist relations of production weakens and constantly threatens the populist political alliance. While the state as the new society's organizing principle could purge the social system of vestigial forms of privilege, a capitalist-led growth economy only substituted new forms of privilege which in the 1970s jeopardized mass acquiescence in the social system.

Mass Mobilization, Mass Control

Class control was a necessary aspect of the populist solution. The working class had to be impelled toward higher productivity and more rational forms of organization. At the same time, their political power necessarily resided with the state, lest they threaten the organization of production. The *campesinos* have been the instrument of modernizing Mexico's agricultural production, which provided the economic basis for industrial development. But their role was limited also; they were to be mobilized for the struggle against prior political and productive forms, not to assume power themselves (see Chapter 5).

Finally, the bourgeoisie also had to fall into line, to ensure the façade of class political and social equality against individual proprietary interests, and to perpetuate the aspect of class compromise built on income and land redistribution. Of course, the regimentation of the bourgeoisie in Mexico has never been as great as that of the working class and *campesinos*. The state-as-regulator has mainly acted as a check on the well-known class tendency of the bourgeoisie to fragment. Likewise, the state's goals for the leading class included an eventual strengthening of its position vis-à-vis the economy and the working class. That is, *another facet of the inequality inherent in the populist pact stems from the guarantee of economic domination for the bourgeoisie. The working class, on the other hand, never receives sanction from the state to act independently as a class*, because its interests may adversely affect capitalist growth. In the 1970s, this maldistribution of class power became more apparent.

It is in this context that the Cárdenas epoch takes clearer shape. As we saw in Chapter 5, the roots of *cardenismo* lie in recognizing the need for a stronger state to guarantee revolutionary precepts, and a modern political party to guide class organization and institutionalize economic growth under the aegis of the state.[27] The populist "social pact" instituted by Cár-

---

ernment to be that practiced in capitalist states; that is to say, liberty for their interests and imposition of their rules; they would like the workers to be left as individuals, because they know that organization will eliminate their privileges. This is why they fear and combat it; but if the workers intelligently use their own power they will quickly achieve a better distribution of public and private wealth." Lázaro Cárdenas, *Apuntes, 1913–1940*, p. 334.

27. Córdova, *La política*, p. 24. Though Mosk suggests that *cardenismo* had little to do with subsequent industrial development, many of the state institutions and policies support-

denas was struck between the masses and the state, with the partial goal of mutual reinforcement. That the contract ultimately meant state control over class conflict would become apparent only after 1940.

Two aspects of the populist social pact proved crucial to Mexican politics after the Revolution. The first was the organizational mode by which the state achieved political control over the classes in civil society. The state exercised more or less control, depending on which class was involved; the specific political and economic conjuncture; and the policy orientation of the regime in power. The second aspect involved the extent to which the state was willing—or able—to fetter the need of capitalist production to extract surplus value from the working class and to concentrate capital. These features surfaced clearly in Mexico when the state attempted to control inflation and the declining worker-share of income. They also fueled the continual battle over the terms of the state's social obligation to the underclasses, an expense necessary to continued populist political legitimacy.

Corporate Organization, Economic Growth, and Populist Decline

Chapters 4 through 7 have shown how various regimes either mobilized or demobilized the country's agrarian forces generally, and the Sonoran campesinos specifically. It is appropriate to conclude that analysis with some comments at a more abstract level. As we saw in Chapter 5, the mass mobilization of the 1930s guaranteed the eradication of certain traditionally privileged groups, mainly reactionary latifundistas. However, mobilization was a temporary political strategy; the production and credit requirements of the Mexican economy needed social acquiescence and the rationalization of the political realm. The state, at the end of the Cárdenas epoch, had to demobilize the campesinos and working class for production purposes. It also feared both its limited control over popular organizations and indefinitely prolonged mobilization.

Corporate reorganization of the official political party on December 19, 1937, sealed off the working class by economic sector. The reorganization of the party solidified the boundaries of the class compromise by including representation for industrial workers, ejidatarios, and various capitalist and service organizations, and by excluding acasillados and rural day-workers (jornaleros) from independent representation.

One important effect of rationalizing the political process through control of the reformed party structure was the denial of class struggle in civil society. Working-class organizations and campesino groups smothered

---

ing that development originated with Cárdenas. By 1940 the major political mobilization and organization of the working class had been completed, and the economic structure of production was well in place in the agrarian sector. (Sanford A. Mosk, *Industrial Revolution in Mexico*, esp. pp. 53–60; Calvin P. Blair, "Nacional Financiera: Entrepreneurship in a Mixed Economy," pp. 208–209; Rafael Izquierdo, "Protectionism in Mexico," pp. 241–289.)

under the weight of subsequent state domination (see Chapter 6). Class leadership itself became bureaucratized in the administrative advance of the state. The economy, then, could be administratively manipulated to a certain extent, which has had equivocal effects. It eventually detracted from performance of the state's social-obligation functions, as we saw in the case of the agrarian reform (especially after 1940). On the other hand, this bureaucratization reduced much of Mexican public policy to a function of bureaucratic trends and whims. It also burdened the state with more responsibilities, and correspondingly lightened the burdens of the bourgeoisie in civil society. The state provides social security and the administration of many worker benefits, to a great extent through foreign borrowing rather than domestic taxation. Tripartite arrangements for labor arbitration pit the demands of the working class against the state as arbiter of the work contract, not against the capitalist. Also, in the conflict over land tenure, the state has become the direct focus of *campesino* discontent, partly because of the organizational preeminence and populist promises which symbolize the state's commitment to equity.

The political equality posited by populist ideology cannot reconcile the subtle linkages among economic power, political authority, state legitimacy, and social obligation. In fact, as we saw in Chapters 6 and 7, the state and the bourgeoisie, after 1940, began to consolidate a development plan which was based, not on social obligation, but on more traditional grounds of legitimation through capitalist accumulation. Nevertheless, it inevitably relied also on organizational control and pacification of leading sectors of the working class and *campesinos*.

THE MEXICAN STATE AFTER 1940

This conceptual treatment of the Mexican state has thus far generally concentrated on the pre-1940 period, an era of mass organization and the sometimes chaotic construction of a new social order. Social obligation cemented the original postrevolutionary political pact. But the promises of social obligation, incurred by the state as a cost of that pact, ultimately had to be discarded as a main consideration in public policy toward the developing economy. This abandonment occurred as a product of post-World War II economic development.

When the Mexican state pledged itself to expanding and industrializing under a capitalist mode of production, the terms of class compromise began to slant more obviously. Stimulating the growth of the dependent capitalist economy meant enhancing the conditions of bourgeois economic domination. *The populist state, in one sense, became merely the political instrumentality of this mission.* When it is recognized that capitalist economic expansion is based on wage-labor and exploitation, the state can no longer truthfully claim to act in the economy as a neutral arbi-

ter of class conflict. It is by its own definition more committed (in economic terms) to the growth of capitalism than to the elimination of class
privilege.

We might see state support of domestic growth over economic distribution as a "natural" phase in the progress of the Mexican political economy—and in a limited sense it is. But it also conflicts with the third term
of the populist pact: social obligation to the *campesinos* and the industrial working class. At one point, roughly from 1930 to 1940, the goals of
domestic economic growth, class political conciliation, and agrarian and
worker redistribution were temporarily consistent. When some regional
capitalists disagreed with the goals of the state, they were chastised by the
state–worker alliance (see Chapter 5). The agricultural sector became the
base for the revolutionary economy, the *campesinos* wresting control of
the land from the remnants of the old regime. The organization and mobilization of the industrial working class solidified the terms of the populist
political pact; it also streamlined control of and communication with the
working class, in the absence of mechanisms to perform these functions
in the private realm. But these years were only the preamble to the modern Mexican economy.

In the years 1940–1970, the rules of the game began to change, affecting
all aspects of populist politics: a bourgeois development plan was implemented, and concessions to capital were broadened.[28] Capitalization and
productivity goals overshadowed distribution and equity in the rural sector as well as in industry.[29] With these changes, the original populist compromise began to decay. The promise of land reform became the *ideology*
of land reform.[30] Worker power meant representation in tripartite arbitration councils, not genuine political or economic power. Large numbers of
workers and *campesinos* were marginalized from the benefits of growth
as well as excluded from the organizational umbrella of the state and its
ancillary organizations.

The corporate political structure envisioned in the 1938 reorganization
of the PNR appeared for nearly thirty years to be able to control the delicate compromise with a traditional mixture of *pan y palo*. After the
reorganization, the power of national politics definitely flowed from the

28. See Mosk, *Industrial Revolution*, and Izquierdo, "Protectionism," for the specific
terms of these concessions. A brief treatment appeared in Chapter 6.

29. Clark W. Reynolds, *The Mexican Economy: Twentieth-Century Structure and
Growth*, pp. 37 and 64–79. Reynolds shows that development in the 1940s came primarily
from sectoral labor shifts and suppressed worker shares of income, along with negative interest from borrowing during times of high inflation. The working class and *campesinos*,
needless to say, did not experience similar benefits from inflation.

30. This interpretation is more appealing than assigning the state the insidious role of
lying on a wholesale basis throughout the land-reform period of 1920–1977. One of the main
contentions of this study is that the political and economic terms of the revolutionary compromise changed after 1940, and that as a product of these changes, the land-reform obligation gradually became more fiction than reality.

party—and, by association, from the state. The class constituents of the PRI were (and still are, to some extent) dependent upon a benevolent state attitude. The goal of the state, as displayed through *presidencialismo*, has been in some measure to control class goals through the apparatus of the state and the party.

What then generated a crisis in the political equation of the late 1960s and early 1970s, given that economic growth and consumption had succeeded in making the post-World War II Mexican economy the "miracle" of Latin America? The crisis evolved from a partial disintegration in almost all the principal class supports of the regime. Leading factions of the bourgeoisie became more willing, in the 1970s, to act as rulers of civil society *independent of the political will of the state*, as was intended under the plans of developmental populism. After many years at the breast, the bourgeoisie—especially after the Echeverría years—are no longer willing to trust the state with planning political and economic priorities, except under close scrutiny (though they are perfectly willing to entrust high-risk investments and infrastructure costs to the state). Leaders of the economy want the reins of the economy, or at least control of the major public-sector economic decisions.

Further weakening the state's position, the bulk of the working class, especially in the agricultural sector, is rapidly escaping the organizations controlled by the state. The workers are being marginalized from the corporate political system of rewards by the economic dynamics of dependent capitalism. Organized labor—or at least its leadership—finds itself forced into the curious position of supporting a government policy of wage suppression with only vague promises of future improvement. Rank-and-file discontent is growing with the dimensions of the crisis.

In the countryside, the *campesinos* are calling in the promise of land reform. Even though the capitalist development plan of 1940–1970 laid more emphasis on aggregate economic growth than on income and product redistribution, the promises and demagogy of the agrarian reform have not been forgotten. A main prop of state control of the social peace has always been the promise of land division and *campesino* expropriation of *latifundia*. Accompanying this promise, the state has made a point of always publicizing the small amounts of land distributed. The CNC, now accompanied by most other *campesino* groups in the Pact of Ocampo, vies for membership by using the glib promise of land to the *campesinos*. As we saw in the case of Sonora, the government often encourages, even plans, *campesino* land seizures as a means of further enhancing the prestige of the government-dominated *campesino* organizations such as the CNC, and defusing possible opposition to official agrarian-reform policy.

Of course it must be understood that the bourgeoisie could not appreciate the need for the state to continue with land reform, especially in the "irrational" manner of Echeverría. It is in this sense that there was, and still is, a serious conflict between the state and the bourgeoisie in Mexico—conflict between a political strategy of integration, cooptation, legitimation, and survival straining against the classic bourgeois tendencies of capitalist accumulation, worker marginalization, and the concentration of capital.

Essentially then, in class terms, the populist state has to face pressure from conflicting social forces which were theoretically reconciled in the "populist pact." The bourgeoisie, feeling put upon particularly over the politicization of land tenure and attempted fiscal reform, know they have the strength to shake the economic roots of the state's legitimacy. The *campesinos*, still poor after years of agrarian reform, are demanding payment on the revolutionary ideology which has so long been used as a means of social control. To them, Gross Domestic Product is not an adequate indicator of the success of the Revolution. Social obligation, in the form of land and capital redistribution, cannot be resolved merely through aggregate economic growth. It must respond to the seemingly eternal quest for land by the Mexican *campesino*. As such, the state, to fulfill the ideology of the Revolution, must contravene its needs as a capitalist state in crisis to fulfill its social obligation as a populist state with a social pact.

In addition to these domestic problems, the Mexican state is presiding over enormous balance-of-payments deficits (about 2.5 billion dollars U.S. in current account at the end of 1978), rising external public debt (26.3 billion dollars U.S. in 1978), and a shaky monetary system resulting from two devaluations in one year.[31] Due to its debt position in the international economic system, Mexico is increasingly dependent upon negotiations with the Inter-American Development Bank, the World Bank, and private international organs of finance. Naturally, these organizations are also quite concerned with social peace, investment climate, growth potential, and the like.

Obviously the state cannot fulfill the obligations of land reform and ignore the more important (in terms of survival) needs of the now-powerful industrial bourgeoisie. The Echeverría years must be viewed in these terms. Echeverría—if we momentarily disregard his own personal sense of historical mission—tried to achieve a powerful coup: to satisfy the bourgeoisie and the economy with production through the expansion of public spending and the revitalization of land reform. The attempt was crushed by fiscal debt, bourgeois resistance, bureaucratic intrigue, and

31. Figures from Banco de México, *Informe Anual*, 1978, resumen. For a fuller summary of the roots of Mexico's problems, see Olga Pellicer de Brody, "Mexico in the 1970s and Its Relations with the United States"; see also Richard R. Fagen, "The Realities of U.S.–Mexican Relations."

the substantial weaknesses inherent in the ejidal system of land reform. In one sense, it may be said that Echeverría invoked the class compromise long after it had become an artifact of the past, unrelated to the political and economic power of the Mexican bourgeoisie in the 1970s. His personal failure was but a dim reflection of the suffering and shattered hopes which were visited upon the *campesinos* manipulated in this short-lived populist resurgence.

FUTURE PROSPECTS FOR MEXICAN POPULISM

It is clear that, for the time being at least, the populist agrarian-reform movement is over. The López Portillo administration has reissued the call for an "alliance for production," a plea for national unity among classes reminiscent of the Ávila Camacho and Alemán governments of the 1940s. The 1976 presidential campaign slogan *"La solución somos todos"* (roughly, "We are all part of the solution") neglected the six-year conflict between the parties to the populist pact of the Mexican Revolution. López Portillo has posted some short-term successes in his campaign to root out corruption in the bureaucracy and to restore investors' faith in the Mexican economy. Likewise, with the indemnification of expropriated lands in Sonora and the long summit meetings between cattlemen, capitalist farmers, and representatives of the state, the new president has at least achieved some accord with the national agricultural elite. But despite all these successes and their potential for overcoming the excesses of the Echeverría *sexenio*, Mexican political society still has not addressed the most significant issues—political legitimacy, state authority, and revision of the ideology of the Mexican Revolution. The roots of these issues date back to the nineteenth-century origins of Mexican land policy and state development.

As we have seen in some detail, the liberal-oriented Constitution of 1917 has served the purpose of delaying or denying the revolutionary character of the land conflicts which have at times faced the Mexican landholding classes. While elements of the revolutionary alliance have consistently fought for significant reforms in the distribution of land, credit, water, and machinery, the national political leadership—with the partial exception of Cárdenas and Echeverría—has used the limited legal-bureaucratic approach to land tenure ultimately to eviscerate any serious progress in agrarian reform. In the years 1940–1970, the agrarian-reform bureaucracy provided a cover for the increasing concentration of rural wealth and the construction of a durable "counter-reform" juggernaut which has systematically crushed independent *agrarista* movements. And despite the heat and fury of the Echeverría *sexenio*, there is little prospect that the Mexican state in its present condition will address the fundamental problems of redistributing existing resources and ensuring the equitable distribution of future increments of growth, regardless of projected oil earnings.

As for the Cárdenas and Echeverría years, we have seen that these periods were characterized by a different political process in the *campo*. During Cárdenas' presidency, working-class and *campesino* leaders became part of the first rank of political power, propelling the regime to the left and ensuring a temporary gain for many of their followers. The LNC and LCAEV of the early 1930s forced Cárdenas to take an early position on the question of land reform, and the rebellion of *campesinos* in the Laguna, Yucatán, and other important agricultural areas forced him to reform land tenure in order to improve agricultural productivity. In the 1960s, independent threats from the left and the increasing militance of some *campesino* leaders provided a similar impetus for Echeverría. The result in both cases was populist mobilization by the state.

But both Cárdenas and Echeverría faced the mobilization of the countryside from a political perspective which differed from the more parochial interests of the *campesinos* and workers. For reasons that should be obvious to us from earlier chapters, neither Cárdenas nor Echeverría had the political power or the will to forsake private property and private accumulation in any serious way. The ideology of agrarian reform has always stood to the left of real agricultural policy. Rather than undertaking an agrarian revolution, the populist state in its formative years under Cárdenas used the agrarian reform as another political and organizational weapon against the enemies of the Revolution—reactionary capitalists and *latifundistas*. In the Echeverría years, the state again used *campesino* militance and reform threats to fight political enemies such as COPARMEX and the CCE. One effect, as manifest in the hard line taken by these two groups toward land reform, was to entrench bourgeois opposition to even moderate redistribution. Meanwhile, for reasons of political control and authority, the state itself, parading as the exclusive agent of *campesino* affairs, crushed independent popular organizations which threatened state power. In this respect, the Echeverría years differed very little from the counter-reform.

Cárdenas' legacy to the populist state included the transformed liberal perspective carried over from the Constitutionalist influence on the Revolution. The postrevolutionary state faced the problem of protecting the *campesinado* while destroying its independent class organizations in civil society. When Cárdenas incorporated working-class and *campesino* organizations into the party apparatus (i.e., the state apparatus), he preserved the limited liberal legacy to the *campesino*. While the bourgeois organizations with representation in the party already had assemblies of their own which existed outside the state apparatus (e.g., CONCAMIN, CONCANACO), the representation of *campesinos* and workers relied for political power on the CNC and CTM exclusively. Both organizations (and subsequently the UGOCM, CAM, and CCI) quickly became bogged down in bureaucratic form and moved progressively further away from the constituencies they alleged to represent. Even in the best of circumstances, the relation of party to social class has not been an easy or effective one in Mexico. Relying strictly on the CNC and CTM for popular political power in organized form has been disadvantageous for the *campesinos*, because the state has not always taken a benevolent attitude toward popular power. During the entire counter-reform, popular organization came to mean limits to popular reforms, not access to state power and policy formation. Meanwhile, the bourgeoisie thrived and grew during the "development decades" until their formal political representation in the party meant less than their power in civil society. At this point the populist equation began to break down in the radical ferment of the late 1960s and the populist revival of the Echeverría presidency. We have seen some of the results of the ensuing friction among state, capital, *campesino*, and worker.

By 1978, the second year of the dismantling of Echeverría's populist revival, it was clear that the Mexican state had emerged from the latest crisis with a substantial loss of power. The terms by which López Portillo had to preside over the return of Mexican capital to the economy, the negotiations for exploitation of national oil reserves, and the security of agricultural exports have required a fundamental denial of the mass base of Mexican political power. There is no expectation that CONASUPO, rural health programs, and other redistributive mechanisms of the state will expand under the official program of fiscal austerity. The agrarian reform will not continue except in the expedition of existing petitions. The steady deterioration of food production continues. And the tripartite organizations for agrarian and worker negotiation are unlikely to take an aggressive popular stance.

The cynicism of official agrarian and worker organizations showed through the populist veneer of *echeverrismo* and detracted from the genuine popular mobilization of 1975–1976. As a result, support in the countryside for the CNC and the Pact of Ocampo has suffered. And belief in the ability of the López Portillo government to treat fairly with unions has declined, especially after the regime crushed the 1977 National University strike with force. In short, the Mexican state, although benefitting from a disorganized and often fractionated opposition, has done little to shore up its sagging popular base.

Instead, the López Portillo government has fallen back on the main supports of the national economy: international capital and the internationally-linked domestic entrepreneurs represented in the CCE. The state also loses power by reaffirming its reliance on the bourgeoisie, however, because the conditions for CCE support are a reduced state presence in the economy, except as a source of capital; "fiscal responsibility," which translates into severely reduced social-capital and social-welfare expenditures; security in private agricultural property; and guaranteed incentives for the private sector. The state, then, is expected to discard inefficient state enterprises, reduce public spending for health and welfare, and suspend the agrarian reform. Even partial agreement to these principles means a loss of state power and increased dependence on private capital to forward national economic goals. Reliance on the private sector to lead economic growth means that the CCE and affiliates will be the prime arbiters of the revised concept of "balanced growth" in the Mexican economy. Clearly the state loses something in this arrangement; the *campesinos* and working class obviously lose more.

Lurking behind the rejection of revived populism is the political necessity that is the focus of our analysis in this study: legitimacy. Growth under the counter-reform was based on a dynamic of increasing concentration of productive wealth and the progressive maldistribution of shares of the national income. Dismantling the social-welfare and social-capital expenditures of the state—to whatever degree—exacerbates that inequality and compounds the problems of legitimating state authority. To guarantee social peace in the countryside, which has been a permanent goal of revolutionary government since Carranza, the state has relied traditionally upon populist appeals to agrarian reform, workers' rights, and so on. With ever-sharpening differences in the material standard of living available to the underclasses, and a reduced apparatus for institutionalized redistribution, the state will ultimately have to redress deficiencies in revolutionary ideology, or perhaps use force to coerce the unemployed and underemployed of the countryside to stay within the law. The possibility of genuine redistribution and balance in national production seems slight, in view of the diminished political capacity of the repentant populist state. The CCE-led faction of national capitalists seems equally unlikely to prescribe socially productive economic growth, since they and their multi-national allies provide the most capital-intensive, expensive consumer and producer goods to the international market (and to part of the domestic economy), and are not inclined to undertake the abandoned role of *patron* of the disenfranchised underclasses.

The reason the demise of state populism (whether permanent or cyclical) represents a crisis of legitimacy lies at the heart of the nature of the Mexican state. Mexican populism, as a product of both bourgeois liberalism and factionalized rural revolution, stems from two contradictory sources, which exacerbates the already-difficult issue of accumulation versus equity. On the one hand, the postrevolutionary institutional and spiritual alliance with nineteenth-century liberal forebears has demanded that the state fill the role of capitalist promoter and marketing agent. The result, if we discount the distortions caused by the Mexican economy's position in the international economic system, is not radically different from other interventionist liberal states in history. As national capital (and, in Mexico, foreign capital) becomes stronger and more dynamic, more of the public decisions affecting the economy can be expected to move to the private realm, to civil society. This tendency is apparent not only in the López Portillo administration, but also in other administrations since Cárdenas.

On the other hand, the populist pact which sealed the social peace guaranteeing the "economic miracle" included a promise of social obligation to the underclasses, especially the *campesinos*. The encroachment of dominant organizations of civil society on state power has meant effective neutralization of the state's "autonomous" power over the disposition of private property. The logical incapacity of capital to organize its own redistributive measures combines with the structural incapacity of Mexican capital to effect sufficient growth in employment to cement its own hegemony in civil society. The reduced state, by previous agreement, is left to answer for its promised social peace, which now offers few benefits to its key participants—marginal workers and *campesinos*. The state in its reduced role is expected to keep the peace for one sector of the populist alliance, while denying its legitimate appeal for allegiance from its potentially rebellious opposite partner in the populist pact. In its worst aspect, the state becomes merely the gendarme of the bourgeoisie.

Because the state adopted an expanded commitment to social equality after the Revolution, and continued to expound a revolutionary ideology, the Echeverría *sexenio* has a certain logic and place in Mexican history. It was a political conjuncture in a literal sense, in which the leaders of bourgeois civil society, led by the CCE and COPARMEX, wrestled with a populist ideologue and his *campesino* affiliates for the right to distribute the scarce resources of Mexican society. As the dust settles from that struggle, one suspects that the newly-purged state and ascendant capital, like Jacob and the angel of the Old Testament, will bind up their wounds and rest.

The temptation to draw apocalyptic conclusions from the powerful battles of the 1960s and 1970s is almost too great. The Mexican state for all its crises has always been remarkable for its resilience. But if the events of the Sonoran frontier in 1975–1976 are an index of the strength of Mexican populism, the agrarian reform as a genuine reallocation of national wealth and a call to the masses for allegiance is dead.

Appendix

Table A1
Definitive[a] Distribution of Land, 1920-1924[b]

TYPE OF STATE ACTION	(1) MEXICO	(2) SONORA	PERCENTAGE (2/1)
Restitution			
Number	40	3	7.0
Area (hectares)	227,092	23,085	10.1
Beneficiaries	12,412	273	2.2
Dotación (grant)			
Number	641	10	1.5
Area (hectares)	992,586	45,992[c]	4.6
Beneficiaries	138,076	1,827	1.3
Confirmation			
Number	3	—[d]	——
Area (hectares)	77,022	5,266	6.8
Beneficiaries	525	—[d]	——
Amplification			
Number	12	——	——
Area (hectares)	10,961	——	——
Beneficiaries	323	——	——
Totals			*Averages*
Number	696	13	1.8
Area (hectares)	1,307,661	74,343	5.6
Beneficiaries	151,336	2,100	1.3

[a]Provisional possessions are not included, as they are frequently altered, withdrawn, or inflated for political reasons.

[b]Data from Mexico, Secretaría de Agricultura y Fomento, Comisión Nacional Agraria (CNA), *Estadística, 1915-1927*, pp. 78 and 88.

[c]This total inexplicably excludes the *ejido* Torreón, in the *municipio* of San Miguel de Horcasitas. Torreón is included in the list of *poblados* receiving a definitive possession. It received 200 hectares of non-irrigated cultivable land by presidential resolution of Jan. 15, 1920, published in *Diario Oficial* on March 11, 1920.

[d]Included in another category.

Table A2

Classification of Sonoran Lands Granted/Restored Definitively, 1920-1924[a]

(in hectares)

COMMUNITY/DATE GRANTED	LAND CLASSIFICATION				
	CULTIVABLE		NOT CULTIVABLE		
	IRRIGATED	NOT IRRIGATED	PASTURE	WASTE	TOTAL
Agua Prieta (5/22/24)			10,000		10,000
Caborca (9/10/20)			5,266		5,266
Cajeme (4/29/24)		324			324
Huachinera (10/7/20)		26	1,974		2,000
La Misa (6/5/24)		800	469		1,269
Moroncarit (2/7/21)[b]	250		5,000	111	5,361
Navojoa (8/15/22)[e]	1,117		14,282		15,399
Oquitoa (7/9/24)[c]	783[d]		6,406		7,189
Querobabi (5/9/24)[e]		224	356		580
San Juan Tubutama (3/11/21)		789	4,388		5,177
Santa Marta (12/23/20)	350		1,076		1,426
Saric (6/4/24)		402			402
Tonibabi	3	1,500	18,400		19,903
TOTALS	2,503	4,065	67,617	111	74,296

[a]SOURCES: CNA, *Estadística, 1915-1927*, pp. 177 and 120; *Diario Oficial*, dates cited. The presentation in the CNA is misleading and confusing. Their summary of land grants to Sonora lists three restitutions in 1922 and none in other years. Of the four restitutions in Sonora between 1920 and 1924, none occurred in 1922.

[b]All of this grant came from national lands. The significance of this fact is that the grant could be achieved easily without expropriation or other methods of affecting land-tenure patterns already existing.

[c]All of Oquitoa except 115 hectares of pasture came from national lands.

[d]This figure seems exaggerated, since Oquitoa presently holds only 200 hectares of irrigated land.

[e]All of Querobabi's and Navojoa's pasture-land came from national lands.

Table A3
Definitive[a] Distribution of Land, 1925-1928[b]

TYPE OF STATE ACTION	(1) MEXICO	(2) SONORA	PERCENTAGE (2/1)
Restitution			
Number	43	——	0.0
Area (hectares)	566,789	——	0.0
Beneficiaries	12,713	——	0.0
Dotación (grant)			
Number	1,503	13	0.8
Area (hectares)	2,351,000	27,614	1.1
Beneficiaries	280,364	1,164	0.4
Confirmation			
Number	47	——	0.0
Area (hectares)	297,519	——	0.0
Beneficiaries	2,576	——	0.0
Amplification			
Number	46	——	0.0
Area (hectares)	44,295	——	0.0
Beneficiaries	3,137	——	0.0
Totals			*Averages*
Number	1,639	13	0.8
Area (hectares)	3,259,603	27,614	0.8
Beneficiaries	298,790	1,164	0.4

[a]Provisional possessions are not included, as they are not infrequently withdrawn or inflated for political reasons.

[b]Dates for 1925-1927 from CNA, *Estadística, 1915-1927*, pp. 78 and 88; for 1928, from Eyler N. Simpson, "The Mexican Agrarian Reform," p. 73, and from data elaborated in Table A4.

Table A4

Classification of Sonoran Lands Granted Definitively, 1925-1928[a]

COMMUNITY/DATE GRANTED	LAND CLASSIFICATION				
	CULTIVABLE		NOT CULTIVABLE		
	IRRIGATED	NOT IRRIGATED	PASTURE	WASTE	TOTAL
Carbó (8/10/27)			918		918
El Claro (6/10/25)	945				945
Guisamopa (8/20/27)	50	650	2,100		2,800
Huepac (12/9/25)[b]		198			198
Jécori (9/5/28)			3,063		3,063
Macoyahui (8/9/26)[c]		650	1,823		2,473
Maquipo (8/14/26)[d]		247	1,227		1,474
Miguelito (9/7/27)[d]			7,610		7,610
Nácori Chico			2,538		2,538
Pantanico y Calera (5/14/25)	520				520
Pozo Verde (6/22/28)			2,832		2,832
La Sangre (5/10/28)[e]		400	150		550
Sonoita Pápagos (9/14/28)			2,232		2,232
Totals	1,515	2,145	24,493		28,153[f]

[a]Data for 1925-1927 from CNA, *Estadística, 1915-1927*, and *Diario Oficial*, dates cited; 1928 from *Diario Oficial* and Manuel Corbalá Acuña, "El problema agrario en Sonora."

[b]Almost 73 hectares of the Huepac grant came from national lands.

[c]568 hectares of Macoyahui was national land.

[d]All of Maquipo and Miguelito were from national lands.

[e]This is the date of the presidential resolution granting the *ejido* of La Sangre, not the publication in *Diario Oficial*.

[f]This total should balance with the total area granted in Sonora from Table A3. The imbalance comes from errors in CNA data, not uncommonly found. CNA data occasionally conflict with *Diario Oficial* as well.

Table A5

Land Granted and Ejidatarios Benefitted,

1929-1934[a]

YEAR	PRESIDENT	AREA (hectares)	NUMBER OF EJIDATARIOS
1929	Portes Gil	1,853,589	126,603
1930	Ortiz Rubio	584,922	60,666
1931	Ortiz Rubio	976,403	41,532
1932	Ortiz Rubio/ A. Rodríguez[b]	249,349	16,462
1933	Rodríguez	542,239	43,008
1934	Rodríguez	1,517,989	115,385
	Totals	5,724,491	403,656

[a]SOURCE: CDIA, *Estructura agraria y desarrollo agrícola en México*, Table I-2, p. 50. Note that Portes Gil and Rodriguez both stand out during these years as grantors of large amounts of land. Portes Gil, in fact, later became known as a staunch *agrarista*. Rodríguez benefitted from repeal of the *Ley de Responsabilidades*. In any case, neither presidency forwarded the cause of the *campesinos* in any durable institutional sense.

[b]Ortis Rubio left office on Sept. 2, 1932, and was succeeded by Abelardo Rodríguez.

Table A6

Ejidos Granted in the Yaqui Valley, May 1938[a]

EJIDO	EJIDATARIOS		CLASSIFICATION OF LAND (in hectares)		
	1938	1941	IRRIGATED	WASTE	TOTAL
Cajeme[b]	69	57	556	3,000	3,556
El Castillo	54	43	432	600	1,032
Cuauhtemoc	173	162	1,384	1,850	3,234
Guadalupe Victoria	24	23	216	940	1,156
F.I. Madero	139	100	1,112	1,650	2,762
F.J. Mina[c]	98	95	790	4,050	4,840
Morelos	52	52	416	2,300	2,716
N. Casa de Teras	97	56	761	2,239	3,000
1º de Mayo[c]	258	208	2,120	3,400	5,520
Progreso	205	185	1,654	3,400	5,054
Providencia	238	171	1,904	2,500	4,404
Quechehueca	184	183	1,472	4,000	5,472
31 de Octubre	104	92	832	2,170	3,002
El Yaqui	464	383	3,768	4,000	7,768
Totals	2,159	1,810	17,417	36,099	53,516

[a]SOURCE: Mexico, Banco Nacional de Crédito Ejidal, S.A., *El sistema de producción colectiva en los ejidos del Valle del Yaqui, Sonora*, p. 29.

[b]Cajeme was already granted by 1938, and this represents an *ampliación* (amplification) of ejidal territory.

[c]The *ejidos* 1º de Mayo and F.J. Mina are in Bácum; the rest are in Cajeme.

Table A7

Lands Distributed in the Mayo Valley,
Initiated During the Governorship of Román Yocupicio,
1937-1939[a]

MUNICIPIO AND EJIDO	NUMBER OF EJIDATARIOS	LAND AREA GRANTED (hectares)	DATE OF POSSESSION[b]
Etchojoa			
Bacobampo	802	10,056	5-19-40
Basconcobe y Sahuaral	268	5,623	9-08-40
Baynorillo	75	810	7-20-47
Buaysiacobe	72	1,562	5-01-40
Etchojoa	499	6,585	9-24-40
Guayabas	25	404	9-24-40
Huichaca	53	516	12-09-39
Jitonhueca	89	——	9-06-40
Mochipaco	46	518	9-24-40
Vasconia	59	400	8-14-41
Huatabampo			
Bachantahui	71	656	9-20-42
El Cahuteve	96	679	7-04-40
El Citavaro	77	637	12-20-42
La Cuchilla	92	503	7-03-39
Etchoropo	121	579	11-07-42
Huatabampo	996	11,808	12-10-42
El Júpare	162	238	10-01-42
Las Parras	99	979	11-16-42
Pozo Dulce	38	656	11-25-42
La Primavera	21	213	11-04-42
Rancho Chapo	35	862	8-11-41
El Riyito	30	190	10-23-43
Navojoa			
Tres Hermanos	53	1,929	11-12-42
Totals	3,879	46,403	

[a]SOURCE: Estado de Sonora, *Informes que rinde el C. General Román Yocupicio, 1º de Abril de 1937 al 15 de Septiembre de 1937;* y *1º de Septiembre de 1937 al 16 de Septiembre de 1938;* y *Memoria de la gestión gubernamental, 1937-1939.*

[b]Dates of possession are taken from Manuel Corbalá Acuña, "El problema agrario en Sonora."

Table A8
Ejidos Granted Before 1940 in the Sonoran Sierra[a]

MUNICIPIO AND EJIDO	DIARIO OFICIAL	LAND AREA GRANTED (hectares)	IRRIGATED (hectares)	DATE OF POSSESSION
Alamos				
Basiroa	6-18-37	6,529		5-16-37
El Cajón del Sabino	7-01-40	1,466		9-14-40
Los Camotes	— —	5,727		12-11-35
El Chino	12-27-33	7,175		3-31-34
Cochibampo	2-18-30	6,850		4-13-30
Conicarit	11-25-33	11,392		10-12-38
El Copas	8-05-40	1,530		2-04-47
El Frijol	5-26-40	1,216		7-18-39
Guirocoba	12-30-33	1,452		12-10-35
Jerocoa	9-08-34	6,086		3-08-36
Macoyahui	8-09-26	3,361		7-06-27
El Maquipo	8-14-26	3,158		7-06-27
Los Muertos	3-21-34	2,501		12-15-35
Palos Chinos	10-17-36	1,587		5-01-37
El Paso	4-12-34	1,500		8-22-41
Potreros de Alcántar	9-27-38	2,326		8-06-41
San Antonio	7-12-36	3,078		— —
Sombrerito	10-16-35	1,521		5-01-37
El Tabelo	11-11-33	1,788		6-22-35
Tapizuelas	6-25-40	2,271		7-31-39
Techobampo	— —	1,585		6-05-27
Arivechi				
Arivechi	10-06-36	5,140	17	5-29-37
Bacanora				
Guáycora	— —	2,220		5-29-34
Milpillas	— —	1,524		5-22-33
Bacerac				
Ciénega de Bacerac	10-13-37	6,696	88	12-24-38
Huachinera	10-07-20	2,000		— —
Bavispe				
Bavispe	10-13-37	8,963	152	11-25-50
San Miguelito	9-07-27	16,975	11	8-22-27

(continued)

Table A8 (continued)

MUNICIPIO AND EJIDO	DIARIO OFICIAL	LAND AREA GRANTED (hectares)	IRRIGATED (hectares)	DATE OF POSSESSION
La Colorada				
Cobachi	11-26-39	3,866	184	4-27-34
La Colorada	1-22-38	8,300		3-10-46
Cumpas				
Divisadero	2-11-30	17,172		7-17-30
Los Hoyos	3-17-30	2,460		6-10-30
Jécori	9-05-28	3,063		8-08-28
Nacozari de García	8-02-34	5,016		11-24-35
Col. Á Obregón	6-31-34	5,995		11-24-35
Ojo de Agua	8-19-33	18,124		11-08-51
Fronteras				
Agua Prieta	5-22-24	10,000		4-29-24
Cuquiriachi	1-30-30	13,756		12-01-29
Esqueda	9-13-34	7,630		7-13-35
Fronteras	1-30-30	16,525		11-27-29
Kilómetro 47	11-12-38	1,399	22	5-17-49
Huachinera				
Aribabi	2-14-30	3,468		7-30-31
Mazatán				
Mazatán	3-19-30	1,236		12-16-31
Moctezuma				
San Clemente	2-11-30	150		7-15-30
Tonibabi	8-30-20	19,903		2-22-20
Tonibachi	——	28,095		11-22-20
Nácori Chico				
Nácori Chico	12-12-25	12,538		12-25-26
El Tecorinami	——	12,350		3-26-38
Nacozari de García				
Nacozari de García	7-20-37	14,770		10-10-38
Nacozari Viejo	7-19-37	3,300		9-30-38
Pilares de Nacozari	7-19-37	7,000		11-20-38

(continued)

Table A8 (continued)

MUNICIPIO AND EJIDO	DIARIO OFICIAL	LAND AREA GRANTED (hectares)	IRRIGATED (hectares)	DATE OF POSSESSION
Quiriego				
Batacosa	3-28-33	9,419		3-09-37
Quiriego	7-19-37	4,327		5-25-39
Sahuaripa				
Guáycora	10-11-32	2,220		5-29-34
Guisamopa	8-20-27	5,500		8-10-27
Meseta de Cuájari	9-13-38	4,685		3-31-38
Santo Tomás	8-04-37	4,656		4-28-33
San Pedro de la Cueva				
Suaqui	6-28-37	11,186		5-01-37
Tepupa	1-27-38	83		7-09-41
Soyopa				
Soyopa	3-25-37	13,792		4-01-37
Tepache				
Divisadero	2-11-30	17,172		7-17-30
Tepache Nuevo Sur	11-30-37	12,350		3-26-38
Yécora				
Yécora	12-07-33	3,341		10-24-34
Totals		422,464		474

aSOURCES: *Diario Oficial* and Manuel Corbalá Acuña, "El problema agrario en Sonora."

Table A9
Land Grants Initiated under Rodolfo Eliás Calles, 1934[a]

MUNICIPIO AND EJIDO	(1) GOVERNOR'S RESOLUTION	(2) PRESIDENTIAL RESOLUTION	(3) DIARIO OFICIAL	(4) DEFINITIVE POSSESSION	LAG A (1-2)	LAG B (1-4)
Agua Prieta						
Cabullona	1934	1936	1936	1937	2	3
Alamos						
La Labor	1934	—	—	—	—	—
Palmarito	1934	—	—	—	—	—
San Antonio	1934	—	1936	—	—	—
Arizpe						
Sinoquipe	1934	1938	1941	1938	4	4
Bacadehuachi						
El Sauz	1934	1936	1936	1937	2	3
Bacoachi						
Unámichi	1934	1937	1937	1946	3	9
Caborca						
La Grullita	1934	1937	1943	1937	3	3
Fronteras						
Turicachi	1934	1938	—	1938	4	4
Granados						
Granados	1934	1955	1955	1956	21	22

Hermosillo						
La Calera	1934	1944	1945	—	10	—
Codorachi	1934	1937	1937	1938	3	4
La Labor	1934	1937	1937	1938	3	4
El Molino de Camou	1934	1936	1936	1936	2	2
Topahue	1934	1937	1937	1938	3	4
Huatabampo						
Tábare	1934	—	1936	1937	—	3
Imuris						
Babasac	1934	1936	1936	—	2	—
Quijano	1934	—	—	—	—	—
Magdalena						
Bachantal	1934	1936	1936	—	2	—
Cerro Blanco	1934	—	1937	1937	—	3
Quelital	1934	—	1937	1937	—	3
Santa Ana Viejo	1934	—	—	1936	—	2
Navojoa						
Etchoguacuila	1934	1936	1936	1937	2	3
Sahuaripa						
La Mesa del Campanero	1934	—	—	—	—	—

(continued)

Table A9 (continued)

MUNICIPIO AND EJIDO	(1) GOVERNOR'S RESOLUTION	(2) PRESIDENTIAL RESOLUTION	(3) DIARIO OFICIAL	(4) DEFINITIVE POSSESSION	LAG A (1-2)	LAG B (1-4)
Tubutama						
La Reforma	1934	—	1935	1936	—	2
Tubutama	1934	—	1935	1935	—	1
Ures						
Ranchito de Aguilar	1934	1937	1938	1937	3	3
San Rafael	1934	—	1934	1937	0	3
Average					4.1	4.3

aThe list of ejidal grants comes from Estado de Sonora, *Informe que rinde el C. Rodolfo Elías Calles, 1934*, p. 81. Dates of presidential resolutions come from Leonel Argüelles Mendes, *La reforma agraria en Sonora*; dates of possession are taken from Manuel Corbalá Acuña, "El problema agrario en Sonora," and *Diario Oficial*, 1934-1955.

Table A10
Ejidal Grants Initiated under Román Yocupicio, 1937-1938[a]

REGION MUNICIPIO AND EJIDO	(1) GOVERNOR'S RESOLUTION	(2) PRESIDENTIAL RESOLUTION	(3) DIARIO OFICIAL	(4) DEFINITIVE POSSESSION	LAG A (1-2)	LAG B (1-4)
Yaqui Valley Grants						
Bácum						
Francisco J. Mina	1937	1938	1938	1938	1	1
1º de Mayo	1937	1938	1938	1938	1	1
Cajeme						
Campo 60	1937	1938	1938	—	0	—
Campo Yaqui	1937	1938	1938	1938	0	1
El Castillo	1937	1938	1938	1938	0[b]	1
Cuauhtemoc	1937	1938	1938	1938	0	1
Francisco I. Madero	1937	1938	1938	1938	0	1
Guadalupe Victoria	1937	1938	1938	1938	0	1
Morelos	1937	1938	1938	1938	0	1
N. Casa de Teras	1937	1937	1938	1938	0	1
Progreso	1937	1938	1938	1938	0	1
Providencia	1937	1938	1938	1938	0	1
Quechehueca	1937	1938	1938	1938	0	1
31 de Octubre	1937	1938	1938	1938	0	1
El Yaqui	1937	—	—	1938	—	1

(continued)

Table A10 (continued)

REGION MUNICIPIO AND EJIDO	(1) GOVERNOR'S RESOLUTION	(2) PRESIDENTIAL RESOLUTION	(3) DIARIO OFICIAL	(4) DEFINITIVE POSSESSION	LAG A (1-2)	LAG B (1-4)
Mayo Valley Grants						
Etchojoa						
Bacobampo	1938	1939	1940	1940	1	2
Basconcobe and Sahuaral	1938	1939	1940	1940	1	2
Baynorillo	1938	——	——	1947	——	9
Buaysiacobe	1938	1939	1940	1940	1	2
Etchojoa	1938	1939	1942	1940	1	2
Las Guayabas	1938	1939	1940	1940	1	2
Huichaca	1938	1939	1940	1939	1	1
Jitonhueca	1938	——	——	1940	——	2
Mochipaco	1938	1939	——	1940	1	2
Vasconia	1938	1939	1940	1941	1	3
Huatabampo						
Bachantahui	1938	1939	1940	1942	1	4
Cahuteve	1938	1939	1940	1940	1	2
El Citavaro	1938	1939	1940	1942	1	4
La Cuchilla	1938	1939	1940	1939	1	1
Etchoropo	1938	1939	1940	1942	1	4
Júpare	1938	1939	1940	1942	1	4
Huatabampo	1938	1939	1940	1942	1	4
Las Parras	1938	——	——	1942	——	4
Pozo Dulce	1938	1939	1940	1942	1	4
La Primavera	1938	1939	1940	1942	1	4
Rancho Chapo	1938	1939	1940	1941	1	3
El Riyito	1938	1939	——	1942	1	4

	Col 1	Col 2	Col 3	Col 4	Col 5	Col 6
Navojoa						
Bacabachi	1937	1937	1937	1937	0	0
Yenobari	1938	1939	1940	1940	1	2
Sierra Grants						
Alamos						
El Cajón del Sabino	1938	1938	1940	1940	0	2
El Copas	1938	1940	1940	1947	2	9
El Frijol	1937	1938	1940	1939	1	2
Potreros de Alcántar	1938	1938	1938	1941	0	3
Tapizuelas	1937	1937	1940	1939	0	2
Bacerac						
Ciénega de Bacerac	1937	1937	1937	1938	0	1
Bavispe						
Bavispe	1937	1937	1937	1950	0	13
La Colorada						
La Colorada	1938	1938	1938	1946	0	8
Fronteras						
Kilómetro 47	1937	1938	1938	1949	1	12

(continued)

Table A10 (continued)

REGION MUNICIPIO AND EJIDO	(1) GOVERNOR'S RESOLUTION	(2) PRESIDENTIAL RESOLUTION	(3) DIARIO OFICIAL	(4) DEFINITIVE POSSESSION	LAG A (1-2)	LAG B (1-4)
Nacozari de Garcia						
Nacozari de G.	1937	1937	1937	1938	0	1
Nacozari Viejo	1937	1937	1937	1938	0	1
Pilares de Nac.	1937	1937	1937	1938	0	1
Quiriego						
Quiriego	1937	1937	1937	1939	0	2
Sahuaripa						
Cajón de Onapa	1937	1937	1938	1938	0	1
Meseta de C.	—	1937	1938	1938	—	—
San Pedro de la Cueva						
Suaqui	1937	1937	1937	1937	0	0
Tepupa	—	1937	1938	1941	—	—
Tepache						
Tepache Nuevo Sur	—	1937	1937	1938	—	—
Average Yaqui Valley					0	1
Average Mayo Valley					1	3
Average Sierra					0	4

aSOURCES: Same as Table A7.
bThe apparent discrepancy in Lag A for Yaqui Valley grants results from the fact that almost all of the grants were adjudicated in January 1938, after initial resolution at the end of October 1937. As the time involved was less than three months, there was no substantial lag.

Table A11
Public and Private Credit Available to Agriculture, 1940-1970[a]

PERIOD	EJIDAL BANK		AGRICULTURAL BANK[b]		PRIVATE CREDIT[b]	
	CREDIT LEVEL[a]	AVERAGE ANNUAL PERCENTAGE OF GROWTH	CREDIT LEVEL[a]	AVERAGE ANNUAL PERCENTAGE OF GROWTH	CREDIT LEVEL[a]	AVERAGE ANNUAL PERCENTAGE OF GROWTH
1940-1950	4,443,611	2.6	3,283,520	68.0	3,984,000[c]	8.8
1951-1960	12,583,296	12.9	4,405,088	4.4	14,452,000	13.7
1961-1970	8,689,591	0.9	7,208,651	3.4	40,957,000[d]	11.8
1940-1970	25,716,498	5.4	14,897,259	25.2	59,393,000[e]	11.7

[a]SOURCE: CDIA, *Estructura agraria y desarrollo agrícola en México*; Tables XI-2, XI-5, XI-13. Credit levels in thousands of pesos.
[b]Supplies credit to the private sector only; called the *Banco Nacional de Crédito Agrícola*.
[c]Date for 1943-1950 only.
[d]Data for 1961-1969 only.
[e]Data for 1943-1969 only.

Table A12

Index of the Value of Agricultural Production Relative to Other Sectors of the Economy, 1934-1945[a]

YEAR	VALUE OF AGRICULTURAL PRODUCTION (pesos)	PERCENTAGE OF NATIONAL INCOME	PERCENTAGE OF GROWTH	INDEXES OF VALUE OF PRODUCTION					
				GENERAL	AGRICULTURE	MANUFACTURING	CATTLE	MINING	PETROLEUM
1934	319,000,000	9.8	—	48	58	27	47	48	68
1935	361,000,000	9.7	+13.2	55	66	37	62	64	74
1936	472,000,000	11.1	+30.7	63	86	49	62	64	73
1937	535,000,000	10.7	+13.3	74	98	60	78	76	97
1938	546,000,000	10.3	+ 2.1	78	100	68	88	87	83
1939	625,000,000	10.2	+14.5	90	114	86	97	95	98
1940	548,000,000	8.1	−12.3	100	100	100	100	100	100
1941	681,000,000	8.9	+24.3	113	124	116	110	96	95
1942	889,000,000	10.0	+30.5	131	162	133	105	118	76
1943	1,022,000,000	10.1	+15.0	150	186	151	141	123	70
1944	1,115,000,000	10.1	+ 9.1	163	203	170	162	110	76
1945	1,214,000,000	10.1	+ 8.9	176	222	183	181	109	84
Averages		9.9	+12.4						

[a]Elaborated from Sanford A. Mosk, *Industrial Revolution in Mexico*, Table 9, pp. 314-315.

Table A13

Public Spending in Agriculture, 1935-1970[a]

PRESIDENCY	BUDGET OF AGRARIAN DEPARTMENTS (pesos)
Cárdenas, 1935-1940	50,415,000
Ávila Camacho, 1941-1946	60,795,000
Alemán, 1947-1952	88,051,000
Ruiz Cortines, 1953-1958	163,254,000
López Mateos, 1959-1964	462,703,000
Díaz Ordaz, 1965-1970	10,832,566,000

[a]SOURCES: CDIA, *Estructura agraria y desarrollo agrícola en México*, app. IX-5. 1968-1970 data from Merilee S. Grindle, *Bureaucrats, Politicians, and Peasants in Mexico: A Case Study in Public Policy*, app. C.

Table A14
Land Area Benefitted by Federal Irrigation Projects, Sonora, 1926-1970[a]

YEAR	NATIONAL		IRRIGATION DISTRICT[b]									
			MAYO (38)		YAQUI (41)		SONORA RIVER		ALTAR (84)		TOTAL SONORA	
	NEW	IMPROVED	NEW	IMPROVED	NEW	IMPROVED	NEW	IMPROVED	NEW	IMPROVED	NEW	IMPROVED
1926-1946	419.9	396.4	—	2.0	50.4	65.9	—	—	—	—	50.4	67.9
1947-1952	386.7	278.8	11.9	5.4	—	—	8.0	2.0	1.5	0.5	21.4	7.9
1953	81.4	80.8	—	—	50.0	—	—	—	1.0	—	51.0	—
1954	131.9	72.2	—	17.0	43.0	—	—	—	—	—	43.0	—
1955	100.4	110.3	13.0	—	—	—	—	—	—	—	13.0	17.0
1956	156.4	69.2	10.0	—	—	—	—	—	—	—	10.0	—
1957	68.1	157.4	6.7	—	5.0	—	—	—	—	—	11.7	—
1958	53.6	41.5	—	—	3.5	—	—	—	—	—	3.5	—
1959	28.8	13.7	—	—	—	—	—	—	—	—	—	—
1960	21.1	20.1	—	4.0	4.0	—	—	—	—	—	4.0	4.0
1961	29.2	13.4	—	—	—	—	—	—	—	—	—	—
1962	25.4	11.2	—	—	—	—	—	—	—	—	—	—
1963	48.5	12.7	—	—	—	—	—	—	—	—	—	—
1964	25.3	12.2	—	—	—	—	—	—	—	—	—	—
1965	35.9	3.2	—	—	—	—	—	—	—	—	—	—
1966	54.9	8.9	—	—	—	—	—	—	—	—	—	—
1967	50.9	7.3	—	—	—	—	—	—	—	—	—	—
1968	72.9	26.3	—	—	—	—	—	—	—	—	—	—
1969	43.7	39.3	—	—	—	—	—	—	—	—	—	—
1970	46.3	7.9	—	—	—	—	—	—	—	—	—	—

[a]SOURCE: Secretaría de Recursos Hidráulicos (SRH), *Informe anual*, 1947-1971.
[b]Area given in thousand hectares.

Table A15

Property and Production by Land Type and Region, Sonora, 1970[a]

REGION	LAND TOTALS			VOLUME OF CROP PRODUCTION		
	EJIDAL (hectares)	PRIVATE (≤5) (hectares)		EJIDAL (tons)	PRIVATE (>5) (tons)	PRIVATE (≤5) (tons)
Irrigation Districts						
District 37	2,717.1	42,418.0	(56.7)	6,053,787	112,109,710	188,839
District 51	6,011.4	110,888.9	(59.7)	17,470,271	361,225,154	183,586
District 84	21,105.4	31,243.3	(12.0)	50,533,008	82,429,872	23,089
District 38	51,322.5	89,112.9	(1,599.1)	127,941,239	232,712,320	2,160,017
District 41	83,256.5	139,605.9	(162.0)	203,356,942	355,871,964	291,633
San Luis R.C.	11,686.4	10,473.7	(14.7)	25,425,301	20,957,303	38,100
Totals	176,099.3	423,742.7	(1,904.2)	430,780,548	1,165,306,323	2,885,264
Sierra	22,929.3	12,222.8	(1,652.9)	19,307,326	25,803,027	2,984,383
Other Municipalities	11,842.1	19,650.8	(1,614.0)	30,916,934	69,795,843	4,402,667

[a]SOURCE: Censo agrícola-ganadero y ejidal, 1970.

Table A16

Irrigation and Production by Region and Crop Type, Sonora, 1970[a]

REGION	IRRIGATED/TOTAL (hectares)		CASH CROPS (tons)	VOLUME STAPLE CROPS (tons)
Irrigation Districts	567,640	599,842.0	1,584,346,444	14,625,691
District 37	44,287	45,135.1	117,614,859	737,477
District 51	113,653	116,900.3	378,184,442	694,569
District 84	47,460	52,348.7	130,554,432	2,431,537
District 38	131,968	140,435.4	355,930,431	6,883,144
District 41	209,006	222,862.4	555,801,175	3,719,364
San Luis R.C.	21,266	22,160.1	46,261,104	159,600
Sierra	10,750	35,152.1	39,824,436	8,270,300
Other Municipalities	25,477	31,492.9	90,652,624	14,462,820

[a]SOURCE: *Censo agrícola-ganadero y ejidal,* 1970. The crop tonnage figures do not include all crops cultivated, but only those reported in the census. Staple crops include corn and beans, both as primary and secondary cultivation. Squash, chile, and other staples are not included in the census, but there is little reason to think that the substance of the tables would be changed, as the Yaqui and Mayo valleys are also the leading producers of vegetables in the state.

Table A17

Proportion of Capital Investment in Units of Production, Sonora, 1970[a]

	>5 HECTARES			≤5 HECTARES			EJIDOS		
	IRRIGATION DISTRICT	SIERRA	OTHER MUNICIPIOS	IRRIGATION DISTRICT	SIERRA	OTHER MUNICIPIOS	IRRIGATION DISTRICT	SIERRA	OTHER MUNICIPIOS
Total capital invested (millions)	6,233.0	1,504.2	1,376.4	376.2	112.9	103.5	1,784.2	461.4	455.2
Total hectares harvested	421,838	10,570	18,037	1,904	1,653	1,614	176,099	22,929	11,842
$\bar{X}$ capital investment per hectare of harvest (000's pesos)	14.8	142.3	76.3	197.6	68.3	64.1	10.1	20.1	38.4
$\bar{X}$ value of machinery as % of capital investment	33.4	6.0	8.3	50.5	2.8	4.7	4.4	4.0	6.6
$\bar{X}$ value of irrigation work as % of capital investment	5.3	0.9	2.3	0.2	0.4	0.7	1.2	0.5	2.5
$\bar{X}$ value of land as % of capital investment	49.7	18.8	25.4	2.6	6.1	9.1	83.4	24.1	22.2
Worked	45.3	2.3	5.8	2.3	5.8	8.8	76.0	7.0	8.2
Idle	4.4	16.5	19.6	0.3	0.3	0.3	7.4	17.1	14.0
$\bar{X}$ value of livestock as % of capital investment	11.7	74.2	64.0	46.7	90.7	85.5	11.7	71.6	68.6

[a]SOURCE: Elaborated from *Censo agrícola-ganadero y ejidal*, 1970.

Table A18

Agricultural and Cattle Areas by Region, Sonora, 1975[a]

(hectares)

MUNICIPALITY	IRRIGATED BY GRAVITY	IRRIGATED BY PUMP	IRRIGATED BY NORIA	SEASONAL	TOTAL AGRICULTURAL	TOTAL WASTELAND
PART I: IRRIGATION DISTRICTS						
District 37						
Altar	1,363	2,700	642	2,384	7,089	248,241
Caborca	—	29,238	3,376	5,892	38,506	833,788
Oquitoa	1,115	—	—	63	1,178	62,486
Pitiquito	1	3,957	1,794	3,186	8,938	1,189,000
Trincheras	1,206	1,265	226	3,229	5,926	370,500
District 51						
Hermosillo	30,198	143,262	9,346	8,382	191,188	1,276,833
District 84						
Guaymas	37,146	16,000	6,792	16,556	76,494	1,140,000
District 38						
Etchojoa	76,235	335	345	2,816	79,731	42,292
Huatabampo	25,323	—	—	3,390	28,713	88,000
Navojoa	41,087	383	37	7,735	49,242	368,828
District 41						
Bácum	24,470	—	24	1,213	25,707	114,263
Cajeme	102,472	63	181	4,392	107,108	285,627
Empalme	4,078	1,056	7,556	2,599	15,289	55,563

District	15,191	189	19,040	50	34,470	141,879
San Luis Río Colorado	15,191	189	19,040	50	34,470	141,879
PART II: SIERRA REGION						
Álamos	19	18	128	16,934	17,099	674,648
Arivechi	286	—	—	947	1,233	71,000
Bacadehuachi	1,922	—	—	1,298	3,220	92,164
Bacanora	169	—	—	289	458	89,850
Bacerac	561	—	6	134	701	117,290
Bavispe	812	—	—	71	883	200,699
La Colorado	83	—	446	1,165	1,694	468,460
Cumpas	1,139	—	102	3,131	4,372	196,978
Divisaderos	—	—	—	1,298	1,298	60,471
Fronteras	1,142	132	108	2,766	4,148	258,489
Granados	367	—	—	12	379	35,748
Huachinera	88	—	1	356	445	118,042
Huasabas	636	—	—	56	692	70,422
Mazatán	16	3	8	1,283	1,310	63,601
Moctezuma	674	—	3	360	1,037	175,302
Nácori Chico	37	—	—	180	217	274,652
Nacozari	5	—	—	10	15	189,925
Onavas	—	—	6	227	233	37,000

(continued)

Table A18 (continued)

MUNICIPALITY	IRRIGATED BY GRAVITY	IRRIGATED BY PUMP	IRRIGATED BY NORIA	SEASONAL	TOTAL AGRICULTURAL	TOTAL WASTELAND
Quiriego	90	—	10	2,354	2,454	268,118
Rosario	275	—	306	1,729	2,310	257,109
Sahuaripa	1,252	—	—	3,398	4,650	400,450
San Javier	2	—	—	—	2	66,389
San Pedro de la Cueva	8	—	503	29	540	66,391
Soyopa	53	—	—	606	659	83,974
Suaqui Grande	64	—	17	80	161	88,767
Tepache	1,259	—	—	114	1,373	73,912
Villa Hidalgo	759	—	—	653	1,412	73,658
Villa Pesqueira	76	16	—	517	609	182,809
Yécora	249	—	—	1,990	2,239	90,542
PART III: OTHER MUNICIPIOS						
Aconchi	680	—	1	175	856	35,018
Agua Prieta	1,494	22	—	694	2,210	359,000
Arizpe	1,964	—	5	1,294	3,253	276,415
Átil	2,096	—	—	17	2,113	37,930
Bacoachi	814	—	13	769	1,596	124,470
Banámichi	1,382	—	—	252	1,634	75,672
Baviácora	879	—	2	403	1,284	84,612
Benjamín Hill	15	—	—	1,089	1,104	84,300
Cananea	12	—	34	223	269	392,059
Carbó	195	136	100	517	948	168,000
Cucurpe	765	96	—	50	911	153,467
Huepac	429	—	4	292	725	36,412
Imuris	2,640	—	166	1,089	3,895	166,139

Magdalena	1,797	—	30	2,303	4,130	140,000
Naco	1	—	—	60	61	63,000
Nogales	551	—	62	352	965	164,000
Opodepe	900	75	7	1,889	2,796	277,628
Puerto Peñasco	12	—	—	586	673	400,000
Rayón	1,059	—	582	229	1,870	108,714
San Felipe	337	—	—	32	369	14,155
San Miguel de Horc.	1,153	973	—	310	2,436	174,410
Santa Ana	781	1,315	—	3,972	6,068	155,996
Santa Cruz	1,008	—	—	555	1,563	86,479
Saric	498	35	25	509	1,067	166,556
Tubutama	1,285	89	—	1,338	2,712	124,377
Ures	3,118	208	149	2,056	5,531	242,170

aSOURCE: Data from Sonora, Departamento de Asuntos Rurales.

Table A19
Average Annual Rates of Agricultural Growth
in the Mexican Economy[a]
(percent)

PERIOD	NET NATIONAL PRODUCT	ALL AGRICULTURE	CROPS	LIVESTOCK
1940-1960	7.0	4.7	6.1	3.2
1940-1950	7.8	4.7	7.5	2.8
1950-1960	6.2	4.6	4.8	3.7
1960-1970	7.7	3.3	3.0	4.5
1940-1970	7.2	4.2	5.1	3.7
1950-1970	7.0	4.0	3.9	4.1
1960-1965	8.4	3.9	4.8	3.4
1965-1970	6.9	2.7	1.2	5.6

[a]SOURCE: Data elaborated from CDIA, *Estructura agraria y desarrollo agrícola en México*, Table II-1.

Table A20
Usable Capacity in Reservoirs Controlled by SRH, and Stored Water Available, 1950-1975[a]

YEAR	RÍO ALTAR CUAUHTEMOC	RÍO YAQUI ANGOSTURA	RÍO YAQUI A. OBREGON	RÍO YAQUI P. E. CALLES	RÍO MAYO A. RUIZ C.
Total Capacity[b]	43.0	917.0	2,737.0	2,417.5	1,089.7
1950	—	—	—	—	—
1951	—	—	—	—	—
1952	18.2	160.5	782.5	—	—
1953	18.0	337.2	455.5	—	—
1954	17.1	234.4	1,452.1	—	—
1955	20.7	740.0	2,141.6	—	825.2
1956	12.0	565.6	1,851.3	—	560.6
1957	7.3	518.3	1,388.0	—	429.3
1958	21.2	815.3	2,500.0	—	716.4
1959	23.4	856.0	2,500.0	—	892.7
1960	28.2	856.0	2,404.0	—	851.7
1961	18.8	847.3	1,898.5	—	989.7
1962	17.9	710.3	1,604.6	—	871.7
1963	8.3	648.5	2,011.5	—	753.0
1964	14.4	668.4	1,508.2	1,704.7	989.7
1965	31.2	593.0	792.2	1,316.5	822.0
1966	43.0	528.4	2,318.0	2,350.6	989.7
1967	43.0	617.0	1,169.0	2,385.0	889.8
1968	43.0	917.0	2,723.5	2,399.1	1,081.1
1969	36.0	885.8	2,407.0	2,101.7	923.0
1970	35.5	214.0	1,995.0	1,428.4	649.8
1971	40.8	269.4	1,640.0	1,336.0	1,089.7
1972	41.3	388.0	1,117.2	1,303.0	1,015.1
1973	39.2	834.1	1,156.4	2,153.7	983.9
1974	29.0	423.0	1,083.6	1,317.3	706.5
1975	20.8	347.0	900.0	1,266.8	557.1

[a]SOURCE: Secretaría de Recursos Hidráulicos (SRH), *Informe anual*, 1971-1976.
[b]Total capacity is measured in millions of cubic meters.

Table A21
Presidential Resolutions in Agrarian-Reform Matters, 1967-1977[a]

ACTION/YEAR	1967	1968	1969	1970	1971	1972	1973	1974	1975	1976	1977*
Restitutions											
Actions	1	1	1	1	1	1	1	—	1	—	21
Beneficiaries	102	173		120	750	750	4,522	—	—	—	1,138
Area (in thousand hectares)	0.1	15.4	5.8	16.9	50.0	50.0	71.0	—	0.2	0.2	40.7
Grants											
Actions	230	365	318	284	127	95	115	102	106	191	21
Beneficiaries	8,298	14,873	13,632	11,996	7,811	5,964	6,286	6,762	7,463	10,723	1,138
Area (in thousand hectares)	1,076	1,478	2,516.2	3,615.7	790.1	189.6	368.5	253.7	248.6	393.1	40.7
New Centers of Ejidal Population											
New Centers	136	131	41	210	78	69	98	36	95	178	11
Beneficiaries	14,039	8,704	2,752	12,271	4,637	5,046	5,924	2,755	7,873	13,926	440
Area (in thousand hectares)	687.2	1,028.4	301.6	596.9	1,409.1	1,253.2	94.7	94.7	1,571.2	416.0	24.1
Expropriations											
Actions	29	19	14	53	22	99	106	80	156	523	10
Area (in thousand hectares)	2.6	3.5	0.3	16.6	2.3	9.3	23.6	47.2	23.3	45.9	0.1

[a]SOURCE: Mexico, *Primer informe de gobierno que rinde al H. Congreso de la Unión José López Portillo, Presidente Constitucional de los Estados Unidos Mexicanos,* Sept. 1, 1977.

*First three quarters of 1977 only.

Table A22

Area and Crops Affected by Official Agricultural Credit, 1967-1977[a]

YEAR/CROP	RICE	BEANS	CORN	WHEAT	SESAME	SAFFLOWER	SOYA	COTTONSEED	SORGHUM
1966-1967	50	108	425	264	32	38	27	149	161
1967-1968	46	86	405	253	36	58	32	187	166
1968-1969	46	90	383	237	46	62	38	186	167
1969-1970	43	133	578	217	65	122	74	146	184
1970-1971	59	192	598	217	65	122	45	238	200
1971-1972	64	153	517	259	47	99	85	279	261
1972-1973	42	140	666	254	53	76	136	269	423
1973-1974	101	165	1,161	381	94	122	143	387	535
1974-1975	140	179	1,434	447	112	160	184	505	705
1975-1976[b]	579	762	2,040	428	181	186	171	163	904
1976-1977[c]	646	789	1,588	405	98	146	83	156	712

[a]SOURCE: Same as Table A21. Area in thousands of hectares.
[b]Preliminary figures.
[c]Estimated figures.

Table A23

Amount of Short-Term Official Agricultural Credit, 1967-1977[a]

YEAR/CROP	RICE	BEANS	CORN	WHEAT	SESAME	SAFFLOWER	SOYA	COTTONSEED	SORGHUM
1966-1967	91	46	284	391	20	49	21	643	110
1967-1968	61	33	273	376	24	60	87	827	142
1968-1969	87	38	271	375	32	77	105	769	142
1969-1970	84	58	478	353	38	70	62	687	174
1970-1971	132	83	446	322	44	158	70	1,121	194
1971-1972	113	93	401	440	33	129	148	1,468	258
1972-1973	102	99	632	464	47	113	257	1,479	489
1973-1974	283	236	1,714	701	99	183	319	2,028	761
1974-1975	377	303	2,108	862	130	234	363	2,651	940
1975-1976[b]	188	1,824	4,377	1,914	378	584	692	292	1,502
1976-1977[c]	97	780	4,115	1,731	267	436	522	2,178	2,569

[a]SOURCE: Same as Tables A21 and A22. Amounts in millions of pesos.
[b]Preliminary figures.
[c]Estimated figures.

Glossary

Acasillados, peones acasillados: Agricultural workers who reside rent-free on the estates they work on and receive a wage for their services.

Agrarismo: The general movement for agrarian reform. An *agrarista* is an advocate of agrarian reform.

Agricultor: Farmer.

Amparo: Judicial protection of the individual against government action, applicable here in agrarian-reform matters.

Baldíos: Uncultivated public lands.

Cacique: Chieftain; political boss of a village or town. *Caciquismo* refers to a system of domination centering around local *cacique* rule.

Campesinos: Literally, country people; roughly, peasants. From *campo*, the countryside. *Campesinado* is the collective noun referring to *campesinos*.

Cardenismo: The brand of populism ascribed to Lázaro Cárdenas, whose followers are called *cardenistas*. The policies and followers of Francisco Madero are termed *maderismo* and *maderistas*; of Luis Echeverría, *echeverrismo* and *echeverristas*, etc.

Caudillo: Military leader or commander; chieftain.

Científicos: Positivist elites important in the cabinet of Porfirio Díaz.

Colonos: Colonists; proprietors of land under official colonization schemes of the government.

Denuncia: Announcement; proclamation; application for a concession.

Ejido: Agricultural land held in usufruct; farmland formally owned by the Mexican nation and granted to rural residents under the agrarian reform. Members of such cooperatives are called *ejidatarios*.

Encomienda: The entrustment of Indians granted to a Spanish *conquistador* by the Crown, with the idea of providing for their spiritual conversion and material welfare.

Fuero Militar: The army's privilege to maintain its own court system.

Hacienda: A large landed estate. The owners of haciendas are *hacendados*.

Henequén: Sisal, henequen.

Jornaleros: Day-workers, agricultural wage-laborers.

Latifundia: Large landholdings; rural property in excess of the legal limits set by the agrarian-reform laws. A system of rural property dominated by latifundia is called *latifundismo*; the landowners are *latifundistas*.

Manos muertos: Mortmain; inalienable estates.

Maximato: The period from 1929 to 1934, dominated by Plutarco Elías Calles, *el jefe máximo* and former president (1924–1928).

Minifundio: A very small landholding, generally less than ten hectares.

Obrerista: Referring to a person, organization, or administration oriented toward the needs of the organized labor movement.

Pan y palo: Bread and a stick; reward and punishment.

Patrón: Protector; landlord; boss—the dominant partner in traditional *patrón–campesino* dyads.

Pelele: Literally, a stuffed figure; puppet; nincompoop. Refers to the popular characterization of the presidents during the *Maximato*: Emilio Portes Gil, Pascual Ortiz Rubio, and Abelardo Rodríguez.

Peon, peones: Worker(s), day-laborer(s).

Peso: The official Mexican unit of currency, with a 1980 floating value of 22–23 pesos equivalent to $1 U.S.

Porfiriato: The regime of Porfirio Díaz, dictator of Mexico from 1876 to 1911.

Predio: A plot of agricultural land; a farm.

Prestanombres: The practice of loaning a name, generally to hide illegal land tenure or business dealings.

Rancho: A small ranch or farm, whose proprietors are *rancheros*.

Repartimiento: A colonial distribution of land or Indians on a temporary basis.

Rurales: The infamous rural police of the *Porfiriato*.

Sexenio: The six-year presidential term of office.

Tiendas de raya: Company or *hacienda* stores.

Bibliography

PRIMARY SOURCES

General

Banco Nacional de México, S.A. *Examen de la situación económica de México.* 1970–1979.

Cabrera, Luis. "La reconstitución de los ejidos de los pueblos como medio de suprimir la esclavitud del jornalero mexicano." Speech given in the Cámara de Diputados, Dec. 3, 1912; reprinted in *Colección de folletos para la historia de la Revolución mexicana,* vol. 2. *La cuestión de la tierra,* pp. 279–310. Mexico: Instituto Mexicano de Investigaciones Económicas, 1961.

Cárdenas, Lázaro. *Apuntes,* 1913–1940, vol. 1 of *Obras.* Mexico: Universidad Nacional Autónoma de México, 1972.

———. *Ideario político* (Leonel Durán, ed.). Mexico: Ediciones ERA, 1972.

Fábela, Isidro. *Documentos históricos de la Revolución mexicana;* 26 volumes. Mexico: Fondo de Cultura Económica, 1960. (Published under the auspices of the Comisión de Investigaciones Históricas de la Revolución Mexicana.)

Huerta, Adolfo de la. *Memorias.* Mexico: Ediciones Guzmán, 1958.

Obregón Salido, Álvaro. *Discursos;* 2 volumes. Mexico: Biblioteca de la Dirección General de Educación Militar, 1932.

———. *Ocho mil kilómetros en campaña,* vol. 5 of *Fuentes para la historia de la Revolución mexicana.* Mexico: Fondo de Cultura Económica, 1959.

Portes Gil, Emilio. *Quince años de política mexicana,* 2nd ed. Mexico: Ediciones Botas, 1941.

United States Congress, Joint Economic Committee, Subcommittee on Inter-American Economic Relationships. *Recent Developments in Mexico and their Economic Implications for the United States.* 95th Congress, first session, hearings Jan. 17 and 24, 1977.

Mexican Government Publications

Banco de Comercio, S.A. *La economía del estado de Sonora.* Colección de Estudios Económicos Regionales (Medardo Tirado Aramburu, dir.), 1969.

Banco Nacional de Crédito Ejidal, S.A. *El sistema de producción colectiva en los ejidos del Valle del Yaqui, Sonora.* 1945.

Banco Rural, S.A., Ciudad Obregón office. Untitled memorandum covering production and evaluation of 1976–77 crop year in the new ejidos of the Yaqui valley.

Cámara de Diputados. *Los presidentes ante la nación, 1821–1966,* vol. 4. 1966.

Congreso de los Estados Unidos Mexicanos. *Diario de los debates del Congreso Constituyente,* vol. 1, 1916–1917.

———. *Diario de los debates,* vol. 41. Oct. 18, 1946.

Departamento Agrario. *Ideario agrarista del General de División Lázaro Cárdenas, presidente constitucional de los Estados Unidos Mexicanos.* 1935.

Departamento de Asuntos Agrarios y Colonización. *Memorias de labores del 1° de Septiembre de 1968 al 31 de Agosto de 1969.* 1969.

———. *Seis años de política agraria del Presidente Adolfo López Mateos, 1958–1964.* 1964.

Departamento de la Estadística Nacional. *Sonora, Sinaloa, y Nayarit.* 1927.

Nacional Financiera, S.A. *Sonora: fideicomiso para la promoción de conjuntos, parques, y ciudades industriales.* 1971.

Secretaría de Agricultura y Fomento. *Comisión Nacional Agraria, Estadística, 1915–1927.* 1928.

———. *Memoria de la Secretaría de Agricultura y Fomento, Septiembre de 1937–Agosto de 1938,* vol. 2. Comisíon Nacional de Irrigación. 1938.

———. *Memoria . . . , Septiembre de 1938–Agosto de 1939,* vol. 2. Comisión Nacional de Irrigación. 1939.

———. *Sugestiones presentadas por la Secretaría de Agricultura y Fomento a la Secretaría de Gobernación para la formulación del Segundo Plan Sexenal que se someterá a la consideración de la Convención Plenaria del Partido de la Revolución Mexicana.* 1939.

Secretaría de Agricultura y Ganadería, Secretaría de Hacienda y Crédito Público, and Banco de México, S.A. *Projections of Supply and Demand for Agricultural Products in Mexico to 1970 and 1975.* 1965.

Secretaría de la Economía Nacional. *Geografía económica. Sonora, Sinaloa, y Nayarit.* 1927.

———, Dirección General de Estadística. *Estadísticas sociales del Porfiriato, 1877–1910.* 1956.

Secretaría de Prensa y Propaganda del Comité Ejecutivo Nacional del Partido Nacional Revolucionario. *La gira del General Lázaro Cárdenas.* 1934.

Secretaría de la Presidencia. *El gobierno mexicano.* 1971–1976.

Secretaría de Recursos Hidráulicos (SRH). Distrito de Riego no. 51, Costa de Hermosillo, Sonora, Document 51-498, Aug. 22, 1958. Sonora State Archives.

———. "Estudio agrícola–ganadero de una area del río Sonora." *Recursos Hidráulicos* 1, no. 4 (1972):405–413.

———. "Plan Hidráulico del Noroeste." *Ingeniería Hidráulica en México* 22, no. 1 (1969):46–62.

―――. Subsecretaría de Construcción, Dirección General de Grande Irrigación y Control de Ríos, Dirección de Estudios Específicos. *Estudio para el mejoramiento integral y incremento de la productividad en los Distritos de Riego del Río Fuerte, Río Mayo, Río Yaqui, y Colonias Yaquis. November 1971.*
―――. Subsecretaría de Planeación. *Plan Nacional Hidráulico.* 1975.
Secretaría de la Reforma Agraria. "Plan Nacional Agrícola: Sonora." 1973.

Mexican Government Serials

Banco de México, S.A. *Informe anual.* 1941–1978.
Banco Nacional de Comercio Exterior, S.A. *Mexico, 1976: Facts, Figures, Trends.* 1977.
Banco Nacional de Crédito Ejidal, S.A. *Boletín de Estudios Especiales.* 1955–1960.
Diario oficial de la Federación. 1920–1977.
Nacional Financiera, S.A. *Informe anual.* 1945–1975.
Secretaría de la Economía Nacional, Dirección General de Estadística. *Primer censo agrícola–ganadero, 1930.* (Published 1936; includes *Primer censo ejidal* of 1935.)
―――. *Censo agrícola–ganadero y ejidal*, vols. 2–5. 1940, 1950, 1960, 1970.
Secretaría de Industria y Comercio. *Anuario estadístico.*1970–1971.
Secretaría de Recursos Hidráulicos (SRH). *Informe anual.* 1947–1976.
Sonora, Gobierno del Estado. *Boletín oficial.* Various dates, 1919–1976.

Presidential and Gubernatorial Reports (in chronological order)

MEXICO, PRESIDENTIAL REPORTS

Informe del Ciudadano General Porfirio Díaz, Presidente de los Estados Unidos Mexicanos, a sus compatriotas acerca de los actos de su administración en los períodos constitucionales comprendidos entre el 1° de Diciembre de 1884 y 30 de Noviembre de 1896.
Informes rendidos por el Ciudadano General Plutarco Elías Calles, Presidente Constitucional de los Estados Unidos Mexicanos, ante el H. Congreso de la Unión los días 1° de Septiembre de 1925 y 1° de Septiembre de 1926, y contestación de los CC. Presidentes del Citado Congreso.
Informe rendido por el Ciudadano Lic. Emilio Portes Gil, Presidente Provisional de los Estados Unidos Mexicanos, ante el H. Congreso de la Unión el día 1° de Septiembre de 1929.
Informe que rinde al H. Congreso de la Unión el C. Presidente de la República General Lázaro Cárdenas, correspondiente al quinto año de su gestión, del 1° de Septiembre de 1938 al 31 de Agosto de 1939.
Primer informe de gobierno que rinde al H. Congreso de la Unión José López Portillo, Presidente Constitucional de los Estados Unidos Mexicanos, 1° de Septiembre de 1977.

ESTADO DE SONORA, GOVERNORS' REPORTS

Informes dados por el Ciudadano Ramón Corral, Vice-Gobernador Constitucional del Estado de Sonora, en ejercicio del poder ejecutivo, a la legislatura del mismo estado sobre la marcha de la administración pública, 1888.
Informe del C. Gobernador Interino del Estado Sr. Carlos E. Randall, presentado el

1° de Septiembre de 1911 ante el H. Congreso del mismo, al hacer entrega del ejecutivo al Gobernador Constitucional Sr. José María Maytorena.

Informe presentado por el C. José María Maytorena, Gobernador Constitucional del Estado de Sonora, ante la XXIII legislatura del mismo, y contestación del Presidente de la Cámara C. Flavio A. Bórquez, 1912.

Informe que rinde al H. Congreso del Estado de Sonora el Gobernador Provisional C. Adolfo de la Huerta, por el período de su gobierno, comprendido entre el 19 de Mayo de 1916 al 18 de Junio de 1917.

Informes que rinde el C. General Plutarco Elías Calles, Gobernador Constitucional del Estado de Sonora, ante la XXIV legislatura del mismo, 1918–1919.

Informe que rinde el C. Francisco S. Elías, Gobernador Constitucional del Estado de Sonora, ante la legislatura del mismo, 1929.

Informes que rinde el C. Rodolfo Elías Calles, Gobernador Constitucional del Estado de Sonora, ante la XXXI legislatura del mismo, 1933–1934.

Informe que rinde el C. General Román Yocupicio, Gobernador Constitucional del Estado de Sonora, por el período de su gobierno del 1° de Abril de 1937 al 15 de Septiembre de 1937.

Informe que rinde el C. General Román Yocupicio, Gobernador Constitucional del Estado de Sonora, por el período de su gobierno del 1° de Septiembre de 1937 al 16 de Septiembre de 1938.

Memoria de la gestión gubernamental del C. General Román Yocupicio en el Estado de Sonora, 1937–1939.

Informes rendidos ante la XXXVII (and XXXVIII) legislatura constitucional del estado, de la gestión realizada por el poder ejecutivo y de la situación que guardan los diversos ramos de la administración pública, de Abelardo Rodríguez, 1943–1944, 1946–1947.

Informe rendido ante la XXXIX legislatura constitucional del estado, de la gestión realizada por el poder ejecutivo y de la situación que guardan los diversos ramos de la administración pública, del 1° de Septiembre de 1950 al 31 de agosto de 1951.

Informes de gobierno del C. Álvaro Obregón, Gobernador Constitucional del Estado de Sonora, 1956–1961.

Informes de gobierno del C. Faustino Félix Serna, Gobernador Constitucional del Estado de Sonora, 1970–1973.

Informe de gobierno del C. Carlos Armando Biébrich, Gobernador Constitucional del Estado de Sonora, 1974.

Important Laws, Decrees, and Compendia of Statutes

Fábela, Isidro. Documentos históricos de la Revolución mexicana, vol. 1. Mexico: Fondo de Cultura Económica, 1960.

Galván Rivera, Mariano. Ordenanzas de tierras y aguas, o sea formulario geométrico-judicial para la designación, establecimiento, mensura, amojonamiento y deslinde de las poblaciones y todas suertes de tierras, sitios, caballerías y criaderos de ganados mayores y menores, y mercedes de agua, 3rd ed. Mexico, 1849.

Orozco, Wistano Luis. Legislación y jurisprudencia sobre terrenos baldíos. Mexico: Ediciones El Caballito, 1974 (reprint of the 1895 edition).

Villarreal Muñoz, Antonio. Restitución y dotación de ejidos, el problema agrario en México: leyes, decretos, circulares, y disposiciones expedidas ultimamente en la materia. (Published with the authorization of the Comisión Nacional Agraria.) Mexico, 1921.

Ley de 6 de Enero de 1915 que declara nulas todas las enajenaciones de tierras, aguas y montes pertenecientes a los pueblos, otorgadas en contravención a lo dispuesto en la ley de 25 de Junio de 1856.

Decreto de Carranza contra los trabajadores, de 1° de Agosto de 1916.

Ley Agraria de 27 de Junio de 1919 (Sonora). Boletín oficial del Estado de Sonora no. 51, July 6, 1919.

Ley de Tierras Ociosas de 23 de Junio de 1920. Diario Oficial, June 28, 1920.

Ley de Ejidos de 28 de Diciembre de 1920. Diario Oficial, Jan 8, 1921.

Ley sobre Bancos Refaccionarios de 29 de Septiembre de 1924. Diario Oficial, Nov. 12, 1924.

Ley reglamentaria sobre repartición de tierras ejidales y constitución del patrimonio parcelario ejidal de 29 de Diciembre de 1925. Diario Oficial, Dec. 31, 1925.

Ley de Crédito Agrícola de 2 Marzo de 1926. Diario Oficial, March 4, 1926.

Ley de Bancos Ejidales de 16 de Marzo de 1926. Diario Oficial, April 9, 1926.

Ley Federal de Colonización de 5 de Abril de 1926. Diario Oficial, May 11, 1926.

Ley de Dotaciones y Restituciones de Tierras y Aguas, Reglamentaria del Artículo 27 de la Constitución, de 26 de Abril de 1927. Diario Oficial, April 27, 1927.

Ley de Crédito Agrícola de 7 de Febrero de 1934. Diario Oficial, Feb. 9, 1934.

Código Agrario de los Estados Unidos Mexicanos de 9 de Agosto de 1934. Diario Oficial, Aug. 12, 1934.

Decreto que reforma varios artículos del Código Agrario de los Estados Unidos Mexicanos, de 9 de Agosto de 1937. Diario Oficial, Aug. 12, 1937.

Ley de Crédito Agrícola de 31 de Diciembre de 1942. Diario Oficial, March 27, 1943.

Código Agrario de los Estados Unidos Mexicanos de 31 de Diciembre de 1942. Diario Oficial, April 27, 1943.

Ley Federal de Reforma Agraria de 22 de Marzo de 1971. Diario Oficial, May 1, 1971.

Ley Federal de Aguas de 30 de Diciembre de 1971. Diario Oficial, Jan. 11, 1972.

Decreto que crea la Comisión de Desarrollo de la Tribu Seri del Estado de Sonora, con personalidad jurídica y patrimonio propio, con el objeto de promover el desarrollo integral de dicha comunidad. El Gobierno Mexicano 51 (February 1975):297–303.

PERIODICALS

Análisis Político (weekly, Mexico City). 1971–1976.

El Día (daily, Mexico City). 1975–1976.

Excelsior (daily, Mexico City). 1929–1977.

El Imparcial (daily, Hermosillo, Sonora). 1938–1977.

Proceso (weekly, Mexico City). 1976–1977.

BOOKS, ARTICLES, AND THESES

Acuña, Rodolfo F. Sonoran Strongman: Ignacio Pesqueira and His Times. Tucson: University of Arizona Press, 1974.

"Agrarismo y política." *Análisis Político*, Nov. 26, 1976, p. 2.

Aguilar Camín, Hector. *La frontera nómada: Sonora y la Revolución mexicana.* Mexico: Siglo XXI, 1977.

———. "La Revolución sonorense, 1910–1914." Ph.D. dissertation, Centro de Estudios Históricos, El Colegio de México, 1975.

Aguilera Gómez, Manuel. "Balance de la Nueva Ley de Reforma Agraria." *Cuadernos Americanos* 178, no. 5 (September–October 1971):49–68.

———. *La desnacionalización de la economía mexicana.* (Series Archivo del Fondo no. 47.) Mexico: Fondo de Cultura Económica, 1975.

———. *La reforma agraria en el desarrollo económico de México.* Mexico: Instituto Mexicano de Investigaciones Económicas, 1969.

Aguirre Avellaneda, Jerjes. *La política ejidal en México.* Mexico: Instituto Mexicano de Sociología, 1976.

Alamán, Lucas. *Historia de Méjico, desde los primeros movimientos que prepararon su independencia, en el año de 1808, hasta la época presente; 5 volumes.* Mexico: J. M. Lara, 1851.

Almada, Francisco R. *La Revolución en el Estado de Sonora.* Mexico: Biblioteca del Instituto Nacional de Estudios Históricos de la Revolución Mexicana, 1971.

Almond, Gabriel, et al. (eds.). *Crisis, Choice, and Change: Historical Studies of Political Development.* Boston: Little, Brown, 1973.

Anguiano, Arturo. *El estado y la política obrera del cardenismo.* Mexico: Ediciones ERA, 1975.

Aranda, Sergio. "La crisis del capitalismo y sus repercusiones en América Latina." *Problemas del Desarrollo* 6, no. 24 (November 1975–January 1976):19–48.

Argüelles Mendes, Leonel. "La reforma agraria en Sonora." Senior thesis, Facultad de Derecho, Universidad de Sonora, Hermosillo, 1977.

Arriola, Carlos. "Los grupos empresariales frente al estado mexicano, 1973–1975." In El Colegio de México, Centro de Estudios Internacionales, *Las fronteras del control del estado mexicano*, pp. 33–81. Mexico: El Colegio de México, 1976.

Ashby, Joe C. *Organized Labor and the Mexican Revolution Under Lázaro Cárdenas.* Chapel Hill: University of North Carolina Press, 1963, 1967.

Ballesteros Porta, Juan. "Ejidos y comunidades: los modelos de organización." In *La reforma agraria en México*, pp. 199–207. Mexico: Archive of the Instituto de Estudios Políticos, Económicos, y Sociales, Partido Revolucionario Institucional, 1975.

Bancroft, Hubert Howe. *History of the North Mexican States and Texas*, vol. 2. *1801–1899.* (Vol. 16 of *The Works of Hubert Howe Bancroft*.) San Francisco: The History Company, 1889.

Barkin, David. "Mexico's Albatross: The United States Economy." *Latin American Perspectives* 2, no. 2 (Summer 1975):64–80.

———, and Timothy King. *Regional Economic Development: The River Basin Approach in Mexico.* Cambridge, Eng.: Cambridge University Press, 1970.

Bartra, Roger. *Estructura agraria y clases sociales en México.* Mexico: Ediciones ERA, 1975.

———, et al. (eds.). *Caciquismo y poder político en México rural*, 2nd ed. Mexico: Siglo XXI, 1976.

Bassols, Narciso. *Obras.* Mexico: Fondo de Cultura Económica, 1964.

Bassols Batalla, Ángel. *El Noroeste de México: un estudio geográfico-económico.*

Mexico: Instituto de Investigaciones Económicas, Universidad Nacional Autónoma de México, 1972.

Bazant, Jan. *Alienation of Church Wealth in Mexico: Social and Economic Aspects of the Liberal Revolution, 1856–1875* (ed. and trans. Michael P. Costeloe). Cambridge, Eng.: Cambridge University Press, 1971.

———. "Desamortización y nacionalización de los bienes de la iglesia." In Luis González et al., *La economía mexicana en la época de Juárez*, 2nd ed., pp. 155–190. Mexico: SepSetentas, 1976.

Benassini, Oscar. "Estudio general de gran visión del aprovechamiento de los recursos hidráulicos del Noroeste." *Ingeniería Hidráulica en México* 8, no. 4 (1954):18–31.

Blair, Calvin P. "Nacional Financiera: Entrepreneurship in a Mixed Economy." In Raymond Vernon (ed.), *Public Policy and Private Enterprise in Mexico*, pp. 191–240. Cambridge, Mass.: Harvard University Press, 1964.

Blancornelas, Jesús. *Biébrich, crónica de una infamia*. Mexico: EDAMEX, 1978.

Bonilla, Arturo. "El desarrollo económico de México y la agricultura." *Problemas del Desarrollo* 6, no. 2 (November 1975–January 1976):101–118.

Brack, Gene M. *Mexico Views Manifest Destiny, 1821–1846: An Essay on the Origins of the Mexican War*. Albuquerque: University of New Mexico Press, 1975.

Brandenburg, Frank. *The Making of Modern Mexico*. Englewood Cliffs, N.J.: Prentice-Hall, 1964.

Brothers, Dwight S., and Leopoldo Solís M. *Mexican Financial Development*. Austin: University of Texas Press, 1966.

Business Trends: The Mexican Economy, 1976. Mexico: Publicaciones Ejecutivas de México, 1977.

Calderón Francisco R. "Los ferrocarriles." In Daniel Cosío Villegas (ed.), *Historia moderna de México*, vol. 7. *El Porfiriato: la vida económica*, 2nd ed., pp. 483–634. Mexico: Editorial Hermes, 1974.

Calderón Salazar, Jorge Alfonso. "Algunos aspectos de la dinámica económica y social de México en el período 1920–1935." Senior thesis, Escuela Nacional de Economía, Universidad Nacional Autónoma de México, 1973.

Callcott, Wilfrid Hardy. *Liberalism in Mexico, 1857–1929*. Stanford, Calif.: Stanford University Press, 1931.

Calzadíaz Barrera, Alberto. *Dos gigantes: Sonora y Chihuahua*; 2 volumes. Hermosillo: Escritores Asociados del Norte, 1964.

Camp, Roderic A. *Mexican Political Biographies, 1935–1975*. Tucson: University of Arizona Press, 1976.

Campbell, Hugh G. *La derecha radical en México, 1929–1949*. Mexico: SepSetentas, 1976.

"Candado a la fuga de dólares." *Proceso* 1, no. 4 (Nov. 27, 1976):32.

Cardoso, Fernando Henrique, and Enzo Faletto. *Dependencia y desarrollo en América Latina*, 9th ed. Mexico: Siglo XXI, 1974. Published in English as *Dependency and Development in Latin America* (trans. Marjorie M. Uriquidí). Berkeley and Los Angeles: University of California Press, 1979.

Centro de Investigaciones Agrarias (CDIA). *Empleo, desempleo y subempleo en el sector agropecuario*; 2 volumes. Mexico: Centro de Investigaciones Agrarias, 1977.

———. Estructura agraria y desarrollo agrícola en México. Mexico: Fondo de Cultura Económica, 1974.

Chevalier, Francois. "The Ejido and Political Stability in Mexico." In Claudio Veliz (ed.), The Politics of Conformity in Latin America, pp. 158–191. New York: Oxford University Press, 1967.

———. Land and Society in Colonial Mexico: The Great Hacienda (trans. Alvin Eustis; ed. Lesley B. Simpson). Berkeley and Los Angeles: University of California Press, 1963.

Chilcote, Ronald, and Joel C. Edelstein (eds.) Latin America: The Struggle with Dependency and Beyond. Cambridge, Mass.: Schenckman, 1974.

Cinta, Ricardo. "Burquesía nacional y desarrollo." El pérfil de México, 1980, vol. 3, 3rd ed., pp. 165–199. Mexico: Siglo XXI, 1974.

Cline, Howard. "The 'Aurora Yucateca' and the Spirit of Enterprise in Yucatán, 1821–1847." Hispanic American Historical Review 27, no. 1 (February 1947): 30–60.

Coatsworth, John. "Railroads, Landholding, and Agrarian Protest in the Early Porfiriato." Hispanic American Historical Review 54, no. 1 (February 1974): 48–71.

El Colegio de México, Centro de Estudios Históricos. Historia general de México; 4 volumes. Mexico: El Colegio de México, 1976.

Conchello, José Ángel, et al. Los partidos políticos de México. (Series Archivo del Fondo nos. 49–51.) Mexico: Fondo de Cultura Económica, 1975.

Connor, Seymour V., and Odie Faulk. North America Divided: The Mexican War, 1846–1848. New York: Oxford University Press, 1971.

Corbalá Acuña, Manuel. "El problema agrario en Sonora." Unpublished; approx. 1973.

Córdova, Arnaldo. La formación del poder político en México, 4th ed. Mexico: Ediciones ERA, 1975.

———. La ideología de la Revolución mexicana. Mexico: Ediciones ERA, 1973.

——— La política de masas del cardenismo. Mexico: Ediciones ERA, 1974.

"Cosechas de violencia." Proceso 1, no. 2 (Nov. 13, 1976): 13.

Cosío Villegas, Daniel. El estilo personal de gobernar, 8th ed. Mexico: Cuadernos de Joaquín Mortiz, 1976.

———. El sistema político mexicano. Mexico: Cuadernos de Joaquín Mortiz, 1972.

———. The United States Versus Porfirio Díaz (trans. Nettie Lee Benson). Lincoln: University of Nebraska Press, 1963.

——— (ed.). Historia moderna de México; 9 volumes. Mexico: Editorial Hermes, 1955–1965.

Cossío Silva, Luis. "La agricultura." In Daniel Cosío Villegas (ed.), Historia moderna de México, vol. 7. El Porfiriato: la vida económica, 2nd ed., pp. 1–133. Mexico: Editorial Hermes, 1974.

Costeloe, Michael P. La Primera República Federal de México, 1824–1835. Mexico: Fondo de Cultura Económica, 1975.

"Crédito condicional al campo." Análisis Político 2, no. 7 (Feb. 19, 1973): 5.

Cronon, E. David. Josephus Daniels in Mexico. Madison: University of Wisconsin Press, 1960.

Crumrine, N. Ross. The Mayo Indians of Sonora: A People Who Refuse to Die. Tuscon: University of Arizona Press, 1977.

Cumberland, Charles C. *Mexican Revolution*, 2 volumes. Austin: University of Texas Press, 1952, 1969.

———. *Mexico: The Struggle for Modernity*. New York: Oxford University Press, 1968.

Dabdoub, Claudio. *Historia del Valle del Yaqui*. Mexico: Editorial Porrúa, 1964.

Dávila, Francisco T. *Sonora histórico y descriptivo*. Nogales, 1894.

Delli Sante, Angela M. "The Private Sector, Business Organizations and International Influence: Mexico, a Case Study." Paper delivered at a conference on United States Foreign Policy and Latin American and Caribbean Regimes, Washington, D.C., March 27–31, 1978.

"Desequilibrios económicos del sexenio anterior." *Proceso* 1, no. 33 (June 20, 1977):26–27.

Díaz, Lilia. "El liberalismo militante." In El Colegio de México, Centro de Estudios Históricos, *Historia general de México*, vol. 3, pp. 85–162. Mexico: El Colegio de Mexico, 1976.

Dobb, Maurice. *Studies in the Development of Capitalism*. New York: International Publishers, 1947.

Dorronsoro, José María. "La mecanización de la agricultura en los distritos de riego en México." *Ingeniería Hidráulica en México* 18, nos. 1–2 (January–June 1964): 102–111.

Dunbier, Roger. *The Sonoran Desert: Its Geography, Economy, and People*. Tucson: University of Arizona Press, 1970.

Durán, Marco Antonio. *El agrarismo mexicano*, 2nd ed. Mexico: Siglo XXI, 1972.

Eckstein, Salomón. *El ejido colectivo en México*. Mexico: Fondo de Cultura Económica, 1966.

"El ejército en Chiapas." *Análisis Político* 5, no. 21 (May 24, 1976): 5.

"El ejido colectivo." *Análisis Político* 2, no. 9 (March 5, 1973): 5.

Fagen, Richard R. "The Realities of U.S.–Mexican Relations." *Foreign Affairs* 55, no. 4 (July 1977):685–700.

———. "Studying Latin American Politics: Some Implications of a *Dependencia* Approach." *Latin American Research Review* 12, no 2 (Spring 1977):3–27.

Falcón, Romana. *El agrarismo en Veracruz: la etapa radical, 1928–1935*. Mexico: El Colegio de México, 1977.

Fernández y Fernández, Ramón. "La organización económica del ejido." *Revista del México Agrario* 9, no. 1 (January–February 1976):13–66.

Florescano, Enrique, and María del Rosario Lanzagorta. "Política económica: antecedentes y consecuencias." In Luis González et al., *La economía mexicana en la época de Juárez*, 2nd ed., pp. 57–106. Mexico: SepSetentas, 1976.

Friedrich, Paul. *Agrarian Revolt in a Mexican Village*. Englewood Cliffs, N.J.: Prentice-Hall, 1970.

Fuentes Díaz, Vicente. *Los partidos políticos en México*, 2nd ed. Mexico: Editorial Altiplano, 1969.

García Cantú, Gastón. *El socialismo en México*. Mexico: Ediciones ERA, 1969.

———. *Las invasiones norteamericanas en México*. Mexico: Ediciones ERA, 1971.

Gilly, Adolfo. *La Revolución interrumpida*. Mexico: Ediciones El Caballito, 1971.

"El gobierno define: colectivizar, única salida agraria." *Proceso* 1, no. 13 (Jan. 29, 1977):18–22.

Gómez-Jara, Francisco. *El movimiento campesino en México*. Mexico: Editorial Campesina, 1970.

Gómez Tagle, Sylvia. *Organización de las sociedades de crédito ejidal de La Laguna*. (Cuadernos del CES no. 8.) Mexico: El Colegio de México, 1974.

González, Luis. "La era de Juárez." In Luis González et al., *La economía mexicana en la época de Juárez*, 2nd ed. pp. 11–55. Mexico: SepSetentas, 1976.

———. "El liberalismo triunfante." In El Colegio de México, Centro de Estudios Históricos, *Historia general de México*, vol. 3, pp. 163–281. Mexico: El Colegio de México, 1976.

———, et al. *La economía mexicana en la época de Juárez*, 2nd ed. Mexico: SepSetentas, 1976.

González Navarro, Moisés. *La Confederación Nacional Campesina: un grupo de presión en la reforma agraria mexicana*. Mexico: Costa-Amic, 1968.

———. "Mexico: The Lopsided Revolution." In Claudio Veliz (ed.), *Obstacles to Change in Latin America*, pp. 206–229. New York: Oxford University Press, 1965.

González Ramírez, Manuel. *La revolución social de México*, vol. 3. *El problema agrario*. Mexico: Fondo de Cultura Económica, 1966.

González Villarreal, Fernando J. "Plan Nacional Hidráulico." *Recursos Hidráulicos* 4, no. 1 (1975):8–29.

Gramsci, Antonio. *Selections from the Prison Notebooks* (ed. and trans. Quintin Hoare and Geoffrey Nowell Smith). New York: International Publishers, 1971.

Green, Rosario. *El endeudamiento público externo de México, 1940–1973*. Mexico: El Colegio de México, 1976.

Griffin, Keith. *The Political Economy of Agrarian Change: An Essay on the Green Revolution*. Cambridge, Mass.: Harvard University Press, 1974.

Grindle, Merilee Serrill. *Bureaucrats, Politicians, and Peasants in Mexico: A Case Study in Public Policy*. Berkeley and Los Angeles: University of California Press, 1977.

Guerrero, Francisco Javier. "La colectivización capitalista del campo y otros límites del reformismo." *Cuadernos Políticos* 3 (January–March 1975):70–81.

Guzmán, Rodolfo. "Gómez Villanueva en el escenario de Bahía de Banderas." *Proceso* 1, no. 34 (June 27, 1977):6–11.

Habermas, Jurgen. *Legitimation Crisis* (trans. Thomas McCarthy). Boston: Beacon Press, 1975.

Hale, Charles A. *Mexican Liberalism in the Age of Mora, 1821–1853*. New Haven: Yale University Press, 1968.

Hansen, Roger D. *The Politics of Mexican Development*. Baltimore: Johns Hopkins Press, 1971.

Hellman, Judith Adler. *Mexico in Crisis*. New York: Holmes and Meier, 1978.

Herrera Canales, Inez. "Comercio exterior." In Luis González et al., *La economía mexicana en la época de Juárez*, pp. 129–154. Mexico: SepSetentas, 1976.

Herrera Gómez, Hugo. "Análisis económico de la unidad agropecuaria de Cananea." Banco Nacional de Crédito Ejidal, *Boletín de Estudios Especiales* 13, no. 147 (Dec. 27, 1958).

Hewitt de Alcántara, Cynthia. *Modernizing Mexican Agriculture: Socioeconomic Implications of Technological Change, 1940–1970*. Geneva: United Nations Research Institute for Social Development, 1976.

Hu-Dehart, Evelyn. "Development and Rural Rebellion: Pacification of the Yaquis in the Late Porfiriato." *Hispanic American Historical Review* 54, no. 1 (February 1974):72–93.

Huizer, Gerret. *La lucha campesina en México.* Mexico: Centro de Investigaciones Agrarias (CDIA), 1970.

Ianni, Octavio. *El estado capitalista en la época de Cárdenas.* Mexico: Ediciones ERA, 1977.

"Invasiones agrarias y rigidez política." *Análisis Político* 5, no 20 (May 10, 1976): 149.

"Isla Tiburón, vedada a los Seris." *Proceso* 1, no. 20 (March 19, 1977):19–20.

Iturriaga de la Fuente, José. *La revolución hacendaria: la hacienda pública con el presidente Calles.* Mexico: SepSetentas, 1976.

Izquierdo, Rafael. "Protectionism in Mexico." In Raymond Vernon (ed.), *Public Policy and Private Enterprise in Mexico*, pp. 241–289. Cambridge, Mass.: Harvard University Press, 1964.

Jardines Moreno, José Luis. "Los Distritos de Riego por bombeo del centro y norte de Sonora." *Recursos Hidráulicos* 5, no. 1 (1976):8–25.

Jiménez Ricárdez, Rubén. "Movimiento campesino en Sonora." *Cuadernos Políticos* 7 (January–March 1976):67–78.

Jiménez Villalobos, Ángel. "Condiciones de las aguas subterraneas en el Distrito de Riego #51, Costa de Hermosillo, Sonora." *Ingeniería Hidráulica en México* 19, no. 3 (1965):65–80.

Johnson, Kenneth F. *Mexican Democracy: A Critical View.* Boston: Allyn and Bacon, 1971.

Johnson, William Weber. *Heroic Mexico.* New York: Doubleday, 1968.

Katz, Friedrich. "Labor Conditions on Haciendas in Porfirian Mexico: Some Trends and Tendencies." *Hispanic American Historical Review* 54, no. 1 (February 1974):1–47.

Keremitsis, Dawn. *La industria téxtil mexicana en el siglo XIX.* Mexico: SepSetentas, 1973.

King, Timothy. *Mexico: Industrialization and Trade Policies Since 1940.* London: Oxford University Press, 1970.

Labastida M. del Campo, Julio. "Nacionalismo reformista en México." *Cuadernos Políticos* 3 (January–March 1975):33–51.

———. "Proceso político y dependencia en México, 1970–1976." Unpublished; 1977.

Lara y Torres, Leopoldo. *Documentos para la historia de la persecución religiosa en México.* Mexico: Editorial Jus, 1954.

Leal, Juan Felipe. "The Mexican State, 1915–1973: A Historical Interpretation." *Latin American Perspectives* 2, no. 2 (Summer 1975):48–63.

———. *México: estado, burocracia y sindicatos.* Mexico: Ediciones El Caballito, 1975.

Leyva, Emilio. "Burguesía agrícola y dependencia." In Ramiro Reyes Esparza et al., *La burguesía mexicana: cuatro ensayos*, pp. 101–139. Mexico: Editorial Nuestro Tiempo, 1973.

Lieuwen, Edwin. *Mexican Militarism: The Political Rise and Fall of the Revolutionary Army, 1910–1940.* Albuquerque: University of New Mexico Press, 1968.

Loaeza, Soledad. "La política del rumor: México, Noviembre–Diciembre 1976." In

El Colegio de México, Centro de Estudios Internacionales, *Las crisis en el sistema político mexicano, 1928–1977*, pp. 121–150. Mexico: El Colegio de México, 1978.

López Saucedo, Miguel. "Ineficiencia y pillaje en Bahía de Banderas." *Proceso* 1, no. 33 (June 20, 1977):6–11.

Loyo, Gilberto. "La concentración agraria en 28 paises." *Investigaciones Económicas* 1, no. 1 (1941).

Luna, Jesús. *La carrera pública de don Ramón Corral*. Mexico: SepSetentas, 1975.

Magdaleno, Mauricio. *José María Luis Mora, el civilizador*. Mexico, 1935.

Malloy, James M. (ed.). *Authoritarianism and Corporatism in Latin America*. Pittsburgh: University of Pittsburgh Press, 1977.

Manero, Antonio. *The Meaning of the Mexican Revolution*. Mexico, 1915.

Manzanilla Schaffer, Victor. *La colonización ejidal*. Mexico: Asociación Nacional de Abogados, 1970.

Martínez, Orlando. *The Great Landgrab: The Mexican–American War, 1846–1848*. London: Quartet Books, 1975.

Marx, Karl. *Grundrisse* (ed. Martin Nicolaus). New York: Penguin Books, 1973.

McBride, George McCutchen. *The Land Systems of Mexico*. New York: American Geographical Society, Conde Nast Press, 1923.

Medina Ruiz, Fernando. *Calles: un destino melancólico*. Mexico: Editorial Jus, 1960.

Mena, Mario A. *Álvaro Obregón: historia militar y política, 1912–1929*. Mexico: Editorial Jus, 1960.

Mendieta y Nuñez, Lucio. *Política agraria*. Mexico: Instituto de Investigaciones Sociales, Universidad Nacional Autónoma de México, 1957.

———. *El problem agrario de México*, 9th ed. Mexico: Porrúa, 1966.

Meyer, Jean. *La Cristiada*, 4th ed.; 3 volumes. Mexico: Siglo XXI, 1976.

Meyer, Lorenzo. *México y los Estados Unidos en el conflicto petrolero (1917–1942)*, 2nd ed. Mexico: El Colegio de México, 1972.

Michaels, Albert L. "The Crisis of Cardenismo." *Journal of Latin American Studies* 2, no. 1 (May 1970):51–79.

Miliband, Ralph. *The State in Capitalist Society: An Analysis of the Western System of Power*. New York: Basic Books, 1969.

Millon, Robert Paul. *Vicente Lombardo Toledano: Mexican Marxist*. Chapel Hill: University of North Carolina Press, 1966.

Moirón, Sara. "A falta de información, el rumor." *Proceso* 1, no. 4 (Nov. 27, 1976): 16.

Moisés, Rosalio, et al. *The Tall Candle: The Personal Chronicle of a Yaqui Indian*. Lincoln: University of Nebraska Press, 1971.

Moncada, Carlos. *Años de violencia en Sonora, 1955–1976*. Mexico: V Siglos, 1976.

Mora, José María Luis. *Mexico y sus revoluciones*. Paris: Librería de Rosa, 1836.

———. *Obras sueltas*, 2nd ed. Mexico: Porrúa, 1963.

Mosk, Sanford A. *Industrial Revolution in Mexico*. Berkeley and Los Angeles: University of California Press, 1950.

Muñoz, Hilda (ed.). *Lázaro Cárdenas: síntesis ideológica de su campaña presidencial*. Mexico: Fondo de Cultura Económica, Archivo del Fondo, 1976.

O'Brien, Philip J. "A Critique of Latin American Theories of Dependency." In Ivar

Oxaal et al. (eds.), *Beyond the Sociology of Development: Economy and Society in Latin America and Africa*. London: Routledge and Kegan Paul, 1975.

O'Connor, James. *The Fiscal Crisis of the State*. New York: St. Martin's Press, 1973.

O'Donnell, Guillermo A. *Modernization and Bureaucratic Authoritarianism: Studies in South American Politics*. Berkeley: University of California Institute of International Studies, 1973.

————, and Delfina Linck. *Dependencia y autonomía*. Buenos Aires: Amorrortú, 1973.

Orive Alba, Adolfo. "Programa de irrigación del C. Presidente Miguel Alemán: posibilidades de un financiamiento parcial." *Ingeniería Hidráulica en México* 1, no. 1 (January–March 1947):17–32.

Otero, Mariano. *Obras*; 2 volumes. Mexico: Porrúa, 1967.

Paré, Luisa. "Caciquismo y estructura de poder en la Sierra Norte de Puebla." In Roger Bartra et al. (eds.), *Caciquismo y poder político en México rural*, 2nd ed., pp. 31–61. Mexico: Siglo XXI, 1976.

Pellicer de Brody, Olga. "Mexico in the 1970s and Its Relations with the United States." In Julio Cotler and Richard R. Fagen (eds.), *Latin America and the United States: The Changing Political Realities*, pp. 314–333. Stanford, Calif.: Stanford University Press, 1974.

Peña, Moisés T. de la. *El pueblo y su tierra: mito y realidad de la reforma agraria en México*. Mexico: Cuadernos Americanos, 1964.

Peña, Sergio de la. *La formación del capitalismo en México*, 2nd ed. Mexico: Siglo XXI, 1976.

Poulantzas, Nicos. *Poder político y clases sociales en el estado capitalista*, 13th ed. Mexico: Siglo XXI, 1976.

Purcell, John F. H., and Susan Kaufman Purcell. "El estado y la empresa privada." *Nueva Política* 1, no. 2 (April–June, 1976):229–250.

Quirk, Robert E. *The Mexican Revolution and the Catholic Church, 1910–1929*. Bloomington: Indiana University Press, 1973.

Ramírez Rancaño, Mario. "Los empresarios mexicanos: las fracciones dominantes." *Problemas del Desarrollo* 6, no. 24 (November 1975–January 1976):49–82.

Reed, Nelson. *The Caste War of Yucatán*. Stanford, Calif.: Stanford University Press, 1964.

Restrepo, Ivan, and Salomón Eckstein. *La agricultura colectiva en México: la experiencia de La Laguna*. Mexico: Siglo XXI, 1975.

Retchkimán K., Benjamín. "La política fiscal mexicana." *Problemas del Desarrollo* 6, no. 24 (November 1975–January 1976):83–100.

Reyes Heroles, Jesús. *El liberalismo mexicano*; 3 volumes. Mexico: Fondo de Cultura Económica, 1961.

Reynolds, Clark W. *The Mexican Economy: Twentieth-Century Structure and Growth*. New Haven: Yale University Press, 1970.

Rivera, Antonio G. *La Revolución en Sonora*. Mexico, 1969.

Roeder, Ralph. *Hacia un México moderno: Porfirio Díaz*; 2 volumes. Mexico: Fondo de Cultura Económica, 1973.

Rosenzweig, Fernando. "El desarrollo económico de México de 1877 a 1911." *El Trimestre Económico* 32, no. 3 (July–September 1965):405–454.

Ross, Stanley R. *Francisco I. Madero: Apostle of Mexican Democracy*. New York: Columbia University Press, 1955; AMS, 1970.

Schmitter, Phillippe. "Still the Century of Corporatism?" *Review of Politics* 36 (January 1974):85–131.

Segovia, Rafael. "La reforma política: el ejecutivo federal, el PRI, y las elecciones de 1973." In El Colegio de México, Centro de Estudios Internacionales, *La vida política en México, 1970–1973*, pp. 49–76. Mexico: El Colegio de México, 1974.

———. "Tendencias políticas en México." In El Colegio de México, Centro de Estudios Internacionales, *Las fronteras del control del estado mexicano*, pp. 3–10. Mexico: El Colegio de México, 1976.

Sevilla Mascareñas, Mario. *Aquí, Sonora, S.O.S.* Mexico: Ediciones Calpuleque, 1977.

Shelton, David H. "The Banking System: Money and the Goal of Growth." In Raymond Vernon (ed.), *Public Policy and Private Enterprise in Mexico*, pp. 111–189. Cambridge, Mass.: Harvard University Press, 1964.

Silva Hérzog, Jesús. *El agrarismo mexicano y la reforma agraria: exposición y crítica*. Mexico: Fondo de Cultura Económica, 1959.

———. *Breve historia de la Revolución mexicana*, 2nd ed.; 2 volumes. Mexico: Fondo de Cultura Económica, 1973.

———. "Opiniones heterodoxas sobre la Revolución mexicana." *Cuadernos Americanos* 206, no. 3 (May–June 1976):7–24.

Simons, Marlise. "Behind the Scandal Rocking Mexican Politics." *San Francisco Chronicle*, April 19, 1978, p. A3.

Simpson, Eyler N. *The Ejido: Mexico's Way Out*. Chapel Hill: University of North Carolina Press, 1937.

———. "The Mexican Agrarian Reform: Problems and Progress." Unpublished; Mexico: Institute of Current World Affairs, Agricultural Studies, series I, no. 9, July 1933.

Smith, Robert Freeman. "The Morrow Mission and the International Committee of Bankers on Mexico: The Interaction of Finance Diplomacy and the New Mexican Elite." *Journal of Latin American Studies* 1, no. 2 (1969):149–166.

———. *The United States and Revolutionary Nationalism in Mexico, 1916–1932*. Chicago: University of Chicago Press, 1972.

Solís, Leopoldo. "Hacia un análisis general a largo plazo del desarrollo económico de México." *Demografía y Economía* 1, no. 1 (1967).

———. *La realidad económica mexicana: retrovisión y perspectivas*, 6th ed. Mexico: Siglo XXI, 1976.

Sonnichsen, C. L. *Colonel Greene and the Copper Skyrocket*. Tucson: University of Arizona Press, 1974.

Spicer, Edward H. *Cycles of Conquest: The Impact of Spain, Mexico, and the United States on the Indians of the Southwest, 1533–1960*. Tucson: University of Arizona Press, 1962.

Stavenhagen, Rodolfo. "Aspectos sociales de la estructura agraria en México." In *Neolatifundismo y explotación de Emiliano Zapata a Anderson Clayton y Cía.* Mexico: Editorial Nuestro Tiempo, 1968.

———. "Reflexiones sobre el proceso político actual." *Nueva Política* 1, no. 2 (April–June 1976):15–22.

Stevens, Evelyn P. *Protest and Response in Mexico*. Cambridge: Massachusetts Institute of Technology Press, 1974.

"Tiempo de la reconstrucción económica." *Proceso* 1, no. 2 (Nov. 13, 1976): 25.

Valadés, José C. *Maximiliano y Carlota en México: historia del Segundo Imperio.* Mexico: Editorial Diana, 1976.

Vargas Alcántara, Vicente. "Perforación de pozos profundos para explotación de aguas subterraneas." *Ingeniería Hidráulica en México* 14, no 1 (January–March 1960).

Vasconcelos, José. *Breve historia de México.* Mexico: Editorial Botas, 1937.

———. *La flama.* Mexico, 1959.

Vernon, Raymond (ed.). *Public Policy and Private Enterprise in Mexico.* Cambridge, Mass.: Harvard University Press, 1964.

Villa, Eduardo W. *Compendio de historia del estado de Sonora.* Mexico: Editorial Patria Nueva, 1937.

Villa, Manuel A. "Las bases del estado mexicano y su problemática actual." In *El pérfil de México, 1980,* vol. 3, pp. 419–460. Mexico: Siglo XXI, 1974.

Villarreal, René. *El desequilibrio externo en la industrialización de México, 1929–1975.* Mexico: Fondo de Cultura Económica, 1976.

Warman, Arturo. "La colectivización en el campo: una crítica." *Cuadernos Políticos* 11 (January–March 1977):47–56.

Weyl, Nathaniel, and Sylvia Weyl. *The Reconquest of Mexico: The Years of Lázaro Cárdenas.* New York: Oxford University Press, 1939.

Whetten, Nathan L. *Rural Mexico.* Chicago: University of Chicago Press, 1948.

Wilkie, James W. *The Mexican Revolution: Federal Expenditure and Social Change Since 1910,* 2nd ed. Berkeley and Los Angeles: University of California Press, 1970.

Wionczek, Miguel S. "Incomplete Formal Planning: Mexico." In Everett E. Hagen (ed.), *Planning Economic Development,* pp. 150–182. Homewood, Ill.: Richard D. Irwin, 1963.

Wolf, Eric R. *Peasant Wars of the Twentieth Century.* New York: Harper, 1969.

Womack, John, Jr. *Zapata and the Mexican Revolution.* New York: Vintage, 1968.

Zea, Leopoldo. *El positivismo en México: nacimiento, apogeo y decadencia.* Mexico: Fondo de Cultura Económica, 1968.

———. *Positivism in Mexico* (trans. Josephine H. Schulte). Austin: University of Texas Press, 1974.

Zevada, Ricardo J. *Calles, El Presidente.* Mexico: Editorial Nuestro Tiempo, 1971.

Zoraida Vázquez, Josefina. "Los primeros tropiezos." In El Colegio de México, Centro de Estudios Históricos, *Historia general de México,* vol. 3, pp. 1–84. Mexico: El Colegio de México, 1976.

Index

Designer:	Wendy Calmenson
Compositor:	G & S Typesetters
Printer:	Thomson-Shore
Binder:	Thomson-Shore
Text:	VIP Melior
Display:	VIP Melior
Cloth:	Holliston Roxite B53665
Paper:	50 lb. P&S offset vellum